NAVIGATING ROMANS THROUGH CULTURES

Romans Through History and Cultures
Receptions and Critical Interpretations

CRISTINA GRENHOLM AND DANIEL PATTE, SERIES EDITORS

Romans Through History and Cultures includes a wealth of information regarding the receptions of Romans throughout the history of the church and today, in the "first" and the "two-thirds" world. It explores the past and present impact of Romans upon theology, and upon cultural, political, social, and ecclesial life, and gender relations.

In each volume, the authors contribute to an integrated practice, "Scriptural Criticism," which takes into account, with contemporary biblical scholars, that different readings can be grounded in the same text by different critical methods; with church historians and practical theologians, that the believers' readings interrelate biblical text and concrete life; and with theologians, that believers read Romans as Scripture.

The cover art skillfully represents that any interpretation of a scriptural text is framed in three ways: a) by an *analytical frame* that reflects each reader's autonomous choice of a textual dimension as most significant—see the individual studying the text; b) by a *contextual/pragmatic frame* shaped by a certain relational network of life in society and community—see the people joining hands; and, c) by a *hermeneutical frame* inspired by a certain religious perception of life—see the bread and chalice and the face-to-face encounter.

By elucidating the threefold choices reflected in various interpretations of Romans through the centuries and present-day cultures, the volumes in the series—which emerge from a three-year Society of Biblical Literature Consultation and an on-going SBL Seminar—raise a fundamental critical question: Why did I/we choose this interpretation rather than another one?

ROMANS THROUGH HISTORY AND CULTURES SERIES

NAVIGATING ROMANS THROUGH CULTURES

Challenging Readings by Charting a New Course

Edited by

Yeo Khiok-khng (K.K.)

t & t clark

T & T Clark International
Madison Square Park, 15 East 26th Street, New York, NY 10010

T & T Clark International
The Tower Building, 11 York Road, London SE1 7NX

T & T Clark International is a Continuum imprint.

Cover art by Elizabeth McNaron Patte

Library of Congress Cataloging-in-Publication Data

Navigating Romans through cultures : challenging readings by charting a new course / edited by Yeo Khiok-Khng (K.K.).
    p. cm. — (Romans through history and culture series)
Includes bibliographical references and index.
ISBN 0-567-02501-2 (pbk.)
1. Bible. N.T. Romans—Criticism, interpretation, etc. 2. Christianity and culture. I. Yeo, Khiok-Khng. II. Series.
BS2665.52.N36 2004
227'.106—dc22
                            2004017574

Printed in the United States of America

04 05 06 07 08 09 10   10 9 8 7 6 5 4 3 2 1

Contents

Part 3
ASIA

–INTRODUCTION–

Navigating Romans Through Cultures

Yeo Khiok-khng (K.K.)

──── ◆ ────

Overview

Navigating Romans Through Cultures contains eight chapters of critical and contextualized readings of Paul's letter to the Romans by scholars from Europe, Africa, Latin America, North America, and Asia. This volume is an interpretive voyage into how the gospel of Paul, as contained in his letter to the Romans, fulfills its original vision of "making known the gospel of Christ in all nations" (Rom 16:26). The challenge of the contributors is to express Paul's gospel in terms of their own cultures. As such their contributions are prophetic writings that strive to make known Paul's gospel to all cultures.

There was no captain on board to steer the ship (Paul's letter to the Romans) when we (contributors) began to chart new courses in different cultures. Initially each contributor brought his or her own navigating gears and steered Romans according to one's hermeneutical interests. It became clear to many of us that, after the first attempted journey on our own, more people were interested in our challenging voyages and surprising discoveries. Thus, the protocol of a more global and critical reflection of each of our journeys was designed before we began our writings. All chapters and most responses in this volume were originally papers presented at 2001-2002 Society of Biblical Literature meetings in the "Romans Through History and Cultures" seminar, chaired by Daniel Patte and Cristina Grenholm. The collective interpretive practice has taken shape not only in the dialogue sessions at the meetings, but also through the engagement of the writers with the respondents and the revisions of their works.

This journey around the world with the letter of Paul to the Romans took no less than four years. Each contributor is familiar with the culture they worked with, since many lived in that culture. Each "travel-log" is not just a report of how we steer the ship (letter to the Romans) through the water of a particular culture (or a sea of cultures for many of us); it is also a life changing critical reflection on our reading and interpretative process. Thus charting a new course involves more than offering new ways of reading Romans; it also involves clarifying the rationales for this new reading, in the light of the contextual, analytical, and hermeneutical frames of Scripture Criticism.

In our voyage we first leave Rome to go to Europe, then to Africa. The first captain is Florin T. Cimpean, who brings us to Pentecostal and Eastern Orthodox communities in Romania and integrates *pro nobis* readings with critical ones. He is convinced that Romans 8 is a central piece of the letter as a "figurative discourse," and he reflects on the struggle and growth of his own biblical hermeneutics. In Africa, Jonathan A. Draper accounts and reflects upon the translation and commentary of Bishop John William Colenso on Romans: how Colenso's "frontier reading" was shaped by the Zulu language, by Colenso's Western training, and by the challenge to communicate the theological issues in Romans within the African context, thus at times "scandalizing the Church of his days."

When Mark D. Baker and J. Ross Wagner grasp the steering wheel of the ship, we cruise with them across the Atlantic Ocean, leaving Europe, into the hurricane-devastated Honduras. They narrate the way the Amor Fe y Vida church struggled theologically with the question of justice of God as vindictive or covenantal faithfulness in the midst of the hurricane Mitch. Our ship took a hard beating, but Baker and Wagner help us to reflect on how a cross-cultural conversation with the Honduras church informed and challenged their readings of Romans in a North American context. Identifying himself as a hybrid creature, a crossing between a chameleon and a scorpion, Juan Escarfuller steers the ship into the assimilated water of academia, in search of a cultural-religious identity for Latina/o theologians in an American context. Considering the Forensic, "New Perspective," and Apocalyptic Interpretative choices, he repudiates assimilation in Romans 9-11 with the resource of an Apocalyptic hermeneutic. Next, Monya A. Stubbs steers the ship with the help of Harriet Tubman's three-dimensional process of empowerment in search of freedom for African American. She reads Romans 13 with the lens of "Subjection-Reflection-Resistance" in the context of a free market economy.

The voyage from North America to Asia across the Pacific Ocean is long and difficult but the *far east* is worth exploring. Daniel C. Arichea from the Philippines has worked with the United Bible Societies in Asia and knows the terrain of Bible translations well. He looks at how Paul's understanding of "righteousness" in Romans is translated into a number of languages in Asia, and the receptions of Romans in Asian communities. Revelation Enriquez Velunta lives in the Philippines as well. With the insight of his mother Nanay, Velunta reads "from faith to faith" in Romans 1:16-17 with the Filipinos' sense of indebtedness (*utang na loob*). Finally, Yeo Khiok-khng (who goes by "K.K."; Yeo is his family name) steers the ship to Confucianist China and reads Paul's language of the predestination of Christ in dialogue with the Confucian political ethics of *Datong* (Great Togetherness), retrieval of the golden age (and Paul's eschatology).

Each contributor is grateful to his or her respondent, whose essay is placed immediately after the chapter upon which it reflects. The respondents have significant roles, though their writings are brief. They raise critical questions for both the contributors and themselves, as all of us are faced with waves of challenges in making Paul's text meaningful to an increasingly diverse world—culturally, religiously, socio-politically, and textually. Respondents keep us awake to stay on course; they make us aware of dangers ahead. Sometimes they are cheerleaders; sometimes "devil's advocates." But all of them are necessary partners for a bon voyage.

Our works are revised and collected here in order to provide a resource for cross-cultural hermeneutics on Romans for the benefit of seminarians, as well as teachers, pastors, and lay leaders of the church. This could well be the first collective volume of modern receptions of Romans, emphasizing the cultural lenses and the contemporary cultural concerns of the interpreters.[1]

In their challenging readings of Romans, the contributors have wrestled with the following issues: (1) An understanding of culture; (2) The cultural background and mission of Paul; (3) Cultural and theological conflicts in the letter of Paul to the Romans; (4) Cultural interpretations of Paul; (5) Navigating equipments in steering Romans through cultures. Let us consider each issue in turn.

Working Definition of Culture in Biblical Interpretation

The word "culture" may not be used in all the chapters in this volume, but it is safe to say they all present cultural readings of the Romans text. Each chapter engages Paul's text with various cultural issues such as ethnic identity, global economy, stories of salvation, and communal living. Daniel Boyarin in his "Introduction" to *A Radical Jew* has explained Paul's criticism of the culture of his days and later readers such as Boyarin himself wrestle with Paul's texts to perform a similar task: "Choice of a hermeneutic and moral center from which to read the text is not a defect in but a starting point for the reading."[2]

The words "culture" and "cultural" are used in this volume in a broad sense to refer to material substance, norms of behaviors, values or significant virtues, beliefs or world-views, expressive symbols or representations.[3]   All these expressions of "culture" are dynamic and changing, and they often fluidly interact with their sub-entities. Thus to speak of a Romanian culture or a Chinese culture requires to spell out the specificities of this culture in as much detail as possible in order to avoid a static view of culture. For example, Draper presents an intriguing case by showing how Bishop Colenso translated Paul's message to the Zulu people in the context of the colonial West; Escarfuller deals with the bi-cultural struggle of being Latina/o in a North American context. Cimpean gives the grid of the Pentecostal and the Orthodox components of the Romanian culture, while Baker and Wagner attend to the people of Amor Fe y Vida in Honduras.

Culture is the life-line of meaning-making for a particular group of people, however we do not want to name people merely in terms of ethnic, class, nationality, belief, or gender categories. Culture is not a non-essential, but "the totality of man's products."[4]   Without culture, a people will not survive. Human beings are compelled by their natures to impose meaningful order upon reality.[5]

Paul does not know the language of social science or anthropology which define culture as the "complex whole" in the making of a society.[6] Yet Paul's language of "Jews and Gentiles," "circumcised and uncircumcised," "male and female," "slaves and free," "Jerusalem" and "Spain" and "Rome," are cultural references. Paul may not know the terms "cultural interpretation," "contextualization" and "indigenization," but his proclamation of the gospel to the Gentiles involved what these terms refer.

It will be helpful to delineate the nuances of the term "cultures" (in the phrase "Navigating Romans Through Cultures") using the cultural understanding of the social sciences and humanities. The purpose of these reflections is to help us become aware of the nuanced connotations of a term such as the word "culture" and to be able to bridge Paul's text with our context.

Perspectives of the Social Sciences

Among the disciplines of social sciences, Edward B. Tylor's expansive definition of culture as the "complex whole" will be useful to all chapters in this volume as they clarify their social locations: "Culture or Civilization, taken in its wide ethnographic sense, is that complex whole which includes knowledge, belief, art, morals, law, custom, and any other capabilities and habits acquired by man as a member of society."[7] The challenge posed by this perspective is the irony that the cultures we know rarely exhibit this complex whole! None of us, contributors to this volume, would want to claim that we have said all what can be said regarding the Filipino, the Chinese, the Zulu, or the African-American cultures. Thus, even with a working definition of the word "culture," each user of the word will take its nuanced meaning slightly different from others. Each society has its own culture, its own pattern of belief, ethical practices, values, ways of life, institutions, etc., formed and reformed in its dynamic historical process.[8]

Despite the difficulty in pinpointing through a clear definition what exactly are the constitutive features of a particular culture, we all agree that culture plays a significant role in biblical interpretation. Culture is one of the essential means for interpreting Romans, because cultures, like theology (interpretive meaning of God), are intertwined in the meaning of a life-world. Theology can be part of a culture, a culture can be a part of theology. Culture without theology is like a corpse, or worse, becomes a narcissistic idol or a demon. Culture does not have spiritual resources of its own to critique and renew itself. Yet theology without culture will die, becoming anemic, because theology cannot feed on itself; it has to feed on "the nitty-gritty" of life.[9]

Many anthropologists in their fieldwork advocate a functional theory of cultures. For example, Bronislaw Malinowski argues that cultural phenomena were determined by basic needs and the possibilities of satisfying them in all societies. This functional concept accounted for the variety of differentiation, as well as for the commonality within the variety.[10] This sociological functional definition packs the complex whole into the definition of culture, so that each culture is communally grounded and ethnographically studied. But it has its own weaknesses. It tends to explain complexity away too easily, reducing its theological aspects into sociological features.

Perspectives of the Humanities

The contributors in this volume use culture along the lines of the social sciences, though they are aware of the benefit of considering the humanities concern for human flourishing—culture as cultured. This approach has its literary and philosophical roots in the Greco-Roman understanding of culture as "cultivating" virtue, pursuing perfection, and attaining excellence in all human potential. Culture enables the human mind and spirit to rise above societal norms and mundane expectations to that which is excellent, truthful, and beautiful. Perhaps, from this view we can appreciate the fact that culture is not simply arbitrary, for culture forms the soul of a people or a society, and if the culture is destroyed, so will be the soul of the community.

Yeo's chapter, one that uses the Confucian lens to read Paul, is probably the most obvious one to deal with "culture as cultured." His ethical reading of Paul's theology and his selection of classical Confucianism reveal a humanistic understanding of culture as cultured. Yeo needs this understanding of culture in order to do an intertextual reading of classical Confucianism and Romans 8. Yeo assumes that, for him and his audience, among the many cultural texts and biblical texts available, Romans 8 and the classical Confucianist texts offer greater "virtues," better cultivated wisdom and beauty. The same can be said of Stubbs, who uses the wisdom of Harriet Tubman, and of Velunta, who finds his mother's lived theology a helpful lens to read Romans. There is a consensus that doing a cultural reading of Romans is not simply an option, but also an inspiring move toward a better way—be it ethically, theologically, hermeneutically, or pragmatically—of reading Paul's text.

Culture is not simply a pursuit of traditionalism or archaism. Cultural interests in all the chapters in this volume foster the aspiration to beauty and wisdom for people today. Living well with beauty and wisdom is part of the benefits of Christ's gospel, which grants all salvation and freedom, righteousness and grace. The two chapters by Stubbs and Arichea also understand this definition of culture. They demonstrate the threat to their different communities of, respectively, free market economy and modern individualism. Stubbs and Arichea's understanding of culture may be akin to that of Matthew Arnold (1822-1888). Arnold argued that a civilization that aims at modernization and progress may end up in a "philistinism" in which technological advancement, instead of bringing cultural refinement, inadvertently brings about the barbaric and the depravation of the human spirit. Thus Arnold advocates that only culture could restore "sweetness and light" (beauty and wisdom) to society and civilization.[11]

A Critical Assessment

Both the humanities and sociological understandings of culture have their weaknesses and strength. While the humanities-based perspective can be elitist, it carries within itself its own value-judgment, something that the sociological understanding does not do. But this value-judgment must not be monopolized by the privileged, powerful, elitist groups. The elitist, humanities-based understanding of culture can inspire people to aspire to the best. Yet, cultural differences in a society may not be as marked as the humanities-based definition suggests. Conversely, leveling these differences by including all human experiences, activities and thinking as part of cultures as the sociological definition does may lead to a definition of culture which is too vague.

Then the question is: By what criteria can one reach the conclusion
that the Chinese have a "high" culture and the non-Chinese have a "low"
culture? That the Europeans have a "high" culture and the Hondurans
and the Zulus have a "low" culture? Are these pairs similar to Paul's
language regarding Jews and Gentiles, civilized (Hellenized) and
barbarians? The broader social scientific definition of culture may avoid
the ethnocentrism of the humanities-based definition, even though the
social scientific definition does not say precisely what culture is. The
humanities-based definition, because of its highly differentiating
function, tends to be perceived from the perspective of the social
sciences as overly critical and elitist. Yet, the assumption of the social-
scientific definition that each culture has its own legitimating way of life
has its own limitations. For example, how can one put into question the
practice of burning alive the wives of the deceased in the funeral service,
if one does not have any ground for judging this cultural practice as
wrong, unethical, and sinful? How does one present child sacrifice in
some tribal groups, if one does not have any ground to point out its
wrong religious assumption?

It will take a prophet to see things beyond the cultural limits and have
the courage and wisdom to preach something new against cultural
blindness so that change will take place. Yet a *cross*-cultural critique
transforms the perception of these cultural limit, distortion, and evil. But
for this cross-cultural critique, I believe, the humanities-based critical
definition will be more helpful than the social-scientific definition that
affirms the self-validation of cultures.

Contributors in this volume have engaged in a cross-cultural
interpretation of Paul.[12] We have amplified this process of crossing over
one's host culture to another culture by inviting respondents to join in the
collective interpretive practice. Much more could be done as readers
travel with Paul and the writers, take the time to immerse themselves in
different cultural particularities, and learn of the power of Paul's
message to different modern audiences.

For present-day interpreters of Paul, cross-cultural interpretation
begins with the translation of Paul's text from Greek to our modern
languages. It involves the two way process of using modern language to
understand Paul's ancient message and seeking to communicate Paul's
text to the modern world. In general, cross-cultural reading values
pluralism, advocates diversity. Thus the term "multi-cultural"
interpretation is used, assuming the kaleidoscopic effect of reading
Paul.[13] But each of the multi-cultural interpretations may happen
independently, and affirmation of each cultural interpretation as
meaningful is easily done. For most critical and faithful readers of the
scriptures, however, cultural interpretations inevitably raise the question

of criteria of "legitimate readings," "rules of adjudication in interpreting scripture," "interpretive will and hermeneutical responsibility."[14] Intercultural interpretation involves the exchanges between two or more cultural readings. Intercultural interpretation is seldom used to refer to cultural exchanges between an ancient and a modern culture. Thus the term cross-cultural is probably the broadest term that refers to a wide range of interpretative issues, processes, and critical reflections on the judgment of cultural readings as well as the criteria that govern such judgment. This volume engages in cross-cultural interpretation in this broad sense.

Cultural Background and Mission of Paul

Cultural World of Paul

Not only interpreters read Paul cross-culturally; Paul's missionary hermeneutics is itself a cross-cultural enterprise. All essays in this volume are not simply cultural, but cross-cultural readings of Romans. This practice of biblical interpretation is consistent with Paul's own life-experience and calling as an apostle to the Gentiles.

Paul was a Diaspora/Hellenistic Jew (Phil 3:5-6; Gal 1:11-24) and had a three-part Roman name, praenomen (given name) of the Hebrew word *Saulos* (Acts 7:58; 8:1, 3; 9:1, 4, 17; 22:7; 26:14), and the cognomen (family name) of the Latin word *Paullus* or Greek word *Paulos*.

Paul was born and raised in the city of Tarsus (Acts 9:11, 30; 11:25; 21:39; 22:3) and was educated within multi-cultural Tarsus as a boy. Being the capital of Cilicia, Tarsus was the political, commercial, intellectual, and cultural center of Cilicia. Jerome Murphy-O'Connor narrates the likelihood that Paul was trained first in the basic skills of reading, writing, arithmetic, but also in an education "inculcating knowledge of and respect for the institutions of state and religion."[15] As a Jewish boy and young man in Tarsus and Jerusalem, Paul studied Hebrew and/or Aramaic and the Septuagint, besides Greek and Latin (Acts 21:40, 22:2, 26:14). Paul was trained in the Greco-Roman rhetorical tradition as the essential aspect of ancient oral and literacy cultures. He was "thoroughly at home in the Greek idiom of his time,"[16] though 2 Cor 10:10 recounts that Paul's words were unimpressive and not eloquently moving, and 1 Cor 2:5 records his ironic contrasts between the wisdom of the world with the power of God; between the power of the Spirit with mere secular rhetorical manipulation. Yet, this is not a total rejection of the rhetorical tradition.

His letters remind us of his Jewish heritage. Paul found pride as an "Israelite, a descendant of Abraham, a member of the tribe of Benjamin" (Rom 11:1). He was "circumcised on the eight day" (Phil 3:5) according to the Torah, but in the eyes of the Roman world, circumcision was a physical mutilation, so he was "marked" as a Jew. Paul was proud of his hybrid identity, foremost that of his ancestral tradition: "Of the people of Israel, of the tribe of Benjamin" (Phil 3:6). When Paul was challenged by his opponents in Galatia—the Judaizers—regarding his apostleship and the truth of the gospel, he defended himself by recounting how steeped his former life was in the Jewish religion and how zealous he was for the traditions of his ancestors (Gal 1:13-14). Likewise, when the Corinthian super-apostles questioned his credentials as the apostle of Christ, Paul replied passionately, "Are they Hebrews? So am I! Are they Israelites? So am I! Are they descendants of Abraham? So am I!" (2 Cor 11:22, RSV)

Despite living in the Diaspora and thus in the mix of Greco-Roman-Jewish cosmopolitan cultures, Paul was familiar with the ancient tongue (Hebrew), the old traditions (Abraham, Torah), and the holy city (Jerusalem). He was able to travel to urban centers like Antioch in Syria, Ephesus in Asia Minor, Philippi, Corinth, Athens in Greece, and Rome in Italy. According to Acts 18:3, Paul learned tent-making to support himself, even after he became an apostle.[17]

Crossing Cultures of Jews and Gentiles

As a loyal Pharisaic Jew, Paul was concerned with how Gentiles could come into the full citizenship of the people of God—by adopting the law of Israel. In the Jewish tradition, Gentiles are sinners because ("by nature," says Paul; Gal 2:15 see also Rom 2:14) they do not have the Jewish law. Lloyd Gaston has shown that some of the writings of Paul's early rabbinic contemporaries express the view that both Jews and Gentiles will have a relationship with God, especially in the end-time, but only through the Torah (directly for the Jews or indirectly for the Gentiles).[18] E. P. Sanders has observed that in some "of Palestinian Jewish literature between Ben Sirach and the redaction of the Mishnah, with . . . the exception of 4 Ezra, membership in the covenant is considered salvation."[19] According to Pharisaic belief, both Jews and Gentiles can achieve and maintain their status in the membership of God only by observing Torah. Paul's zeal for Torah in persecuting the Christian movement can be seen in this light.

Law is a sacred tradition, that which society counts as upright. Torah to Paul is a cultural and religious code that identifies him as a Jew, more particularly as a Pharisee (Phil 3:5; cf. Acts 5:34, 22:3, 23:6, 26:5). Paul's past experience in Romans 7 and Galatians 2 does not stand for

Jews in general but represents Paul's distorted practice of the law when
he was a Pharisee who persecuted the church. The law became a form of
cultural arrogance for Paul, rather than the way of righteousness that it
should have been.[20]

Paul in Gal 1:13-17 recalls that experience explicitly: how in his
former life (*pote*) he "advanced in Judaism" (*proekopton en tô
Ioudaïsmô*).[21] He possessed extreme zeal towards the tradition of his
ancestors—the law. According to the Torah tradition, zeal for God's
commandment is the preservation of Israel's absolute loyalty to Yahweh,
Israel's well being (cf. Sir 48:1-2; 1 Macc 2:23-26), and the redemption
of Israel from God's wrath (cf. Num 25:6-13). Any violation of such
loyalty to the Torah, as in the case of believing in a crucified Messiah
and a Christological critique of the law (cf. Acts 7 and 8) is a threat to
the well being of Israel. Zeal connotes more than commitment and
adoration. In its extreme or distorted form, it may result in the use of
violence ("persecuting to the extreme" in Gal 1:13). Maintaining that
righteousness and zeal across culture and religion often results in
persecution (Gal 1:23; 4:29; 5:11; 6:12; Acts 9:4; 22:7; 26:14) of the
church of God (see 1 Cor 15:9; Phil 3:6).

There was nothing wrong with Paul's commitment to the Jewish faith
and tradition by observing the laws. The problem is not inner-cultural,
but cross-cultural. The problem is that Paul in his zealous obedience to
the Jewish faith and tradition demanded others (Gentiles and Christians)
to do the same. There is nothing wrong for Jews to devote themselves
totally to the law; there is nothing threatening for Christians to believe in
the crucified Messiah. But when a zealous Jew wants a Christian to be a
faithful Jew, expecting them to subscribe to the ancestral tradition of the
Torah, or when the crucified Messiah of the Christian is seen as a threat
to or a betrayal of Torah, then fear, hatred and annihilation take form.

Previously as a Pharisee, Paul might only accept *qahal* Yahweh (the
congregation of Israel) as law observing people, whether they were Jews
or Gentiles. He was not aware that the church *of God* might be the
extension of "the congregation of Israel" (Deut 23:2-3). After his call,
Paul was able to recognize that this Christian church, believing in the
crucified Messiah, is indeed the church *of God*. As a Pharisee, he was
offended by the thought that a Jewish sect (Christian Jews) might confess
the crucified Jesus to be the Messiah of God, because the law is the law
of God, and the law condemned anyone who is crucified as a criminal
(Deut 21:23; Gal 3:13). As a Pharisee, he is sure that anyone confessing
that the crucified Jesus is the Messiah of God and calling themselves the
church *of God* is blasphemous. But that understanding is prior to the
apocalypse (revelation) of God to Paul.

Cross-Cultural Theology of Paul's Conversion[22]

Paul's "conversion" experience (at Damascus; 36 CE) was of cross-cultural significance as he was called to be an apostle to the Gentiles (Rom 11:13, 15:16, cf. Rom 1:13, 11:11, 16:4). Galatians 1:15 is an account of Paul's conversion from an identity as a Jew to that of a Jewish Christian—a turning from a law-abider to a cross-cultural missionary of Christ. Paul gained a new perspective on the Messiah and on the relation of Jews and Gentiles in God's people. The new perspective does not oppose God's passivity in Paul's former life to God's activity in Paul's converted life. Rather, his new perspective confirms God's gracious initiatives (cf. Gal 1:3, 6, 15; 2:9, 21; 5:4; 6:18) throughout the process of "setting him apart in my mother's womb" (Gal 1:15, Rom 1:1)—"setting apart" (*aphorisas*) means consecrated for service. Paul does not trace his call to his Jewish training, education, and culture. Rather, he traces it to the God who is the author of grace and the God of the prophets; although his Jewish tradition is sacred, his prophetic call to service is apocalyptic; it involves God's intruding and claiming acts upon human lives.

Paul's encounter with Christ on the road to Damascus (according to Acts, cf. Gal 1:13-14) brings about a "conversion experience"—not a conversion from one religion to another, but a conversion from one practice of piety to another. Paul saw the danger of being religious, the impotence of the law to break the power of sin, the curse of the law to exclude Gentiles as people of God, and the danger in the segregation of God's heirs. Perhaps it is this kind of critical autobiographical reflection that convinced Paul all the more regarding the crucified Messiah. Claiming that God's Son as Messiah was crucified is neither foolishness, nor weakness, nor profanity. The crucified Messiah symbolized God's wisdom, God's power, and God's holiness. The Cross is a divine paradigm to address the problems of cultural superiority and distorted religious zeal of all humanity.

Violence and persecution result from a cultural and/or religious group that boasts of its wisdom, power, and sacredness as superior to those of other cultural and religious groups. In modern terminologies, we call this ethnocentrism, imperialism, or hegemony. Paul's conversion begins with the realization that the crucified Messiah was absolutely obedient not to the law but to God alone. Christ did not hold on to his right; he did not retaliate on the Cross. On the contrary, the Messiah gave himself up, accepted the violence of the cross from humanity, and thus proved the love of God for all (Rom 5:8).

The second point is the union between Christ and the church of God; they are not the same but they are so intimately related to each other that if Paul persecutes God's church, he actually persecutes Christ. This point focuses the discussion on the elect people of God: Who belongs to God's people, with full-member status? What is the identity symbol for the people of God? The law? or Christ? Romans discusses this issue under the rubric of cultural and theological conflict between "the circumcised and the uncircumcised" (Jew and Gentile Christians).

Cultural and Theological Conflicts in Romans

The Situation of Romans

Scholars study the situation presupposed by Romans for many purposes.[23] Paul wrote Romans approximately in 57 CE (probably at Corinth), partly in preparation to visit Jerusalem (Rom 15:25, 30-32; cf. Acts 21:1-16) for the offering (or collection), but also to seek support from the Roman churches for his gospel mission.[24] Romans is also written to address the polemical tensions in the Roman churches. At that time the Roman house-churches, which Paul probably knew quite well,[25] were not unified (15:7-13). Relationships within these ethnically, ideologically, and religiously mixed congregations had produced conflicts. Romans 14:1-15:13 suggests that the conflict was between "the weak," the Law-observant Jewish Christians and "the strong," the Law-free Gentile Christians. While the "weak" might have included a few Gentile Christians who practiced the law, the "strong" might have included a few Jewish Christians who felt freedom from the law because of the advent of the Messiah.[26] Romans 15:1-6 and 7-13 show that "Gentile" and "Jewish" are not only ethnic designations, but also terms that distinguish attitudes toward the Law. Most of the Jewish Christians at Rome emphasized the traditional observances of their ancestral faith; most of the Gentile Christians felt it unnecessary to subscribe to Torah because they were now in Christ.

The ugliness of this conflict is seen in the name-calling between Jewish and Gentile Christians. The Jewish Christians used the "circumcision/ uncircumcision" terminology, while the Gentile Christians used the "weak/strong" terminology.[27] Fourteen of the thirty-five instances of "circumcision" and eleven of the twenty uses of "uncircumcision" in the New Testament appear in Romans. Marcus surveys these two terms against the rabbinic usage of *mîlâ* (circumcised penis) and *'orlâ* (foreskin) and concludes that "circumcision/ uncircumcision" should be translated concretely as "circumcised penis" and "(glans)/foreskin," rather than with the abstractions of "state of being circumcised/uncircumcised."[28] These "circumcision/uncircumcision" terms are epithets designating groups of people in Romans (2:26-27; 3:30; 4:9; 15:8) for a dual purpose, both to insult others and to lift up one's own pride.[29] Notice also that the use of circumcision in Rom 2:25-

27 is preceded by a citation of Isaiah 52:5 in Rom 2:24, "which speaks of
the name of God being *blasphemed* among the Gentiles because of the
Jews."[30] One of the problems in the Roman congregations was therefore
one group's assertion of superiority over the other (cf. 1:7, 16, 2:25-29,
8:33, 9:6-13, 11:5-7, 28-32).

Theological Response of Paul

Paul responds to this cultural and theological conflict among the
house-churches in Rome by talking about the righteousness of God. As a
pastoral theologian working in the concreteness of a missionary
situation, he exhorts the Roman Christians to live and cooperate for the
sake of the gospel mission and so that both Jews and Gentiles (11:17-24)
may eventually worship God together (15:8-12). Indeed, God is the God
of Jews and Gentiles (cf. Rom 3:29). Paul's theological reflection on this
issue can be summarized by the following outline of Romans. The
outline reflects a reading that takes as most significant Paul's thesis:
Equality of all peoples (Jew and Gentile) in the Righteousness of God
(against all cultural boastings) as manifested in the Gospel of Christ.

Exordium (Introduction): Romans 1:1-17
    Definition of the inclusive gospel in relation to the gospel
    partnership between Paul and the Roman Christians
First Proof: Romans 1:18-4:25
    On the Righteousness of God in setting right all (sin of all and
    justification of all by God's righteousness) to imply equality of
    sinfulness, thus elimination of cultural boastings
Second Proof: Romans 5:1-8:39
    On the Righteousness of God in the new life of the spiritual
    community (righteousness of faith as a reality of eschatological
    freedom from cultural boastings)
Third Proof: Romans 9:1-11:36
    On the Righteousness of God and salvation history to imply
    equality between Jewish and Gentile Christians under the faithful
    God
Fourth Proof: Romans 12:1-15:13
    On Righteousness of God in communal practice to imply equality
    in gifts and graces
Peroratio (Conclusion): Romans 15:14-16:27
    On Christian solidarity and recommendations for the gospel
    mission to imply Oneness (impartiality) of God and celebration of
    cultural diversity of the people of God

Given the audience of Jewish and Gentile Christians (not Jews and Gentiles in general), and if we assume that the main theme is Christian unity in and for the sake of the gospel of Christ, the word "righteousness" is so significant that it is discussed in every chapter of the letter. "Made right" (*dikaioun*), "set right" (*dikaioô*), or "righteousness" (*dikaiosynê*) are traditionally understood as justification or justified, meaning God imputing his righteousness on a person so that he or she can enter the covenant of salvation. Some have used the words "set right" to translate *dikai-* Greek words in the sense that a person or people group maintains the covenant-relation, a set-right relationship that defines this people. The root *dikai-* can also mean to show justice, to vindicate someone as just, or to acquit someone. The emphasis may not necessarily be upon the sinlessness of the just; rather it is upon the one (in this case, God) who graciously vindicates or acquits others. The meaning can be about acquittal from guilt and sin in the sense of wrong; it can also be about setting right by God from shame and curse so that propriety, honor, and freedom characterize the rightful relationship a group of people has with God.

Returning to the cross-cultural significance of Paul's "conversion" experience, it is possible to read Romans 7 metaphorically as describing *not* the typical behavior of a Pharisee but the distorted zeal of Paul the Pharisee whose strict conformity to the law resulted in his persecution of the Christian church. This behavior, viewed retrospectively, does not reveal a fault of the Jewish law, for Paul affirms the holiness and goodness of the law/cultural ideal and attributes his frustrated experience to the power of sin working through the law. His devotion to the law, to his own cultural and religious traditions, blinded him to the new act of the righteousness of God in Christ, who has opened up salvation to the (Gentile) world. Looking back, Paul arrives at a new view of the law, which has now become for him the new law of the Spirit. Paul finds victory over his dilemma in "the law of the Spirit of life in Christ Jesus" (Rom 8:2), which is more inclusive than Paul's old conception of the law and is essential for the co-existence and salvation of both Jews and Gentiles (all people).

Rom 7:7-25 serves to remind Jewish Christians not to abuse the Jewish law (like Paul once did) but to live in the Spirit before God and with Gentile Christians. It encourages Gentile Christians not to take pride in their own traditions and not to consider themselves strong and Jewish Christians weak (cf. Romans 14). For both Jewish and Gentile believers are now in Christ Jesus (Rom 8:1), and the law of the Spirit has led both groups into victory over sin and death (8:2-13) and into confession that they are all children of God (8:14). Those in Christ (7:25) and in the Spirit (8:2) do not abrogate but fulfill the law (8:4).

Gentile Christians are reminded not to boast of their cultural uniqueness, for the thesis of the "priority of Israel" in Romans 9-11 has shown that Gentiles owe their spiritual blessings to the Jews. It is not the Gentiles who support the Jewish root, but the root supports the engrafted branch of the Gentiles (Rom 11:18). Gentiles have come to share the spiritual blessings of the Jews (Rom 15:27). There seems to be divine warrant for the privilege of the Jews when Paul writes of the Jewish distinctions: "They are Israelites, and to them belong the sonship, the glory, the covenants, the giving of the law, the worship, and the promises; to them belong the patriarchs, and of their race, according to the flesh, is the Christ" (Rom 9:4-5). The gospel of Christ was promised long ago through the Jewish prophets in the holy scriptures (Rom 1:3; cf. 3:21). This is the gospel of God's Son, who was descended from David (Rom 1:4).

William S. Campbell argues that, in Romans, Paul makes a positive connection between Jewish law and the gospel:

> This is demonstrated in the phrases, law of faith (3:27); the law of the Spirit (8:3); the just requirement (*dikaioma*) of the law (to be fulfilled in us) (8:4); God's law (8:7); Christ, the goal (*telos*) or end of the law (10:4); love is the fulfilling of the law (13:10). These taken together with Paul's concluding argument that 'Christ became a servant to the circumcised to show God's faithfulness in order to confirm the promises given to the patriarchs . . .' (15:8), reveal a concern unique in Paul's letters to demonstrate positive continuity between the new way and the parent faith in Judaism.[31]

In Christ there is no discrimination and no boasting by either Jews or Gentiles because God is the impartial (Rom 2:11, 16:27) God of Jews and Gentiles (3:29).

One of the implications of Paul's cross-cultural theology for Jews and Gentiles in Romans is the way interpreters of Paul continue his hermeneutical legacy. The gospel of Christ has traveled throughout the world, propelled by the impetus of bringing the salvation of Christ to all that began in Paul's time. Yet the theological footprints of Paul in Africa, South America, Asia, and many faith communities in North America are often washed offshore. This volume aims at allowing Paul's gospel in Romans to take new steps in these new territories and at discovering those that it has already taken there.

Cultural Interpretations of Paul[32]

We have mentioned the cross-cultural character of Paul's mission and theology. Yet, not all Pauline scholars would see their works as following in the footsteps of Paul. Most of us are familiar with Paul the apostle to Europe and North America. Pauline scholarship has been greatly enriched by European and North American scholars. When we recommend commentaries on Romans to students or Bible study group leaders in our churches, the works of Karl Barth, C. E. B. Cranfield, James D. G. Dunn, Ernst Käsemann, and Joseph A. Fitzmyer seem to set the standard imprint for Paul's meaning.[33] There is nothing wrong with the "standard imprint." In a global village of biblical interpretation, however, our challenge is "to edify one another" (Rom 14:19), especially for "the strong" to help "the weak" (Rom 14:1-15:13).

There is "Paul the Apostle to America" but there is no Paul the Apostle to Africa.[34] Behind the Chinese-script cover of commentaries on Romans, the Paul I often encounter seems unaware of China and Chinese situations, issues, and thoughts. Worse, the impression I often have is, that Paul is articulated within European contexts, and "Paul" seems eager to use a particular worldview and methods of reading foreign for the Chinese readers. I hope that my experience with Chinese scholarship on Paul is unique, and that this experience does not prove to be true in Latin American, African, and other Asian contexts—although I know that in many cases my experience is repeated.

The critical issue raised here is *not* that of minimizing the contributions of European and North American biblical scholarship on Paul. That Paul, an Hellenist Jewish Christian apostle, is conversant with the European and North American academic and pastoral readings of Romans. The issue is *not* whether Asian scholars should use methodologies or hold to the interpretations proposed by European scholars—of course all methodologies have their own validity. The question is how to challenge Pauline interpreters to do critical and faithful readings of Romans as they navigate Paul's message in less sailed waters into less traveled lands. This challenge is consistent with Paul's original intention to bring the gospel of Christ to Spain (Rom 15:24, 28), the end of the (ancient) world.

This advocacy (of learning from those who have done cultural readings of Romans) is *not* to criticize the works of "first" world scholars but to consult with them regarding the cultural ways they exegete Romans, and perhaps to glean from their fruits how to read Romans culturally in the "two-thirds" world.

Throughout the history of biblical interpretation, Paul was interpreted culturally. In these cultural interpretations Paul was in the images (direct reflections or inverted reflections) of his interpreters. For example, the

Ebionites, a conservative Jewish Christian movement, read Paul as an apostate Jew because Paul to them seemed to reject their Jewish laws.[35] Marcion (2nd century) read Paul as a Gnostic thinker whose ten epistles (excluding the Pastorals) and his antitheses between law and gospel, flesh and spirit, works and faith in turn reinforced Marcion's theology. In partial reaction to Marcion, the church fathers (Greek and Latin), such as Irenaeus, Origen, Chrysostom, and Jerome regarded Paul as the champion of Gentile Christianity, defender of orthodoxy, legislator of morality. Paul was interpreted in the Hellenistic perspective that the church fathers embodied.[36] Again, we see the nineteenth century's Hellenistic Paul was projected through the religious and philosophical lenses of the Enlightenment, and Paul's Jewishness faded into the background. F. C. Baur and the Tübingen School employed the Hegelian philosophy of their times to read Paul, with the result that Pauline freedom and Jewish legalism were perceived in a similar Hegelian relationship (i.e., eventually producing second century early catholicism out of Pauline Christianity).[37] Paul was read in the nineteenth century using rationalistic or mythological lenses, with the result that the heart of Pauline theology was interpreted not as the objective, redemptive, historical event of Christ's incarnation, death, and resurrection (the "Christ event"). Rather, the ethical, mystical (non objective) communion of believers with Christ, leading to a life of love and liberty was perceived as the core of Pauline theology.[38] For example, Albert Schweitzer interpreted Jesus as an apocalyptic visionary who proclaimed the Kingdom of Heaven.[39] In *Die Mystik des Apostels Paulus*, Schweitzer argued that since the kingdom of God failed to arrive at Christ's death and resurrection, Paul faced a new situation and he turned to Christ-mysticism. The mystical doctrine of dying and rising with Christ became the central feature of Pauline theology. Schweitzer believed that "being in Christ is the prime enigma of the Pauline teaching: once grasped it gives the clue to the whole."[40]

Building on the Tübingen dichotomy between Palestinian and Hellenistic Christianity, the twentieth century comparative religious school (*religionsgeschichtliche Schule*) read Paul's Christology using the contexts of the mystery religions and the pagan cults.[41] Richard Reitzenstein read Paul using a cultural lens of Eastern Gnosticism and concluded that Gnostic terminology (e.g. *gnosis, doxa, nous, pneuma, pnematikos,* etc.) was the source of Paul's Christology.[42] R. Bultmann's *religions-geschichtliche* approach to New Testament used Heideggeran existential philosophy to read Paul, seeking to make the Cross understandable and acceptable to modern readers. The result of the Bultmannian reading is to remove the historical basis of redemptive event and transfer it to the realm of purely experiential.[43] Thus,

Bultmann understands Pauline theology regarding God's work of salvation through Christ's death and resurrection as a non-historically verifiable space-time event.[44] For Bultmann, the significant point is that, through the Christ event, the *kerygma* (proclamation) is preached, calling people to a decision of faith. As to the source of Paul's thought, Bultmann finds it not in the mystery religions' myth of the dying-rising redeemer god but in an alleged pre-Christian Gnosticism (the myth of a preexistent heavenly Redeemer who descends, conquers, and frees people from the threatening powers of the cosmos).

It will not be difficult to show that Paul was read in the context of the Roman culture, especially in Peter Ramsay and F. F. Bruce's works. Ramsay's research led him to abandon F. C. Baur's thesis and accept Luke's reliability as a historian. Ramsay further argues for the influence of Paul's Roman citizenship on his personality and missionary practices: his cosmopolitan vision to spread the gospel throughout the Roman Empire; his adaptability to changing circumstances; his organizational and administrative gifts by means of postal, transportation, and political resources of his world; his respect of civil government (in Rom 13:1-7).[45]

As cultural lenses of interpreters change, Paul's images shift as well. Joachim Jeremias, F. F. Bruce, Seyoon Kim find the ultimate key to Pauline theology not in Tarsus, Jerusalem, or Rome, but on the road to Damascus; i.e., Paul is a Christian and his Christian identity supersedes all his cultural backgrounds. Jeremias maintains that the key that unlocks the mindset of the apostle, such as the Law, election, Christology, the apostolate and its missionary obligation, ecclesiology, is his conversion experience (i.e., his meeting with the risen Lord).[46] Bruce speaks of the significant Christophany event at the Damascus Road.[47] Kim emphasizes Jesus' exalted lordship and divine sonship, Christ as the image of God, the "in Christ" concept, the body of Christ, human's solidarity with Adam and the believers' solidarity with Christ the Second Adam.[48]

The omnipresent principle of a cultural reading of Paul is evident throughout the history of hermeneutics, though most traditional exegetes neither admit nor make explicit their cultural lenses. The above review of the history of Pauline interpretation has shown that no interpreter of Paul is ever free from a cultural reading.

Navigating Equipments in Cultural Interpretation

How to empower the voices of interpreters of Romans from all lands, so that they are equipped with broader equipments to sail in new territories? The consciousness of (cross-)cultural reading of Paul is sensitized by social-scientific methodologies. The major trend of sociological study helps scholars to look for the horizontal coordinates (cultural anthropology, philosophy, sociology, or psychology) as they employ "a hermeneutics of social embodiment"[49] to understand Paul. For example, John Gager, *Kingdom and Community: The Social World of Early Christianity* reads Paul within the millenarian politics of his day.[50] Abraham J. Malherbe examines Pauline theology and community among the Greek manual laborers and Greek philosophical traditions.[51] Bruce J. Malina's cultural anthropological studies and Wayne A. Meeks' social world analysis provide scholars new insights into the cultural environment of Pauline community and personality.[52]

Since every reading is inevitably a cross-cultural reading in the sense that interpreters cannot recover completely the cultural meaning of Paul, the way to help us overcome our biases is to be truthful to ourselves regarding our presuppositions, self-critical of our readings, and engage in a "collective interpretive practice" of "scriptural criticism."[53] Grenholm and Patte have articulated the blueprint of scriptural criticism in the first volume of this series. I want to highlight one point and raise a critical question that I see as relevant to cultural interpretation of Romans for writers of this volume.

Scriptural criticism uses three frames or criteria for making truth-claims and interpretations of the text. Grenholm and Patte write:

> [I]nterpreters use certain *contextual-pragmatic criteria* when they make truth-claims in their social roles in life as responsible members of a given society and culture—and, in the academic world, as practical theologians and activists. They use certain *analytic* criteria in their roles as responsible readers of biblical texts—and, in the academic world, as biblical scholars. Finally, they use certain *hermeneutical* criteria in their roles as responsible believers—and, in the academic world, as systematic theologians.[54]

These three basic modes of interpretation interact with each other in any given reading process. In the cultural and cross-cultural readings of Romans, the discussion on scriptural criticism is helpful as it aims towards interpretations that are critical and receptions that are contextual. The tripolar practice of scriptural criticism is taken seriously—the scriptural text, the believers' life-context, and the believers' religious perceptions of life.[55] Throughout the volume the markings of **C A H**

C Contextual/pragmatic frame.

A Analytical frame.

H Hermeneutical frame.

and **I** in the footnotes are guide to readers who wish to know how this heuristic tool of scripture criticism works. They are by no means comprehensives.

The critical question I want to ask regarding "scripture criticism" is suggested by the subtitle of the first volume of the series—"legitimacy and plausibility of divergent interpretations." Each chapter in this volume will have a different response to that question. Appropriately, they are "divergent interpretations." But since the practice and critical reflection of the (cross-)cultural reading of Romans has been practiced in relatively few published works, none of the chapters is ready to offer a confident response to the question of the "legitimacy and plausibility" of the proposed interpretation. This is not to say we are suspicious of our work; we are confident they are "legitimately" grounded in the text. But navigating Romans through cultures is a challenging task, for there are too many icebergs in the uncharted territories. These challenging readings in this volume pose many questions to traditional understandings of what is legitimate without entering in this discussion at this time. Yet we can say that the voyage has given us surprising discoveries.

The criteria for the "plausibility of divergent interpretations" is similarly beyond the scope of this book. We all admit that we cannot know for certain what Paul actually means, for example, in Romans 8. But in light of our life-contexts and religious perceptions of life, each of us offers a particular reading and test its plausibility, knowing that more than one interpretation can be reasonable. This assumption is based on the conviction that the interaction among the three poles constitutes the dynamic reading process. Thus, it is not just the scriptural text that determines the meaning. The purpose of (cross-)cultural interpretation in this volume is neither to resolve the exegetical impasse of some texts nor to differentiate competing interpretations. Rather, the goal is to work on a contextual hermeneutic of faithful interpretations of Romans for the global village. The globally-sensitive hermeneutic process brings about dialogue which entails negotiating old boundaries of traditional readings of Romans, and to move beyond vantage points of "first" world scholars. We hope the intended result is a more richly interpreted Pauline text.

The volume will enable readers to appreciate biblical scholarship of reading Romans from diverse cultural locations. It is hoped these studies will challenge the voyage of our readings of Romans, bring us surprises upon surprises in our discovery of the interactions between Romans and cultures, and help interpreters to chart new ways beyond old boundaries.

I   Interplay between two or more frames.

Notes

1. The existing cross-cultural reading of Romans are discussed in this volume: Elsa Tamez, *The Amnesty of Grace: Justification by Faith from a Latin American Perspective*, trans. Sharon H. Ringe (Nashville: Abingdon Press, 1993), 93-117, is discussed in chapter five; Loretta Dornisch, *Paul and Third Women Theologians* (Collegeville: Liturgical Press, 1999), 69-95, is discussed in the last chapter.

2. Daniel Boyarin, *A Radical Jew: Paul and the Politics of Identity* (Berkeley: University of California Press, 1994), 5. The introductory essay in Boyarin's book is instructive regarding both Paul's own cultural reading and plausible readings of Paul by his interpreters, including our own cultural readings of Romans.

3. See Richard Peterson, "Revitalizing the Culture Concept," *Annual Review of Sociology* 5 (1979), 137-166. I have added "material substance," which might overlap with his "expressive symbols." For further, see Kathryn Tanner, *Theories of Culture: A New Agenda for Theology* (Minneapolis: Fortress Press, 1997).

4. Peter L. Berger, *Sacred Canopy: Elements of a Sociological Theory of Religion* (Garden City: Doubleday, 1967), 6.

5. Berger, *Sacred Canopy*, 22. See also, Tanner, *Theories of Culture*, 33.

6. See for example the usage of culture by Edward B. Tylor, *Primitive Culture: Researches into the Development of Mythology, Philosophy, Religion, Art, and Custom*, Vol. 1: *The Origins of Culture* (London: J. Murray, 1871), 1.

7. Tylor, *Primitive Culture*, 1.

8. See Tanner's helpful critique of modern understanding of culture in her *Theories of Culture*, 38-58.

9. See a similar understanding in Stephen Neill, "Religion and Culture: A Historical Introduction," in John Stott and Robert T. Coote ed., *Gospel and Culture: The Papers of a Consultation on the Gospel and Culture* (Pasadena, California: William Carey Library, 1979), 1.

10. Bronislaw Malinowski, *A Scientific Theory of Culture and Other Essays* (New York: Oxford University Press, 1960), esp. chaps. 4-7.

11. Matthew Arnold, *Culture and Anarchy* (Cambridge: Cambridge University Press, 1932), 48-49.

12. See Charles H. Cosgrove, Herold Weiss, Yeo Khiok-khng, *Cross-cultural Paul* (Grand Rapids: Eerdmans, forthcoming), Yeo, "Culture and Intersubjectivity as Criteria of Negotiating Meanings in Cross-cultural Interpretations," in Charles H. Cosgrove ed., *The Meanings We Choose* (Edinburgh: T&T Clark, 2004), 81-100.

13. See Boyarin, *A Radical Jew*, 5.

14. See Daniel Patte, *Discipleship according to the Sermon on the Mount: Four Legitimate Readings, Four Plausible Views of Discipleship, and Their Relative Values* (Valley Forge: Trinity Press International, 1996). Also, Charles H. Cosgrove, *Elusive Israel: The Puzzle of Election in Romans* (Louisville: Westminster/John Knox, 1997), 38-45 on "interpretive will and hermeneutical responsibility"; *idem, Appealing to Scripture in Moral Debate: Five Hermeneutical Rules* (Grand Rapids: Eerdmans, 2002), passim on rules of adjudication in moral debate of interpreting scripture.

15. Jerome Murphy-O'Connor, *Paul, A Critical Life* (Oxford: Clarendon, 1996), 47.

16. George Kennedy, *New Testament Interpretation Through Rhetorical Criticism* (Chapel Hill: University of North Carolina Press, 1984), 10.

17. See R. F. Hock, *The Social Context of Paul's Ministry: Tentmaking and Apostleship* (Philadelphia: Fortress, 1980).

18. L. Gaston, *Paul and the Torah* (Vancouver: University of British Columbia Press, 1987), 28.

19. E. P. Sanders, "The Covenant as a Soteriological Category and the Nature of Salvation in Palestinian and Hellenistic Judaism," R. Hamerton-Kelly and R. Scroggs ed., *Jews, Greeks and Christians* (Leiden; Brill, 1976), 15.

20. See my article, "Culture and Intersubjectivity as Criteria for Negotiating Meanings in Cross-Cultural Interpretations," 81-100. In it I use Romans 7 to reconstruct Paul's pharisaic experience of wanting to love the law and the result of persecuting the church. This interpretation was first suggested by Robert Jewett (in a class lecture at Garrett-Evangelical Theological Seminary).

21. A term coined in the Hellenistic period referring to the religion of the Jews (cf. 2 Macc 2:21; 8:1). In the New Testament, it occurs only in Gal 1:13, 14, cf. 2:14. See J. Louis Martyn, *Galatians: A New Translation with Introduction and Commentary* (Anchor Bible; New York: Doubleday, 1997), 163-164.

22. "Conversion" is used here not in the anachronistic sense of Paul changing religious faith from Judaism to Christianity; in Paul's day, these two religious faiths are not yet differentiated. "Conversion" is used here to refer to Paul's taking a radical view of his own Torah tradition as well as of the way Christ as Messiah fits into the picture of God's salvation for Jews and Gentiles. I think the experience is so radical the term "conversion" is appropriate. Gaventa's position is that Paul's Damascus experience is a transformation, rather than a conversion or alternation: "Paul does not reject the past, rather it has been subjected by the advent of the Messiah." Beverly Roberts Gaventa, *From Darkness to*

Light: Aspects of Conversion in the New Testament (Philadelphia: Fortress, 1988), 40.

23. See Karl P. Donfried ed., *The Romans Debate* (Minneapolis: Augsburg Publishing House, 1977).

24. Robert Jewett, "Roman as an Ambassadorial Letter," *Interpretations* 36 (1982), 5-20.

25. In chapter 16, Paul greets most of the thirty individuals by name, which enables Paul to write to their local, specifi͜c situation.   However, T. W. Manson disagrees and suggests that chapter 16 is an addendum to a letter originally sent to the church of Ephesus; K. P. Donfried and R. E. Brown have given a response to Manson's argument.   See, T. W. Manson, "St. Paul's Letter to the Romans—and Others," *The Romans Debate*, 1-16.

26. As suggested by Ulrich Wilckens, *Der Brief an die Römer*, 3 volumes (Zürich: Benziger; Neukirchen-Vluyn: Neukirchener Verlag, 1978-1982), 3:111-115.

27. For detailed analysis, see Joel Marcus, "The Circumcision and the Uncircumcision in Rome," *New Testament Studies* 35 (1989): 73-81.

28. Marcus, "The Circumcision," 75.

29. Marcus, "The Circumcision," 75; and Wilckens, *Römer*, 1:155 n. 398.

30. Marcus, "The Circumcision," 79.

31. William S. Campbell, *Paul's Gospel in an Intercultural Context. Jew and Gentile in the Letter to the Romans* (Frankfurt, Bern, New York, Paris: Peter Lang, 1991), 144.

32. I am indebted to John Gillman, "Recent Perspectives in Pauline Studies," *Living Light* 3 (1988) 255-266; Don N. Howell, Jr., "Pauline Thought in the History of Interpretation," *Bibliotheca Sacra* 150 (1993): 303-326, for the review of interpretations on Paul.

33. Karl Barth, *The Epistle to the Romans*, trans. Edwyn C. Hoskyns (London: Oxford University Press, H. Milford, 1933), C. E. B. Cranfield, *A Critical and Exegetical Commentary on the Epistle to the Romans*, 2 vols. (Edinburgh: T&T Clark, 1975-1979), James D. G. Dunn, *Romans 1-8; Romans 9-16* (2 vols.) (Dallas: Word, 1988), Joseph A. Fitzmyer, *Romans: A New Translation with Introduction and Commentary* (Doubleday: Anchor Bible, 1992), Ernst Käsemann, *Commentary on Romans*, trans. Geoffrey W. Bromiley (Grand Rapids: Eerdmans, 1980).

34. Robert Jewett, *Paul, Apostle to America: Cultural Trends and Pauline Scholarship* (Louisville: Westminster/John Knox, 1994).

35. Jaroslav Pelikan, *The Emergence of the Catholic Tradition (100-600)* (Chicago: University of Chicago Press, 1971), 23-24.

36. Pelikan, *The Emergence of the Catholic Tradition*, 71-81, 112-113.

37. F. C. Baur, "Die Christuspartei in der korinthischen Gemeinde, der Gegensatz der petrinishchen und paulinischen Christenthums in der ältesten Kirche, der Apostel Petrus in Rom," in Klaus Scholder ed., *Ausgewählte Werke in Einzelausgaben* (Stuttgart: Frommann, 1963), 1:1-146: cleavage between the church of Jerusalem and the churches of the Pauline mission. The former's (Peter and James's) concern was with the adherence to the Law and circumcision, and the latter's (Paul's) concern gospel of faith in Christ for the Gentiles. Therefore, the Jerusalem leadership sent emissaries to undermine Paul's authority. The documents that do not reflect this cleavage (Acts, Pastorals) are deutero-Pauline from the second century.

38. E.g., Albert Schweitzer, *Paul and his Interpreters* (London: Adam and Charles Black, 1950); W. Wrede, *Paulus* (1908; see *Paul* [Lexington: American Library Association Committee on Reprinting, 1962]) argues that the person of Jesus had little influenced on Paul, but the apostle "Christianized" the ethical teaching of Jesus that Paul's gospel is different from the Galilean prophet.

39. *The Quest of the Historical Jesus: A Critical Study of Its Progress from Reimarus to Wrede*, 3rd ed. (London: Black, 1954).

40. *Mysticism of Paul the Apostle*, trans. William Montgomery (New York: Macmillan, 1956), 3.

41. They found the origin of Paul's more developed Christology in mystery religions and pagan cults, of Greece (Eleusian), Egypt (Isis and Osiris), Syria (Adonis), Asia Minor (Cybele), and Rome (Mithras). E.g., dying-rising redeemer god, the exalted *kyrios,*" the sacramental redemption, initiation into mystic participation in the deity, gnosis, and pneumatic experience of mystery, all these conditioned Paul's thought. The pioneer of this school is W. Bousset, *Kyrios Christos: A History of Belief in Christ from the Beginnings of Christianity to Irenaeus*, trans. John E. Steely (Nashville: Abingdon, 1970).

42. Richard Reitzenstein, *Hellenistic Mystery-Religions: Their Basic Ideas and Significance*, 3rd ed., trans. John E. Steely (Pittsburgh: Pickwich, 1978).

43. H. Ridderbos, *Paul: An Outline of His Theology* (Grand Rapids: Eerdmans, 1975), 33: "What in Baur was Hegelian idealism, however, is in Bultmann Heideggerian existentialism."

44. R. Bultmann, *Theology of the New Testament*, trans. Kendrick Grobel, 2 vols. in 1 (New York: Charles Scribner's Sons, 1951, 1955), 1:viii, 191.

45. See F. F. Bruce, *Paul: Apostle of the Heart Set Free* (Grand Rapids: Eerdmans, 1977), read *the pax Christus* along side the context of *pax Romana*.

46. Joachim Jeremias, *Der Schlüssel zur Theologie des Apostels Paulus* (Stuttgart: Calwer, 1971).

47. *Apostle of the Heart Set Free*, 74-76.

48. Seyoon Kim, *The Origin of Paul's Gospel* (Grand Rapids: Eerdmans, 1982); see also Timothy J. Ralston, "The Conversion of Paul and Its Significance within His Theological Construct," *Bibliotheca Sacra* 147 (April-June 1990), 198-215.

49. Wayne A. Meeks, "A Hermeneutics of Social Embodiment," *Harvard Theological Review* 79 (1986), 176-186.

50. (Englewood Cliffs: Prentice-Hall, 1975).

51. Abraham Malherbe, *Social Aspects of Early Christianity* (Baton Rouge: Louisiana State University Press, 1977; 2nd edition 1983); *idem*, *Paul and the Popular Philosophers* (Minneapolis: Fortress Press, 1989). See also Hock, *The Social Setting of Paul's Ministry*.

52. Bruce Malina, *Christian Origins and Cultural Anthropology: Practical Models for Biblical Interpretation* (Atlanta: John Knox Press, 1986); Wayne A. Meeks, *The First Urban Christians: the Social World of the Apostle Paul* (Philadelphia: Fortress, 1983), *idem*, *The Moral World of the First Christians* (Philadelphia: Westminster, 1986); J. H. Neyrey, *Paul, in Other Words: A Cultural Reading of His Letters* (Louisville: Westminster, 1990); Francis Watson, *Paul, Judaism and the Gentiles: A Sociological Approach* (Cambridge: Cambridge University Press, 1986).

53. See Cristina Grenholm and Daniel Patte, "Overture: Receptions, Critical Interpretations, and Scriptural Criticism," in Cristina Grenholm and Daniel Patte ed., *Reading Israel in Romans: Legitimacy and Plausibility of Divergent Interpretations* (Harrisburg: Trinity Press International, 2000), 1-54.

54. Grenholm and Patte, "Overture: Scriptural Criticism," 7.

55. *Ibid.*, 19-30.

Works Cited

Arnold, Matthew. *Culture and Anarchy*. Cambridge: Cambridge University Press, 1932.

Barth, Karl. *The Epistle to the Romans*. Trans. Edwyn C. Hoskyns. London: Oxford University Press, H. Milford, 1933.

Baur, F. C. "Die Christuspartei in der korinthischen Gemeinde, der Gegensatz der petrinishchen und paulinischen Christenthums in der ältesten Kirche, der Apostel Petrus in Rom." In Klaus Scholder ed., *Ausgewählte Werke in Einzelausgaben*, 1:1-146. Stuttgart: Frommann, 1963.

Berger, Peter L. *Sacred Canopy: Elements of a Sociological Theory of Religion*. Garden City: Doubleday, 1967.

Bousset, W. *Kyrios Christos: A History of Belief in Christ from the Beginnings of Christianity to Irenaeus.* Trans. John E. Steely. Nashville: Abingdon, 1970.

Boyarin, Daniel. *A Radical Jew: Paul and the Politics of Identity.* Berkeley: University of California Press, 1994.

Bruce, F. F. *Paul: Apostle of the Heart Set Free.* Grand Rapids: Eerdmans, 1977.

Bultmann, R. *Theology of the New Testament.* Trans. Kendrick Grobel. 2 volumes. New York: Charles Scribner's Sons, 1951, 1955.

Campbell, William S. *Paul's Gospel in an Intercultural Context. Jew and Gentile in the Letter to the Romans.* Frankfurt, Bern, New York, Paris: Peter Lang, 1991.

Cosgrove, Charles H. *Elusive Israel: The Puzzle of Election in Romans.* Louisville: Westminster/John Knox, 1997.

_____. *Appealing to Scripture in Moral Debate: Five Hermeneutical Rules.* Grand Rapids: Eerdmans, 2002.

Cosgrove, Charles H., Herold Weiss, and Yeo Khiok-khng. *Crosscultural Paul.* Grand Rapids: Eerdmans, forthcoming.

Cranfield, C. E. B. *A Critical and Exegetical Commentary on the Epistle to the Romans.* 2 volumes. Edinburgh: T&T Clark, 1975-1979.

Donfried, Karl P., ed. *The Romans Debate.* Minneapolis: Augsburg Publishing House, 1977.

Dornisch, Loretta. *Paul and Third Women Theologians.* Collegeville: Liturgical Press, 1999.

Dunn, James D. G. *Romans 1-8; Romans 9-16* (2 vols.) Dallas: Word, 1988.

Fitzmyer, Joseph A. *Romans: A New Translation with Introduction and Commentary.* Doubleday: Anchor Bible, 1992.

Gager, John. *Kingdom and Community: The Social World of Early Christianity.* Englewood Cliffs: Prentice-Hall, 1975.

Gaston, L. *Paul and the Torah.* Vancouver: University of British Columbia Press, 1987.

Gaventa, Beverly Roberts. *From Darkness to Light: Aspects of Conversion in the New Testament.* Philadelphia: Fortress, 1988.

Gillman, John. "Recent Perspectives in Pauline Studies." *Living Light* 3 (1988) 255-266.

Grenholm, Cristina, and Daniel Patte. "Overture: Receptions, Critical Interpretations, and Scriptural Criticism." Pages 1-54 in *Reading Israel in Romans: Legitimacy and Plausibility of Divergent Interpretations.* Edited by Cristina Grenholm and Daniel Patte. Harrisburg: Trinity Press International, 2000.

Hock, R. F. *The Social Context of Paul's Ministry: Tentmaking and Apostleship.* Philadelphia: Fortress, 1980.

Howell, Jr., Don N. "Pauline Thought in the History of Interpretation." *Bibliotheca Sacra* 150 (1993): 303-326.

Jeremias, Joachim. *Der Schlüssel zur Theologie des Apostels Paulus.* Stuttgart: Calwer, 1971.

Jewett, Robert. "Roman as an Ambassadorial Letter." *Interpretations* 36 (1982): 5-20.

_____. *Paul, Apostle to America: Cultural Trends and Pauline Scholarship.* Louisville: Westminster/John Knox, 1994.

Käsemann, Ernst. *Commentary on Romans.* Trans. Geoffrey W. Bromiley. Grand Rapids: Eerdmans, 1980.

Kennedy, George. *New Testament Interpretation Through Rhetorical Criticism.* Chapel Hill: University of North Carolina Press, 1984.

Kim, Seyoon. *The Origin of Paul's Gospel.* Grand Rapids: Eerdmans, 1982.

Malherbe, Abraham. *Social Aspects of Early Christianity.* Baton Rouge: Louisiana State University Press, 1977.

_____. *Paul and the Popular Philosophers.* Minneapolis: Fortress Press, 1989.

Malina, Bruce. *Christian Origins and Cultural Anthropology: Practical Models for Biblical Interpretation.* Atlanta: John Knox Press, 1986.

Malinowski, Bronislaw. *A Scientific Theory of Culture and Other Essays.* New York: Oxford University Press, 1960.

Manson, T. W. "St. Paul's Letter to the Romans—and Others." Pages 1-16 in Karl P. Donfried ed., *The Romans Debate.* Minneapolis: Augsburg Publishing House, 1977.

Marcus, Joel. "The Circumcision and the Uncircumcision in Rome." *New Testament Studies* 35 (1989): 73-81.

Martyn, J. Louis. *Galatians: A New Translation with Introduction and Commentary.* Anchor Bible; New York: Doubleday, 1997.

Meeks, Wayne A. *The First Urban Christians: the Social World of the Apostle Paul.* Philadelphia: Fortress, 1983.

_____. *The Moral World of the First Christians.* Philadelphia: Westminster, 1986.

_____. "A Hermeneutics of Social Embodiment." *Harvard Theological Review* 79 (1986): 176-186.

Murphy-O'Connor, Jerome. *Paul, A Critical Life.* Oxford: Clarendon, 1996.

Neill, Stephen. "Religion and Culture: A Historical Introduction." Pages 1-20 in John Stott and Robert T. Coote ed., *Gospel and Culture: The Papers of a Consultation on the Gospel and Culture.* Pasadena, California: William Carey Library, 1979.

Neyrey, J. H. *Paul, in Other Words: A Cultural Reading of His Letters.* Louisville: Westminster, 1990.

Patte, Daniel. *Discipleship according to the Sermon on the Mount: Four
    Legitimate Readings, Four Plausible Views of Discipleship, and
    Their Relative Values*. Valley Forge: Trinity Press International,
    1996.
Pelikan, Jaroslav. *The Emergence of the Catholic Tradition (100-600)*.
    Chicago: University of Chicago Press, 1971.
Peterson, Richard. "Revitalizing the Culture Concept." *Annual Review of
    Sociology* 5 (1979), 137-166.
Ralston, Timothy J. "The Conversion of Paul and Its Significance within
    His Theological Construct." *Bibliotheca Sacra* 147 (April-June
    1990): 198-215.
Reitzenstein, Richard. *Hellenistic Mystery-Religions: Their Basic Ideas
    and Significance*. 3rd ed. Trans. John E. Steely. Pittsburgh:
    Pickwich, 1978.
Ridderbos, H. *Paul: An Outline of His Theology*. Grand Rapids:
    Eerdmans, 1975.
Sanders, E. P. "The Covenant as a Soteriological Category and the
    Nature of Salvation in Palestinian and Hellenistic Judaism." Pages
    11-44 in R. Hamerton-Kelly and R. Scroggs ed., *Jews, Greeks and
    Christians*. Leiden; Brill, 1976
Schweitzer, Albert. *Paul and his Interpreters*. London: Adam and
    Charles Black, 1950.
_____. *The Quest of the Historical Jesus: A Critical Study of Its
    Progress from Reimarus to Wrede*. 3rd ed. London: Black, 1954.
_____. *Mysticism of Paul the Apostle*. Trans. William Montgomery. New
    York: Macmillan, 1956.
Tamez, Elsa. *The Amnesty of Grace: Justification by Faith from a Latin
    American Perspective*. Trans. Sharon H. Ringe. Nashville: Abingdon
    Press, 1993.
Tanner, Kathryn. *Theories of Culture: A New Agenda for Theology*.
    Minneapolis: Fortress Press, 1997.
Tylor, Edward B. *Primitive Culture: Researches into the Development of
    Mythology, Philosophy, Religion, Art, and Custom*, Vol. 1: *The
    Origins of Culture*. London: J. Murray, 1871.
Watson, Francis. *Paul, Judaism and the Gentiles: A Sociological
    Approach*. Cambridge: Cambridge University Press, 1986.
Wilckens, Ulrich. *Der Brief an die Römer*. 3 volumes. Zürich: Benziger,
    Neukirchen-Vluyn: Neukirchener Verlag, 1978-1982.
Wrede, W. *Paul [Paulus, 1908]*. Lexington: American Library
    Association Committee on Reprinting, 1962.
Yeo Khiok-khng. "Culture and Intersubjectivity as Criteria of
    Negotiating Meanings in Cross-cultural Interpretations." Pages 81-
    100 in Charles H. Cosgrove ed., *The Meanings We Choose*.
    Edinburgh: T&T Clark, 2004.

PART 1

EUROPE AND AFRICA

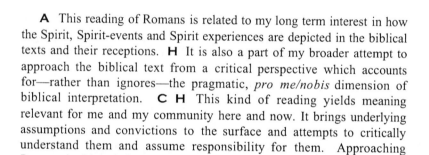

– O N E –

From Margins to Center

Pentecostal and Orthodox Readings of Romans 8 in Romania[1]

Florin T. Cimpean

A This reading of Romans is related to my long term interest in how the Spirit, Spirit-events and Spirit experiences are depicted in the biblical texts and their receptions. **H** It is also a part of my broader attempt to approach the biblical text from a critical perspective which accounts for—rather than ignores—the pragmatic, *pro me/nobis* dimension of biblical interpretation. **C H** This kind of reading yields meaning relevant for me and my community here and now. It brings underlying assumptions and convictions to the surface and attempts to critically understand them and assume responsibility for them. Approaching Romans in this way becomes a challenge.

C As a Pentecostal, I have to deal with the question of how a book like Romans, considered often as a theological treatise and one of the most difficult writings in the New Testament,[2] could be relevantly read by a community that values and places the pneumatic experiential complex at the center of its system of beliefs. Keck and Furnish suggest that the experience of the Spirit was a vital feature of early Christian life[3] and, arguably, of the communities addressed by Paul. With this in mind, a question arises: **I** Did these communities read this letter from the standpoint of their life experiences or did they read it theologically as most modern interpreters do? To push the issue further, could this

---

A Spirit event in the biblical texts.

H *Pro me/nobis* dimension of biblical interpretation.

C H Hermeneutical interest of interpreting biblical texts to one's community and culture.

C Pentecostal culture.

I An interplay question between historical meaning and hermeneutical significance.

difficult letter be read from a pneumatic standpoint at all?[4] This is what this paper will partially attempt to answer.

C As a Roman(ian) I approach Romans with the awareness that it has over time become the defining center of Western Christianity and consequently the West seems to have a monopoly on this text. Yet, from the margins this center seems often distant and its readings sound as strange voices. Communities outside the West face difficulties in identifying themselves with the standard Western readings of Romans. Therefore, this paper seeks to decenter such Western readings by presenting two alternative receptions of Romans from Romania—a Pentecostal reading and an Orthodox one—which ironically are focused on the center of Romans, namely chapter 8. These Romanian readings originate in a twofold marginality. Politically, Romania belongs to a world that is often unnamed—a world between the First and the Third World, sometimes called the Second World. Religiously, Pentecostalism and Eastern Orthodox Christianity are often viewed in the West as second class Christianity. From this marginal position, both the Pentecostal and the Eastern Orthodox readings under consideration view chapter 8 as the key for understanding Romans, where the Spirit functions as the integrating principle of Pauline theology and of the whole Christian experience.

A The paper argues that these alternative readings could be supported by a scholarly interpretation which is focused upon the figurative dimension of the rhetorical structure of Romans that forms a chiasm with chapter 8 at its center.

H C Therefore, this paper's aims are: (a) to provide a Pentecostal *pro me/nobis* pneumatic reading of Romans from Romania; (b) to present an alternative Romanian Eastern Orthodox interpretation of Romans; (c) to offer textual grounding for these readings and (d) finally, to place these readings in the arena of competing receptions of this text and understand them as legitimate interpretations of the text in the history of receptions of Romans.

Identifying the Center: Western Readings of Romans

H Given the amount of Western scholarly work on Romans, it is impossible to do justice to all the important interpretations of Romans.

C Explaining cultural influence on interpreter.

A An attempt to history as an analytical frame.

H C Hermeneutical interest influenced by one's context.

H Hermeneutical category influenced by one's epistemology.

Therefore, this section simply seeks to identify predominant readings of Romans, that is, interpretive approaches that are distinctive because of the epistemological categories they use for making sense of the many features of the letter to the Romans.

A. The Theocentric Perspective on Romans

H The foremost and the widest held view about this text centers on the fact that Romans is ultimately a letter about God and his intervention in the history and his dealings with humanity. This theocentrism is expressed in several ways.

1. Luther and his heirs stressed that the heart of Romans *is* justification by faith, in the sense that through faith in Jesus Christ every human being receives forgiveness and a share of a "foreign righteousness" which is manifested in Christ's graceful work at calvary.[5] The theological concept of justification by faith, which in Luther bears also an anthropological dimension, became more theocentric in the work of later scholars, being understood as the righteousness of God.[6]

2. A different theocentric view of Romans was presented by Calvin who basically says that only those marked by God for election are able to partake of the benefits and freedoms of grace.[7] In chapter 8 the Spirit functions as the sign of the saving grace, as a mark of distinction for the elect in the world. The Spirit is the agent by which God's election is made manifest.[8] In a sense, the elect become God's center in the world; all others are marginalized.

3. Bartlett emphasizes the universalist view of God in Romans. God is God of every human being, of all of human history and of the whole universe. God's claim over all people is demonstrated by the cross and resurrection of Jesus Christ. The appropriate response is faith, as the way by which all humanity can acknowledge God's claim.[9] This universalist view of God is facilitated and implemented by the Spirit.

B. Reconstructing the Symbolic World of Romans

H In an attempt to shift away from the theocentric perspective on Romans some proposed that the pulsating heart of Romans is the mystical union of the believer with Christ and the work of the Spirit as expressed in Romans 5-8.[10] Morgan asserts that Paul, in his attempt to articulate a vision of the world and human life under God, projects a symbolic world which is structured on three levels: 1. The transcendental level of God, the ultimate symbol which is the focus of religious activity;

H An attempt to understand meaning of God in Romans.

H An attempt to understand meaning of the symbolic world of Romans.

2. The level of revelation in the crucified and risen Lord through whom God is known—it determines how the transcendental is encapsulated in personal terms and communicated to the human life; and 3. The level of community—the locus of religious experiences and practices, meanings and values.[11]   This symbolic world becomes the lens through which Romans should be read.

C. Christian-Life Perspective

H Some readings point to the fact that Romans deals at great extent with Christian living and embarks on the ethical and moral dimensions of Christian existence. In his commentary Fitzmyer's ultimate aim is some kind of expected ecclesial pay off.[12]   Humans are not only liberated but also empowered to live a new life of action before God and for God through the Spirit which is the powerful source for the new Christian *modus operandi*.[13] Morgan also delves into the ethical dimension of Romans, stressing that salvation results in the re-evaluation of behavior, both positively and negatively, as expressed by the dichotomy Spirit-flesh. For him Romans presents us with a Spirit ethics.[14] Focusing on the systems of convictions also opens the door for an ethical perspective.[15]

D. The Christological Perspective

H Douglas J. Moo asserts that christology along with salvation history represent the theological ground and the starting point of Romans as the only topics broad enough to unify the various themes of the letter.[16]

E. The New Perspective On Paul

H Recently, an important shift has taken place in the process of interpretation of Romans which challenges the Lutheran hermeneutical grid of justification by faith imposed on Romans and makes space for the role of the Jews in salvation history.[17] As Dunn states:

> Paul's treatment of the law. . . becomes one of the chief integrating strands which binds the whole letter into a cohesive and powerful restatement of Jewish covenant theology in the light of Christ.[18]

H An attempt to understand Christian life in Romans.

H An attempt to understand Christ in Romans.

H An attempt to understand Law in Romans.

A Pentecostal *Pro Me/Nobis* Reading of Romans 8 From Romania: Integrating Text, Theology And Life Experience

Exclusion of Romans from the Functional Canon of Most Romanian Pentecostals

My first meeting with Romans took place in my childhood, when the only professing Christian in our household, my great-grandfather, asked me to read aloud for him from the Bible. He could not read but he loved the Bible and he was able to recite by heart long pericopae he learned by hearing. **H C** In his "towering" presence I perfected my reading skills and I developed attitudes toward the different biblical texts. Romans had become the book-to-avoid for two reasons: first, I was rarely asked to read from it and second, when I was asked to do so, I did not understand it and I did not like it. Therefore, I developed an aversion toward Romans. Later on, I discovered the same aversion toward this text among the Romanian Pentecostals. The ethos of the Romanian Pentecostals is an ethos of poverty, suffering, oppression both by the government and other religious bodies, sorrow, humility, longing, eschatological tension, existential struggle and Spirit encounters.[19] The Romanian Pentecostal discourse is made up from stories that have at their center the unending presence of the Spirit. They are not about the success achieved through the Spirit, but about the divine participation in our struggles, sufferings and longings. As my great-grandfather repeatedly told me, the Spirit is at the center of everything, in the midst of unutterable suffering and unspeakable joy, in seasons of persecution and in seasons of liberation. Therefore, the Spirit has become the great *hermeneute* of our experiences and of the biblical text.

C Without a history, without a written legacy, and without heroes and models, Romanian Pentecostals claimed the biblical text as their history and legacy, and the biblical events, teachings and characters as their models. Time, distance and space collapsed and the horizon of the community and that of the biblical text fused. Characters and events came alive in our experiences in a great sense of identification with the world of the text. Read aloud the biblical text was there to ignite and legitimate our experiences, to recreate the worlds of the individual believers and community and to sparkle imagination, vision and action. Sermons were not aimed at systematizing grand teachings but at "re-storying" the text for today, at recapturing the passion of the text, at helping Pentecostals to cope with the passion of their existence. Pushed

---

H C A Romanian reading of the Bible.

C Romanian Pentecostals.

to the margins by both the Communists and previous regimes as well as
by the religious establishment, the Romanian Pentecostal community
held to the biblical text and the Spirit as the necessary ingredients for
subsistence and resistance. But what about Romans?

Because we were told that Romans was basically a treatise of
abstract theology, in Melanchtonian terms a *doctrinae Christianae
compendium*[20] which has little to say about the experience of the Spirit
within the real constraints of life, the letter was somehow excluded from
our functional "canon."[21] In retrospect, I have to say that this was a sort
of "false consciousness" about this book.

When Romanian Pentecostals Read Romans: Chapter 8 as the Center

A When Romanian Pentecostals enter Romans they do so at the
center, chapter 8. But they are told that they should have started at the
beginning and if possible with the great theological key concept of
justification by faith. The point is that justification by faith, however
popular in the West, does not ring a bell in a Romanian Pentecostal
context. Thus we felt compelled to stay away from this text.

Yet, Romans has the potential to revitalize the Romanian Pentecostal
ethos. By entering the world of Romans through chapter 8 we gain a new
perspective on Romans and new teachings for our life experience.
However pregnant with theological motifs (according to a Western
perspective), this letter grew from concrete situations in the life of Paul
and the communities which he interacted with.[22] It is also about how one
experiences the reality of life; and again and again it is brought into
concrete experiences of life and death. When my great-grandfather was
taking his last breath of earthly air after almost one century of struggle
and passion (I was 13 years old), he was doing so at the center of
Romans: "and we know that all things cooperate together toward good
for those who love God, who are called according to his purpose."[23]

Romans 8 as Vital for Our Understanding of the Text and for Our Self-understanding

C H When chapter 8 is taken as the key for understanding the rest of
the letter, this chapter is viewed as a representation of the pneumatic
vision that Paul has of his teaching and practice. It is the basis for
moving from *theoria* to *praxis*. The Spirit functions as the *integrating
principle* by means of which Paul brings together his theological
categories and the Christian praxis. Furthermore, the Spirit is the

---

A Romans 8 as center.

C H A Romanian interpretation of the Romans text.

integrating principle through which the readers' struggling, fractured, suppressed identities are made whole, their muted voices, their hopelessness, their alienation are overcome; and the creation itself is renewed.

A For us chapter 8 becomes the lens through which we are reading Romans.[24] It helps us to understand both chapters 1-7 and chapters 9-16.[25] This is in agreement with Bartlett who states that everything in chapters 1-7 leads to chapter 8, and everything in chapters 9-16 grows out of it.[26] Such a reading provides the evidence which justifies the Pentecostal emphasis on the importance of the Spirit in the hermeneutical task, in the ordering of Christian life and praxis and in the cosmological and eschatological vision.

The Main Tenets of Romanian Pentecostal Reading of Romans

A C The main tenets of this reading by the Romanian Pentecostals can now be presented.

1. The Spirit offers the possibility of *liberation* (8:1-4). To begin with, we understand *katakrima* and the rest of 8:1 in an ideological sense, as referring to a liberationist act, and not just in a legal sense. "There is no condemnation" encompasses the idea of justification by faith as freedom from bondage (oppression).[27]

2. This liberationist language becomes very important for a Romanian Pentecostal community that has continuously faced oppression during its history. In our interpretation, Paul presents a liberation which intervenes at four levels.

First, at the ideational level: Paul places his theological developments and statements in a context of experiential encounter, where his arguments become *"pro me/nobis"* teaching for our community and its members. All of Paul's theological categories— christology (vv. 1-4), adoption (vv. 14-17), justification (vv. 3-4, 10-11), grace (vv. 2-4), sin (vv. 2-10, 12-13), ethics, eschatology, etc (see verses 1-4—are set in a pneumatic horizon where semantic boundaries are torn apart. Christology becomes pneumatic and is liberated from its rigid constraints to be open to new possibilities of meaning. Different understandings are not condemned, but encouraged.

Second, at the individual level, immersion in this pneumatic universe is an exercise in freedom (v. 2).[28] He is liberated from the constraints of sin, selfish ego and from identity suppression. There is no condemnation, neither self-condemnation for oneself nor for the others. The individual is affirmed.

A Romans 8.

A C A Pentecostal reading.

Third, the community as a whole enters this pneumatic liberation and becomes the locus where the Spirit interprets doctrines, human life and the Other. From the singular pronoun in v. 2, Paul switches to a more holistic language as is evident in the frequency of *hymeis* and *hêmeis* (see vv. 9,12,15 just to mention a few instances). In this way, adoption, for instance, becomes a community affair (vv. 14-17). The community is the place where the disinherited are adopted, the lame walk in the Spirit, the muted speak, the blind see, the unnamed receive identity and the excluded receive adoption. Community is not the place where identities are denied, but affirmed. Verses 9-10 underscore the fact that those dispossessed find already eschatological locus, or rather their unlivable conditions become divine locus "since the Spirit of God dwells in you."[29]

Fourth, the whole cosmos enters this pneumatic liberation. Not only is the Spirit present in/with us, but it is also present in the universe creating cosmological equilibrium (vv. 18-23).[30] Liberation is a painful process and the whole creation partakes in the destiny of the liberated children of God (specifically vv. 19-22).

3. This pneumatic vision offers *orientation and identity* for us, both as a community and as individuals (4-8, 12-17). In the pneumatic context, as a liberated community and liberated individuals we do not fall back in fear and oppression because we are given an identity as the children of God (v. 15); we receive a sense of direction in life. To "walk according to the Spirit" is to have a direction induced by the Spirit, to have mobility and a life of action (v. 4). The Spirit orients us toward God and toward each other. We understand *phronema* in v. 6 not simply as "mind" but as orientation of life which underscores an experiential mode of living. We find purpose in life and in service. Confusion and alienation is sorted out when the Spirit prompts us to identify ourselves with the divine Other and with the human others (vv. 15-16). Now, no one could claim a privileged relationship, identity, knowledge, for all of us are children of God. The problem is not a lack of knowledge, or of ability or of will, but a lack of vision. The Spirit provides us with this vision.

4. In such a context, a pneumatic tension appears in Rom 8:9-11, 18-21. The vision of liberation, orientation and identity provided by the Spirit is not just a utopian dream. It is an actualized reality, a shared experience (v. 23). Yet, this vision is not suddenly fully actualized; this teaching is not final; this experience is not ultimate; this liberation is not total. While there is a present realization, there is also an eschatological aspiration. *Hypomonê* in v. 25 is not fatalistic patience but rather dynamic perseverance in the struggle. The Spirit integrates the two ages and makes life livable. Life becomes a process through which the new condition of the children of God is actualized in the midst of this old age. The new age is breaking in the old aeon, but is not yet consummated.

The old age still resists, and therefore, liberation, orientation and search for identity become a continuous process (vv. 15-16 versus vv. 23-25—already liberated and adopted/yet waiting for liberation and adoption). Waiting for the full consummation becomes a transforming action. Those who are still oppressed, who are still searching for their identities continuously long for liberation. This pneumatic tension is the engine of the experience of life. By the indwelling of the Spirit, the Other participates in our experiences and we participate in the experience of the others and of the whole creation. Such a pneumatic vision presupposes that everything should be kept in tension: individual and community, theology and praxis, spirit and flesh, present and future, etc. Despite the sufferings and frustration associated with this long process of actualization, we hope for liberation, for eschatological consummation (v. 24). In a sense, God participates in our journey of suffering, in our hope, in our aspirations and in our tears, in our ecstatic joy and our deepest cry of desperation (vv. 26-27). There is a profound solidarity between God, humanity and creation.[31]

5. In such a vision, the Spirit offers pneumatic discourse (vv. 26-27). Those who are mute, the inarticulate, those who do not possess the "right" knowledge, the weak, the marginal who do not know the mainline prayer, those who are not represented are given speech, pneumatic discourse, glossolalic power.[32] The Spirit speaks a common language with those whose feelings could not be expressed, "sighs too deep for words" (v. 26).[33] Glossolalia is usually understood as speech addressed to God by humans. Yet, glossolalia is also a sign and a wonder of the divine self-disclosure and takes place primarily because of this disclosure. Then it can also be communication from God to humans.[34] The groaning of the Spirit discloses the divine participation in our struggle. In the midst of oppression, or in our eschatological journey, the Spirit gives us speech, an existential cry for freedom.[35] This speech becomes a protest against any manipulation and oppression of humanity.[36] And since God overcame the barriers that separated humanity from him, this pneumatic discourse should bring down all human barriers.

6. Paul exalts in a pneumatic doxology (vv. 28-39), because he is liberated and receives an identity, because his speech and his teaching are Spirit-rearticulated. This section of chapter 8 presents a Paul who is liberated from the struggle of chapter 7, who is now certain of his identity, has eschatological direction in life and utters a pneumatic speech. This section could easily characterize a Pentecostal entering charismatic worship. Indeed, from our perspective, once liberated we have nothing to fear. Who or what will once again oppress us? Who or what will erase our identity? Who or what will mute our voices? Who or what will diminish our hope? Nothing will separate us from the

pneumatic vision of Christ and God (v. 39). It is precisely the way we
see christology, and consequently any Pauline teaching, that is, through
pneumatological lenses.

For us as a community, this alternative reading offers us
hermeneutical lenses for reading the rest of Romans. As chapter 8 is the
center of Romans, so in our experience the Spirit is the center and plays
the integrative role. Our beliefs are liberated from the constraints of
dismay and stigma. We feel valued for what we are and what we
practice. Our obliterated horizons are reoriented; our search for
significance receives fulfillment in the matrix of our identity;
relationships with others are bridged, the future becomes hopeful and our
inept babbling becomes articulate speech.

Paul writes Romans to bridge the East with the West, his Eastern
mission with his Western missionary intentions, Jews with Gentiles and
theology with praxis. Likewise, this text grants us as Roman(ian)
Pentecostals our identity. As Roman(ians) belonging to a land between
the West and the East this text helps us to integrate this geo-political
split. As Pentecostals, we are able to integrate our experience and our
theology, to deal with our past of oppression and to clear the confusion
brought about by the fall of Communism. This reading compels us to
give Romans a place of honor in our functional canon.

The Spirit of God Or A New Spiritual Conscience?—An Alternative Eastern Orthodox Reading From Romania

C H At this point I introduce a kind of interpretation that situates
itself at the interface of the theological and exegetical reading. It is a
different kind of approach because it springs from a different
understanding of the biblical text. This Romanian Greek Eastern
Orthodox interpretation of Romans starts with several hermeneutical
assumptions. First, if Romans played an important role in shaping
Western Christianity, it did not have the same prominent role in the
context of Eastern Christianity. This is very evident from the scarcity of
Romanian Orthodox commentaries on Romans.[37] This interpretation of
Romans also takes on a polemic tone, especially against the Protestant
views on Romans. Cornitescu explicitly rejects as a gross exaggeration
Luther's designation of Romans as the "summa theologiae Pauli"; even
though Romans presents a theological richness, it cannot replace the
other Pauline letters. It rather needs to be read with the others.[38] A
second underlying assumption is that Romans needs to be read in terms
of its intertextual relations with other biblical texts and traditions.

C H An Eastern Orthodox (from Romania) reading of Romans.

Cornitescu favors a holistic approach to the text: different verses and pericopae should be interpreted in the context of the theological flow of the letter and of the whole biblical text.[39] These interpretations are very much interested in the historical issues such as authorship, place, purpose, authorial intent, original readers, authenticity and integrity, critical, problematic and philological questions. Yet, these commentaries are for the church, as is evident from the theological structure of the letter: the first section of the letter (1-11) is the dogmatic part, the second section (12-15) is the moral part.[40] The third thing worth mentioning is the weight the writings of the early church get as intertexts for these readings[41] and the sacramental inferences in the process of interpretation.[42]

For the Eastern Orthodox interpretation of Romans, chapter 8 becomes very important since Orthodox christology and ecclesiology are by definition pneumatological.[43] These interpretations envision that Christians receive a new conscience which is materialized through adoption. In fact, this new conscience is the new spirit the Christian receives through adoption at the time of baptism.[44] This new spirit is not the Holy Spirit as a divine person or as the power of God, but it is the new state of being of the Christian life; it is a new attitude and orientation toward God and the other, the conscience that God exists. This is the spirit in which Jesus performed his ministry, a spirit of good works.[45] Living in the flesh means focusing on the material things, while living in the spirit means transcending the impulse of the material condition and focusing on God and the good that springs out of him.[46] This is the spirit in which Christian culture, thought, and morality develop. Not only individuals but also, their community (culture) and the whole of nature participate in this salvation framework. Salvation is never final, never accomplished in this realm; therefore we need to continue to actualize our new spirit in moral behavior and good works.

This Romanian Eastern Orthodox reading challenges the traditional Western readings of Romans and confirms the importance of the Romanian Pentecostal interpretation. Now the question is: Are these readings legitimate, even though as any faith-interpretation must do, they blur the lines which separate Paul's text from the theological and existential concerns of today's believers? Can chapter 8 be legitimately viewed as the key to understanding Romans? As its center? Is there any textual grounding for such a claim? The next section of this chapter will sketch in a preliminary way possible answers to these questions.

Textual Grounding:
Understanding Paul's Structural Rhetoric

A My Romanian Pentecostal *pro me/nobis* reading of Romans starts with chapter 8 assuming that this chapter is the hermeneutical key to the whole epistle. Essential for my reading is also the assumption that the Spirit functions as the integrating principle of theology and Christian experience. The alternative Eastern Orthodox reading confirms this claim. These assumptions can be grounded in the text, following Cranfield's descriptive observations.

Cranfield points out that, even though the Spirit is mentioned only five times in chapters 1-7 and only nine times in chapters 9-16, in chapter 8 the Spirit takes prominence, being mentioned some twenty one times.[47] In this regard, chapter 8 comes like a surprise; it abounds in pneumatic discourse. Moreover, there is a sense of excitement and puzzlement and a personal rhetorical presence on Paul's side starting with 8:1 through the end of the letter.[48]

The centrality of chapter 8 in the economy of Romans is widely acknowledged. As I already noted, Bartlett emphasizes clearly that chapter 8 is the central chapter of Romans.[49] Fitzmyer asserts that chapter 8 is the third most important part of the letter equaling the discussion of justification in 3:21-31, forming a certain peak in the theological development.[50] Hahn suggests that the whole argument in chapters 9-15 is built on chapter 8.[51]

Yet, other authors barely pay attention to this chapter in their reading of Romans or their theological reconstructions.[52] Furthermore for some, in the larger context of Romans, the section that includes chapters 5-8 generates a series of problems. Thielman points out that for some scholars, chapters 5-8 break the logical and theological flow and sequence of the letter and could very well be an independent composition dropped by Paul or someone else in the letter.[53] According to others, these chapters could function as a "backwater" text.[54] These kind of suggestions pose serious questions about the whole of Romans. Dunn shows that some scholars consider Romans as a combination of two letters, or an amalgation of two homilies.[55] This brief survey of issues concerning chapter 8 and its surrounding context shows that there is no consensus on how to treat the chapter and confusion still persists about its role in the economy of the letter.

The above readings of Romans call us to pay closer attention to chapter 8, and its potential role in the structure of Romans. Scholars have often proposed that the key to the structural and theological understanding of Romans is chapter 1,[56] or chapter 3:21-26,[57] or chapter

---

A Paul's structural rhetoric.

5,[58] or perhaps, in recent times, chapters 9-11.[59] In turn, I propose that the key to understanding Romans is chapter 8. These different proposals signal that the interpreters focus their attention on different kinds of structure of Romans.

The traditional structuring of Romans divides the letter in two parts: chapters 1-8 which encompasses the mature theology of Paul, and chapters 9-16 dealing with some practical implications.[60] Such a structure cannot be denied. Yet its nature needs to be clearly understood: This is the structure of Romans as a theological/moral discourse. This is appropriate because, among other things, Romans conveys to its readers theological ideas and moral instructions.

What I propose is to consider Romans as a figurative discourse—that is, as a discourse which aims at establishing a symbolic world for its readers. This is also appropriate, because there is not doubt that this letter is a religious discourse, which like other such discourses sets a symbolic world that provides the framework necessary for making sense of the theological and moral teachings of this text.[61] This figurative structure is not unrelated to the rhetorical power of the letter and thus to the arrangement of the argument that reflects the use of principles promoted by the ancient schools of rhetoric.[62] Very often, when rhetorical techniques are applied to the biblical text, Romans is used as a case study because it fits nicely in such categories.[63]

More specifically, in this figurative structure, chapter 8 functions as the climax of the letter and offers grounds for transition and a framework for integration for what precedes and what follows. Chapters 8 helps us to move back and forth in a journey of understanding. This becomes clearer when we note that Romans is arranged in a chiastic fashion.

Even though the theoretical information about chiasmus as a rhetorical technique is scarce, its presence can be traced as early as Homer.[64] Chiasmus belongs to the *figurae elocutionis, to the figurative* complex and could be defined as the presence in a text of " bilateral symmetry of four or more elements about a central axis, which may itself lie between two elements, or be a unique central element, the symmetry consisting of any combination of verbal, grammatical or syntactical elements, or, indeed, of ideas and concepts in a given pattern."[65] Thomson proposes six characteristics of a chiasm: 1. It is frequent for a chiasm to exhibit a shift at, or near the center, consisting of a change in the person of the verb, or introduction of a new idea, etc. After the change, the train of thought is resumed; 2. At times, a chiasm is introduced or followed by a frame passage which functions either as a spring-board to launch the chiasm, or as a tail piece; 3. Passages that present a chiastic structure may also contain parallelism of elements; 4. Identical arguments may occur at the extremities and at the center of a certain system; 5. Balancing elements have approximately equal lengths; 6. Generally, the center contains the focus of the author's thought.[66]

A This raises the question: Does Romans as a whole have such a framework? Generally, a chiastic pattern is looked for in smaller units. Such a study of Romans has already been done on short passages in Romans. Thomson identifies a chiasm in Rom 5:12-21,[67] Gordon Fee finds chiastic structures in 1:3-4 and 7:13-8:4,[68] and De la Potterie demonstrates that Romans 8:14-30 is organized in a chiastic fashion.[69] There seems to be no doubt that there are chiastic structures in Romans. But what I propose is a macro-chiasm in Romans, which is more difficult to study—there are less possibilities for control. An application of the rules for identifying chiasms provided by Thomson will serve as one kind of control.

My interpretation argues for a major shift in chapter 8, which I see as the center of the letter and, thus as the center of the chiastic pattern. Chapter 8 presents both a change in the person of the verb—from "I" to "you"— and an introduction of new ideas, such as the prominence of the Spirit. Since I argue for a macro-chiasm I will apply the second rule to the center of the pattern: chapter 8 is preceded by a springboard, that is chapter 7, and is followed by a tailpiece, namely chapters 9-11. This addresses much debated issues about the structural position of these latter chapters. Romans is also filled with parallelisms and antithesis, both thematically and structurally.[70] Furthermore, there is a parallelism between chapters 1-7 and 9-16.   In addition, chapter 8 presents, in a remarkably symmetrical way, a concentration of ideas which are also found both in the beginning and end of the letter and also in the surrounding pericopae.[71] For instance, chapter 8 deals with justification and sin, with persecution, with practical living and mission. Also, according to Thomson's rules, the structure I propose is well balanced from a thematic and quantitative standpoint; chapter 8 is in the middle of the theological and quantitative flow. Finally, as I suggested above, chapter 8 can be viewed as the climax of the letter, and therefore, as the focus of Paul's discourse. Thus this preliminary investigation suggests that Romans as a whole meets the minimal requirements for a chiastic structure. In the next page I present a rough chiastic scheme in Romans:

A Does Romans as a whole have a framework?

1 Salutation 1:1-7
  2 Wishing to visit Rome 1:8-15
    3 Power and Sin 1:16-32
      4 Jews, Judgment, Sin 2:1-29
        5 Jews, Gentiles, Equality 3:1-20
          6 Need for Forgiveness—Solution 3:21-31
            7 Illustration 4:1-25
              8 Consequences 5:1-21
                9 Grace over sin 6:1-23
                  10 Struggle at personal level 7:1-25
                    11 Pneumatic Visions 8:1-27
                    11' Christological Visions 8:28-39
                  10' Paul and Jews—A Personal Struggle 9:1-5
                9' Mercy and sin 9:6-33
              8' Consequences 10:1-21
            7' Illustration 11:1-24
          6' Need for Salvation—Solution 11:25-36
        5' Equality in the Spirit 12:1-21
      4' Social Ordering and Relationships 13:1-15:13
    3' Paul, Power and Mission 15:14-33
  2' Wishing 16:1-20
1' Benediction 16:21-27

I want to make a few general concluding comments on the chiastic structure of Romans. I first want to acknowledge that this chiastic pattern is not perfectly symmetrical. Yet this is not a problem in and of itself. Thomson shows that perfect symmetry is not always desirable in practice. On the contrary, asymmetries often emerge in the architecture of certain chiasms.[72] This is also the case with Pauline literature. Thomson proposes several possible explanations for the break in symmetry: (a) the author has intentionally or accidentally created the break; (b) the author was unable to sustain the pattern, or perhaps was distracted; (c) the author may have taken some flexibility generated by his need to communicate or by cultural aversion against perfect symmetry, and (d) the author may have used the imbalance deliberately as an emphasizing device.[73]

Yet, all this needs to be put in the context of the chiasm's figurative functions. Watson points to two main functions of the chiasm as a structuring and an expressive device.[74] One of Paul's interests in writing to the Romans was to be persuasive. Therefore he had to be concerned both with the aesthetic aspect of his message and with the didactic ends.[75] These concerns yield an architectural structure that creates an integrating connection between form and content. As the architectural analysis shows, these concerns were commonplace in the classical ancient period, were expressed in a balanced concentric construction around a main point, pedimental modes of compositions and chiastic parallelisms. The biblical texts could not be neutral to these trends.[76]

A In sum, the structure I propose suggests that Paul used such figurative devices. Developing a systematic study of Romans from this perspective promises to show that Eastern readings of Romans, be they in Romanian Pentecostal or Orthodox circles, reflect responses to a significant dimension of this letter as figurative discourse.

Romans 8: A Hermeneutical Center for the Margins

H This paper has been envisioned as an experiment in integration of *pro nobis* readings with critical ones. It attempted to challenge the Western monopoly on the text of Romans and to show that readings from the margin could highlight dimensions of the text that were for long overlooked by the interpretive and academic center. The chiastic reconstruction of Romans hints that it is legitimate to focus one's reading of Romans on chapter 8. Such a reading represents my struggle with Romans better than the introspective conscience of the Western world. I hold to this interpretation because I cannot easily renounce my identity as a Pentecostal, and more specifically as a Romanian Pentecostal—an identity which implies a history of persecution and marginalization, a complex of inferiority vis-à-vis articulate discourses, perpetual redefinition, and a universe of practices that we know are perceived as strange by modern observers.

A H However tempting is the Western interpretive and academic center, I cannot easily integrate myself into it. I cannot just renounce my marginality—though it is painful, it is nevertheless exciting. By considering the different existing readings I was able to decipher and better understand my choices and the value judgments that prompted them. The reading I chose also helps me and my community rediscover Romans as a text for us and include it in our experiential and faith canon. While the other kinds of interpretations mentioned above are appealing, they continue to estrange us from Romans. They impose a clear dichotomy between faith, creative and critical reading. The West created professions defined by clear boundaries: one is a minister, a theologian, or a biblical scholar. It rarely happens that these boundaries are transgressed. These boundaries keep these fields in isolation, separated by huge gaps. In this way, Romans is disenfranchised and truncated.

A Figurative device in the rhetoric of Paul.

H Hermeneutical center for the margins.

A H Tension between academic and hermeneutical readings?

Indeed, one fragment belongs to Paul, another to Cephas and another to Apollos (to use the Corinthian division as a metaphor for these gaps). In the world where my community exists, we see Romans holistically. Similarly, I am at once minister, theologian and biblical scholar. My task is not just to make faith statements and systemize them in articulated speech but also to bring these statements to critical understanding. In fact, my reading attempts to re-marry faith, creative readings and critical interpretations, to bring them into an interrelationship. In this way Romans is back into the community; it becomes once again a community text.

Finally, I hold on to my reading because it reflects not only my effort to understand an old text and to draw meaning from it, but also the fact that this text read, shook and reshaped, my experience. I acknowledge that I come to this text with a limited understanding about the text and its world, as well as a limited understanding about life, salvation, the Spirit and my own experience. The text exposes my lack of understanding and illuminates both itself and my own experience. In this way this reading is both an exercise in text understanding and self-understanding. This paper is a statement about how I rediscovered Romans and with it, the legitimacy of my experience. For me, a critical study of Romans—that is, a study which makes explicit its interpretative processes—requires that I acknowledge the pragmatic, dimension of my interpretation, including the way this text as scripture affects me and my community, even as I verify that it is indeed an aspect of the text of Romans that affects us in this way.

Notes

1. I wish to thank Professor Daniel Patte, Professor of New Testament and Early Christianity, Vanderbilt University, Nashville, for editing the paper and valuable insights.

2. C. K. Barrett, *Reading Through Romans* (Philadelphia: Fortress, 1977), 2 points to the fact that Romans is considered by many, the hardest book among Paul's writings.

3. L. E. Keck and V. P. Furnish, *The Pauline Letters* (Nashville: Abingdon Press, 1984), 95.

4. Interestingly, Barrett (*Reading Through Romans*, 2) suggests that anyone who wants to read Romans seriously should do it with the same dependence on the Spirit of truth as Paul had in writing it. But he goes further and reads it theocentrically and christologically.

5. Martin Luther, *Lectures On Romans*, Vol. XV (Philadelphia: The Westminster Press, 1961).

6. To mention a few: Adolf Schlatter, *Romans—The Righteousness of God,* trans. by S. S. Schatzmann (Peabody: Hendrickson, 1995, originally 1935). Ernst Käsemann, *Commentary on Romans,* trans. by G. W. Bromiley (Grand Rapids: Eerdmans, 1980). Peter Stuhlmacher, *Paul's Letter to the Romans,* trans. by S. J. Hafemann (Louisville: Westminster/John Knox Press, 1994).

7. John Calvin, *The Epistle of Paul the Apostle to the Romans and to the Thessalonians,* trans. by R. Mackenzie (Edinburgh/London: Oliver and Boyd, 1961).

8. Calvin, *The Epistle to the Romans,* 164, 167, 179-181.

9. David L. Bartlett, *Romans* (Louisville: Westminster/John Knox Press, 1995), especially pages 1-7, 71-72.

10. Albert Schweitzer, *The Mysticism of Paul the Apostle* (London: A&C Black, 1931); Robert Morgan, *Romans* (Sheffield: Sheffield Academic Press, 1995).

11. Morgan, *Romans,* 102-108.

12. Joseph A. Fitzmyer, *Romans: A New Translation with Introduction and Commentary* (New York/London, 1993). This is also obvious in the fact that his Anchor Bible commentary is followed by a companion volume of spiritual exercises targeted at the believing communities: *Spiritual Exercises Based on Paul's Epistle to the Romans* (New York: Paulist Press, 1995).

13. Fitzmyer, *Romans,* 479-480.

14. Morgan, *Romans,* 47-49.

15. See Daniel Patte, *Paul's Faith and the Power of the Gospel* (Philadelphia: Fortress, 1983).

16. Douglas J. Moo, *The Epistle to the Romans* (Grand Rapids: Eerdmans, 1996), 25. Fitzmyer also has christological leanings in his treatment of Romans.

17. See especially, Krister Stendahl, *Paul Among Jews and Gentiles* (Philadelphia: Fortress, 1976), E. P. Sanders, *Paul, the Law and the Jewish People* (Philadelphia: Fortress, 1983). James D. G. Dunn, "The New Perspective on Paul: Paul and the Law," in *Romans Debate* (Peabody: Hendrickson, 1991), 299-308 and *Romans 1-8* (Dallas: Word Books, 1988), especially pp. lxiii-lxxii.

18. James D. G. Dunn, "The New Perspective on Paul," 308.

19. Trandafir Sandru, *Biserica Crestina—Evolutie si Spiritualitate* (Bucuresti: Editura Institutului Teologic Penticostal, 1995), 262-268. *Biserica Penticostala in Istoria Crestinismului* (Bucuresti: Editura Institutului Teologic Penticostal, 1992). Professor Sandru embodies in his writing the empirical and existential realities that led to the emergence of such an ethos.

20. Peter Stuhlmacher, "The Purpose of Romans," in Karl P. Donfried ed., *The Romans Debate* (Peabody: Hendrickson, 1991), 231-242, points

to the perceived supremacy of Romans in the Western hemisphere in terms of theology and doctrine. Also, Krister Stendahl, "The Apostle Paul and the Introspective Conscience of the West," in *Paul Among Jews and Gentiles* (Philadelphia: Fortress, 1976), 78-96, shows that the West claims the eastern Paul as the hero and promoter of introspective conscience.

21. An American friend who spent quite some time in Romania visiting churches told me on one occasion that he very rarely heard a sermon from Romans in the churches he visited. This made me aware that I was not paying a great deal of attention to this epistle. As a community we were alienated from this text.

22. Beverly R. Gaventa, "Romans" in C. A. Newsom & S. H. Ringe, *The Women's Bible Commentary* (Louisville: Westminster John Knox Press, 1992), 313-320 provides a concise argument to explain why this book is not solely a manual of systematic theology. There are major reasons: (a) There are key Pauline theological concepts missing from this letter and, (b) It is improbable that Paul will take the leisure to write a systematic theology without a clear pastoral goal as finality (314). She also points to the possibility that this letter emerged as a response to concrete situations in either Paul's life or of the Roman community, or maybe both (314-315).

23. This is my own translation; "for him all things" meant the whole package: freedom, suffering, persecution, resurrection, glory, Spirit, life and death.

24. Reading the text as a Pentecostal and bringing my experience to the text does not necessarily mean a sublime plunge in eisegesis (reading my own experience into the text) because whatever I bring to the text is transformed by it. There are some hermeneutical implications for such a reading. First, there is a claim by the charismatic community I belong to, that there is a certain experiential correspondence between the experience of the Spirit in the early church and the modern Pentecostal experience. Second, in this line, the Spirit and pneumatology become the theological and hermeneutic lenses by which the biblical text is approached. Third, the issue of identity becomes very important. Pentecostalism emerged as a "protest against modernity" and the hegemony of reason, denouncing the "dominant patterns of status quo and its ideology." It developed as a radical counterculture identity, as a "haven" for the marginalized which "became centered in a new society for a new identity" (Quote from Cheryl Bridges Johns, "The Adolescence of Pentecostalism: In Search of a Legitimate Sectarian Identity" (Presidential Address) *Pneuma* 17:1 (Spring 1995), 4. In this context, the process of reading becomes also a search for identity whereas identity shapes reading and reading shapes identity.

25. Even though chapter 16 may be an addition written to adapt the letter for another audience, for the sake of this paper I will treat the letter as a whole.

26. David Bartlett, *Romans* (Louisville: Westminster John Knox, 1995), 72.

27. I usually tend to translate *katakrima* as "oppression" over the most common translation "condemnation" because I understand the context to be more anthropological than legal. The idea in v. 1 could also underscore "guilt" pointing to the conscience as a "judge."

28. In verse 2 we find individualist language: the pronoun *"se"* (second person singular) is generally preferred over other variants that have *"me"* or *"hêmas."* See, K. Aland *et al., The Greek New Testament*, 4th edition (Stuttgart: United Bible Societies, 1993), 538.

29. Quote from New Revised Standard Version (RSV).

30. Again Paul employs holistic language to create an effect in his audience and to stress how important is his vision.

31. A brilliant creative description of the pneumatic tension in Pentecostal theology is provided by Steve Land, *Pentecostal Spirituality: A Passion for the Kingdom* (Sheffield: Sheffield Academic Press, 1993).

32. I would argue with others that Paul refers in these verses to glossolalia—"sighs too deep for words." So does E. Käsemann, *Commentary on Romans* (Grand Rapids: Eerdmans, 1980), 230-44 and Krister Stendahl, "Glossolalia—The New Testament Evidence," 109-124. But Cranfield argues that Paul would not have confused human groaning with that of the Spirit. Rather these sighs are imperceptible to the Christians. They do not need to be expressed because God knows the intention of the Spirit: C. E. B. Cranfield, *Romans* (Grand Rapids: Eerdmans, reprint 1988), 201-202.

33. Frank D. Machia, "Sighs Too Deep For Words: Toward a Theology of Glossolalia," *Journal of Pentecostal Theology* 1 (1992*)*, 55-60.

34. *Ibid.*

35. E. Käsemann, "The Cry for Liberty in the Worship of the Church," in *Perspectives on Paul* (Philadelphia: Fortress, 1971), 122-137.

36. Machia, "Sighs Too Deep For Words," 61.

37. In my research I found only four commentaries on Romans during the past century. These are: Fericitul Teofilact, Arhiepiscopul Bulgariei, *Trimiterile cele Patrusprezece ale Slavitului si prea Laudatului Apostol Pavel* (Bucuresti: Tipografia Cartilor Bisericesti, 1904); Iosif Olaroiu, *Epistolele S. Apostol Pavel* (Caransebes: Tipografia Diocezana, 1910); Vasile Gheorghiu, *Epistola catre Romani* (Cernauti: Societatea Tipografica Bucovineana, 1923); Constantin Cornitescu, *Studiul Biblic al Noului Testament*, Vol. 1 (Bucuresti: Universitatea Bucuresti, facultatea

de Teologie Ortodoxa, 1995). My discussion with Fr. Ioan Sauca of the World Council of Churches, Geneva helped a great deal.

38. Cornitescu, *Studiul Biblic al Noului Testament*, 32

39. Ioan Sauca, "Romans 8" manuscript (Geneva: World Council of Churches, 1998)

40. Cornitescu, *"Studiul Biblic al Noului Testament,"* 32.

41. Gheorghiu, "Epistola catre Romani," xxviii-xxxi. The bibliography is an evidence for this.

42. Sauca, "Romans 8," 1.

43. Sauca, "Romans 8," 2.

44. Gheorghiu, "Epistola catre Romani," 55-57.

45. Gheorghiu, "Epistola catre Romani," 59.

46. Cornitescu, "Studiul Biblic al Noului Testament," 47-49.

47. Cranfield, "Romans," 172.

48. James R. Edwards, *Romans* (Peabody: Hendrickson, 1992), 197-98 suggests indirectly that such excitement exists. He also points to the fact that this chapter has the most mentions of the Spirit in the New Testament.

49. Bartlett, "Romans," 72.

50. Fitzmyer, *Romans,* 481.

51. Roger L. Hahn, "Pneumatology in Romans 8: Its Historical and Theological Context", *Wesleyan Theological Journal* 21 (Spring-Fall, 1986), 76.

52. Such are Stanley K. Stowers, *A Rereading of Romans* (New Haven/London: Yale University Press, 1994); Daniel Patte, *Paul's Faith and the Power of the Gospel* (Philadelphia: Fortress, 1983); Charles B. Cousar, "Continuity and Discontinuity: Reflections on Romans 5-8," in David M. Hay and Elizabeth Johnson eds., *Pauline Theology,* Vol. III (Minneapolis: Fortress, 1995), 196-210.

53. Frank Thielman, "The Story of Israel and the Theology of Romans 5-8, in *Pauline Theology,* 169-72.

54. See, James D. G. Dunn, "The Formal and Theological Coherence of Romans" in Karl P. Donfried ed., *The Romans Debate* (2nd ed.; Peabody: Hendrickson, 1995), 247.

55. See Dunn, "The Formal and Theological Coherence of Romans," 247 pointing to Kinoshita and Scroggs.

56. See, for instance, Peter Stuhlmacher, "The Theme of Romans" in *The Romans Debate,* 333-345.

57. See, William S. Campbell, "Romans III as a Key to the Structure and Thought of the Letter", in *Romans Debate,* 251-264.

58. Anders Nygren, *Commentary on Romans,* trans. by Carl C. Rasmussen (Philadelphia: Muhlenberg Press, 1949), 26-37.

59. After the Holocaust, these chapters raised serious questions about Pauline theology and have drawn a great deal of debate being contoured

as the starting point for the understanding of the theology of Romans. A brief overview of the issues at stake is offered by E. Elizabeth Johnson, "Romans 9-11—The Faithfulness and Impartiality of God", in *Pauline Theology*, Vol. III, 211-239.

60. Probably a good indirect example of this division is James Dunn's two volume commentary on Romans, *Romans 1-8 and Romans 9-16* (Waco: Word, 1988, 1989).

61. While this figurative structure is, like the convictional structure, to be distinguished from the theological structure (as proposed by Patte. *Paul and the Power of the Gospel*, chapter 6), it remains that the figurative structure is different from the convictional (or thematic) structure. See Patte, *Religious Dimensions of Biblical Texts* (Atlanta: Scholars Press, 1990), chapters 2 and 4.

62. Robert Jewett, "Following the Argument of Romans" in *Romans Debate*, 267.

63. So G. A. Kennedy, W. Wuellner, R. Jewett in *The Romans Debate*, 268.

64. Ian H. Thomson, *Chiasmus in the Pauline Letters* (Sheffield: Sheffield Academic Press, 1995), 17.

65. Thomson, *Chiasmus,* 25-26.

66. Thomson, *Chiasmus*, 27. He goes further and identifies certain requirements and constraints that one has to face when working with chiasms. Such are: the chiasm should be present in the text as it stands, without further modification; the symmetrical elements need to be present in inverted order; the chiasm should begin and end at reasonable points; macro-chiasm should avoid arrangement by headings; focus on recurring words could be misleading; one should avoid laying out a chiasmus in an exegetical vacuum, etc. (pp. 28-33).

67. Thomson, *Chiasmus,* 186-212.

68. Gordon D. Fee, *God's Empowering Presence* (Peabody: Hendrickson, 1994), 479-80, 525-26. If this chiasmus is textually grounded, it points to the damage done to the flow of the text by the breaks in the text caused by the chapters divisions.

69. Ignace De La Potterie, "Le Chretien Conduit Par L'Esprit Dans Son Cheminement eschatologique" in Lorenzo De Lorenzi ed., *The Law of the Spirit in Rom 7 and 8* (Rome: St Paul's Abbey, 1976), 228-232.

70. Cousar, *Pauline Theology*, III: 207-208.

71. Jewett, "Following the Argument of Romans," 275

72. Thomson, *Chiasmus*, 39.

73. Thomson, *Chiasmus*, 39-40.

74. W. G. E. Watson, "Chiasmus in Biblical Hebrew Poetry" in J. W. Welch ed., *Chiasmus in Antiquity: Structures, Analyses, Exegesis* (Hildesheim: Gerstenberg Verlag, 1981), 145.

75. Whether Paul prepares himself for the Jerusalem audience, whether his main aim is to introduce himself to the church in Rome, whether he addresses certain circumstances, he needs to be interested in the effects of his message, in its power of persuasion.

76. For detailed discussion of the architectural analysis and its implications for the biblical criticisms see, Charles H. Talbert, *Literary Patterns, Theological Themes and the Genre of Luke Acts* (Missoula: Scholar Press, 1974), 1-10.

Works Cited

Dunn, James D. G. "The New Perspective on Paul: Paul and the Law." Pages 299-308 in Karl P. Donfried ed., *The Romans Debate*. Peabody: Hendrickson, 1991.

Johns, Cheryl Bridges. "The Adolescence of Pentecostalism: In Search of a Legitimate Sectarian Identity" (Presidential Address). *Pneuma* 17:1 (Spring 1995): 4.

Machia, Frank D. "Sighs Too Deep For Words: Toward a Theology of Glossolalia." *Journal of Pentecostal Theology* 1 (1992): 55-60.

Thomson, Ian H. *Chiasmus in the Pauline Letters*. Sheffield: Sheffield Academic Press, 1995.

Centrality of the Spirit

A Response to Cimpean,
"From Margins to Center"

Herold Weiss

———— ◆ ————

Cimpean's very helpful paper opens and closes on the same note. Three times he tells us that he wishes to do critical work on the text of Romans to demonstrate how it can "account for" the pragmatic "pro me/nobis" application of the biblical text in the praxis of the life of faith. In other words, critical readings must "acknowledge" the validity of the readings of faith and "verify that it is indeed an aspect of the text of Romans that affects us in this way." Therefore, he characterizes his paper as "an experiment in integration of *pro nobis* readings with critical ones." Cimpean also tells us that a critical study is "a study which makes explicit its interpretative process." A great deal depends on acceptance of this definition. True to his definition, before engaging in his critical study of Romans and after having described Pentecostal and Orthodox readings, Cimpean places his assumptions on the table. He says that he assumes both that chapter 8 is the hermeneutical key to Romans, and that the Spirit functions as the integrating principle of theology and praxis. He then goes on to "ground" these assumptions in the text. Some, including myself, have reservations about calling this a critical study. Some time ago Bultmann acknowledged that an exegesis without presuppositions is a chimera. But then he distinguished presuppositions of results from presuppositions of method, and argued that critical exegesis can only have presuppositions of method. Methodologically, therefore, this essay raises some important questions.

Cimpean's essay turns around two arguments to two different audiences. In the first place, the paper argues to fellow Pentecostals that rather than excluding Romans they should be giving a place of honor to Romans in their functional canon. The argument is that Paul's vision of liberation by the Spirit in chapter 8 provides ample scriptural grounding to Romanian Pentecostal identity, and that the Pauline exposition of the power of the Spirit confirms the legitimacy of a pneumatological hermeneutic. Thus, he takes a quick look at Romanian Eastern

Orthodoxy only to find in it confirmation for the centrality of the Spirit as the force that energizes Christian life and thought, and, by extension, that the chapter on the Spirit is the core of the letter to the Romans. Of course, Cimpean is quite aware that this argument is for the benefit of a wider audience.

Secondly, Cimpean develops an argument for understanding chapter 8 as the key to Romans. As he sees it, this is the contribution which the Romanian margin can make to the Western center in the study of the letter to the Romans. In a brief survey of studies from the center, Cimpean finds that the path leading to Romans' gateway is littered with proposals. Among the suggestions, however, chapter 8 and its emphasis on pneumatology is conspicuously absent. Here, Cimpean argues, is where the Romanian margin, both in its Orthodox and its Pentecostal spiritualities, can make a significant contribution to the center.

I find Cimpean's contribution to this discussion of great value and most timely. It is not at all rare to see concerns with the relative significance of faith and works, Salvation History, the identification of the actual circumstances that prompted Paul to write, the nature of the relationship between theology and ethics in Paul or whether Paul's Christology is to be read anthropologically or theologically leaving no room for a balanced consideration of the role of the Spirit in the letter to the Romans. Cimpean's effort to make room for the Spirit in this conversation is a most welcomed contribution. The value of his suggestion is not to be denied even if one is not convinced that Paul structured his letter chiastically. I find his, admittedly sketchy, description of a chiastic macro pattern unconvincing due to the tendentious characterizations of the sections that are supposedly in counterpoint. This, however, does not, in my view, disqualify chapter 8 as a contender for the hermeneutical key to Romans, or, indeed, to the Pauline corpus. The centrality of the Spirit as the power that raised the living Lord and thereby constituted a new creation in the Spirit that is in tension with the creation in the flesh, as envisioned by Paul, is worthy of a careful and elaborate argument. In this connection, much is to be learned from Eastern Orthodox understandings of the Spirit as the power that restores the image of God in humans to the point that they become, like Christ, individuals with a human and a divine nature. Therefore, I thank Cimpean for expanding the conversation about the key to Romans.

I would also like to commend Cimpean for giving us a beautiful demonstration of the importance of experience to meaningful theology. His essay is ample proof that in the elaboration of Christian theology to scripture and tradition must be added experience as a full partner in the hermeneutical task because, as he points out, experience played a significant role when Paul wrote his letters. Since experience is filtered by culture, Cimpean considers that the assumptions present in a cultural matrix must be allowed to exercise their power. One may judge that when as a Romanian Pentecostal Cimpean chooses to see any Pauline teaching "through pneumatological lenses," he has unnecessarily adopted a reductionist perspective. Still, one must admit that looking through these lenses he perceives some wonderful vistas of the divine that give authenticity to human experience in the margin. I find his pneumatological paraphrase of Paul's exaltation of the power of love to be most revealing and, it would seem, fully within the Pauline thought world. Does not Paul, in reference to the effectiveness of the power of God, speak of the power of the Spirit, the power of the cross, the power of the gospel, the power of love, interchangeably?   Cimpean's paraphrase is both illuminating and a most appropriate expression of his experience and of my gratitude for his contribution to our common task:

> [O]nce liberated we have nothing to fear. Who or what will once again oppress us? Who or what will erase our identity? Who or what will mute our voices? Who or what will diminish our hope? Nothing will separate us from the pneumatic vision of Christ and God.

A "Frontier" Reading of Romans

The Case of
Bishop John William Colenso (1814-1883)

Jonathan A. Draper

——— ◆ ———

Introduction

C John William Colenso (1814-1883) was born into a lower middle class Nonconformist family in Cornwall, which fell on hard times. He converted to Anglicanism as a young man and worked his way through university at St. John's College, Cambridge. A brilliant scholar, especially in mathematics, he became a fellow of the college before leaving to take the parish of Forncett St. Mary's in order to be able to marry. Through his wife, Francis Sarah Bunyon, Colenso was introduced to the intellectual elite of Broad Church Anglicanism centred around the philosophy of Samuel Taylor Coleridge (1772-1834) and the universalist theology of F. D. Maurice (1805-1872). **H** Colenso became interested in mission work as local secretary of the Society for the Propagation of the Gospel. He was proposed to Bishop Robert Gray, Bishop of Cape Town, as a suitable candidate for the newly created Diocese of Natal in the fledgling British colony of the same name on the South-East coast of Africa, which had been seized from Dutch settlers trekking northwards to evade British rule. Consecrated bishop in 1853, Colenso threw his considerable energy, vision and intellectual ability into the work of mission to the Zulu people, though his work also required him to minister to the disparate and restless English settlers in his new diocese.

C Cultural background of John William Colenso.

H Colenso's hermeneutical interest in mission work.

I Unlike Gray, who spent his energies in organizing a colonial church, and for whom mission to the indigenous people was a secondary interest, Colenso concentrated on mastering the Zulu language and understanding their culture. The Coleridgean universalism which had inspired him before he left England predisposed him to find among the Zulu people a knowledge of God and an ethical sense based on this. His reflections on his dialogue with Zulu people were published in a series of books, the first of which was his *St. Paul's Epistle to the Romans: Newly Translated, and Explained from a Missionary Point of View*, published at his mission press at Ekukhanyeni in 1861.[1] Although he is better known for his seven volume work, *The Pentateuch and Book of Joshua Critically Examined*,[2] which denied the inerrancy of Scripture head on, it was largely his *Commentary on Romans* which led to his trial and conviction for heresy by the metropolitan, Bishop Gray, in 1863.[3] Although the trial was pronounced invalid by the supreme court of appeal, the Privy Council, Gray stood by his decision and excommunicated Colenso in 1866 and consecrated a new bishop, sparking a major crisis in the world wide Anglican communion. Colenso continued as Bishop of Natal on the strength of the Privy Council ruling, but was increasingly marginalized and pilloried by metropolitan English society and expansionist settler Natal. He turned more and more to his work on behalf of justice for the Zulu people, for which he is widely admired in post-apartheid South Africa.[4]

In an article which preceded his biography (1964) of Bishop John William Colenso, the ecclesiastical historian and apologist for the Anglican Church in South Africa, Peter Hinchliff, writes: "Colenso was, in fact, a Peter Pan amongst angry young men, and an unwillingness to grow up can be extremely irritating when found in a bishop and theologian."[5] The interesting implication of this picture of Colenso is that he inhabits an unreal world of crocodiles, pirates, Red Indians and fairies. The real world is the world of London, of commerce and empire: in a word, of Europe, not the "exotic" world of the Zulu people and their culture. Hinchliff, indeed, situates Colenso in what David Chidester describes as the world of the "frontier."[6] Here competing world views meet in a first encounter characterized by fluid and unstable exchanges. The equivalencies of ideas and linguistic concepts are not yet negotiated, and the opposing cultures have not yet been made safe by incorporation into existing categories and understandings. Things are not what they seem, and fixed understandings are constantly being subverted. No wonder Hinchliff concludes that although Colenso was "an honest, moral and courageous man," he was "forced by his very honesty to make a public defence of ideas and beliefs which he did not perhaps entirely

I Interplay of Colenso's cultural background and his hermeneutical interest.

understand himself and which he could not really deal with adequately."[7] Partial understanding is a characteristic of the "frontier," where it takes courage and integrity to survive. Writing a hundred years after the publication of Colenso's *Commentary on Romans*, when Europe has "domesticated" Africa by exploration and conquest, Hinchliffe sees Colenso's problem as an unwillingness to return from his adventure in Africa to the real world, to grow up, and to subordinate his traveller's experience to the wisdom of the imperial and colonial Western establishment.

I In a recent article on Colenso's *Commentary on Romans*, Timothy Larsen has placed Colenso's exegesis entirely within the context of metropolitan English Anglicanism. Colenso is "the bishop who didn't give a damn." Colenso, he argues, makes no contribution to the field of biblical criticism since his reading is "skewed by his theological agenda." Colenso is simply a typical liberal churchman in the Coleridgean tradition who breaks "the unwritten rule among liberal Anglicans that they were to be careful not to push matters too far" and publishes whatever the consequences, presumably because his location on the margins of power gives him the licence to do so. He discounts the bishop's interaction with his Zulu converts entirely in his discussion of Colenso's work both in this article and in an earlier article on Colenso's interpretation of the Pentateuch.[8] On the other hand, my own recent studies have advanced the view that Colenso's "conversations" with his Zulu interlocutors can be somehow overheard in his exegesis and commentary.[9] In this paper, I hope to rethink the question and revisit Colenso's exegesis in the light of further research and discussion. Colenso himself believed his exegesis to have been fundamentally shaped and framed by his contact with the Zulu culture and religion, so that it is "explained from a missionary point of view," as the subtitle says, and this should be given its due weight. In addition, it is important to resist the tendency to reduce all debates to the issues of the imperial centers of power and to disguise their origin on the colonized margins.[10] If Colenso broke the unwritten rules of the metropolis, what was it in his experience of the margin which occasioned such reckless behavior and what were the consequences for the center?

I Interplay of Colenso's cultural background, hermeneutics, and analytical skill in his biblical interpretation.

Frontier Readings

H Chidester's model of the "frontier" draws on the work of post-colonial hermeneutics, and views the conflictual meeting point of cultures as not only a sphere of contested power relations, but also a sphere of creativity and new understanding, as Homi Bhabha states it, **I** "It is the 'inter'—the cutting edge of translation and negotiation, the *in-between* space—that carries the burden of the meaning of culture":[11]

> I define a frontier as a zone of contact, rather than a line, a border, or a boundary. By this definition, a frontier is a region of intercultural relations between intrusive and indigenous people. Those cultural relations, however, are also power relations. A frontier zone opens with the contact between two or more previously distinct societies and remains open as long as power relations are unstable and contested, with no one group or coalition able to establish dominance. A frontier zone closes when a single political authority succeeds in establishing its hegemony over the area.[12]

C The first meaningful contacts between cultures on the frontier are made by the travellers, missionaries and administrators of the metropolis. Central to the world of the missionaries, in the tradition of the Reformation, was the Bible. Reading the Bible and preaching the Word in the indigenous languages, where there were no agreed equivalencies and analogies, opened up a dangerous and fruitful challenge. The frontier was thus an area not only of spatial contestation but also an area of hermeneutical crisis.

A Imperial readings of the Bible configure readings of the text on the basis of the indigenous people as the other, the outsiders, who must be instructed in the revealed truth of the Bible as this is construed in the metropolis. "Frontier" readings of the text problematize such hegemonic "truths" because they begin with the questions and practice of the other. Chidester argues that the first emergence of comparative religious studies and religious tolerance can be seen to emerge from this frontier situation and he situates Colenso and his Biblical exegesis within this context: "Taking this [Zulu] context seriously, Colenso tried to confront the

---

H Hermeneutics of John William Colenso, read from the hermeneutical lens of Chidester's "frontier" readings.

I Interplay between translation and negotiation, "space" and meaning.

C Cultural hermeneutics.

A Analytical frame on indigenous reading and imperial reading.

factual and moral dimensions of the biblical text in conversation with Zulu converts."[13] Zulu idiom also affected his reading of the Bible, in discussion, in translation, asking their questions of the text:

> As a result of such questions, Colenso rewrote the Bible, not only into the Zulu language, but also into a comparative religion that included Zulu religion among the religions of the world.[14]

H However much Colenso used the tools of modern criticism in his interpretation of the Bible, he always viewed it as a response to the crisis posed by his discussions with his Zulu converts.

Colenso's Biblical criticism is ambivalent, bipolar. It is located between the debates of Europe and the experience of mission. On the one hand, he is writing his *Commentary on Romans* for Western readers in the metropolis, hoping by means of this intervention to influence imperial attitudes and practice. As Jeff Guy has eloquently stated:

> His missionary writings, his preaching, and his political work were all undertaken in the belief that the indisputable facts which his work revealed would touch the good in the 'English People' and turn them towards 'their old principles of truth and justice.'[15]

C Colenso assumes the superiority of Christianity and Western culture. He remains a bishop of the realm, whose authority and status depend on Letters Patent of the crown. He dedicates his *Commentary on Romans* to the colonial Secretary for Native Affairs in Natal, Theophilus Shepstone, who was responsible for the development of a system of "native reserves" and "native law" on which later South African governments based their segregationist policies. Edward Said has astutely noted in his *Culture and Imperialism*, "how it was that the imperial European would not or could not see that he or she was an imperialist and, ironically, how it was that the non-European in the same circumstances saw the European *only* as imperial."[16]

H On the other hand, Colenso was able, despite his inevitable ethnocentricity, through his dialogue and constant involvement with the Zulu people, "to gain some insight into the colonial world as it was perceived by the colonized."[17] He also campaigns tirelessly in the local colonial situation and in the imperial parliament on behalf of the Zulu

---

H Colenso's hermeneutical critique.

C Western culture influenced Colenso's cultural reading of the Bible.

H Colenso overcame his ethnocentricity.

people. He seeks to defend their humanness in the face of attempts to depict them as savages past their evolutionary "sell-by date," legitimate targets for genocide or slavery. He seeks to defend their right to independent government in the face of colonial land grabs. He and his family, especially his daughter Harriette, come in the end to be wholly identified with the struggle of the Zulu people. He spends his days in Natal in constant dialogue with Zulu converts. Colenso's conversations with William Ngidi, his first Zulu interlocutor are well known, since Colenso explicitly acknowledges his debt to him in his *Commentary on the Pentateuch*. Indeed, he is pilloried for this in a famous limerick as the Bishop who was converted by a Zulu.[18]

    H "Conversation" for Colenso means opening himself to counter questions and answers from his dialogue partners: "I am afraid William meant to include in this talk hearing and answering their questions also."[19] The same may be said of his ongoing relation with Magema Fuze, who became supervisor of the mission press, and who wrote the first book in Zulu by a Zulu setting out the history of the Zulu people as he understood it, *The Black People and Whence They Came*, which comments on Colenso's historical discussions of affairs in Natal and interpolates his own perspectives on this "white narrative" or *esilungwini*.[20]   **A** The first teacher Colenso employed at his school at Ekukhanyeni, Walter Baugh, gives an insight into Colenso's habits in a report on July 1st, 1856 to the Society for the Propagation of the Gospel:

> The Kafir Sunday Service, which takes place in the Afternoon, is conducted by the Bishop himself. Sunday after Sunday this service becomes of more interest and profit to the people. His Lordship usually expounds a portion of Scripture and then induces the audience to ask questions. I could not but observe on recent occasions a deep interest exhibited on the part of the people when questions were asked and answers given by the Bishop. I should remark that everything that occurs at this Service is worthy of notice, inasmuch as it is a Congregation of Heathen Kafirs, their being usually but one Christian Kafir in the whole Congregation. The number of hearers latterly has been from 60 to 100 inclusive of the Schoolboys.[21]

    C Baugh is impressed by Colenso's conversational style in view of "the great barrier of prejudice to be broken down before a Kafir will

---

H "Conversation" as an essential of Colenso's hermeneutics.

A Baugh's analysis on Colenso.

C Cultural background of Colenso.

listen with any attention to anything about instruction in belief in religion." The teacher who succeeded Baugh, Charles Septimus Grubbe, in a letter of February 6th 1860,[22] on the other hand, found Colenso's method to be an intolerable one of "indulgence and favouritism" to the senior boys (Undiane and probably Fuze). He himself never learned Zulu and resorted to frequent flogging of the boys for their "dirty habits," before he was removed.

The school at Ekukhanyeni was pivotal in the emergence of a new Zulu missionary elite, the *amakholwa*, even though it shared in the kind of ambivalence we have already noted.[23] Colenso regarded it as a "kafir Harrow" and wrote school textbooks for the boys on Zulu grammar,[24] mathematics (he had already published a textbook on algebra in England in 1849, and followed this with one on arithmetic in 1855, trigonometry in 1859, Euclid in 1861), science, including evolution (1861), as well as religious books (apart from Bible and liturgy, see also his *Izindaba Zokupilo kuka'Jesu-Kristu indodana ka/dio unkulunkulu Inkosi yetu* [A Narrative of the Life of Jesus Christ, the Son of Dio God our Lord] 1857). He was determined they should attain the same knowledge and education required of a Western school child in the best schools in England. **C** Yet the constant process of translation of words and concepts into Zulu, not indeed just simple mission oriented concepts but also fundamental Western "truths" of science and culture, via discussion with his converts, also reconfigured that knowledge. Things look different on the "frontier."

I So Colenso essentially faces in two directions at once. While his book on Romans is directed at Western readers and clearly interacts with the burning issues of the age in England, it is answering questions and facing issues which arise for the Zulu people confronted by Christianity and colonialism, two aspects of the same intrusive reality. It is not only the cultural universe of the Zulu people which is placed in question by the activity of the missionaries, but also their own, as "these Europeans had eventually to come to terms with the disconcerting image of themselves that the "wilderness" gave back."[25] The act of re-presentation of our own culture in a frontier situation (where the other culture "holds up a mirror to our own," as the Comaroffs put it) unmasks the "taken for granted" or hegemonic nature of our own social universe and puts it in question. This calls for the formulation of an ideological defense of what has previously needed no defense, and there will always be a residue which can no longer be defended in a "frontier" situation.

C Cultural background changed; frontier changed.

I Interplay of different audiences; interplay of different issues.

A This was particularly true for Colenso, who had already been questioning some of the normative ideas of the English establishment before he left England, under the influence of Coleridge and Maurice. It is the gaps (and the existential need to fill them) which the re-presentation of our own image by the other in the "frontier" situation opens up, the spaces for play and experimentation or *bricolage*,[26] which produce the kind of "boundary jumping" noted by Larsen. Giving this a positive valuation, the Comaroffs describe this as the "poetics of history." **I** Colenso believes that his situation on the "frontier" engaged in missionary work among the heathen gives him a unique insight into Paul's Epistle, since Paul was also a "missionary among the heathen." As he writes in his preface of scholars in the metropolis:

> Those scholars have written from a very different point of view, in the midst of a state of advanced civilization and settled Christianity. Hence they have usually passed by altogether, or only touched very lightly upon, many points, which are of great importance to Missionaries, but which seemed to be of no immediate practical interest for themselves or their readers.[27]

I Colenso's *Commentary on Romans* can be read, then, as an act of *bricolage*, produced by the interaction of English and Zulu culture in a sensitive and intelligent observer. To put it in another way, we need to note both aspects in Colenso's reading of Romans, imperialism *and* resistance, which Said describes as "contrapuntal reading,"[28] which does justice to the "intertwined and overlapping histories"[29] of the colonial frontier.

Romans "Newly Translated"

C A H Well equipped by his Cambridge education and by his seven years of study of the Zulu language, which issued in publishing his pioneering Zulu *Grammar*[30] and *Dictionary*,[31] Colenso set about the work of translating Romans. In his *Commentary on Romans*, he presents us with an English translation from the Greek, but the purpose of the

---

A Questioning of Colenso on the normative ideas of English establishment.

I Interplay of Colenso's culture and his analysis on his hermeneutics.

I Colenso's reading as a "bricolage"; the relationship between imperialism and resistance; "contrapuntal reading."

C A H Colenso's translation comprises of the cultural, analytical, and hermeneutical frames.

work was to prepare for his Zulu translation of Romans, *Inncwadi ka'Paulo Umpostole Wenkosi, ayilobela Ibandla Las'eRoma* [The Letter of Paul, Apostle of the Lord, written to the Church of Rome] which appears in his full Zulu New Testament: *Izindab' ezinhle Ezashunyayelwa Ku'bantu ng' uJesus-Kristo Inkosi Yetu Kanye Nezinncwadi Ezalotshwa Ng' abapostole Bake* [The Good News Preached to the People by Jesus Christ Our Lord Together with the Letters Written by His Apostles] (1876). **I** It is significant that Colenso never claims to be *the* translator or author of the translation. He developed his translation in dialogue with his converts at a time when there were no agreed linguistic and grammatical equivalencies.[32] **H** This makes it particularly significant as part of the wider study of *translation* as a hermeneutical category, as this has been argued by Lamin Sanneh and Bediako.[33] **I** On this understanding, the insistence of the missionaries on the translation of the Bible into the vernacular opened up, not only the semantic potential of the text itself, but also the dynamic, creative semantic and cultural potential of African societies under colonialism.[34] Sanneh argues that it was this introduction of vernacular literacy which accounts for the success of the mission, rather than theological persuasion or spiritual conversion.

A Colenso's translation made a lasting contribution both to the development of modern Zulu grammar and also to modern translations of the Bible. However, the first and most significant point of translation was the choice of the name for God. This was already a matter of heated debate among missionaries when Colenso arrived in Natal.[35] Most had adopted names for God that were borrowings from other languages to avoid the possibility that "heathen" associations would subvert the preaching of the gospel. Most popular was the Khoikhoi word for God, *uThixo*, which is still used among the Xhosa and sometimes by Zulu people today as well, but others used *uYehova* or *uDio*. Trying to avoid specificity, some experimented with the Zulu word *iThongo*, to express an impersonal divine power, only to find it referred to the influence of the ancestral spirits.[36] What is significant is that Colenso advocated the normative names for God in Zulu culture, *uNkulunkulu* and *uMvelinqangi*, not in spite of their indigenous connotations but rather because of them. In his *Dictionary* he defines *uNkulunkulu* to mean

---

I Interplay between Colensa and his converts.

H Colenso's translation as a hermeneutic.

I Interaction between translation, semantic potential, and creative semantic of the text.

A On the name of God.

"Great-Great-One, Supreme Being, traditional Creator of all things, called also *uMvelinqangi*." **I** He found in the traditional Zulu understanding of divinity the universal creator God worshipped by all human beings of good will, the same God as the God of Jesus Christ.

This choice of the name for God had profound consequences, since it allowed for a maximum of **C** cultural continuity in the "translation" of the gospel. It opened up in a particularly meaningful way, the possibility for Zulu people to question the presentation of the Christian God by the missionaries, to begin a dialogue in terms of how they themselves already understood this God. It is also a fundamental step in Colenso's *Commentary on Romans*, since, as his translation of 1:19-20 shows particularly clearly, it enables him to apply the Jew-Gentile dichotomy in Romans in the same terms as Paul does, whereas other missionaries were apt to claim either that the heathen had no God at all, or else that they worshipped demons. **A** Colenso translates:

> Inasmuch as that which is knowable of God is manifest among them; for God manifested it to them. For His invisible *things*, from the creation of the world, being understood by his works, are being clearly seen, to wit, His Eternal Power and Deity, so that they are without excuse.[37]

I What Colenso translates in English as "manifest" is rendered in his Zulu translation *kuhlalukiswa* (having been made to come to light), a passive of the causative *hlalukisa*, which he translates in his dictionary as "make to come to light" (where the American Board of Mission translation of 1865 has *ku ya bonakaliswa*, "having been made visible" and the modern Bible Society translation has *yambulwa*, "having been revealed"[38]). Colenso argues that this manifestation is not a thing of the past, but a continuing process, on the basis of **A** Paul's use of the Aorist tense:

> In fact, the Greek Aorist can often be expressed best by one of the forms of the English present, "God manifests it," which English expression does not point to any one particular time, past, present,

---

I Interplay between cultural background of God and analytical understanding of God of Jesus Christ.

C Cultural continuity in the "translation."

A Colenso's translation of Rom 1:19-20.

I The meaning of "manifest" in the interplay of culture and cognitive understanding of the word.

A Paul's use of aorist.

or to come, or to any continually progressing manifestation, but implies the frequently recurring acts in all time by which God manifests his Glory to men.[39]

Colenso's translation also removes the implication of 1:21 in the Authorized Version that real knowledge of God is impossible through nature ("became vain in their imaginations") by translating "became silly in their reasonings," which is repeated in his Zulu translation *ubuphukuphuku* ("foolishness"; in Colenso's dictionary he defines such a person as a "silly, empty-headed, frothy, fellow, simpleton, blockhead").

A The Zulu people, then, have an implicit knowledge of God from creation. They see it all about them in the world he has created. Their own cultural understanding of God represents "that which may be attained by human faculties, enlightened by the Divine Spirit, without special revelation."[40] They are not depraved and without moral sense, since they have a moral sense through natural revelation:

> The recognition of the Eternal Power and Deity of our glorious Maker involves a natural and necessary consequence, the duty of fearing, loving, trusting, and obeying Him, in proportion to the Light He gives us.[41]

I Thus Paul cannot mean to include all Zulu people indiscriminately in the condemnation "they are without excuse." That would be manifestly unjust, since "infants and young children" and imbeciles are clearly without culpability by reason of ignorance. **H** Likewise, heathen people of good will, from the time of ancient Greece and Rome until today, living their best according to their lights, cannot be included under a blanket condemnation. Instead the "without excuse" applies to individuals, heathen or Christian, who sin knowingly (according to their lights), and who yet look to experience the mercy of the God of love, who will deal mercifully with us and "so too, we may be sure, will He deal with the heathen."[42]

Of course it would be impossible to discuss Colenso's translation of the whole of Romans in a short paper. However, **I** this sample already clearly demonstrates the way in which Colenso's work of revisiting the

---

A The Zulu people and their implicit knowledge of God.

I Between Paul's word and the Zulu people.

H Hermeneutical issue of meaning from the past to the present.

I A sample of Colensa's works that take the cultural, hermeneutical, and analytical frames seriously.

Greek and English translation in the context of producing his Zulu
Grammar, Dictionary and translation of the Bible, creates a rich
potential for his "frontier" reading of Romans.

"Explained from a Missionary Point of View"

4.1 Who are the true Jews?

If Colenso's translation of Romans is profoundly influenced by issues
of "translation," beginning with the question, "Who is the God of the
Zulus?" then his "explanation" of Romans is profoundly influenced by
the question, "Who are God's chosen people? Who are the Israel of
God?" **H** David Chidester has noted the way in which the Western
imperial venture began by denying that the indigenous people had any
religion and then moved on to "discovering" that they had a religion after
all and finding ways of incorporating it into the imperial religious
system. **H** One common way of doing this was to see the indigenous
people as a "lost tribe of Israel." Africans then became descendents of
Ishmael in the case of the Xhosa[43] or else descended from the Jews in the
case of the Zulu,[44] who still held on to monotheism and some of the laws
of God, but who had degenerated and lost their original glory. **I** Colenso
toyed with this idea of the Zulus as debased descendants of ancient
Israel,[45] since it enabled him to take their culture and religious beliefs
and practice seriously. However, it had a particular ironic significance in
his interpretation of Romans, enabling him to understand the question of
Paul with a new intensity: **H A** Does God have favorites? Who are
God's people?

    H Colenso's hermeneutical key is to understand the epistle as written
to Jews and proselytes, not to Christians as such. They had been present
at the first Pentecost in Jerusalem and had brought back with them a
belief in Jesus as Messiah, but had not yet understood the implications of
this, namely that in Christ all humankind is redeemed. Instead, they
continued to insist that Gentiles who believed should become Jews and
that obedience to the Torah was the only path to salvation. They
continued to worship in the synagogue and live as Jews. Paul knew of
the situation in Rome through Priscilla and Aquila, who had learned the

---

H Hermeneutical issue of conveying meaning across religions and cultures.

H Who are the "lost tribes of Israel" in Africa?

I Colenso's hermeneutics and cultural understanding.

H A "Does God have favorites?"—a hermeneutical and an analytical question.

H Colensa's hermeneutical key.

good news of salvation for all human kind without works of law from Paul in Ephesus. Paul wished in his letter to share the gospel with them before he visited them on his way to Spain.

A What Paul addresses in the letter are the "three great pre-possessing errors of the Jewish mind": they thought they had a special status before God; they thought they had thus a special claim on the Messiah over against the Gentiles, and they insisted that Gentiles must keep the Jewish law and rituals if they wished to be equal to Jews.[46] In other words, Paul is attacking reliance on election and race and arguing that salvation is a pure gift of God ("without special favor or distinction"). Of course, there is, from our post-holocaust point of view, an unsettling element of what Said (1978) calls "essentialism" here. The "Jew" is given fundamental oppositional characteristics, which are used to construct an alternative world. Yet Colenso has in mind a symbolic value for the category "Jew," which does not extend to the Jews of his own day, whom he explicitly excludes from any special condemnation. Quite the reverse, the persecution of Jews by Christians had made it virtually impossible, he argues, for them to believe the Christian gospel:

> But, as for the Jews of the present day, we cannot presume to say that they too have been given over to a reprobate mind, or that their eyes are darkened as a penal consequence of their continuing in unbelief. It may be so in certain individual cases, where light has reached the inner man, and been rejected. But, probably, in our days, amidst the great body of the Jewish people, such cases are very rare. It is far more likely that the acts of abominable cruelty, injustice, and contemptuous bigotry, with which, in Christian lands and by Christian people too often, alas! by Christian ministers they have been so frequently, and are even now, treated, have gone far to fix them in holy and righteous horror of a religion, which taught that such outrages were right. All, surely, that an humble-minded Christian can allow himself to say of the present state of the Jews generally is that they are not actually incurring great moral *guilt* (he cannot judge of that,) but suffering great moral and spiritual loss from the acts of their forefathers.[47]

H In any case, he could argue, the Zulus are also Jews by descent, however degenerate their understanding of their Jewish heritage might have become! His purpose is quite the opposite of anti-Semitism in his

---

A An understanding of Paul's text.

H Zulus are Jews by descent.

own context (however much essentialisms might play into the hand of such prejudice).

H For Colenso, his question, "Who are the chosen people of God? Who are the real Jews?" has the ironic double answer: the very people the colonists despise as savages may be by descent the chosen people of God, Israel. Moreover, their belief in God and their ethical life may, in many ways, put the unbelieving, dissolute and greedy colonists to shame:

> The great drawback here is that the country is already saturated with a corruption of Christianity, and the natives have acquired such a view of the character of God and of the Gospel as keeps them back from desiring to have a much closer acquaintance with it. This they have obtained partly from the example they have constantly before them in the lives of the unfaithful Christians partly from the mistaken teaching of the missionaries.[48]

H On the other hand, when the question of the "pre-possessing errors of the Jewish mind" are opened up for discussion in the *Commentary*, it is quite clear that Colenso has in mind the English imperialists and colonists, who rely on pride of election and race. **A** Just as Paul was concerned to persuade the Jews to whom he writes that the Gentiles are now, through Christ, equally the beloved people of God, saved by grace alone and not by works of law, so Colenso seeks to persuade the colonists and the metropolis that the Zulu people are also equally the beloved people of God, saved by grace alone and not by the adoption of Western culture and lifestyle. In other words, the colonists and the English at home are the Jews of today, vis-à-vis the "Gentile" Zulus.

H Colenso turns around Paul's argument in 2:25, concerning circumcision as a grounds for confidence before God, so that it applies to Christians who pride themselves on their election and race over the indigenous people they have conquered:

> The baptism of a Christian has a meaning and use, if he walks faithfully; otherwise his baptism becomes a mere nullity. If, then, an unbaptised heathen does that which is good and right and true, shall not his unbaptised state be reckoned for baptism? and they, which are heathens by nature, and walking according to the light vouchsafed to them, judge those, who, baptised Christians as they

---

H Zulus are chosen people of God.

H Colenso's hermeneutic in the *Commentary*.

A Paul's understanding of the Jews.

H Colenso's re-interpretation of 2:25.

are, yet knowingly transgress the law of their Lord? For he is not a Christian, who is so merely in name and profession, nor is that true baptism, which is only outwardly with water. But the Christian in God's sight is he who is one inwardly; and the baptism, which is of value before Him, is that of the heart, in the spirit, not in the outward form.[49]

H Of course, this raises for Christian theology the same question as it raised for Jewish people addressed by Paul: what benefit circumcision? He answers in his exegesis of 4:2: just as Abraham was declared righteous before he received circumcision, so too is every human being, through the work of Christ, and baptism is simply the sign or ratification of something already freely given to all. The child of Abraham is anyone who "walks patiently in the path of duty according to the light vouchsafed to them, receiving God's blessed gift, not earned by their works, poor and unworthy at the best, but bestowed by His free grace."[50]

H What, then, do Christian sacraments such as baptism and eucharist mean? Colenso paraphrases Paul's answer in startling fashion:

It might be asked, 'If you say the heathen may be saved without the knowledge of the Gospel, what advantage then, hath the Christian, or what profit is there in Christian Baptism?' And a similar answer might be given: Much, in every way: in the very first place, because to them are entrusted the Holy Scriptures, the books of the New Testament as well as the Old?—And to this we might go on to add, 'To them are given the means of grace, and the hope of glory.'[51]

H Colenso does not hesitate to adopt the logic of Paul's argument, namely that the blessing of salvation has been given in Christ to all humankind in solidarity with him, and through the sacraments the individual is "receiving each for himself, personally, in baptism a formal outward sign of ratification of that adoption, which they have shared already, independently of the sign, with the whole race."[52] Likewise, the eucharist is given to all humankind in their daily experience of God's sustaining love

---

H Colenso's re-interpretation of 4:2.

H Colenso's interpretation of the sacraments.

H Colenso's interpretation of the logic of Paul.

... of which we are partaking, day by day, at every moment, as redeemed creatures, though we may not know it or may not heed it, of which every man everywhere is partaking, though he may not know what the Word made Flesh has done at His Father's bidding, for the children of men.[53]

A Colenso uses the phrase, "the whole race" no less than 16 times in the commentary to express human solidarity in Christ regardless of conversion to Christianity. The answer to the question, "Who then are God's people?," is that it consists of all human beings without exception, whether they know it or not. Christ as the new Adam is the "Head" (this word is used no less than 49 times in the *Commentary on Romans*) of a new humanity under the Fatherhood of God, as Colenso says in his commentary on 6:4:

> What He, our Head, did, that we, the members of His Body, share in, we, the whole brotherhood of Man, we, the whole race, whose nature He took upon Him.[54]

The "Jews," on the other hand, become the symbolic type of human groups who pride themselves on election and race, to the exclusion of others. Colenso, for his part, identifies the Jews of Paul's argument with the English Christians of his own day, who condemn, despise and exclude the indigenous peoples they have conquered.

Who then shall be saved?

A If God has no favorites, but pours out his love in the work of the Son on all alike, the good and bad, the believers and the unbelievers, who then is saved? **H** Of one thing Colenso is sure: salvation does not depend on the fallible and half-understood work of the missionary, "laying down the law to them, often with the most obscure and defective utterance, in some difficult native tongue, upon matters of the deepest personal and social interest."[55] The intensity of Colenso's feeling here reflects the questions of his Zulu converts. **H** For them the idea that their "living dead" ancestors, the focus of identity, stability and ethical conduct in the African community, are condemned to eternal damnation because they did not respond to the missionary preaching, is an

---

A Meaning of "the whole race."

A An analytical question on the impartiality of God.

H Colenso's hermeneutical answer on salvation.

H Colenso's interpretation for his Zulu converts.

intolerable injustice. Colenso had already expressed doubts about the concept of eternal damnation in his *Village Sermons* before he left England, following the teaching of his early mentor, F. D. Maurice, but had been pressured into backing off somewhat.[56] His "conversations" on the "frontier," however, left him no more room for doubt: "as in Adam all die, so in Christ shall all be made alive." If the first half of the statement is true of all men, in the emergence of original sin, then the second half must be taken in the same sense, in the emergence of "original salvation" for all human beings from creation to eternity. **H** He translates 5:18 as follows (italics his), "So then, just as through one fault, *it* [death] *passed* unto all men, unto condemnation, so also, through one righteous act, *it* [the gift of righteousness] *passed* unto all men, unto justification of life." He interprets this as follows,

> For 'the many' who died in Adam, were, of course, the whole race; and therefore also, blessed be God! 'The many', to whom 'the grace of God abounded, and the free gift by grace of the one man Jesus Christ', the gift of righteousness, must be the whole race, the whole family of man.[57]

Colenso does not deny that there will be punishment for those who have sinned willfully and wickedly, for that would also impugn the justice of God. Yet even such punishment will be a process of purification and preparation for eternal life, since to punish without hope would be cruel and unjust. Human beings are accountable for what they do now "according to their lights," following the dictates of their conscience, but in the end, in God's good time, all will be saved and all will be restored in Christ to the fullness and glory of God's purpose in creation. **A** His sustained discussion of this point is given in his commentary on 8:18-39.[58] In the end, Love would conquer all.

In the meantime, we are saved by faith without works of law. But what exactly does it mean to have faith? The missionaries working in Natal when Colenso arrived were in no doubt: it meant a personal act of conversion and separation. Here again, however, **H** Colenso's reflections are profoundly influenced by his dialogue with his Zulu converts. He saw at first hand the damage done by indiscriminate applications of this understanding of faith, breaking up families, putting away wives and turning loose children of polygamous marriages, the

---

H Colenso's interpretation.

A Meaning of 8:18-39.

H Colenso's reflection with his Zulu converts.

creation of dependent mission farm communities. **H** In his early work at translating the Bible, he found no satisfactory Zulu translation for the Greek word, *pistis*. The word favored by the American Board of Mission was *ukukholwa*, which means "to be satisfied, have enough of a thing, to be satisfied with the evidence of a thing," as Colenso puts it in his *Dictionary*, commenting trenchantly (using the old Zulu orthography),

> N.B. The word *kolwa* only expresses *belief* in the sense of *assent*, not of *trust* or *affiance*, for which *temba* must be employed. Hence it is a very improper word to be used generally, for the faith of a Christian.[59]

The use of *ukukholwa* was, however, too firmly established in missionary usage, and Colenso was not successful in his attempt to supplant it. Colenso uses instead the Zulu word *ukuthemba* ("trust, hope, rely on, confide in").[60] **H** He translates 1:17, *olungileyo uya'uhamba ngokwokutemba*, literally, "the righteous person walks by trust" (while the American Board of Mission translates it *olungileyo wo hlala ugenkolo*, "the righteous person stays being satisfied with the evidence"; and the modern Bible Society translates it *olungileyo uzakuphila ngokukholwa*, "the righteous person shall live by faith" (since *ukukholwa* has become the fixed term for this in modern Zulu). This understanding of the meaning of *pistis* determines Colenso's picture of the life of faith, "Being justified by faith, by simple trust in God's Fatherly forgiving Mercy and restoring Love, he [the true Christian] has peace again with God."[61] **H** This experience of peace, springing out of a life of confident trust in the Creator God, is available not only to the Christian, but to all who live the ethical life "according to their lights," that is, according to their experience of God "by means of any one of Earth's ten thousand voices," whatever their culture and creed.[62] It also characterizes the kind of conversion and Christian faith experienced and practiced by the influential Zulu elite produced by Ekukhanyeni, who placed a largely positive valuation on Zulu culture, history and tradition.[63]

Conclusion

If ancient cartographers wrote on the blank spaces of the maps, "Here be dragons," then they signal their deep fear and distrust of the unknown

---

H Colenso's translation.

H Colenso's interpretation of 1:17.

H An analysis of Colenso's interpretation.

spaces of the earth, the frontiers where danger and ambiguity lurk to ensnare the unwary traveler. It is the world of Peter Pan, of Never Never Land. The missionaries who went out to preach the gospel in the "blank spaces" dreamed, perhaps, of creating the perfect world away from the "dark Satanic mills" of England, the Kingdom of God in Africa. However, there were no real "blank spaces," any more than there were "unclaimed lands," in Africa or anywhere else.[64] The dragons in the blank spaces turned out to be their own reflections in the mirrors held up to them by the indigenous people they found there. Colenso's long, hard and courageous look into the mirror of Africa transformed him and pushed him to take the intellectual and political steps he would probably never have taken had he stayed in England. However, he was certainly not a Peter Pan who never grew up. Nor was he someone who "didn't give a damn": he cared deeply. He simply could not return to the "ordinary world" of Victorian orthodoxy and "normality," even though the cost of his "eccentricity" to himself and his family was considerable.

C A H It is not surprising that Colenso's *Commentary on Romans* scandalized the Church of his day. His conclusions seemed a step too far. However, in the globalized world of the twenty first century they seem attractive and strangely "sensible," even if sometimes couched in tiresome Victorian sentimentality. It is also interesting to see that several Pauline scholars today are also moving towards a view of Paul as facing in two directions, like Colenso, a Jew writing to other Jews but trying to create a new reality on the "frontier" with Gentiles, a new inclusive humanity.[65] Colenso's work was never properly studied in his own time, once it had been declared heretical, but it bears rich testimony to the fruitfulness of reading with the "other," listening to other voices on the margins of power. This is something which modern scholars located in the metropolis need to hear also. Colenso's insights, born of the European Enlightenment and an emerging Zulu cultural identity, may be closer to Paul's thought than could otherwise have been conceived a hundred and fifty years ago.

Notes

1. For the sake of brevity, this work is referred to as *Commentary on Romans*. All references to the work are from the edition of 2003: Bishop John William Colenso, *Commentary on Romans*, edited by J. A. Draper. Pietermaritzburg: Cluster Publications. The page numbers from the

---

C A H Colenso's *Commentary* uses contextual, hermeneutical, and analytical frames.

original Ekukhanyeni edition are provided there for convenience in the
body of the text in square brackets.

2. J. W. Colenso, *The Pentateuch and Book of Joshua Critically
Examined: Parts I-VI* (London: Longmans, Green, 1862-1871).

3. See J. A. Draper, "The Trial of Bishop John William Colenso," in
Draper ed., *The Eye of the Storm: Bishop John William Colenso and the
Crisis of Biblical Interpretation* (London & New York: T&T Clark
International/Pietermaritzburg: Cluster Publications, 2003) (hereafter
The Eye of the Storm), 306-325 for an account of the tangled and bitter
legal controversy.

4. J. A. Draper, "Bishop John William Colenso and History as
Unfolding Story," *Journal of Theology for Southern Africa* 117 (2003):
97-105.

5. P. Hinchliff, "John William Colenso: A Fresh Appraisal," *Journal
of Ecclesiastical History* 13.2 (1962): 203.

6. D. Chidester, *Savage Systems: Colonialism and Comparative
Religion in Southern Africa* (Charlottsville and London: University Press
of Virginia, 1996). I am indebted to Halvor Moxnes, who responded to
my paper in the "Seminar on Romans through History and Culture" at
the Society of Biblical Literature Annual Meeting in Nashville 2000
("Bishop John William Colenso's Interpretation to the Zulu People of the
Sola Fide in St. Paul's Letter to the Romans," in *Seminar Papers of the
Society of Biblical Literature Annual Meeting 2000* [Atlanta: Scholars
Press, 2000], 465-493), for his suggestion that I should explore the
potential of Chidester's "frontier" model further. I would like to thank
Sharon D. Welch as well for her insightful response on the same
occasion, which also has influenced this rewriting of the original.

7. Hinchliffe, "John William Colenso," 216.

8. T. Larsen, "Bishop Colenso and His Critics: The Strange
Emergence of Biblical Criticism in Victorian Britain," in Draper ed., *The
Eye of the Storm* [1997], 45-48; for a different perspective see D.
Jobling, "Colenso on Myth or Colenso as Myth: A Response to Timothy
Larsen," in Draper ed., *The Eye of the Storm,* 64-75; J. W. Rogerson,
"John William Colenso," in J. W. Rogerson ed., *Old Testament Criticism
in the Nineteenth Century: England and Germany* (London: SPCK,
1985), 220-237.

9. J. A. Draper "Hermeneutical Drama on the Colonial Stage: Liminal
Space and Creativity in Colenso's Commentary on Romans," *Journal of
Theology for Southern Africa* 103 (1998), 13-32; *idem,* "The Bishop and
the Bricoleur: Bishop John William Colenso's Commentary on Romans
and Magema kaMagwaza Fuze's The Black People and Whence They
Came," in G. O. West & Musa W. Dube ed., *The Bible in Africa:
Transactions, Trajectories and Trends* (Leiden: Brill, 2000), 415-454;
idem, "Bishop John William Colenso's Interpretation to the Zulu People

of the *Sola Fide* in St. Paul's Letter to the Romans," in *Seminar Papers of the Society of Biblical Literature Annual Meeting 2000* (Atlanta: Scholars Press, 2000), 465-493; *idem,* "Colenso's Commentary on Romans: An Exegetical Assessment," in Draper ed., *The Eye of the Storm,* 465-493.

10. Chidester, *Savage Systems,* 1.

11. *Ibid.,* xv.

12. *Ibid.,* 20-21.

13. *Ibid.,* 135.

14. *Ibid.,* 135-136.

15. J. Guy, *The Heretic: A Study of the Life of John William Colenso 1814-1883* (Johannesburg: Ravan/ Pietermaritzburg: University of Natal Press, 1983), 354.

16. E. W. Said, *Culture and Imperialism* (New York: Vintage, 1993), 162.

17. Guy, *The Heretic,* 358.

18. Cited by *ibid.,* 133.

19. J. W. Colenso, *Bringing forth Light: Five Tracts on Bishop Colenso's Zulu Mission,* edited with an introduction by Ruth Edgecombe (Pietermaritzurg: University of Natal Press/ Durban: Killie Campbell Africana Library, 1982 [1865]), 228.

20. See J. A. Draper, "The Bishop and the Bricoleur: Bishop John William Colenso's Commentary on Romans and Magema kaMagwaza Fuze's The Black People and Whence They Came," in G. O. West & Musa W. Dube ed., *The Bible in Africa: Transactions, Trajectories and Trends* (Leiden: Brill, 2000), 415-454; H. Mokoena, "The Black People and Whence They Came: Christian Converts and the Production of Kholwa Histories in the Nineteenth-Century Colonial Natal—The Case of Magema Magwaza Fuze" (Unpublished paper presented at the Centre of African Studies, University of Cape Town, September 2003; cited with permission of the author).

21. United Society for the Propagation of the Gospel (hereafter USPG) (Rhodes House, Oxford, C/AFS/6).

22. *Ibid.,* 14.

23. See P. Kearney, "Success and Failure of 'Sokululeka' Bishop Colenso and African Education," in Draper ed., *The Eye of the Storm,* 195-206; V. Khumalo, "The Class of 1856 and the Politics of Cultural Production(s) in the Emergence of Ekukhanyeni, 1855-1910," in Draper ed., *The Eye of the Storm,* 207-241; Mokoena, "The Black People and Whence They Came."

24. J. W. Colenso, *First Book in Zulu-Kafir: An Introduction to the Study of the Zulu Language* (Ekukhanyeni, Natal: Mission Press, [1855] 1859).

25. Jean Comaroff & John Comaroff, *Of Revelation and Revolution: Christianity, Colonialism and Consciousness in South Africa* (Chicago: University of Chicago Press, 1991), 171, cf. 99.

26. *Ibid.*, 25, 29.

27. *Ibid.*, xliii.

28. J.W. Colenso, *Commentary on Romans*, edited with an introduction by J. A. Draper (Pietermaritzburg: Cluster Publications, 2003), 66.

29. *Ibid.*, 18.

30. J. W. Colenso, *An Elementary Grammar of the Zulu-Kafir Language* (Ekukhanyeni, Natal: Mission Press, 1859).

31. J. W. Colenso, *Zulu-English Dictionary* (Pietermaritzburg: P. Davis, 1861).

32. S. T. Tshehla, "Colenso, John 1.1-18 and the Politics of Insider and Outsider Translating," in Draper ed., *The Eye of the Storm,* 30-31.

33. Lamin Sanneh, *Translating the Message: The Missionary Impact on Culture* (Maryknoll, New York: Orbis, 1989); *idem, Encountering the West: Christianity and the Global Cultural Process* (Maryknoll, New York: Orbis, 1993); K. Bediako, *Theology and Identity: The Impact of Culture upon Christian Thought in the Second Century and in Modern Africa* (Akropong-Akuapem, Ghana: Regnum Books, 1992).

34. For a critique see T. S. Maluleke, "Black and African Theologies in the New World Order: A Time to Drink From Our Own Wells," *Journal of Theology for Southern Africa* 96 (1996): 3-19; *idem,* "Half a Century of African Christian Theologies: Elements of the Emerging Agenda for the Twenty-First Century," *Journal of Theology for Southern Africa* 99 (1997): 4-23; for a positive evaluation and application of this theory see Tshehla, "Colenso, John 1.1-18 and the Politics," 29-41; Mokoena, "The Black People and Whence They Came."

35. Chidester, *Savage Systems*, 132-136.

36. G. R. Dent and C. L. S. Nyembezi, *Scholars Zulu Dictionary* (Pietermaritzburg: Shuter & Shooter, 1969), 496.

37. Colenso, *Commentary on Romans*, 37.

38. *Ambula* is given the meaning in Colenso's *Dictionary*, "take off, strip off, (as a blanket, mist, fog, smoke, &c.); remove, (as any broad thing laid over something else); open, (as a book)." In Dent and Nyembezi, *Scholars Zulu Dictionary*, "uncover; unveil; reveal."

39. Colenso, *Commentary on Romans*, 41.

40. *Ibid.*

41. *Ibid.*, 42.

42. *Ibid.*, 43.

43. Chidester, *Savage Systems*, 92-94.

44. *Ibid.*, 124-129

45. Chidester, *Savage Systems*, 137-138.

46. Colenso, *Commentary on Romans*, 29.

47. *Ibid.*, 33.

48. Letter to Rev. Ferguson on August 9, 1859 in G. W. Cox, *The Life of John William Colenso, D.D., Bishop of Natal* (2 vols.) (London: W. Ridgeway, 1888), 119-120.

49. Colenso, *Commentary on Romans*, 68.

50. *Ibid.*, 97.

51. *Ibid.*, 69-70.

52. *Ibid.*, 90, 203.

53. *Ibid.*, 126.

54. *Ibid.*, 124.

55. *Ibid.*, 98.

56. Guy, *The Heretic*, 42-46.

57. Colenso, *Commentary on Romans*, 114.

58. *Ibid.*, 177-212.

59. J. W. Colenso, *St. Paul's Epistle to the Romans: Newly Translated, and Explained from a Missionary Point of View* (Ekukhanyeni: Mission Press, 1861), 234; cf. Dent and Nyembezi, *Scholars Zulu Dictionary*, 392.

60. Colenso, *St. Paul's Epistle to the Romans*, 502.

61. *Ibid.*, 168.

62. *Ibid.*, 115.

63. Cf. Mokoena, "The Black People and Whence They Came."

64. Cf. the poignant letter to the press written by Colenso's daughter Francis, cited by J. Guy, *The View Across the River: Harriette Colenso and the Zulu Struggle against Imperialism* (Cape Town: David Philip/ Charlottesville: University of Virginia/ Oxford: James Currey, 2001), 168.

65. E.g., H. Moxnes, *Theology in Conflict. Studies in Paul's Understanding of God in Romans* (Leiden: Brill, 1980); M. D. Nanos, *The Mystery of Romans: The Jewish Context of Paul's Letter* (Minneapolis: Fortress, 1996); D. Boyarin, *A Radical Jew: Paul and the Politics of Identity* (Berkeley: University of California Press, 1994).

Works Cited

Bediako, K. *Theology and Identity: The Impact of Culture upon Christian Thought in the Second Century and in Modern Africa.* Akropong-Akuapem, Ghana: Regnum Books [1992] 1999.

Boyarin, D. *A Radical Jew: Paul and the Politics of Identity.* Berkeley: University of California Press, 1994.

Chidester, D. *Savage Systems: Colonialism and Comparative Religion in Southern Africa.* Charlottsville and London: University Press of Virginia, 1996.

Colenso, J. W. *First Book in Zulu-Kafir: An Introduction to the Study of the Zulu Language.* Ekukhanyeni, Natal: Mission Press, [1855] 1859.

_____. *St. Paul's Epistle to the Romans: Newly Translated, and Explained from a Missionary Point of View.* Ekukhanyeni: Mission Press, 1861.

_____. *Zulu-English Dictionary.* Pietermaritzburg: P. Davis, 1861.

_____. *The Pentateuch and Book of Joshua Critically Examined: Parts I-VI.* London: Longmans, Green, 1862-1871.

_____. *Bringing forth Light: Five Tracts on Bishop Colenso's Zulu Mission.* Edited with an introduction by Ruth Edgecombe. Pietermaritzurg: University of Natal Press/ Durban: Killie Campbell Africana Library, 1982.

_____. *Commentary on Romans.* Edited with an introduction by J. A. Draper. Pietermaritzburg: Cluster Publications, 2003.

Comaroff, Jean and John Comaroff. *Of Revelation and Revolution: Christianity, Colonialism and Consciousness in South Africa.* Chicago: University of Chicago Press, 1991.

Cox, G. W. *The Life of John William Colenso, D.D., Bishop of Natal* (2 vols.). London: W. Ridgeway, 1888.

Dent, G. R. and Nyembezi, C. L. S. *Scholars Zulu Dictionary.* Pietermaritzburg: Shuter & Shooter, 1969.

Draper, J. A. "Magema Fuze and the Insertion of the Subjugated Historical Subject into the Discourse of Hegemony." *Bulletin for Contextual Theology* 5/1-2 (1998): 16-26.

_____. "Archbishop Gray and the Interpretation of the Bible." Pages 44-54 in J. Suggit and M. Goedhals ed., *Change and Challenge: Essays Commemorating the 150th Anniversary of Robert Gray as First Bishop of Cape Town (20 February 1848).* Johannesburg: CPSA, 1998.

_____. "Hermeneutical Drama on the Colonial Stage: Liminal Space and Creativity in Colenso's Commentary on Romans." *Journal of Theology for Southern Africa* 103 (1998): 13-32.

_____. "The Bishop and the Bricoleur: Bishop John William Colenso's Commentary on Romans and Magema kaMagwaza Fuze's The Black People and Whence They Came." Pages 415-454 in G. O. West & Musa W. Dube ed., *The Bible in Africa: Transactions, Trajectories and Trends.* Leiden: Brill, 2000.

_____. "Bishop John William Colenso's Interpretation to the Zulu People of the *Sola Fide* in St. Paul's Letter to the Romans." Pages

465-493 in Seminar Papers of the Society of Biblical Literature Annual Meeting 2000. Atlanta: Scholars Press, 2000.

_____. "Colenso's Commentary on Romans: An Exegetical Assessment." Pages 104-125 in J. A. Draper ed., *The Eye of the Storm: Bishop John William Colenso and the Crisis of Biblical Interpretation*. London & New York: T&T Clark International/ Pietermaritzburg: Cluster Publications, 2003.

_____. "The Trial of Bishop John William Colenso." Pages 306-325 in J. A. Draper ed., *The Eye of the Storm: Bishop John William Colenso and the Crisis of Biblical Interpretation*. London and New York: T&T Clark International/Pietermaritzburg: Cluster Publications, 2003.

_____. "Bishop John William Colenso and History as Unfolding Story." *Journal of Theology for Southern Africa* 117 (2003): 97-105.

Guy, J. *The Heretic: A Study of the Life of John William Colenso 1814-1883*. Johannesburg: Ravan/ Pietermaritzburg: University of Natal Press, 1983.

_____. *The View Across the River: Harriette Colenso and the Zulu Struggle against Imperialism*. Cape Town: David Philip/ Charlottesville: University of Virginia/ Oxford: James Currey, 2001.

Hinchliffe, P. *John William Colenso: Bishop of Natal*. London: Nelson, 1964.

_____. "John William Colenso: A Fresh Appraisal." *Journal of Ecclesiastical History* 13.2 (1962): 203-216.

Jobling, D. "Colenso on Myth or Colenso as Myth: A Response to Timothy Larsen." Pages 64-75 in J. A. Draper ed., *The Eye of the Storm: Bishop John William Colenso and the Crisis of Biblical Interpretation*. London & New York: T&T Clark International/ Pietermaritzburg: Cluster Publications, 2003.

Kearney, P. "Success and Failure of 'Sokululeka' Bishop Colenso and African Education." Pages 195-206 in J. Draper ed., *The Eye of the Storm: Bishop John William Colenso and the Crisis of Biblical Interpretation*. London & New York: T&T Clark International/ Pietermaritzburg: Cluster Publications, 2003.

Khumalo, V. "The Class of 1856 and the Politics of Cultural Production(s) in the Emergence of Ekukhanyeni, 1855-1910." Pages 207-241 in J. A. Draper ed., *The Eye of the Storm: Bishop John William Colenso and the Crisis of Biblical Interpretation*. London & New York: T&T Clark International/ Pietermaritzburg: Cluster Publications, 2003.

Larsen, T. "Bishop Colenso and His Critics: The Strange Emergence of Biblical Criticism in Victorian Britain." Pages 42-63 in J. A. Draper ed., *The Eye of the Storm: Bishop John William Colenso and the Crisis of Biblical Interpretation*. London & New York: T&T Clark International/ Pietermaritzburg: Cluster Publications, 2003. [1997]

_____. "John William Colenso." Forthcoming in J. Greenman and Timothy Larsen ed., *Reading Romans: Encounters with the Epistle to the Romans through the Centuries*.

Maluleke, T. S. "Black and African Theologies in the New World Order: A Time to Drink From Our Own Wells." *Journal of Theology for Southern Africa* 96 (1996): 3-19.

_____. "Half a Century of African Christian Theologies: Elements of the Emerging Agenda for the Twenty-First Century." *Journal of Theology for Southern Africa* 99 (1997): 4-23.

Mokoena, H. "The Black People and Whence They Came: Christian Converts and the Production of Kholwa Histories in the Nineteenth-Century Colonial Natal—The Case of Magema Magwaza Fuze." Unpublished paper presented at the Centre of African Studies, University of Cape Town, September 2003. Cited with permission of the author.

Moxnes, H. *Theology in Conflict. Studies in Paul's Understanding of God in Romans*. Leiden: Brill, 1980.

Nanos, M. D. *The Mystery of Romans: The Jewish Context of Paul's Letter*. Minneapolis: Fortress, 1996.

Rogerson, J. W. "John William Colenso." Pages 220-237 in J. W. Rogerson ed., *Old Testament Criticism in the Nineteenth Century: England and Germany*. London: SPCK, 1985.

_____. "Colenso in the World of Nineteenth-Century Intellectual Ferment." Pages 127-135 in J. A. Draper ed., *The Eye of the Storm: Bishop John William Colenso and the Crisis of Biblical Interpretation*. London & New York: T&T Clark International/ Pietermaritzburg: Cluster Publications, 2003.

Said, E. W. *Culture and Imperialism*. New York: Vintage, 1993.

Sanneh, L. *Translating the Message: The Missionary Impact on Culture*. Maryknoll, New York: Orbis, 1989.

_____. *Encountering the West: Christianity and the Global Cultural Process*. Maryknoll, New York: Orbis, 1993.

Tshehla, S. T. "Colenso, John 1.1-18 and the Politics of Insider- and Outsider-Translating." Pages 29-41 in J. A. Draper ed., *The Eye of the Storm: Bishop John William Colenso and the Crisis of Biblical Interpretation*. London & New York: T&T Clark International/ Pietermaritzburg: Cluster Publications, 2003.

Archives: United Society for the Propagation of the Gospel (USPG), Rhodes House, Oxford.

Comparative and Reception Paradigms

A Response to Draper, "A 'Frontier' Reading of Romans"

Gerald O. West

———— ◆ ————

Introduction

African biblical scholarship has tended to follow the contours of Western biblical scholarship, though with significant adaptations and contextual appropriations. So, for example, much of African biblical scholarship has been dependent on historical-critical scholarship (and its more recent socio-historical incarnations).[1] There are at least three reasons for this. First, most African biblical scholars have been trained in European and/or American institutions where this methodology has held sway. Second, most of the books in the field of biblical studies in most African libraries represent the era in which historical-critical methods have been dominant.[2] And third, African biblical scholars have found resonances between biblical history and society and African history and society.

The Comparative Paradigm

This last factor is particularly important, pointing as it does to the predominant paradigm in African scholarship, namely, the comparative paradigm. Comparative studies have been defined as studies whose major approach is a comparative methodology that facilitates a parallel interpretation of certain Old Testament [and New Testament] texts or motifs and supposed African parallels, letting the two illuminate one another. Traditional exegetical methodology is of course found here, too; however, the Old Testament [and/or New Testament] is approached from a perspective where African comparative material is the major dialogue partner and traditional exegetical methodology is subordinated to this perspective.[3]

Comparative studies form the vast bulk of all academic African biblical interpretation, and can usefully be divided into three overlapping chronological phases.[4] According to the chronology developed by the Nigerian biblical scholar Justin Ukpong, an early reactive phase (1930s-1970s), which legitimized African religion and culture vis-à-vis the western tradition through comparative studies, was replaced by a reactive-proactive phase (1970s-1990s), which more clearly made use of the African context as resource for biblical interpretation, and eventually by a proactive phase (1990s), which makes the African context the explicit subject of biblical interpretation.[5]

In each of these phases, as Holter's definition acknowledges, there is an explicit dialogue between the socio-historical dimensions of the biblical text and the religio-social realities of African life. African biblical interpretation is, therefore, part of a wider historical movement in scholarly research generally in its interest in the historical and sociological; however, African biblical interpretation is also distinctive in that it overtly operates within an African post-colonial and post-independence context. Eric Anum of Ghana is therefore right "when he argues that the comparative approach arose as a response to the negative concepts of traditional African culture and religion prevalent in colonial and missionary circles."[6]

In sum, the comparative method arose as a response to a colonial conception of African traditional religion and culture on the part of missionaries who believed that African cultures were satanic and pagan and needed to be totally abandoned if Christianity was to thrive in Africa. Thus, what African biblical scholars tried to do was to identify similarities between the biblical world and African religio-cultural practices and to use their scholarly and scientific tools to show the relationship between African Traditional Religion and Christianity.[7]

The dialogue between the socio-historical world of the biblical text and the religio-cultural world of African life is two-way. The comparative approach is not simply a strategy for validating anything and everything in the African religio-cultural world that shows some similarities with the socio-historical world of and behind the biblical text. The comparative approach is always evaluative. Ukpong identifies three approaches to evaluation:

> The first approach seeks to evaluate elements of African culture, religion, beliefs, concepts or practices in the light of the biblical witness, to arrive at a Christian understanding of them and bring out their value for Christian witness. The historical critical method is used in analysing the biblical text. The belief or practice is analysed in its different manifestations and its values and disvalues are pointed out against the background of biblical teaching. . . .

The second approach is concerned with what a biblical text or theme has to say in the critique of a particular issue in the society or in the church's life, or what lessons may be drawn from a biblical text of theme for a particular context. It is similar to the first above but with the difference that in the first approach the contextual realities studied are assumed to be values or at least to contain values whereas in this one they are presented as liabilities to be challenged with the biblical message. The study involves analysing the biblical text and pointing out the challenge it issues to the context or drawing its implications for the context. Generally, historical critical tools are used for the study. . . .

In the third approach biblical themes or texts are interpreted against the background of African culture, religion and life experience. The aim is to arrive at a new understanding of the biblical text that would be informed by the African situation, and would be African and Christian. Historical critical tools are used in analysing the biblical text. The basis for this approach is the realization that any interpretation of a biblical text or theme is done from the socio-cultural perspective of the interpreter. Approaching a theme or text from an African perspective is therefore expected to offer some fresh insights into its meaning even though the tools of interpretation still remain Western.[8]

Ukpong here neatly captures many of the methodological impulses of African biblical interpretation. First, African biblical interpretation is predominantly interested in the historical and sociological dimensions of the biblical text. Second, African life interests are consciously and explicitly a part of the interpretative process. Third, African biblical interpretation is always aware of the ambiguous history of the Bible's arrival in Africa, and so is constantly attempting to assert itself over against the dominant discourses of western imperialism and colonialism.

At this point it is worth noting that even this very general characterization of African biblical scholarship does not accurately represent South African biblical scholarship. South African biblical scholarship is deeply problematised by apartheid.[9] While white English-speaking biblical scholarship has been predominantly historical-critical and socio-historical, white Afrikaner-speaking biblical scholarship has tended to take up the structuralist and semiotic strands of literary methodologies.[10] Black South African biblical scholarship, though showing some signs of literary analysis, concentrates on the socio-historical dimensions of biblical scholarship.[11]

I mention the anomalous situation in South African biblical scholarship for three reasons. First, it is the context in which I work and out of which I write this brief response. Second, significant shifts are currently taking place in South African biblical scholarship of which Jonathan Draper's essay is a part. Third, in what I say about Draper's contribution and its place in an emerging paradigm in South African biblical scholarship I am not making claims about whether this new paradigm is manifesting itself more widely in Africa; I suspect the impulses are being felt more widely, but I would not presume to comment on them in their incipient stage elsewhere in Africa.

A Reception/Appropriation Paradigm

Some may argue that what I am here calling a new paradigm is really no more than a development of the comparative paradigm, and I would go along with this, though there are signs that it may turn out to be substantially discontinuous.

Like the historical-critical approach, incorporated and configured for African ends in the comparative paradigm, reader-response criticism too has made its way into African biblical scholarship. As my brief overview above indicates, a real reader has always been overtly acknowledged by African biblical scholarship. The comparative paradigm depends on a reader engaging with the text—an African reader. And as I have argued at length, this reader has been both the scholarly reader and the non-scholarly, ordinary African "reader."[12] Reception has always been an overt constituent of African biblical hermeneutics, long before reader-response criticism became fashionable in the western academy, but the advent of reader-response criticism in Europe and America has provided additional momentum to what I am referring to as a new paradigm. This has particularly been the case for Afrikaner biblical scholarship. The flight from history embodied in their refusal to engage with historical-critical and sociological methods has failed, apartheid has been defeated (though its legacy lives on), and it is now safe to tackle historical and sociological questions. History has returned via the reader.

While this return has generated significant reflection on identity politics among South African readers,[13] it has also had a profound impact on our readings of the Bible text. The return of history, however, is not the rather thin history of early historical-critical studies, but the much "thicker" socio-history that has characterized recent biblical scholarship in both the North and in Africa. Bernard Lategan, a South African biblical scholar, was ahead of his time in recognizing that reader-response criticism called forth a more sociological reading of the biblical text.[14]

Postcolonial criticism has also played a part in "thickening" our sense of history in South African biblical studies, across all the historically-radicalized communities in South Africa.[15] Here there is a considerable convergence with the comparative paradigm of African biblical scholarship. Again, though implicitly present in almost all forms of African biblical scholarship, postcolonial criticism as such has given fresh impetus to South African scholars to explore the territory and the boundaries between the pre-colonial, colonial, and postcolonial.

A final, for now, element in the mix that is giving rise to this new paradigm is the growing recognition of African agency.[16] Again, African agency has always been a mark of African biblical scholarship, but the difference now is that their description has become more important than prescription. The postcolonial context not only provides an important locus for academic African biblical interpretation, its presence also imparts a particular kind of attitude. Our postcolonial context has tended to impart a prescriptive attitude or perspective to academic talk about the Bible among African biblical scholars and theologians. Whether orientated to a hermeneutic of suspicion or a hermeneutic of trust, the prevailing mode of speaking about the Bible by African theologians and biblical scholars is about how we ought to interpret the Bible.

South African biblical scholars, across the racial spectrum, are beginning to realize that we need to describe what is, rather than to prescribe what ought to be. Tinyiko Maluleke says it well when he states that the task before Black Theology in these days is "not only to develop creative Biblical hermeneutic methods, but also to observe and analyze the manner in which African Christians 'read' and view the Bible."[17] Fortunately, just as there are signs of an emerging new paradigm in African theology with African agency at its core,[18] so too there are signs of a more descriptive paradigm with respect to African biblical interpretation. (And it is no coincidence that these have emerged together.) I call this paradigm a reception or appropriation paradigm, though I prefer the latter, the former being too passive.

The work of Takatso Mofokeng and Itumeleng Mosala have made passing reference to how ordinary black South Africans have adopted a variety of strategies in dealing with an ambiguous Bible, including rejecting it[19] and strategically appropriating it as a site of struggle,[20] though neither Mofokeng nor Mosala provide the kind of detail required for Maluleke's project.[21] More detail is available from the fieldwork study conducted by Justin Ukpong in Port Harcourt, Nigeria, between 1991-1994, in which he investigates the attitude of ordinary Nigerian people to the Bible, how they interpret and apply the Bible to their daily lives, and what the differences are between how the Bible is used in mainline churches and African Instituted Churches, though he cannot resist a prescriptive final paragraph.[22] Though they begin with a prescriptive "How should Africans interpret the Bible," Zablon

Nthamburi and Douglas Waruta end their essay with some description of how African Christians actually do read the Bible.[23] In a far more descriptive mode, Nahashon Ndungu identifies the role of the Bible in the rise of the Akurinu Church among the Gikuyu of Kenya and in their worship.[24] Also taking up the descriptive task, but again with a prescriptive twist in the tale, is David Tuesday Adamo's work on the use of Psalms among the Aladura churches in Nigeria.[25] Anthony Nkwoka looks more broadly at the role of the Bible in Igbo Christianity in Nigeria, and though there is an undertone of prescription, he does manage to be systematically descriptive.[26] In his analysis of the use of the Bible in contemporary Tanzanian hymns, Fergus King gives us a sustained description of Bible reading reality, as does Hilary Mijoga in his extended analysis of the use of the Bible in preaching within the African Instituted Churches of southern Malawi.[27] Musa Dube provides considerable descriptive detail of how ordinary Batswana women in African Independent Churches interpret and use (or do not use) the Bible, and how the Bible is interpreted in the corporate cyclical sermons of their churches.[28] A recent volume of the South African journal *Scriptura* (78, 2001) includes a number of articles which analyze the reading processes of a range of South African readers. My own descriptive attempts, though not detailed enough, reflect on and conjure with concepts that elucidate the way in which ordinary black South Africans "read" the Bible;[29] I also make some cursory comments on how black Christians "view" the Bible, though these are far from adequate.[30] A more thorough reflection on the latter can be found in the work of Hezekiel Mafu on the use of the Bible in traditional rain-making institutions in western Zimbabwe.[31] Though by no means exhaustive, this selection does offer a foretaste of things to come if we will persist with a more descriptive and less prescriptive paradigm.

It is precisely here that Jonathan Draper's essay both locates itself and makes a contribution. Draper's careful analysis of the interface between Colenso and the Zulu people he reads the Bible with provides the kind of descriptive detail that characterizes this new paradigm. Though focusing on the colonial figure in this encounter, Draper's essay supplies some of the raw material for our understanding of local indigenous appropriations of Romans in South Africa. We know what Colenso made of this "contrapuntal" reading, and careful analysis will reveal something of the contours of an indigenous "reading" of Romans. If Vincent Wimbush is right, and I think he is, in claiming that the array of interpretative strategies forged in these earliest encounters between Africans and those who bring the Bible among them are foundational, in the sense that all other readings are in some sense built upon and judged by them,[32] then such analysis has tremendous hermeneutical significance for our current context.

While this essay does not go on to describe and analyze how Zulu "readers" appropriated this text, Draper's essay does deal with one end of this encounter in detail. Without this focus we have no notion of what indigenous Africans may have encountered and appropriated, and so this moment is important. My own work on the BaTlhaping's encounters with Bible bearing traders, explorers and missionaries demonstrates the importance of understanding just what was done with the Bible and how it was done.[33] But we must make the next step, and though Draper does not do so in this essay, he does this in great detail in others, where, for example, he examines the appropriation of a particular biblical text by the Zulu prophet, George Khambule.[34] As with the work of other scholars whose research constitutes this new appropriation paradigm,[35] and not all of them are biblical scholars,[36] Draper's essay here gives precedence to a "thick" description of the interpretative context and the Bible's place in it.

Draper's essay also makes an important contribution to understanding the kind of hermeneutic tools we need for exploring the territory of this new paradigm. Drawing on a range of postcolonial resources, specifically David Chidester's notion of "the frontier," Draper explores in depth the transformative effect of reading "in-between," that contested territory of translation and transaction.[37] The colonial encounter, as Draper reminds us via the work of Jean and John Comaroff,[38] is always a two-way gaze. How we describe and delve into this terrain requires taking up well-worn tools, but also forging new ones.

Conclusion

Africans have not negotiated with the Bible empty-handed, nor have they been passive receptors. What they bring to the encounter with the Bible is as important as what was brought. Jonathan Draper's essay reminds us of both, but focuses on the latter, contributing to an emerging paradigm in South African (and African) biblical scholarship, a paradigm that is drawing the full spectrum of South African biblical scholars into its ambit. This is no small feat, given our diverse and contentious histories, and so this new paradigm promises much.

Notes

1. See Grant LeMarquand, "A Bibliography of the Bible in Africa," in Gerald O. West and M. W. Dube ed., *The Bible in Africa: Transactions, Trajectories, and Trends* (Leiden: E.J. Brill, 2000).

2. Knut Holter, *Yahweh in Africa: Essays on Africa and the Old Testament* (New York: Peter Lang, 2000).

3. Knut Holter, *Old Testament Research for Africa: A Critical Analysis and Annotated Bibliography of African Old Testament Dissertations, 1967-2000* (New York: Peter Lang, 2002), 88.

4. Justin S. Ukpong, "Developments in Biblical Interpretation in Africa: Historical and Hermeneutical Directions," *Journal of Theology for Southern Africa* 108 (2000): 3-18.

5. Holter, *Old Testament Research for Africa*, 89.

6. *Ibid.*

7. Eric Anum, "Comparative Readings of the Bible in Africa: Some Concerns," in *The Bible in Africa*, West and Dube eds., 468.

8. Ukpong, "Developments in Biblical Interpretation in Africa," 17-18.

9. Gerald O. West, *Biblical Hermeneutics of Liberation: Modes of Reading the Bible in South Africa* (Maryknoll and Pietermaritzbur: Orbis and Cluster Publications, 1995), 47-59.

10. Dirk J. Smit, "The Ethics of Interpretation and South Africa," *Scriptura* 33 (1990): 29-43; Jonathan A. Draper, "'For the Kingdom Is Inside You and It Is Outside of You': Contextual Exegesis in South Africa," in P. J. Hartin and J. H. Petzer ed., *Text and Interpretation: New Approaches in the Criticism of the New Testament* (Leiden: E. J. Brill, 1991).

11. See, for example, Itumeleng J. Mosala, *Biblical Hermeneutics and Black Theology in South Africa* (Grand Rapids: Eerdmans, 1989).

12. Gerald O. West, "Indigenous Exegesis: Exploring the Interface between Missionary Methods and the Rhythms of Africa: Locating Local Reading Resources in the Academy," *Neotestamentica* 36 (2002): 147-162.

13. Gerrie F. Snyman, "Playing the Role of Perpetrator in the World of Academia in South Africa," *Bulletin for Old Testament Studies in Africa* 12 (2002): 8-20; *idem*, "Being Haunted by the Past," *Bulletin for Old Testament Studies in Africa* 14 (2003): 13-16; Madipoane (Ngwana' Mphahlele) Masenya, "Is White South African Old Testament Scholarship African?," *Bulletin for Old Testament Studies in Africa* 12 (2002): 3-8.

14. Bernard C. Lategan, "Current Issues in the Hermeneutic Debate," *Neotestamentica* 18 (1984): 7 (1-17).

15. Gerald O. West, "Finding a Place Among the Posts for Post-colonial Criticism in Biblical Studies in South Africa," *Old Testament*

Essays 10 (1997): 322-342; Musa W. Dube, *Postcolonial Feminist Interpretation of the Bible* (St. Louis: Chalice Press, 2002); Frank England, "Mapping Postcolonial Biblical Criticism in South Africa," *Neotestamentica* 38 (2004): 88-99.

16. Tinyiko S. Maluleke, "The Rediscovery of the Agency of Africans: An Emerging Paradigm of Post-cold War and Post-Apartheid Black and African Theology," *Journal of Theology for Southern Africa* 108 (2000): 19-37.

17. Tinyiko S. Maluleke, "Black and African Theologies in the New World Order: A Time to Drink from Our Own Wells," *Journal of Theology for Southern Africa* 96 (1996): 15 (3-19).

18. Maluleke, "The Rediscovery of the Agency of Africans," 19-37.

19. Takatso Mofokeng, "Black Christians, the Bible and Liberation," *Journal of Black Theology* 2 (1988): 40 (34-42).

20. Itumeleng J. Mosala, "The Use of the Bible in Black Theology," in I. J. Mosala and B. Tlhagale ed., *The Unquestionable Right to Be Free: Essays in Black Theology* (Johannesburg: Skotaville, 1986), 184; Mofokeng, "Black Christians, the Bible and Liberation," 41.

21. Gerald O. West, *The Academy of the Poor: Towards a Dialogical Reading of the Bible* (Sheffield: Sheffield Academic Press, 1999), 88-89.

22. Ukpong, "Popular Readings of the Bible in Africa and Implications for Academic Readings: Report on the Field Research Carried out on Oral Interpretations of the Bible in Port Harcourt Metropolis, Nigeria under the Auspices of the Bible in Africa Project, 1991-94," in West and Dube ed., *The Bible in Africa* (Leiden: E.J. Brill, 2000), 582-594.

23. Zablon Nthamburi and Douglas Waruta, "Biblical Hermeneutics in African Instituted Churches," in H. W. Kinoti and J. M. Waliggo ed., *The Bible in African Christianity* (Nairobi: Acton Publishers, 1997), 40-57.

24. Nahashon Ndungu, "The Bible in an African Independent Church," in H. W. Kinoti and J. M. Waliggo ed., *The Bible in African Christianity* (Nairobi: Acton Publishers, 1997); *idem*, "The Role of the Bible in the Rise of African Instituted Churches: The Case of the Akurinu Churches of Kenya," in West and Dube ed., *The Bible in Africa*, 236-247.

25. David T. Adamo, "African Cultural Hermeneutics," in R. S. Sugirtharajah ed., *Vernacular Hermeneutics* (Sheffield: Sheffield Academic Press 1999), 66-90; *idem*, "The Use of Psalms in African Indigenous Churches in Nigeria," in West and Dube ed., *The Bible in Africa*, 336-349.

26. Anthony O. Nkwoka, "The Role of the Bible in the Igbo Christianity of Nigeria," in West and Dube ed., *The Bible in Africa*, 326-335.

27. Fergus J. King, "Nyimbo za vijana: Biblical Interpretation in Contemporary Hymns from Tanzania," in West and Dube ed., *The Bible*

in Africa, 360-373; Hilary B. P. Mijoga, *Separate But Same Gospel: Preaching in African Instituted Churches in Southern Malawi* (Blantyre: Kachere, 2000); *idem*, "Interpreting the Bible in African Sermons," in M. Getui, T. S. Maluleke, and J. S. Ukpong ed., *Interpreting the New Testament in Africa* (Nairobi: Acton Publishers, 2001), 123-144.

28. Musa W. Dube, "Readings of Semoya: Batswana Women's Interpretations of Matt. 15:21-28," *Semeia* 73 (1996): 111-129; *idem*, *Postcolonial Feminist Interpretation of the Bible,* 184-192.

29. West, *The Academy of the Poor*, 89-107.

30. Gerald O. West, "Mapping African Biblical Interpretation: A Tentative Sketch," in West and Dube ed., *The Bible in Africa*, 47-49; *idem*, "Indigenous Exegesis," 147-162.

31. Hezekiel Mafu, "The Impact of the Bible on Traditional Rain-making Institutions in Western Zimbabwe," in West and Dube ed., *The Bible in Africa*, 400-414.

32. Vincent L. Wimbush, "Reading Texts through Worlds, Worlds through Texts," *Semeia* 62 (1993): 131 (129-140).

33. Gerald O. West, "Early Encounters with the Bible Among the BaTlhaping: Historical and Hermeneutical Signs," *Biblical Interpretation* (forthcoming).

34. Jonathan A. Draper, "The Closed Text and the Heavenly Telephone: The Role of the Bricoleur in Oral Mediation of Sacred Text in the Case of George Khambule and the Gospel of John," in J. A. Draper ed., *Orality, Literacy and Colonialism in Southern Africa* (Atlanta: Society of Biblical Literature; Pietermaritzburg: Cluster Publications; Leiden: E. J. Brill, 2003), 57-89.

35. See, for example, Johannes Smit, "J. T. van der Kemp's Interpretation of the New Testament on the Frontier (1799-1801)," in J. N. K. Mugambi ed., *Text and Context in New Testament Hermeneutics* (Nairobi: Acton Publishers, 2004), 129-156.

36. See, for example, Duncan Brown, *Voicing the Text: South African Oral Poetry and Performance* (Cape Town: Oxford University Press, 1998), 119-163.

37. David Chidester, *Savage Systems: Colonialism and Comparative Religion in Southern Africa* (Charlottsville and London: University Press of Virginia, 1996).

38. Jean Comaroff and John L. Comaroff, *Of Revelation and Revolution: Christianity, Colonialism and Consciousness in South Africa, Vol. 1* (Chicago: University of Chicago Press, 1991).

PART 2

LATIN AMERICA
AND
NORTH AMERICA

–THREE–

"The Righteousness of God" and Hurricane Mitch

Reading Romans in Hurricane-Devastated Honduras

Mark D. Baker and J. Ross Wagner

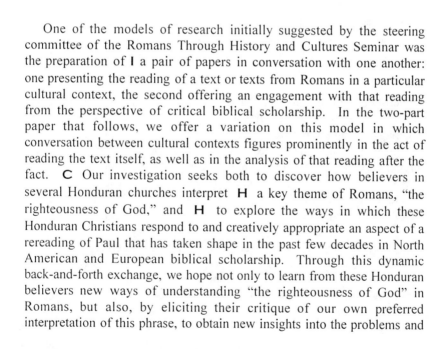

One of the models of research initially suggested by the steering committee of the Romans Through History and Cultures Seminar was the preparation of **I** a pair of papers in conversation with one another: one presenting the reading of a text or texts from Romans in a particular cultural context, the second offering an engagement with that reading from the perspective of critical biblical scholarship. In the two-part paper that follows, we offer a variation on this model in which conversation between cultural contexts figures prominently in the act of reading the text itself, as well as in the analysis of that reading after the fact. **C** Our investigation seeks both to discover how believers in several Honduran churches interpret **H** a key theme of Romans, "the righteousness of God," and **H** to explore the ways in which these Honduran Christians respond to and creatively appropriate an aspect of a rereading of Paul that has taken shape in the past few decades in North American and European biblical scholarship. Through this dynamic back-and-forth exchange, we hope not only to learn from these Honduran believers new ways of understanding "the righteousness of God" in Romans, but also, by eliciting their critique of our own preferred interpretation of this phrase, to obtain new insights into the problems and

---

I A pair of papers in conversation.

C Honduran context.

H "Righteousness of God" in Romans.

H Response of Honduran Christians.

possibilities of the so-called "New Perspective on Paul" that has shaped us as readers of Romans.[1]

I The term "conversation" aptly describes what we have intended to foster by undertaking this project. We are convinced that biblical interpretation requires serious engagement with readers from a multiplicity of social locations different from one's own, in which each reader is willing to learn from, as well as offer insight to, the others. In his book *Cultural Interpretation*, Brian Blount argues convincingly for such an approach, showing that

> one's sociohistorical context influences what one sees in the language [of the text]. Every investigative exercise, historical-critical and literary included, has a powerful interpersonal component. Only when that component is acknowledged can one begin the process of controlling it, not through the establishment of a direct speech [i.e., an "objective" or "neutral" way of accessing the text], but through an awareness that one's interpretative conclusions are sociolinguistically biased. Such an awareness induces an investigator to invite, and subsequently accept analectically,[2] input from other sociolinguistic perspectives.[3]

In both the field research for this paper and in its writing, faithfulness to this ideal of reading-in-conversation has remained our goal, however far we may be deemed to have fallen short of it.[4]

Awareness of the influence one's sociohistorical context exerts on the process of interpretation ought to lead critical biblical scholars to welcome readings from other contexts, precisely because such openness results in a fuller appreciation for the richness of the text itself. Blount eloquently describes the fruitfulness of this type of dialogical reading:

> We see that when ethnographic and popular interpreters approach the texts with a conscious interpersonal agenda, new information constantly bursts on the scene, leading to meanings that push beyond the textual and ideational boundaries established by mainline scholarship. When these conclusions are analectically engaged, a process occurs whereby the full richness of the text begins to be more clearly opened, and we can see how the text comes to life in a new way in a new circumstance. . . . We want to promote an analectical engagement of interpersonal conclusions so

---

I   Interplay between text and cultural context, interpreter and readers of biblical texts.

that the rich potentiality of a text's meaning can be more fully appreciated.[5]

Indeed, it is our goal in this study not to narrow the meaning of "the righteousness of God" in Romans, but rather to explore dimensions of this concept that may be neglected or even unnoticed by biblical critics in North America and Europe. Moreover, by examining the ways in which these Honduran believers interpret and appropriate the biblical text, we hope to allow their *interpretive practices*, as well as the interpretations themselves, to enrich our own understanding of what it means to read Romans as Scripture.

C Part One of our paper describes and analyzes the conversations that took place in Honduras between Mark Baker and a number of groups of Honduran Christians during the period 25 June to 8 July 2000. Part Two then offers further analysis by Ross Wagner, who draws out some implications of the interpretations and interpretive practices of these Honduran believers for readers of Romans in a North American context. Although each of us has taken primary responsibility for one part of the paper (Baker, Part One; Wagner, Part Two), the entire study is a collaborative effort, the fruit of numerous stimulating and enjoyable conversations.

Part One: Reading Romans in Honduras: A Cross-Cultural Conversation

Flor Del Campo and Hurricane Mitch

The Hurricane

C On Friday, 30 October 1998, the rains beat down on the tin roofs of Flor del Campo, one of the numerous squatter neighborhoods dotting the hills surrounding Tegucigalpa, the capital of Honduras.[6] It had been an unusually rainy month. The ground was already saturated, and the dirt streets that navigate the neighborhood's hilly terrain now turned into muddy streams. But that morning's incessant rains were just the beginning of Mitch's assault on the city and its population of over 1.1 million.

Over the past two decades, most of the residents of Flor del Campo have migrated to the city out of desperation or in hope of a better life.

C Honduras context.

C Hurricane context and Flor del Campo.

Although a few have prospered and built small but solid brick homes, some still live in the simple wooden shacks they pieced together twenty years ago. As throughout Tegucigalpa, the poorest in Flor del Campo live in places considered uninhabitable a decade ago. Their shacks cling to steep embankments and line the small river at the edge of the neighborhood. Almost annually, during a heavy rain, a house or two slides down the hill, and those along the river fill with water.

On that stormy October day, those dwelling on the river-banks saw the river rising and began carrying possessions to higher ground. Those who lived a hundred yards or so from the river watched this procession—grateful that they lived out of the river's reach. But the water began to attain heights never seen before, and by nightfall the river was surging into their homes also. They fled, and soon the walls of their houses were smashed by the raging torrent.

It was a night of terror in Flor del Campo. The winds howled as Mitch, now a tropical storm, passed over Tegucigalpa in the middle of the night. The river continued to rise and sweep away everything in its path. It ate away whole hillsides, and houses tumbled into the roaring current. People heard rumors that the dam at the reservoir just a few miles away was about to break. How high did one have to go to be safe?

As it turned out, the dam did not break, but by the time the waters began to recede on Saturday, about one hundred fifty families from Flor del Campo were added to the list of thousands of *"damnificados"*—those who had lost their homes. Yet as many pointed out, to some degree most everyone in Tegucigalpa, if not all Honduras, was *damnificado.* Most were without water and electricity. Many found themselves jobless because Mitch had destroyed their place of employment. Students could not go to classes. If their school still stood, it was now filled with families who had lost their homes. Most bridges had been damaged or destroyed. Tegucigalpa was cut off from the rest of the country, and traffic within the city backed up at the few bridges that remained usable.

God and Mitch

H Why all this death, destruction, and suffering?[7] A common, if not the most common, answer to be heard in Tegucigalpa was that God had sent the hurricane to punish Honduras.[8] Why was Honduras singled out for this punishment? Some pointed to the rampant corruption in the society in general and in the government in particular. Others spoke of the increasing levels of drug use and drug trafficking, or God's desire to wipe out pockets of satanism and witchcraft. Still others stated that God had sent Mitch as a warning to Hondurans to turn back to God, or they

---

H Theological interpretation of context.

would face something even worse on the day of judgment. Many evangelicals saw the hurricane as a direct response to the huge statue of Jesus that had been completed just months before the storm.[9] Standing on a mountain overlooking the city, this statue had become a site of pilgrimage and popular religiosity. Some explained that this "idol" had especially provoked the wrath of God against Honduras because the government had helped pay for it. Yet the statue still stands today, while the Honduran Bible Society office and many church buildings were destroyed. Certainly some drug dealers and corrupt officials died or lost their homes, but so did law-abiding Christians.[10] Even so, many Hondurans unwaveringly continue to interpret Mitch in terms that depict God as a vengeful judge lashing out in anger and sending Mitch as a punishment for their sins.

It would be a mistake, however, to think that the magnitude of the disaster suddenly led Hondurans to view God as an angry, accusing figure. Rather, many saw Mitch as a punishment sent by God because they *commonly* interpret sickness, the loss of a job, and other setbacks as interventions by a vengeful God. Although there is talk of God's love, many live as if God's love is conditional. God rewards those who live morally and fulfill religious obligations, and God punishes those who do not. It must be granted that these general statements do not apply equally to everyone. I am not claiming that this is a universal concept of God among Hondurans. On the other hand, it certainly is a common, if not the most common, view of God held by Hondurans.[11]

Amor Fe y Vida Church

C People from one church in Flor del Campo would acknowledge that what I have just described matches the way they used to think about God. They would also tell you, however, that they now know and experience a God distinctly different from the vindictive judge portrayed above.

In 1991, a few leaders in one of the evangelical churches in Flor del Campo came into conflict with the pastor of the church. They wanted to start using church funds to help the needy—both within the congregation and in the neighborhood. Like the other evangelical churches in Flor del Campo, their church practiced an individualistic-spiritualized version of Christianity that was basically indifferent to issues of justice and to the physical needs of their impoverished neighborhood.[12] Through attending a seminar at a Mennonite church in Tegucigalpa and through reading some pamphlets they obtained there, this group of four or five church

---

C Amor Fe y Vida Church.

leaders had come to see that the Bible in fact has much to say about justice and concern for the poor. The pastor, however, was not sympathetic. He called them "communists," and eventually they left the church. About thirty people left with them, as much for relational reasons as for theological convictions, and they joined with another small church to start Amor Fe y Vida Church in 1992.[13]

The leaders wanted all the people in the new church to embrace the concept of a holistic gospel, and, through a mutual acquaintance, they asked me to come and persuade the people of the church to do so. I was reluctant simply to tell them how they ought to be thinking. Instead, I offered to give a workshop over two weekends on how to study the Bible, intending to give them better tools with which they could discover this holistic gospel themselves. During that workshop, people repeatedly asked questions about various rules the evangelical churches in Flor del Campo imposed on their members and the bearing of these rules on one's salvation and continuing fellowship with a community of believers. Concern and interest were so high that I returned a number of additional weekends to study Galatians with the group. Through reflecting carefully on Galatians, the members of Amor Fe y Vida Church sought not only to exchange an overly individualistic-spiritualized gospel for a more holistic one, but also to exchange their legalistic version of Christianity, with its angry, accusing enforcer-God, for an ethics of freedom that takes Christian behavior equally seriously, but that practices it as a response to a gracious and loving God revealed through Jesus Christ. They would admit that after eight years this theological transformation is still a work in progress, but it is one they undertake with great commitment and hope. I have had the privilege of learning with them through studying the Bible together as a group and through interacting with them in their homes.[14]

Why These Texts, in This Place, with These People?

H The Flor del Campo neighborhood, Hurricane Mitch, a concept of a vindictive, punishing God, and a small church seeking to row against the current form the context of this study. The stage is set, but it is fair to ask why we chose to study texts from Romans about God's righteousness in this church in a hurricane-ravaged neighborhood in Tegucigalpa.

It should be made clear from the outset that both of the authors are sympathetic to and supportive of the course Amor Fe y Vida Church has taken over the past eight years. Because Baker had been living in Honduras during Hurricane Mitch and its immediate aftermath, we knew that some in Amor Fe y Vida Church had been attempting to understand

---

H Wrestling with difficult theological questions in the cultural context.

the hurricane as something other than a punishment sent by God, but we did not know their current thinking about this problem. In part, then, this project was seen as an investigation of—and a possible contribution to—their ongoing reflections about Mitch. We did not, however, go into the project thinking that these texts, by themselves, could answer the question: "Why all the death and destruction?" In fact, we do not even maintain that these are the most important texts for addressing this question.

So why did we choose these particular texts? We have three principal reasons: First, we are interested as scholars and believers in the question of how to interpret "God's righteousness" in Romans, and we hoped to learn more through listening carefully to readings of Romans by believers from a sociolinguistic context quite different from our own.[15] Second, we do believe that one's interpretation of "God's righteousness" is an important component in one's response to the problem of theodicy generally, and therefore to this hurricane specifically. For at stake in debates about the meaning of "the righteousness of God" is nothing less than one's understanding of the very character of God. Third, how one interprets "God's righteousness" in Romans has tremendous ramifications for one's understanding of the shape of the Christian life. Consequently, we hoped that we would contribute to the ongoing quest of Amor Fe y Vida to embrace a more holistic gospel. At the same time, we honestly considered it just as likely that they would contribute significantly to our own understanding of what it means to embody the gospel message in a community of faith.

Reading Romans in Honduras

C The field research for this project involved discussion groups from four churches: La Mizpa, a Central American Mission Church (1 July 2000), Amor Fe y Vida Church (4-6 July 2000), a Roman Catholic Church (8 July 2000), and Tegucigalpa Mennonite Church (25 June 2000 and 2 July 2000).[16] With each group, I first read Romans 3:19-26 and Romans 8 with the people and asked them to explain the meaning of "the righteousness of God" in these passages. I then explained our interpretation of the same texts, and finally I asked them to reread Romans in light of our interpretation and offer their reflections on our understanding of "God's righteousness."[17] This paper focuses on my conversations with the group from Amor Fe y Vida Church. For the purpose of comparison and contrast, however, I will occasionally bring

---

C The four churches.

in interpretations that emerged during my discussions with the other groups.[18]

"The Justice Of God" in Romans as Interpreted by the Members of Amor Fe y Vida

H A Is the "righteousness" of God the same thing as the "justice" of God? For some interpreters it may be, and for others the phrases may have different shades of meaning. This is not a question we can ask Hondurans as we read Romans, however. In English, we translate Greek *dik-* words both with "just" and its cognates, and with "righteous" and its cognates. But in Spanish Bibles we find only one root employed: *justificar, justicia, justo,* etc. Therefore, although our title, with the English text in mind, refers to "the righteousness of God," throughout the rest of this paper we will speak of "the justice of God" in order to reflect more closely the discussion that went on in Spanish.

"The Justice of God" and Hurricane Mitch

Before reading Romans together, I asked each group, "How is the justice of God related to Hurricane Mitch?" The majority of the responses in three of the four groups reflected, to one degree or another, the theme of Mitch as a just punishment from God. However, not one of the dozen participants from Amor Fe y Vida Church answered in this way. A common theme in their written answers,[19] and in the discussion that followed, was the fact that human actions, such as cutting down forests, building houses in inappropriate places, slash and burn practices, and irresponsible mining, had made Mitch much more destructive than it would have been otherwise. So, as one person wrote, "God allowed us to suffer the consequences of our inappropriate actions." Another explained, "The relation is that God permits us to enter into self-evaluation and see that we are destroying ourselves. In that way the justice of God is manifested."[20]

"The Justice of God" in Romans 3:19-26

In relation to Romans 3:19-26 and the question, "How is the justice of God manifested?" we can see two general approaches in the answers of the participants from all the groups. One approach, which I will call "juristic," envisions God both enforcing and complying with a certain standard of justice. So, for instance, Ines, a member of La Mizpa Church who lost her house and all her possessions to Mitch, stated, "We need to be cleaned because, since God is just, he needs everything to be

---

H A "Justice of God" in Romans understood by Amor Fe y Vida.

clean—to be pure and in order."[21] Others described God as a judge who gives us what we deserve. In contrast, the second approach, which I will term "relational," places God's justice in the larger context of God's loving and compassionate relationship with people. Ines asserted, "God is just because he loves us and always gives us an opportunity."[22] Rather than seeing God as just because God punishes us as we deserve, she explained that God is just because God recognizes that we are unable to live without sin and therefore forgives us.[23] Significantly, the juristic and relational perspectives were found together not only within a single church group, but also at times within the comments offered by one individual, as in the case of Ines.

All of the responses from the members of the Amor Fe y Vida Church, however, clearly lined up with the relational approach. For example, Bertilia Fuentes, a middle-aged woman who runs a shoemaking business from her home, stated, "God manifests his justice by not holding our sins against us and by graciously giving us salvation . . . . God is a just God, not a God who is focused on punishing us." Juan Ernesto Hernández, a man about nineteen years old and in his first year of university studies, observed, "One can have different concepts of God's justice. Some understand it in terms of love, compassion, and mercy; others put the emphasis on God giving people what they deserve." Astrid Rivera, a woman about twenty years old and in her last year of high school, added: "It is not just how one thinks about God's justice, but how one thinks about justice in general."[24] Thus very early in the conversation, long before I had mentioned anything about the contrast between juristic and relational concepts of justice,[25] a few people from Amor Fe y Vida were already emphasizing that interpretations of these texts in Romans could differ considerably depending on the concept of "justice" employed.

Some preliminary analysis may be helpful at this point. As Abraham Smith has commented, "Received traditions of reading usually come with a history."[26] What are the factors, then, that help to explain these variant understandings of "God's justice"? Though there is no simple answer to this question, a number of influences must be considered. First, with regard to the "juristic" interpretation, it is safe to say that a traditional protestant understanding of the justice of God and of justification—deeply influenced by a greco-roman "juristic" conception of justice—has been taught in most evangelical Bible institutes in Honduras by North American missionaries. This is still by far the most common view being presented by their Honduran students who are now teaching the courses on Romans. So, although the participants in these study groups have not themselves received formal theological instruction about the meaning of "the justice of God," they have listened to

preachers who have.[27] Moreover, the common Honduran conception of
God as a stern and distant judge described earlier would certainly favor
the juristic interpretation of "God's justice." And, of course, the
participants are all familiar with the type of justice dispensed by the
Honduran judicial system, which operates within a greco-roman model.
For all these reasons, it does not surprise us that many described the
justice of God in terms of a judge intent on punishing wrongdoers.

What *is* surprising is that many described God's justice so
differently—in relational terms such as mercy, compassion, and
deliverance—and that, in fact, everyone from Amor Fe y Vida did so.
How can we explain this relational understanding of "the justice of God"
by many of the Honduran believers? One contributing factor is that
when Hondurans describe a person or an action as "just" (*justo*), they
most commonly mean that the person or the action is "fair."[28] For
instance, a person who says, "I have a just employer," probably does not
mean that her employer follows the legal code established by the Labor
Department. Rather, she means that her employer treats her fairly. The
noun "justice" is less frequently used as a synonym for "fairness,"
however. Moreover, when talking about "justice" in relation to courts
and judges, Hondurans tend to think in terms of complying with legal
standards. Yet the concept of a "just person" does provide the semantic
opening for a description of "God's justice" that focuses on God's doing
what is expected in a relationship, and thus it may lead, by extension, to
those definitions that emphasize God's mercy.

In addition, it would seem that some gave the answers they did
because they have *experienced* a God much different from the distant
accusing figure that many Hondurans associate with God. As the
discussion continued, those from Amor Fe y Vida frequently mentioned
that at one time they had understood "the justice of God" to refer to
God's commitment to punish sin. In recent years, however, they had
come to see things differently, and they no longer interpreted the phrase
this way. It is noteworthy that they gave answers very much in line with
the more relational concept of justice that I planned to present to them,[29]
even though they had not done careful exegetical work with Old
Testament texts or read scholarly essays on the topic. Before our final
study together, I asked two of the church members what might account
for this. They simply stated, "Because of the image we have of God, we
could not give answers that put an emphasis on punishment."[30] That is,
they did not articulate a view of the justice of God different from that
held by most of the people I interviewed because they had received a
new teaching from us on God's justice; rather, they articulated a different
perspective on God's justice because their new understanding of God
would not allow them to parrot an explanation of God's justice that

contradicted the character of the God they saw on the pages of the Bible and experienced in daily life.

"The Justice of God" in Romans 8

H A We next read Romans 8, and I asked, "What, if anything, does this passage have to do with the justice of God?" Juan Ernesto, referring to the first four verses, stated that we see a demonstration of God's justice in that "God changed the 'rules of the game' so that we are not condemned, not under the law." In relation to verses 31-34, David Suazo, an eighteen-year-old man who has just started at the university, observed, "God is here not in the role of accuser or judge, but of defense attorney." Mario Cantor, who is the lay pastor of Amor Fe y Vida and with his family runs a shoemaking business out of their home, followed up on David's statement by observing that if God is not the accuser in chapter eight, then perhaps it would be wrong to see God as the accuser in chapter three.[31]

Juan Hernández, a middle-aged man who is a community organizer and educator and who has worked with various development agencies, related what he read in verse 17 to the idea of justification. He noted that since Paul talks of our present suffering with Christ, "justification implies a relation to how we live and what we do in the here and now." Juan also believes we have a role in the redemption of creation in the sense that creation waits for the revealing of the children of God (Rom 8:19). This "revealing of the children of God" would include our displaying "an appropriate stance in relation to creation." Mario agreed, "We are the cause of the suffering of creation and we have a role in its redemption. It is not just something we should be waiting around for, like in the films about the rapture."[32]

"The Justice of God" as Covenant Faithfulness: Insights from Biblical Criticism

A H I have organized the report of my conversation with Amor Fe y Vida Church into units that imply that I first listened to their interpretation, then presented our interpretation (worked out in the context of North American and European biblical scholarship),[33] and finally asked them to respond to our interpretation. In a general sense, this is an accurate description of the course of our study together. But in reality, our conversation was much more fluid and interactive than this outline would suggest. As soon as I began to explain our perspective, the

---

H A "Justice of God" in Romans 8 understood by Amor Fe y Vida.

A H "Justice of God" in biblical criticism.

people of Amor Fe y Vida, through their questions and comments, started evaluating, interpreting, and at times arriving on their own to the place where I was headed. Therefore, I cannot leave Amor Fe y Vida out of this section of the paper, even though this is primarily a report on the ideas I presented to them.

In this part of the study, I first had us read biblical texts together that would elicit the recognition that Paul and his fellow Jews operated with a different concept of "justice" from the one that lies behind the Honduran judicial system. I began by having us read Psalm 145:7-9 together in order to note how the psalmist speaks of God's justice in close connection with God's grace and mercy. I then asked the participants to imagine themselves standing before a Honduran court, admitting that they were guilty, or unjust, but then also pleading not to go to prison. I asked them to complete the following sentence: "Honorable judge, I acknowledge my guilt, but I appeal to your _____! Please don't send me to jail!" Without exception, they each filled the blank with the word "mercy." Next I asked them what would happen if a person appealed to the judge's "justice" rather than to his "mercy." They laughed and said that such a person would be asking the judge for a prison sentence! At that point, we read Psalm 143 and saw that David says exactly what we had just acknowledged would make no sense in a Honduran court. David admits his guilt (v. 2), while all the time appealing to God's "justice" (v. 1). They quickly concluded that David must be using the word "justice" differently from the way we would use it today in a Honduran court.

Once they had made this discovery, I went to the blackboard and listed a number of key differences between what I have chosen to call "juristic" and "relational" conceptions of justice, describing what it would mean for a person to be considered "just" in each one.[34] For instance, I told them that, on the juristic side, justice is an external norm or criterion that is used to measure whether one is just or not. In contrast, the psalmist's concept of justice is relational. One cannot be considered just apart from the question of how one stands in relationship to God and to others. On this understanding of justice, people are considered just when they fulfill their obligations, responsibilities, and agreements with others. Through the lens of the relational perspective, then, we observed a close relationship between "justice" and "faithfulness."

Before I had even begun to talk about God in connection with this relational understanding of justice, Mario saw where all this was heading. He observed,

> It seems that through history the relation between God and humans has been through covenants. So it is when we are unfaithful to

these covenants that God considers us unjust. Nevertheless, God continues to be faithful to the covenants, and therefore God is just.[35]

Since Mario had introduced this theme, I led the group in unpacking his statement. Then, to see if others understood, I asked, "What will we evaluate to determine if God is just according to a relational conception of justice?" David replied, "God's faithfulness to God's covenants and promises."[36] In contrast, they stated that according to the juristic concept of justice, one would measure the justice of God according to "the form in which God applies the law," by evaluating whether or not "God gives each person what he or she deserves."[37] David added, "We would evaluate God's own actions according to the criteria of the laws."[38] In a group from another church, Luis made a similar observation, but recoiled from its implications for his view of God. He said,

> I certainly have very often interpreted God's justice according to the juristic perspective. Now I see that I was not correct to do this. This has led me to ask myself, "Why have I thought of the justice of God in this way? Who is going to impose norms of justice on God? God does not need to ask for norms or moral criteria."[39]

Before turning our attention back to Romans, we quickly looked at a number of additional Old Testament texts, including Isaiah 45:20-25, Isaiah 51:4-8, Psalm 40:9-11, and Psalm 98:1-3. Seeing how "justice" was used in conjunction with words like "salvation," "faithfulness," and "mercy" served to reinforce and expand their understanding of the relational concept of justice.

All of the groups responded positively to my interpretation of "the justice of God" as referring to God's faithfulness to God's covenants and promises. They demonstrated that they understood it, and they communicated in various ways that they found it helpful. A number of things probably contributed to their positive response. First, they all take the Bible quite seriously. Therefore, it was significant for them when they encountered texts in the Psalms and in Isaiah that describe justice in a way different from the juristic concept of justice with which they are familiar from the setting of the court-room. Second, although the Honduran state does, of course, have a juristic approach to justice, Hondurans in general do not hold their judicial system in high regard. In light of that fact, and because of the opportunity their use of "*justo*" affords for conceiving of a person being "just" in other than a juristic way, these Hondurans may have found it easier than people in some other sociolinguistic contexts to imagine that Paul understood justice in a way that differs markedly from the juristic concept. Third, in the case of those from Amor Fe y Vida, it is likely that they readily embraced this new perspective on the justice of God because it meshed well with the way they were already reading Romans. They did not receive it as a challenge or correction to their reading, but as something supportive, enriching, and clarifying. Even so, this particular way of thinking was new to them, and so I was eager to hear how it might affect the way they read these passages in Romans a second time.

Rereading the Texts with Amor Fe y Vida

C H I continued the conversation with the group from Amor Fe y Vida by rereading the two passages in Romans (3:19-26 and chap. 8) and asking them how understanding the justice of God in a relational sense—that is, as covenant faithfulness—might change, confirm, or enrich the way they had read it before. As already mentioned, in 1992 Amor Fe y Vida Church made an intentional break from the typical form of evangelicalism found in other churches in their neighborhood. Their eight-year struggle to become a different kind of church has entailed a good deal of theological reflection. They have sought to identify and to leave behind teachings that produce the legalistic and overly individualistic-spiritualized version of Christianity they faulted for leading to indifference to the needs of the community and for doing little to lessen people's fear of a distant and accusing God. We might say that they are attempting to weed out theological perspectives they consider a barrier to people experiencing true *shalom* through a holistic gospel, while seeking to plant in place of the weeds theological perspectives that are life-giving and that promote the embodiment of a holistic gospel in their particular community of faith.

This process was evident as they reread Romans. They continually talked about the way they would have read Romans some years ago—interpreting the justice of God through the lens of a juristic concept of justice—and they contrasted that old reading with the new possibility of looking at Romans through the lens of justice as covenant faithfulness. Arely Cantor, a woman in her early twenties, observed that from the juristic perspective one would say that "God sent his Son to take our place and pay the penalty we should pay; therefore God is able to forgive and still remain in line with the criteria of justice." She went on to say that from a relational perspective of justice one would say that "God is just because God keeps his promise, his covenant, to bring salvation through Israel to the nations."[40]

C H Biblical interpretation with cultural sensitivity and relevant.

The members of Amor Fe y Vida displayed particular interest in discussing the related issue of justification. Licethe Flores, a woman about twenty years old, stated that whereas evangelicals typically think of justification in an individualistic way—as a matter solely between God and an individual—if one thinks of being justified from the perspective of a relational concept of justice, more people are involved. Mario asked whether justification is instantaneous or gradual. The group agreed that from a juristic perspective it is seen as instantaneous. Mario then wondered whether a relational perspective of justice might allow them to understand justification as both instantaneous and a process. Juan answered,

> I have the impression that God manifests himself to us in a gradual way. We are in a process of growing in and experiencing the grace of God. Not in the sense that we have to reach a certain point in the process in order to be saved, but that we are in the process of more deeply experiencing God's love.[41]

Mario responded,

> The juristic concept of justification in our context ends up having a certain magical character to it; in contrast, the relational concept is real. The relationship between God and the human and that between the human and other humans is real and permanent. Also, on the juristic side there is no cost [to us], but on the relational side there is a cost, implications. God expects something from us when we are brought into relationship with others in the people of God.

Arely added, "We are speaking of a commitment. If I decide to enter this community of faith, there are consequences and implications to joining the community." Juan agreed, "On the juristic side we do not have anything to do, on this other side we have to make decisions in freedom."[42] Although everyone appeared to agree with this, they also observed that churches that present justification in the traditional way do in fact make many demands and do expect people's behavior to change. As Tina Raudales said, "many are living in fear of sinning and losing their salvation."[43] Juan acknowledged that this is true, but observed,

> There may be a program of religious rules, such as having to go to church every night, but it does not flow from the experience of God in justification. Rather it is an individualistic effort to measure up to religious standards.[44]

The group stated that one of the central teachings of Romans 8 is that God is for us and that nothing can separate us from God's love. They observed that there is little relation between the justice of God and these verses if one interprets the justice of God through the lens of a juristic concept of justice, but that there is a strong connection when the justice of God is interpreted as covenant faithfulness. Following up on the discussion of an individualistic versus a more corporate understanding of being justified, Arely pointed out that in Romans 8:31-39 Paul writes in the plural: "It says nothing can separate *us* [from God's love]. It is about community."[45]

In observations like these, the group both appropriated ideas I had shared earlier and also made fresh connections and reached new conclusions on their own. In fact, they contributed to our conversation about the justice of God insights that I had not anticipated. This is especially evident in their emphasis on human responsibility for caring for creation as an implication of Paul's discussion of the redemption of creation in Romans 8. For instance, Juan stated, "As the children of God are made manifest [v. 19], they will work to save the creation. So, as God keeps his promise to bring salvation to humans, God is also bringing salvation to creation."[46]

At the end of our time together, I returned to the question of the justice of God and Hurricane Mitch. I asked the group from Amor Fe y Vida how this conversation had contributed to their thinking about this problem. Mario spoke first, saying,

> From this study it is clear that Hurricane Mitch was not a punishment from God, although that is the common interpretation among many people here—that God sent Mitch to bring justice by giving people the punishment they deserved. But I see in this reading of Romans that God promised to restore rather than destroy, to give life rather than to kill. So the common view does not match up with God's intentions. How does it help us? It liberates us from fear, from fear of the idea that God will punish for whatever thing we might do. It allows us to live more in freedom and have an internal sense of peace.[47]

Astrid asked, "But wasn't there judgment involved in Mitch? Like we said before, people suffered as a consequence of human sin." Bertilia responded,

> We do not have a vengeful God. As Mario said, we do not need to be terrified of God. The negative destruction of Mitch, as we said before, was much worse because of our actions. It could be even

that the hurricane itself, its size, is related to our lack of concern for the environment and the atmosphere.

Francisco Vargas, a middle-aged man with an activist spirit, interjected, "But there still would have been a hurricane." I said, "Right, but is there something in Romans that might help us with that issue?" Francisco replied, "We read here that something is amiss with the creation itself. It is suffering birth pains and awaiting liberation. This implies that things in creation are not as God originally intended."[48] Arely concluded,

> Thinking about this in relation to the corporate sense of the relational concept of justice, we see that the actions of some humans have affected a whole generation of Hondurans, and we are suffering the consequences of these actions. But, as a Christian community of faith, we have the hope of returning to what God originally desired.[49]

Part II: Reading Romans in North America
Lessons from a Cross-Cultural Conversation

C H Mark Baker has recounted his series of conversations with members of Amor Fe y Vida Church and with other believers in Honduras concerning the meaning of "the justice of God" in Romans and its implications for Christian belief and practice. He has also offered an explanation of some of the contextual factors that help to account for the particular readings of Romans that took shape during these discussions.

A H My purpose in the second part of this paper is to reflect, as a North American biblical scholar, on the broad forces at work in the scriptural interpretations of the members of Amor Fe y Vida. In addition, in the spirit of genuine "analectical engagement" with these Honduran Christians, I will suggest a number of ways in which their readings and, perhaps just as importantly, their reading practices, might inform and challenge[50] the readings of Romans we perform in a North American context.[51]

C H Baker's main task of contextual and hermeneutical readings.

A H Wagner's main task of analytical reading with hermeneutical considerations.

Practicing "Scriptural Criticism"

In their "Overture" to the inaugural volume in the Romans through History and Culture Series, Cristina Grenholm and Daniel Patte offer a model for a "scriptural criticism" that attempts to elucidate the ways in which believers read the Bible as Scripture. In doing so, scriptural criticism aims to help readers assess the value of their interpretations in order that they may assume ethical responsibility for them.[52] Grenholm and Patte offer a model of the interpretive process that involves three poles: "the scriptural text, the believers' life-context, and the believers' religious perceptions of life."[53] Corresponding to these three poles are "three basic modes of interpretation (methodologies): the analytical, contextual-pragmatic, and hermeneutical-theological modes."[54] Any reading of scripture involves a dynamic interaction among all three poles and utilizes all three modes of interpretation.

While scriptural criticism enables interpreters to think critically about their own interpretations, it also allows them to evaluate and learn from the interpretations of others "from the outside," so to speak, based on the ways in which the threefold interpretive process is inscribed in the final product of interpretation. Grenholm and Patte explain:

> This assessment from the outside requires the identification of *characteristics of these other scriptural readings as final products*, but not necessarily of the characteristics of the process of interpretation that led to them . . . . Three frames are inscribed in each scriptural interpretation as final product—such as the receptions of Romans. We name them in such a way that their relationship with the modes of interpretations will be clear: . . . the hermeneutical, analytical, and contextual frames.[55]

In what follows, I will employ this model of three interpretive frames standing in dynamic relation to one another as a tool for analyzing aspects of the readings of Romans that emerged from Baker's conversations with the community of Amor Fe y Vida. To keep the discussion within appropriate limits, I will point to representative features of each frame rather than attempt a comprehensive analysis.

The Contextual Frame — C

The most obvious contextual feature of these readings of Romans is, of course, the appalling devastation left in the wake of Hurricane Mitch. This situation functions in Baker's discussions with the Honduran believers as the initial "bridge category," that is, "the life problem or issue that the reader brings to the text with the conviction that the text can address it."[56] The tremendous difficulties for their daily lives created by the hurricane—and exacerbated by a long history of environmental abuses—help to explain why the members of Amor Fe y Vida understand Paul's discussion in Romans 8 concerning the present subjection of creation to futility and the promise of its eschatological redemption to have clear implications for the way in which people should treat the environment in the here and now.[57]

Context may also go a long way toward explaining why the particular issue of theodicy with which Paul wrestles in Romans—the fidelity of God toward Israel in the face of the gospel's reception by many Gentiles and rejection by many Jews—receives no attention in these conversations.[58] The problem of Jewish-Christian relations is simply not an issue impinging on the lives of believers in this community, for there is only a small Jewish presence in Honduras.[59] Moreover, their own history—unlike that of Christians in North America and Europe—is not haunted by the specter of the Holocaust. Consequently, these Honduran believers have not experienced the same post-Holocaust impetus to rethink their understanding of Paul's attitude toward the Jewish people. However, it may be the case that further analectical engagement with North American and European readings of Romans will eventually lead these Honduran believers to grapple with the question of the relationship of the Church to Israel. In doing so from the perspective of their own interpretive context, they may well be able to provide new insights for Christians in North American and European contexts who are wrestling with this crucial theological issue.

Although the hurricane provides the initial bridge category for the discussions, it is interesting to see how quickly the conversations turn away from the issue of theodicy to broader questions of the nature of God and the shape of the Christian life as a new creation brought into existence by "God's justice." This move is illuminated by understanding the particular history of Amor Fe y Vida, which came into being as a community in large part because of the members' growing dissatisfaction with a legalistic form of Christianity focused on individual salvation. Their marked tendency to interpret "the justice of God" in a relational sense and their deep sensitivity to the "horizontal" aspects of justification (i.e., its implications for human relationships) reflect their ongoing struggle to embody what they believe to be a more holistic, community-oriented gospel. Because their community history involved—and continues to require—theological choices influenced to a great extent by the reading of Scripture,[60] we see here a good example of the dynamic interplay among all three interpretive modes: contextual-pragmatic, hermeneutical-theological, and analytical.

As already noted by Baker, the sociolinguistic context of the believers in Honduras exerts a significant influence on the interpretations they offer of "the justice of God." The tendency of these Hondurans to conceive of God's "justice" (*justicia*) primarily in relational, rather than in strictly legal, terms appears to be facilitated by the way Hondurans commonly use the related adjective "just" (*justo*) to describe a person who meets his or her social obligations.[61] As Luis explains, "We say that phrase [viz., "he is a just person"] in a relational sense, that a person does what is normal, what is expected in relation to another person."[62]

This is not to imply that the Hondurans are unfamiliar with a legal setting for the language of "justice." In fact, several of the interpreters strongly contrasted the *relational* connotations of the adjective "just" (when used to describe a person) with both the *legal* connotations the noun "justice" carries in everyday life and particularly with the way the terms "just/justice" are used in the setting of the law-courts.[63] Moreover, they know very well that most of the believers in other faith communities in Flor del Campo—interpreters who inhabit the same sociolinguistic context as the members of Amor Fe y Vida—understand "the justice of God" primarily in a juristic sense.[64] It is clear, then, that those who interpret "the justice of God" in relational terms have made a *choice* to do so. Why they choose to emphasize this relational sense of justice when speaking about God leads us to consider a second interpretive frame.

The Hermeneutical Frame — H

That larger theological conceptions significantly shape the ways in which the members of Amor Fe y Vida read Romans is clear to at least some of the interpreters themselves. In a private conversation with Mario and his daughter, Arely, Baker asks them to comment on the fact that the believers of Amor Fe y Vida place a marked emphasis on the relational, rather than the juristic, connotations of Paul's phrase, "the justice of God." They explain, "Because of the image we have of God, we could not give answers that put an emphasis on punishment."[65] Mario and Arely go on to clarify that they have become more and more convinced that the image of a vengeful, angry, accusing God held by so many Hondurans is simply incorrect. Their thinking about God has changed during the period of their involvement with Amor Fe y Vida. Together, this community has experienced a gracious God of love and mercy, and this, they claim, has affected the character of their church to the extent that people who have come in from other churches in Flor del Campo note the difference. Clearly, then, the theological commitments of this church—shaped over a period of years through hearing and living the Scriptures together in a communal quest to find a more life-giving, holistic gospel in their own particular context—function as lenses for their reading of Romans, filtering out some possible interpretations of the text and allowing others to come sharply into focus. The extent to which Mario and Arely recognize that prior theological commitments underlie their readings of Romans suggests that these are interpreters who are willing to take responsibility for the interpretive choices they have made, to confess with a remarkable degree of critical self-awareness, "*I* believe this interpretation is truly the Word of God for us today."[66]

The significance of the hermeneutical frame chosen by the members of Amor Fe y Vida becomes even more apparent when we consider the interpretation of "the justice of God" in another community located in the same barrio. In Baker's discussions with members of the dispensationalist La Mizpa Church, there is a much stronger sense of the juristic interpretation of "the justice of God." Luis explains that a "just" judge is one who is "impartial, [who] applies the law as written." For him, "the justice of God" refers to the fact that "God will put our works in the balance of justice and judge our works. Nobody can escape facing the justice of God."[67] This interpretation of Paul's phrase may be correlated in significant ways with the larger religious perceptions of life held by the members of this church. The shape of their communal life is, from the perspective of Amor Fe y Vida, much more focused on strict rule-keeping, and their view of God tends to emphasize God as lawgiver and judge.[68] In fact, it is just such a version of the Christian life that the members of Amor Fe y Vida understand themselves to have rejected as an overly legalistic and individualistic embodiment of the gospel. Little wonder, then, that the two churches, despite sharing a similar sociocultural context, should understand "the justice of God" in Romans in such strongly divergent ways.

The Analytical Frame — A

I have suggested a number of ways in which context and theology influence the way the members of Amor Fe y Vida read the biblical text. It is crucial, however, to recognize that the scriptural text, as it is read and interpreted, also challenges and/or reinforces the believers' theological conceptions. Moreover, as the teachings of Scripture are embodied in the life of the community, they in turn help to shape the context in which interpretation takes place.[69]

Among the readerly virtues displayed by the members of Amor Fe y Vida throughout the course of their conversations with Baker is a sincere desire to find warrants for their interpretations in the scriptural text itself. The series of three discussions at Amor Fe y Vida are thus marked by careful attention to the text, where the participants consistently appeal to the Scriptures to justify their interpretations. At times, this close reading leads an interpreter to make a new exegetical connection that brings fresh theological insight. For instance, after considering the court-room drama of Romans 8:31-34, where God acts to vindicate believers, Mario reflects on their earlier reading of Romans 3:19-26 and concludes, "This might mean we would be wrong to view God as accuser in chapter three."[70]

On the whole, however, these studies of "the justice of God" in Romans seem not so much to lead to radically new insights or to challenge deeply-entrenched convictions as to provide a more complete scriptural framework for—and thus a greater confidence in—the community's convictions about God, the gospel, and the nature of the Christian life. For example, by reading Paul's language of "the justice of God" in connection with the ways this concept functions in other scriptural texts—such as Psalm 143, Psalm 145, and Deutero-Isaiah—the members of Amor Fe y Vida find new justification for the relational sense they were giving the phrase during their first pass through Romans with Baker. As Baker leads them to think through the implications of the "juristic" and "relational" models of "justice/justification," they develop a sharper critique of the juristic model for its inability to allow Romans to address their concerns for justice and for helping the poor in the community. At the same time, they see in a fresh way how Paul's concerns in Romans may offer scriptural resources for their struggle to articulate and live out a holistic understanding of the gospel.

Similarly, these conversations appear to deepen the conviction among the members of Amor Fe y Vida that God is one who graciously delivers them from trouble, whose dealings with them are characterized by mercy. As their contributions to these studies make clear, they recognize very well that much more is at stake for them in the interpretation of "the justice of God" than the resolution of an interesting technical problem in Pauline scholarship. At issue is their entire conception of God, with all of the implications for day-to-day life as Christians that follow from it. Though spoken by someone from a different faith-community, these words sum up well the feeling of many members of Amor Fe y Vida at the end of these studies:

> Thinking this way about the justice of God [i.e., in a relational sense, as covenant faithfulness] gives me more confidence to ask for justice as David did [in Psalm 143], with the confidence that the justice of God is a positive thing for me and that it can include God's mercy.[71]

The overwhelmingly positive response to these studies on the part of the members of Amor Fe y Vida suggests that conversations between biblical critics and believers in other sociolinguistic contexts may prove fruitful not only for the scholars, but also for those who seek to shape their lives according to the Scriptures, heard as God's Word addressed to them.[72]

Seeking "Analectical Engagement"

Analectical engagement promises that as one approach honestly encounters another and learns from it, its very conceptual existence will change, as will the manner in which it views the biblical reality it is designed to investigate.[73]

From the inception of this project, we have eagerly expected that our own understanding of Romans and our own practices of scriptural interpretation would be challenged and transformed by reading these texts together with believers in Honduras, and we have not been disappointed. In a similar way, we anticipate continuing to learn from our ongoing discussions in the context of the Romans through History and Culture Seminar. The following reflections are thus offered as an invitation to engage in further conversation both about the readings of Romans that emerged from these Bible studies in Flor del Campo and about the relevance of all of this for our own practices of scriptural criticism.

The Interpretation of Romans

Two aspects of the readings of Romans offered by members Amor Fe y Vida stand out as particularly significant challenges and/or contributions to the interpretation of Romans in North American and European biblical criticism.[74] First, these Honduran believers place a great emphasis on the "horizontal" dimension to justification—that is, on the implications of Paul's conception of "the justice of God" for relationships between human beings. "God expects something from us when we are brought into relationship with others in the people of God," explains Mario.[75] The Hondurans' recognition that a relational understanding of "the justice of God" has clear and direct implications for human life in community poses a strong challenge to versions of "God's justice" and "justification" that focus primarily on the private "vertical" relationship of the individual believer to God. At the same time, this emphasis on the "horizontal" dimension to justification finds its counterpart in many of the more recent scholarly efforts to reconceptualize the contours of Paul's theology in light of the so-called "New Perspective on Paul."[76]

A second interpretation that emerges from our conversations in Honduras offers what for Europeans and North Americans may be an unconventional—though perhaps ultimately compelling—insight into the implications of Paul's argument in Romans 8. Reading Romans in the wake of Hurricane Mitch, the members of Amor Fe y Vida hear in Paul's description of the cosmic effects of the revelation of God's justice (Rom 8:18-22) a clear call to Christians to join in rescuing the environment.

While they resist viewing Hurricane Mitch as a *punishment* sent by God, a number of these Honduran believers find "the justice of God" revealed in this event in the sense that God allowed humans to suffer the consequences of their abuse of the environment:

> It was a natural phenomenon that turned into a threat and a killer because of previous human actions [such as cutting down forests, mining too aggressively, and building homes too close to the river and on steep hillsides]. The justice of God is God's faithfulness to creation and the positive and negative consequences of our stewardship of creation.[77]

> The justice of God is for all of creation. Human beings destroyed creation. Therefore God has manifested his justice. We did bad things [to the environment], and there are consequences to our actions.[78]

In one of the more intriguing interpretations offered during the three nights of study, Juan suggests that Romans 8:18-22 means, "As the children of God are made manifest [v. 19], they will work to save the creation. So, as God keeps his promise to bring salvation to humans, God is also bringing salvation to creation."[79] The idea that "the justice of God" includes God's determination to redeem the entire created order means for them that God holds human beings responsible in the here and now for how they take care of creation.[80] The relationship these Honduran believers see in Paul's argument in Romans between "the justice of God" as God's act of cosmic redemption and a theology of environmental responsibility is not one normally recognized by biblical critics in North America and Europe.[81] Yet perhaps such a connection is waiting to be made in our own interpretive context as well if we are willing to follow the lead of these Honduran interpreters and return to the text with fresh eyes.[82]

Practices of Interpretation

Finally, I would like to suggest three ways in which the reading *practices* of the members of Amor Fe y Vida pose a challenge to the practices of North American and European biblical critics who seek to interpret Romans for the Church.[83] First, these Honduran believers read Romans as Christian Scripture, that is, as part of a larger whole, the Bible. Thus, whatever "the justice of God" might be taken to mean in Romans, for them it ultimately must be integrated into the larger witness of the entire biblical canon to the saving purposes of God. Their belief in the intra-textual nature of the Bible—and their considerable creativity in exploiting its interpretive possibilities—is well illustrated in Mario's contention that "the justice of God" spoken of by Paul in Romans is vividly illuminated by the story of Jesus and the Accused Woman in John 7:53-8:11.[84] The Honduran believers move much more easily from New Testament to Old Testament or from one biblical book to another than biblical critics generally feel comfortable doing, but if we are to nurture and build up the Church through our scholarship, can we afford to read Romans simply as one of several "genuine" letters of Paul without also interpreting it, ultimately, as part of the larger canon of Scripture?

Second, the members of Amor Fe y Vida adopt an interpretive stance that allows them to hear Romans as a word of God *to them*. That is to say, they assume that there is a deep organic continuity between Paul's original addressees in Rome and their own community in Flor del Campo. Though separated by time and space, both belong to the one people that God is calling into being through Jesus Christ from every nation, tribe, and language. Consequently, Romans is addressed as much to them as to those house-churches in Rome centuries ago. For the people of Amor Fe y Vida, reading Romans is not a theoretical exercise interesting in and of itself; rather, the scriptural text makes a claim on their lives and leads to transformation in exceedingly practical terms.[85] Could it be that those of us trained as biblical critics in a North American or European context, though rightly concerned to take account of the historical and cultural *distance* between ourselves, on the one hand, and Paul and his hearers, on the other, ignore for all practical purposes the hermeneutical implications of our ecclesiology—and so fail to receive the scriptural text as a word of God addressed *to us*?[86]

Lastly, the people of Amor Fe y Vida challenge us by their practice of reading to recognize that interpreting Scripture in and for the Church is at heart a communal task.[87] Not only do their readings of Romans emerge in the context of a conversation that allows for a multiplicity of voices and perspectives to be heard, but, even more significantly, these interpretations find their focus in discussions about the shape their communal life should take. In their wrestling with Romans, Paul's notion of "the justice of God" is understood as a teaching about God that has very practical ramifications for their relationships with God and with one another. The believers of Amor Fe y Vida realize that the test of any reading of Scripture is finally whether or not it contributes to the formation of a community that can embody the gospel of "God's justice" manifested through Jesus Christ.[88] Except perhaps as an ideal, such a communal dimension all too often appears to be lacking from our work as biblical critics seeking to serve the Church through our scholarship. The rampant individualism into which we are inculturated, the dominant structures of academy and guild, our own readiness to claim for our interpretations the status of "expert opinion" over against the readings of ordinary believers—all complicate our efforts to allow our readings to be shaped by the community of faith. If we were to take the members of Amor Fe y Vida seriously at this point as a model for our own reading of Scripture as biblical scholars, what might this mean for the shape of our interpretive practice? The question would seem to be one well worth pursuing further—*together*.[89]

Notes

1. For a concise explanation of the character of this "new perspective" by the scholar who coined the expression, see J. D. G. Dunn, "The New Perspective on Paul," *Bulletin of the John Rylands Library* 65 (1983): 95-122.

2. That is, through a process of appropriation and incorporation, rather than through a process of opposition and exclusion.

3. Brian K. Blount, *Cultural Interpretation: Reorienting New Testament Criticism* (Minneapolis: Fortress, 1995): 39.

4. It is obvious that the very process of summarizing these conversations is an act of interpretation no less subject to our own cultural biases than that of reading a text. We necessarily reframe another's thoughts in terms that make sense to us. This fact does not, however, preclude a real exchange of ideas between people or across cultures (for the significance of this insight for cross-cultural studies, see the perceptive discussion of "interpretive sociology" by Nancy Jay in *Throughout Your Generations Forever: Sacrifice, Religion, and Paternity* [Chicago: University of Chicago Press, 1992] xxv-xxvi, 13-14). Recognizing the difficulties of representing our Honduran interlocutors fairly, we nevertheless commit ourselves to a "hermeneutic of love" which seeks as far as possible to understand and articulate another's perspective in terms they would find acceptable (on the rationale for such a dialogical approach to interpretation, see further D. Patte, *The Challenge of Discipleship* [Harrisburg: Trinity Press International, 1999] 52-54; N. T. Wright, *The New Testament and the People of God* [Minneapolis: Fortress, 1992] 50-64).

5. Blount, *Cultural Interpretation*, 85-86.

6. Over 15,000 people make Flor del Campo their home.

7. The Honduran government reported a nationwide toll of 5,657 dead, 8,058 missing, 12,272 injured, and 1.4 million homeless according to *USA Today* on 8 December 1998 (http://www.usatoday.com/weather/news/1998/ wsuspend.htm).

8. The information in this paragraph is based on what I (Baker) heard in conversation with people after Mitch, .when I was still living in Honduras, and on interviews with both Catholic and evangelical believers in Flor del Campo in June and July 2000.

9. In Latin America, the term "evangelical" is used more commonly than "protestant" to refer to non-Catholic Christians. For this reason, and because the number of mainline protestants in Honduras is very small, we will employ the term "evangelical" throughout this paper.

10. This fact is, of course, obvious to the Hondurans who see Mitch as a punishment sent by God. Many of them suffered great personal loss. For instance, "Luis" (fictitious name; see n. 18 below), a Flor del Campo resident who lost his business to Mitch, still describes the hurricane as a punishment aimed at the statue of Jesus and at those who practice a mix of popular religiosity and witchcraft (discussion with La Mizpa Church, 7/1/00).

11. The concept of God described in this paragraph is based upon my reading, ethnographic research, and ten years of field experience in Honduras. For concrete examples and analysis see, Mark D. Baker, *Religious No More: Building Communities of Grace and Freedom* (Downers Grove: InterVarsity Press, 1999): 17-33, 40-48; Stanley Slade, "Popular Spirituality as an Oppressive Reality," Guillermo Cook ed., *New Face of the Church in Latin America* (Maryknoll: Orbis, 1994): 135-49.

12. For a discussion of these phenomena in the wider Latin American context and for examples of how this form of the gospel is articulated and lived out in Flor del Campo, see Mark D. Baker, *Evangelical Churches in a Tegucigalpa Barrio, Do They Fit the Escapist and Legalistic Stereotype?: An Ethnographic Investigation*, Duke–University of North Carolina Program in Latin American Studies Working Paper Series, no. 16 (February, 1995).

13. For a more detailed description of their history, see Baker, *Religious No More*, 49-55, 153-159.

14. I left Honduras in the summer of 1992, but I lived there again for two and a half years during the period 1996-1998. I have visited annually when not living there.

15. Our interpretation of Paul's phrase, "God's righteousness," to mean, "God's covenant faithfulness, God's merciful commitment to deliver God's people," is a fairly common understanding of the phrase within scholarship that has influenced, or been influenced by, the "New Perspective on Paul" (see n. 33 below). This interpretation relies heavily on the uses of this phrase in Israel's scriptures and in Jewish writings of the Second Temple Period. Wagner argues for the importance of Isaiah's language of "the righteousness of God" for Paul's argument in

Romans in *Heralds of the Good News: Paul and Isaiah "In Concert" in the Letter to the Romans* (Leiden: Brill, 2002).

16. Tegucigalpa Mennonite Church is the only one of the four that is not located in Flor del Campo. The discussion with the group from Amor Fe y Vida Church lasted five hours over three evenings; conversations with the other groups were somewhat shorter. The discussions were tape-recorded, and I later translated and transcribed them. All quotations from participants in these conversations are taken from the transcriptions. In addition, the study was field tested in a trial run on 27 June 2000 with David Garcia, the director of the extension program of the Honduran Holiness Church's Bible Institute in Tegucigalpa. I benefited greatly from David's questions, criticisms, and suggestions for improvement.

17. The focus of this paper is how the people of Amor Fe y Vida Church interpret "the justice of God" in Romans, not how we do. Yet, at the same time, the paper is the report of a conversation. Especially in the second and third parts of the discussion I did not just ask questions, but contributed to the conversation. In this sense we chose to follow an approach similar to that of Ernesto Cardenal. In *The Gospel in Solentiname,* he elicits the Nicaraguan *campesinos'* reflections on biblical texts, but he also contributes information and ideas based on his life experiences and formal theological training. He reports not just their ideas, but the conversation itself (Ernesto Cardenal, *The Gospel in Solentiname* [4 vols; Maryknoll: Orbis, 1976-82]). Gerald O. West, a South African biblical scholar, similarly understands his role to be that of a dialog partner with readers in poor and marginalized communities (*The Academy of the Poor: Towards a Dialogical Reading of the Bible* [Interventions 2; Sheffield: Sheffield Academic Press, 1999]).

18. Although the members of Amor Fe y Vida gave us permission to use their real names, participants in the other groups were told that their identity would remain anonymous in order to increase their level of comfort in sharing ideas while a tape recorder was operating. We will use a fictitious name for a person in one of these groups where necessary to enable the reader to identify different comments made by the same person.

19. Because not all of the participants could read and write, almost all of the rest of my questions were answered orally. In a few questions, like this one, however, I wanted to gauge the breadth of thinking of the group, not just the opinions of the most vocal. So I asked those who could do so to write their answers down before all were invited to share their responses verbally.

20. Both comments were anonymous written comments offered during the discussion with Amor Fe y Vida Church, 7/4/00.

21. Ines (fictitious name; see n. 18 above); discussion with La Mizpa Church, 7/1/00.

22. Ines; discussion with La Mizpa Church, 7/1/00.

23. *Ibid.*

24. The three comments were made during the discussion with Amor Fe y Vida, 7/4/00 (NB: The people from Amor Fe y Vida agreed together to allow us to use their real names in this paper).

25. See below, "The Justice of God" as Covenant Faithfulness: Insights from Biblical Criticism.

26. Personal communication with the authors, 11 February 1999. Cf. the comment of Brian Blount: "One witnesses today not *a* political theology, but political theologies, each of which actualizes a life relation and preunderstanding appropriate to its specific sociolinguistic, historical, and existential context" (Blount, *Cultural Interpretation*, 38; italics his).

27. Elsa Tamez makes the similar observation that the understanding of justification by faith that focuses on "liberation from guilt by the blood of Christ on the cross" pervades Latin America. "Justification by faith functions as a sort of code phrase, in which the disjuncture with our reality is evident: Forgiveness of sin is spoken of in an individual and generic sense, and reconciliation too is seen on an individual and abstract plane" (Elsa Tamez, *The Amnesty of Grace: Justification by Faith from a Latin American Perspective,* trans. Sharon Ringe [Nashville: Abingdon, 1993] 19-20).

28. "Fair" and "just" are given as the two English translations of the word *justo* in *The Oxford Spanish Dictionary* (Oxford: Oxford University Press, 1994), 442.

29. See below, "The Justice of God" as Covenant Faithfulness: Insights from Biblical Criticism.

30. Mario Cantor and Arely Cantor, personal conversation, 7/6/00.

31. Comments from the discussion with Amor Fe y Vida, 7/4/00.

32. *Ibid.*

33. Our understanding of "the justice of God" in Romans in relational terms, as expressing God's faithfulness to rescue and redeem God's covenant people—now understood by Paul to embrace Gentiles together with Jews—is based on our own close reading of Romans, which in turn has been shaped in conversation with a number of important studies. These include: S. K. Williams, "The 'Righteousness of God' in Romans," *Journal of Biblical Literature* 99 (1980): 241-90; R. B. Hays, "Psalm 143 and the Logic of Romans 3," *Journal of Biblical Literature* 99 (1980): 107-115; *idem*, "Justification," *Anchor Bible Dictionary* 3:1129-33; J. D. G. Dunn, *The Theology of Paul the Apostle* [Grand Rapids: Eerdmans, 1998] 334-46; E. P. Sanders, *Paul and Palestinian*

Judaism (Philadelphia: Fortress, 1977): 491-92; N. A. Dahl, "The Doctrine of Justification: Its Social Function and Implications," *Studies in Paul* (Minneapolis: Augsburg, 1977): 95-120; E. Käsemann, "The Righteousness of God in Paul," *New Testament Questions of Today* (Philadelphia: Fortress, 1969), 168-82; *idem*, "Justification and Salvation History in the Epistle to the Romans," *Perspectives on Paul* (Philadelphia: Fortress, 1971): 60-78. As J. D. G. Dunn observed in his response to our SBL paper, this relational understanding of "God's righteousness" has a long history in modern scholarship; an important early statement of this view is Hermann Cremer, *Die Paulinische Rechtfertigungslehre im Zusammenhang ihrer geschichtlichen Voraussetzungen* (Gütersloh: Bertelsmann, 1899).

34. The contrasting terms, "juristic" and "relational," are not intended to suggest that there is not a legal aspect to a relational understanding of justice. The question is rather one of the *basis* for this justice—the demands of an abstract set of legal principles, or the obligations of a concrete interpersonal relationship? In fact, one of the ways I helped people understand the difference between the two was asking them to contrast how a judge would operate depending on whether the society held more of a juristic or a relational concept of justice.

35. Mario Cantor; discussion with Amor Fe y Vida, 7/5/00.

36. David Suazo; discussion with Amor Fe y Vida, 7/5/00.

37. Juan Ernesto Hernández; Juan Hernández; discussion with Amor Fe y Vida, 7/5/00.

38. David Suazo; discussion with Amor Fe y Vida, 7/5/00.

38. Luis; discussion with La Mizpa Church, 7/1/00.

40. Arely Cantor, discussion with Amor Fe y Vida, 7/5/00.

41. Juan Hernández; discussion with Amor Fe y Vida, 7/6/00.

42. Comments from the discussion with Amor Fe y Vida, 7/6/00. When in their statements they mention "side," they are referring to the blackboard which we divided in half, listing on one side characteristics of a juristic understanding of justice and on the other side characteristics of a relational understanding of justice.

43. Tina Raudales; discussion with Amor Fe y Vida, 7/6/00.

44. Juan Hernández; discussion with Amor Fe y Vida, 7/6/00.

45. Arely Cantor; discussion with Amor Fe y Vida, 7/6/00.

46. The Spanish translation Juan read from (*Reina-Valera*), literally translated to English, is: "the manifestation of the children of God" (*la manifestación de los hijos de Dios*). I have therefore used his term, "manifest," in my translation of his statement, rather than the NRSV's "revealing."

47. Mario Cantor; discussion with Amor Fe y Vida, 7/6/00.

48. Astrid Rivera, Bertilia Fuentes, and Francisco Vargas; discussion with Amor Fe y Vida, 7/6/00.

49. Arely Cantor; discussion with Amor Fe y Vida, 7/6/00.

50. Blount (*Cultural Interpretation*, 85) argues that it is not enough for scholars simply to acknowledge the fact that one's sociolinguistic context influences one's reading of the text:

> What also needs to take place is the recognition that context is a necessary interpretative ingredient that should be consciously explored and promoted so that not only the contextual influences and strategies of mainline scholars are accepted as legitimate contextual by-products of the investigative enterprise, but also that the contextual perspectives of marginalized communities be recognized as appropriate interpersonal determinants of and challenges to text interpretation.

51. The context I particularly have in mind is the one in which I teach—a graduate school of theology related to a mainline protestant church, one of whose primary missions is to train women and men for various ministries in local churches of this and many other protestant denominations. This social location, of course, plays a significant role in what I select as especially noteworthy, helpful, or challenging about these readings of Romans in Honduras. My intention is not to stand over these Honduran readings and judge them as if from a neutral, objective vantage point, but rather to "invite, and subsequently accept analectically, input from other sociolinguistic perspectives" (Blount, *Cultural Interpretation*, 39).

52. Cristina Grenholm and Daniel Patte, "Overture: Receptions, Critical Interpretations, and Scriptural Criticism," in C. Grenholm and D. Patte ed., *Reading Israel in Romans* (Romans Through History and Culture Series 1; Harrisburg: Trinity Press International, 2000), 1-54. This model is developed for a more popular audience in Patte's *Challenge of Discipleship* (see especially 3-22, 43-63, 211-34).

53. Grenholm and Patte, "Overture," 35.

54. *Ibid.*

55. *Ibid.*, 36.

56. Patte, *Challenge of Discipleship*, 235 n. 2. See further Grenholm and Patte, "Overture," 37-39. This bridge category falls under the general rubric suggested by Grenholm and Patte of "powerlessness" (*ibid.*, 38). Strictly speaking, the selection of this initial bridge category and the particular biblical texts to read together was determined by our invitation to the Hondurans to discuss the ways in which they understood the concept of "the justice of God" in Romans to relate to their experience of the hurricane and its aftermath. However, the problem itself is one very much in the forefront of the Hondurans' minds, since dealing with the consequences of the hurricane has been an unavoidable feature of their daily lives for the past two years.

57. Mario Cantor comments, "We have a role in [the creation's] redemption. It is not just something we should be waiting around for, like in the films about the rapture" (discussion with Amor Fe y Vida, 7/4/00).

58. The only mention of Jews or Israel by Hondurans that I can find in the transcripts is a question, raised on two separate occasions, concerning how the understanding of "justice/righteousness" in modern Judaism compares with the meaning this concept has in the Old Testament (discussion with Amor Fe y Vida, 7/5/00; discussion with the Catholic Church, 7/8/00).

59. According to the Union of Jewish Congregations of Latin American and the Caribbean, there are approximately fifty families associated with the two Jewish communities in Honduras, one of which is located in Tegucigalpa, the other in San Pedro Sula (http://www.ujcl.org/honduras/).

60. For a detailed examination of aspects of this process in the life of Amor Fe y Vida as they wrestle with Paul's letter to the Galatians, see Baker, *Religious No More.*

61. Interestingly, the "contemporary" Spanish-language translation *Dios Habla Hoy* eliminates this point of contact between the relational use of "justo" in Spanish and Paul's thought in Romans by paraphrasing *dikaiosunê theou* in Romans 1:17 as "*Dios nos libra de culpa*" ("God frees us from guilt") instead of translating it "*justicia de Dios*" (as does the *Reina-Valera* version, the translation most commonly used in Amor Fe y Vida and in other evangelical churches). This paraphrase explicitly leads readers to think of the divine-human relationship primarily in juristic, rather than relational, terms. See further Baker, *Religious No More*, 98, 103.

62. Discussion with La Mizpa Church, 7/1/00. In contrast, the ways in which the adjective "just" is used in English do not facilitate an understanding of God's justice in relational terms. One could argue, in fact, that translating *dik-* words into the language of "just/justice/ justification" actually *hinders* understanding of Paul's meaning. Hence, some have preferred to translate Paul using terms exclusively from the "righteousness" word group, even though this entails either reviving or inventing a corresponding verb (such as "to rightwise(n)" or "to righteous," respectively). For the former approach, see K. Grobel's translation of R. Bultmann, *Theology of the New Testament* (2 vols.; New York: Charles Scribner's Sons, 1951-1955), I:253, translator's note. The latter tactic is adopted by E. P. Sanders in *Paul, the Law, and the Jewish People* (Minneapolis: Fortress, 1983), 13-14, n. 18; cf. *idem, Paul and Palestinian Judaism*, 470-71.

63. Mario Cantor describes the difference between these two models of "justice" in relation to a very practical (and painful) matter:

It impresses me that much of the justice that is practiced in the church is more according to the juristic approach than the relational. They base decisions on norms and rules. For instance [before helping to found Amor Fe y Vida] we were involved in our church, and we wanted to do things differently than the leaders of the denomination. We wanted to do things to help the needy in the neighborhood. *We* had paid for the [church] building, but according to the legal documents it belonged to the denomination. So they kept it, and we left with nothing (Discussion with Amor Fe y Vida, 7/5/00).

64. "Many would say that God is not just because God does not give to people as they deserve—God should punish more!" (Juan Hernández and David Suazo; discussion with Amor Fe y Vida, 7/5/00).

65. Conversation with Mario Cantor and Arely Cantor, 7/6/00.

66. The quotation is from Patte, *Challenge of Discipleship* (210 and *passim*; italics his). For believers to be able to make such a confession from a standpoint of critical awareness of the process by which they have arrived at their particular interpretation of scripture is for Patte the ultimate goal of scriptural criticism.

67. Discussion with La Mizpa Church, 7/1/00.

68. Luis himself recognizes this. After Baker's explanation of the difference between juristic and relational concepts of justice, Luis acknowledges, "I certainly have very often interpreted God's justice according to the juristic perspective" (discussion with La Mizpa Church, 7/1/00).

69. In the model offered by Grenholm and Patte to explain what happens when believers read the Bible as Scripture, there is a *dynamic* interaction among all three poles of the interpretive process—the believers' context, their religious perceptions of life, and the scriptural text itself. It is only for analytical purposes that the scriptural critic focuses on one of the three frames at a time.

70. Mario Cantor; discussion with Amor Fe y Vida, 7/4/00.

71. Conversation with David Garcia, director of the extension program of the Honduran Holiness Church's Bible Institute in Tegucigalpa, 6/27/00.

72. Though we have chosen to focus in this paper on Amor Fe y Vida, all of the groups involved affirmed that they found the activity to be helpful, and they all expressed their enthusiasm for studying the Bible together again.

73. Blount, *Cultural Interpretation*, 177.

74. Whether they are viewed as challenges or contributions depends on the way in which one currently reads Romans!

75. Mario Cantor; discussion with Amor Fe y Vida, 7/6/00.

76. See, for example, J. D. G. Dunn, "The Justice of God: A Renewed Perspective on Justification by Faith," *Journal of Theological Studies* 43 (1992): 1-22. Dunn rightly argues that the horizontal dimension to justification must not be viewed in opposition to the vertical dimension; the two are inextricably bound together when justification is understood as God's act of bringing humans into the people of God.

77. Arely Cantor; discussion with Amor Fe y Vida, 7/4/00.

78. Astrid Rivera; discussion with Amor Fe y Vida, 7/4/00. A similar idea is expressed by Luis, a member of La Mizpa Church. Commenting on the decades of environmental destruction by humans in Honduras, he suggests that through the devastation wrought by Mitch, "God has tried to help us see that we must take care of the environment" (discussion with La Mizpa Church, 7/1/00).

79. Juan Hernández; discussion with Amor Fe y Vida, 7/6/00.

80. Such an outlook, however, is by no means the only one to be found among Honduran Christians. Francisco Vargas reports attending a seminar at the Technological University on methods for limiting the amount of destruction and loss of life from natural disasters. There he heard a group of evangelical pastors write off such efforts as futile: "The pastors stated that these disasters are written in the Bible and that what we are seeing today is the fulfillment of what was predicted; they are the judgment of God" (discussion with Amor Fe y Vida, 7/6/00).

81. Sheila E. McGinn notes that feminist interpretations of Romans 8:18-23 often emphasize human responsibility to respect and care for the environment ("Feminist Approaches to Romans: Rom 8:18-23 as a Case Study," Paper presented at the Romans Through History and Cultures Seminar, SBL Annual Meeting, 2000). She goes on to observe, however, that "markedly different from many feminist views, Paul's theology of creation is intricately intertwined with eschatology" (ms p. 17). The members of Amor Fe y Vida appear to be closer to Paul on this point, since it is precisely their "inaugurated eschatology" that functions for them as an explicit warrant for caring for the environment.

82. Patte suggests, "When [believers'] practical conclusions are not comparable to those implied by existing scholarly interpretations, I believe that they call the attention of scholars to a dimension of the text that has been neglected" (*Challenge of Discipleship*, 17).

83. Recognizing the significance of context for all practices of interpretation, I do not presume to address biblical critics in general. Instead, I will direct my comments more specifically toward those of us who locate ourselves within the community that confesses the Bible to be Scripture. Others within this community of faith, and those who locate themselves within different interpretive communities, will doubtless have further insights to offer.

84. Mario Cantor; discussion with Amor Fe y Vida, 7/4/00.

85. Mark Baker relates the following story (Personal correspondence, 25 June 2000):

> After the class [at the Tegucigalpa Mennonite Church], a woman who had been in the discipleship group Lynn and I led when we lived here asked me what the implications of this study were for her relationship with her ex-husband and some things he is asking from her. Should she be "just" even though he has been far from just? That is, should she help him out of a financial problem even though he is not keeping some of his obligations toward her? It impressed me that for her this did not at all remain just an academic discussion.

During the study itself another woman found Paul's understanding of the "justice of God" as God's covenant faithfulness to have similar ramifications for her own personal conduct. She observes, "If a person doesn't deserve something, even as a human I might have mercy and give it to them because I am a just person" (discussion with Tegucigalpa Mennonite Church, 6/25/00).

86. On the hermeneutical significance of ecclesiology for Christian interpretation of the Bible, consider the provocative thesis of Robert Jenson ("The Religious Power of Scripture," *Scottish Journal of Theology* 52 [1999]: 89-105):

> The error of most modern biblical exegesis is a subliminal assumption that the church in and for which Matthew or Paul wrote, or in which Irenaeus shaped the canon, and the church in which we now read what they put together, are historically distant from each other. That is, the error is the assumption that there is no one diachronically identical universal church. And that is, *the initiating error of standard modern exegesis is that it presumes a sectarian ecclesiology.* But while Athens may perhaps have disappeared into the past and been replaced by Paris or London or New York, Paul's church still lives as the very one to which believing exegetes now belong (98; italics his).

Similar concerns are being voiced within the field of biblical criticism as well. Christopher Seitz considers of paramount importance for modern biblical studies the question of "*whose* book is [the Bible] and *why* is it being read in the first place?" (*Word Without End: The Old Testament as Abiding Theological Witness* [Grand Rapids: Eerdmans, 1998], 340). Significantly, recognition of this fundamental hermeneutical problem has not been confined to Christian interpreters of scripture; see, for example, Jon D. Levenson, *The Hebrew Bible, the Old Testament, and Historical Criticism: Jews and Christians in Biblical Studies* (Louisville: Westminster/John Knox, 1993).

87. See further S. E. Fowl and L. G. Jones, *Reading in Communion: Scripture and Ethics in Christian Life* (Grand Rapids: Eerdmans, 1991).

88. See W. A. Meeks, "A Hermeneutics of Social Embodiment," *Harvard Theological Review* 79 (1986): 176-86; R. B. Hays, *Echoes of Scripture in the Letters of Paul* (New Haven: Yale University Press, 1989): 191-92; Fowl and Jones, *Reading in Communion*.

89. We want to express our deep gratitude once again to the members of Amor Fe y Vida Church for their hospitality and for their willingness to engage in substantive conversations with us about Paul's letter to the Romans. We are indebted especially to Juan Hernández, who organized the studies involving participants from La Mizpa church and from the Roman Catholic Church in Flor del Campo. Thanks go also to Professors Jean-Pierre Ruiz and James D. G. Dunn for their thoughtful responses to our paper at the 2000 SBL Annual Meeting and to the members of the Romans through History and Cultures Seminar for the stimulating discussion that followed.

Works Cited

Baker, Mark D. *Evangelical Churches in a Tegucigalpa Barrio, Do They Fit the Escapist and Legalistic Stereotype?: An Ethnographic Investigation*, Duke–University of North Carolina Program in Latin American Studies Working Paper Series, no. 16, February, 1995.

_____. *Religious No More: Building Communities of Grace and Freedom.* Downers Grove: InterVarsity Press, 1999.

Blount, Brian K. *Cultural Interpretation: Reorienting New Testament Criticism.* Minneapolis: Fortress, 1995.

Bultmann, Rudolf. *Theology of the New Testament.* Translated by K. Grobel. 2 vols. New York: Charles Scribner's Sons, 1951-1955.

Cardenal, Ernesto. *The Gospel in Solentiname.* 4 vols. Maryknoll: Orbis, 1976-82.

Cremer, Hermann. *Die Paulinische Rechtfertigungslehre im Zusammenhang ihrer geschichtlichen Voraussetzungen.* Gütersloh: Bertelsmann, 1899.

Dahl, Nils A. "The Doctrine of Justification: Its Social Function and Implications." Pages 95-120 in *Studies in Paul*. Minneapolis: Augsburg, 1977.

Dunn, J. D. G. "The New Perspective on Paul." *Bulletin of the John Rylands Library* 65 (1983): 95-122.

_____. "The Justice of God: A Renewed Perspective on Justification by Faith." *Journal of Theological Studies* 43 (1992): 1-22

_____. *The Theology of Paul the Apostle.* Grand Rapids: Eerdmans, 1998.

Fowl, Stephen E. and L. Gregory Jones. *Reading in Communion: Scripture and Ethics in Christian Life*. Grand Rapids: Eerdmans, 1991.

Grenholm, Cristina and Daniel Patte. "Overture: Receptions, Critical Interpretations, and Scriptural Criticism." Pages 1-54 in *Reading Israel in Romans*. Edited by C. Grenholm and D. Patte. Romans Through History and Culture Series 1. Harrisburg: Trinity Press International, 2000.

Hays, Richard B. "Psalm 143 and the Logic of Romans 3." *Journal of Biblical Literature* 99 (1980): 107-115.

_____. *Echoes of Scripture in the Letters of Paul*. New Haven: Yale University Press, 1989.

_____. "Justification." *The Anchor Bible Dictionary*, 3:1129-33. Edited by D. N. Freedman. New York: Doubleday, 1992.

Jay, Nancy. *Throughout Your Generations Forever: Sacrifice, Religion, and Paternity*. Chicago: University of Chicago Press, 1992.

Jenson, Robert. "The Religious Power of Scripture." *Scottish Journal of Theology* 52 (1999): 89-105.

Käsemann, Ernst. "The Righteousness of God in Paul" Pages 168-82 in *New Testament Questions of Today*. Philadelphia: Fortress, 1969.

_____. "Justification and Salvation History in the Epistle to the Romans." Pages 60-78 in *Perspectives on Paul*. Philadelphia: Fortress, 1971.

Levenson, Jon D. *The Hebrew Bible, the Old Testament, and Historical Criticism: Jews and Christians in Biblical Studies*. Louisville: Westminster/John Knox, 1993.

McGinn, Sheila E. "Feminist Approaches to Romans: Rom 8:18-23 as a Case Study." Paper presented at the Romans through History and Cultures Seminar, Society of Biblical Literature Annual Meeting, 2000.

Meeks, Wayne A. "A Hermeneutics of Social Embodiment." *Harvard Theological Review* 79 (1986): 176-86.

The Oxford Spanish Dictionary. Oxford: Oxford University Press, 1994.

Patte, Daniel. *The Challenge of Discipleship*. Harrisburg: Trinity Press International, 1999.

Sanders, E. P. *Paul and Palestinian Judaism*. Philadelphia: Fortress, 1977.

_____. *Paul, the Law, and the Jewish People*. Minneapolis: Fortress, 1983.

Seitz, Christopher. *Word Without End: The Old Testament as Abiding Theological Witness*. Grand Rapids: Eerdmans, 1998.

Slade, Stanley. "Popular Spirituality as an Oppressive Reality." Pages 135-49 in *New Face of the Church in Latin America.* Edited by Guillermo Cook. Maryknoll: Orbis, 1994.

Tamez, Elsa. *The Amnesty of Grace: Justification by Faith from a Latin American Perspective.* Translated by Sharon Ringe. Nashville: Abingdon, 1993.

Wagner, J. Ross. *Heralds of the Good News: Paul and Isaiah "In Concert" in the Letter to the Romans.* Leiden: Brill, 2002. Reprinted, New York: Brill, 2003.

West, Gerald O. *The Academy of the Poor: Towards a Dialogical Reading of the Bible.* Interventions 2. Sheffield: Sheffield Academic, 1999.

Williams, Sam K. "The 'Righteousness of God' in Romans." *Journal of Biblical Literature* 99 (1980): 241-90.

Wright, N. T. *The New Testament and the People of God.* Minneapolis: Fortress Press, 1992.

A Radical and Holistic Reading

A Response to Baker and Wagner,
" 'The Righteousness of God'
and Hurricane Mitch"

James D. G. Dunn

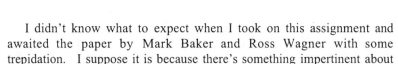

I didn't know what to expect when I took on this assignment and awaited the paper by Mark Baker and Ross Wagner with some trepidation. I suppose it is because there's something impertinent about an outsider to such a disaster, like me, trying to offer a theological rationale to those who have suffered from it. If called upon to make theological sense of hurricane Mitch to the Hondurans I would have to listen long and hard before I ventured to say anything at all.

When the paper arrived, my first reaction was one of relief, relief that it was not a case of non-Hondurans coming along and trying to provide poor Honduran Christians with some biblical sticks and theological sheets to patch their shattered faith. My second reaction was one of admiration at the way the Amor Fe y Vida Church members, who had themselves suffered severely from the hurricane, were handling the disaster theologically.

I confess also to be excited by the fact that they found "the righteousness of God" such a positive theologoumenon in their attempt to understand what had happened theologically. If I have grasped the history of the Amor Fe y Vida church aright, they had already parted from the more established evangelical churches of the region because the latter understood the gospel in too individualistic and legalistic terms. The Amor Fe y Vida leaders had already concluded that the gospel was more holistic, with horizontal and social ramifications as well as vertical and spiritual ones. They were already turning away from the image of God as one who stood at the top of the social pyramid enforcing his law rigorously on all those at the bottom of the pile. In other words, they had already made Luther's discovery that "the righteousness of God" is not to be understood primarily in terms of an angry God punishing those who offend him. But they had made that discovery in social terms and not simply in terms of personal salvation.

133

If I have that right, it means that the Amor Fe y Vida leaders had already made the breakthrough of understanding "righteousness/justice" in relational terms and "the righteousness of God" in terms of concern for the poor. Personally I don't attribute the grasp of righteousness as a relational term to "the new perspective on Paul"; it is an insight with much deeper and longer roots; Hermann Cremer's *Die paulinische Rechtfertigungslehre im Zusammenhange ihrer geschichtlichen Voraussetizungen* (^{2}1900) is usually given prime credit. And in some disagreement with Ross Wagner, I would remind him that an emphasis on a creational dimension of God's righteousness is particularly associated with the work of Ernst Käsemann and Peter Stuhlmacher on the subject: God's righteousness denoting his faithfulness as the Creator to his creation. It may be truer, however, to say that "the new perspective" has helped to liberate the social, national and racial dimensions of Cremer's insight into righteousness as relational in character. But if that is the case, then I would have been very interested to hear more about how the Hondurans had first arrived at that insight, since it seems to have been that prior insight which enabled them to read Romans in such a positive way in relation to hurricane Mitch.

Their reading of Romans 1 is not particularly highlighted in the paper, but seems to underlie their attempt to correlate "the justice of God" with hurricane Mitch—the understanding that God "allows"/"permits" human sin to work out its consequences. Paul did not consider natural disasters in his indictment of Rom 1:18-32, but we should not think of the sins he does indict—idolatry and inappropriate sexual activity—as lacking in social dimensions. And his final examples in Rom 1:28-31 can certainly be characterized in terms of society gone wrong—"jealousy, murder, rivalry, deceit, spite, rumour-mongers, slanderers . . . senseless, faithless, loveless, merciless" (1:29-31). When Romans 8 is also taken into consideration, the portrayal of creation as subject to futility and decay can be fitted into the Rom 1:18-32 schema without difficulty—the extent to which natural disasters are one of the consequences of irresponsible stewardship of the natural world. The significant feature is the very different corollary which can be drawn. The portrayal of God as one who punishes sin with natural disasters evokes the picture of a frightening God who needs to be appeased by repentance and a more strictly ruled personal conduct—as presumably in the larger evangelical churches of the region. The portrayal of God as one who has created a moral universe, where human freedom to sin includes the unrestricted outworkings of the consequences of human greed, encourages rather a concern to identify social sin as sin, to limit its effects and to help those suffering from its consequences - that is, a politically activist agenda and not simply a personal spiritual discipline. Such a reading, it seems to me, makes much better sense of an understanding of God's justice in Romans as it bifurcates into God's wrath on the one hand and into his saving righteousness on the other.

The new element which seems to have come in through the Amor Fe y Vida church's re-reading of Romans is that of God's righteousness as covenant faithfulness. This again is Luther's insight—that God's righteousness draws the sinner back to himself, not simply demands the sinner's punishment. But it is Luther tweaked by the new perspective to bring out the national and social dimensions of righteousness as faithfulness. The concept of God's faithfulness to those he has chosen has, of course, other corollaries which pose equally hard questions of theodicy - particularly, what about the justice of God in regard to those he has not chosen. It would have been good, had it been appropriate, to listen in to how the Amor Fe y Vida Christians handle Romans 9-11. But at least the concept of God's faithfulness enables a more positive theological response to disaster than that of the angry God administering punishment. For the history of the people of God is littered with disasters, and the affirmation of God's continuing faithfulness to his people, despite their sin and failures, can provide a tremendous assurance and reinvigoration to faith under threat. Such assurance can of course be misplaced, as Romans 2 reminds us; here again it would have been interesting to hear how the Honduran Christians handle that chapter. And the question of whether assurance of God's faithfulness is sufficient to cope with a disaster like the Holocaust is, once again, a question which only those who have experienced the Holocaust can answer. But at least in the case of hurricane Mitch it is both humbling and heartening to see how positively constructive the understanding of God's righteousness as coterminous with his faithfulness has been for the Amor Fe y Vida church members.

Ross Wagner also notes that the Honduran Christians had not picked up on another aspect of the new perspective—on Jewish/Christian relations. As he points out, this is hardly surprising in view of the lack of Jewish presence in Honduras. But it reminds us that the Holocaust is a particularly European issue. It has impacted on European theology and the theology of the traditional denominations because it made us conscious of the dark strand of anti-semitism which runs through European church history. In recoiling against the legalistic stereotype of Judaism which had so besmirched our history and misled our exegesis of the New Testament, we rediscovered dimensions of justification by faith which had been lost to sight. What is interesting for me is that the Hondurans seem to have perceived these dimensions of God's righteousness without the stimulus of the Holocaust. In consequence, they may have missed out on the corollaries for Jewish/Christian relations. But their recognition that God's righteousness includes his concern for the poor is derived directly from Christianity's Jewish heritage in the scriptures of Israel (the Old Testament). So we could say that the new perspective insight, that Israel's identity feeds into and is integral to Christianity's identity, is implicit. Still, it would be interesting to see how Amor Fe y Vida handle the idea of the Christian Old Testament as Jewish scripture.

Another question which came to mind was how the Hondurans handle those scriptures which seem to envisage natural disasters as willed by God and used by God to discipline or punish his people. We need only think, for example, of the plagues of Egypt (Exo 7-10), or the fiery serpents in the wilderness (Num 21), or the droughts and pestilence of which Amos 4 speaks, not to mention the fearful visions of Revelation 9. Now of course, the Baker-Wagner project was a limited one, and fascinating enough in itself, without expecting the Amor Fe y Vida church leaders to wrestle with all the issues thrown up by New Testament theology. But it does remind us that there are further dimensions to the subject of God's righteousness as presented in the biblical tradition, and that we must beware lest the new perspective become as blind as the old to important facets of that witness.

One last issue was whether a more radical reading of Romans would have provided any further insight or inspiration for the Hondurans. I have in mind John Draper's edition of Bishop Colenso's treatment of Romans in 19th century Natal. In that, if I recall aright, Colenso read the Jew/Greek dialectic of the letter in terms of the situation of his own day—the British colonial power represented by the "Jew," the Zulus by the Greeks. Apart from its shock value, the treatment raises the central hermeneutical issue of the extent to which there are repeating patterns of relationships between a traditional society which sees itself as superior and a local society marginalized by the system controlled by the superior. And whether Paul's indictment of Jew first but also Greek can be transposed to such other situations in other periods and places.

My final thought is one of renewed admiration for the way the Honduran Christians have been open to the text of Paul's letter to Rome, to hear it as God's Word addressed to them, to be instructed by it, and to draw from it encouragement in the face of disaster and practical action in the face of the indifference of the powerful.

– F O U R –

Repudiating Assimilation in Reading Romans 9-11

A Latino Theologian
Locates His Cultural-Religious Hybridity

Juan Escarfuller

———— ◆ ————

Introduction: Interpretive Strategy

C I construct this interpretation of Romans 9-11 from my social location as a flesh-and-blood reader in conversation with a framework of hermeneutical, analytical, and contextual choices from scriptural criticism.[1] **H** I argue critically and responsibly in favor of my choices within that framework: critically, because I account for the process leading to my concluding interpretation, and responsibly, because I acknowledge the viability of choices different than mine. If others have no choice, then I have no choice and cannot meaningfully claim, "*Creo* ("I" believe)." Such a claim is of paramount importance as I interpret for the sake of particular Christian believers in a present-day flesh-and-blood social location.

C What is that social location? I am a hybrid across place and time: a *dominicano* (Dominican) born in Santo Domingo during the tumult of 1968, an immigrant to the United States since 1975, a "cradle" Catholic with an experience of *iglesia* (church) affected by the Second Vatican Council and the CELAM meeting in Medellín, by the Cuban and Nicaraguan revolutions, by the witness of Father Camilo Torres and Mons. Oscar Romero, among thousands of contemporary Catholic martyrs across the Americas inspired to make a radical, material

———————————

C Contextual frame of the social location.

H Critical hermeneutics.

C Social location of the author.

difference through social change on behalf of oppressed multitudes. At the same time, I am part of an experience of *iglesia* incorporating the hegemonic strategies of dominant groups in order to use institutional church weight against social change. I belong to a church in the Americas which since before the arrival of the *conquistadores* has worked hand in hand with imperial-military powers to provide stability for landowners and other owner groups. With eyes that flinch, I have gained more and more awareness that the history of the expansion of Christianity in the Americas is connected to the history of the occupation of the Americas through the expansion of Euro-centric empires—from those of the Spanish, Portuguese, French and British crowns to the present one of the United States—with the yoke of an all-consuming social organization whose prime purpose is to fatten the bank accounts of a minority.

C In such mixing, at times I am a chameleon; at times a scorpion. As a chameleon, I am the "happy native" who follows the script of a dominating culture: "Tell me who you say that I am that I may show you such colors." As a scorpion, I sting back with what seems to me as subversion of the same script: "Tell me who you say that I am that I may be the opposite." I associate the chameleon with my experiences of assimilation—as in "Speak English, not Spanish!"—and the scorpion with nativism—as in "Get out of the United States; go back to your own kind!" However, I seek to identify myself beyond a chameleon or a scorpion for I see the assimilationist-nativist dichotomy to be an expression of the same logic of hegemony which repudiates hybridity and remains obsessed, transfixed, and bound in either case with the totalizing script of the dominant culture. I see the self-hatred, loss of self and negation of responsibility common to either identity. I see the script as a script and as a knowing one at that in the politics of identity—"You had better know it or else!" Or else what? My conviction is that the conscious repudiation of the assimilation-nativism dichotomy is best for a Latina/o[2] academic professional who, confronted with euphemistic/ pejorative, shifting/shifty, messy/stained, mixed/impure hybrid cultural labels, seeks to articulate something other than cultural hegemony. Because the colonizing discourse on minoritized groups suppresses the contradictions and promises created by cultural hybridity and power asymmetries within those groups, critiquing the logic of hegemony in such a discourse is a liberating act for a hybrid Latina/o theologian.

A What does Paul have to say regarding assimilation-nativism in Romans? As a believer in a United States Catholic Latina/o community

---

C Complex contextual frame.

A Paul on assimilation-nativism.

turning to biblical preaching inside and outside the walls of Sunday Eucharistic worship, I care about how Paul is interpreted in my hybrid life-context. Where do I read the chameleon in Romans? I choose to focus on the assimilating chameleon for I am privileged educationally and economically as a Latino in the New Testament doctoral program at Vanderbilt University. **C H** As such, I find myself exerting effort to "fit in" so that I can remain in prestigious halls of power in the United States. Indeed, I am no stranger to reading Paul in terms of polemics between groups vying for prominence before the imperial backdrop of the *Pax Romana*. How do I read Romans in terms of the assimilation of voices like mine both targeted and privileged? More specifically, how do I engage in the social struggle for liberation if I myself as a Latino academic professional theologian am in the colonizing chains of intellectual assimilation? **C** My interpretation of Romans 9-11 in response to these questions reveals my struggle against assimilation and provides strategies for addressing issues of knowing in the politics of identity within my life-context. The journey to my chosen interpretation proceeds as follows: I detail intellectual and socio-historical commitments from my experiences of cultural and religious hybridity; then, I draw from three interpretive traditions of reading Romans; and I conclude by taking a stance regarding the tradition with which I choose to construct my interpretation.

Social Commitments

C Taking seriously the complexity and on-going development of my hybrid cultural identity, I present four perspectives of reality to which I am committed and from which I choose to launch my interpretation of Romans: postmodernism, postcolonialism, Latina/o religious hybridity, and assimilation by Latina/o academic elites.

Postmodernism

C H Living between distinct worlds, languages, times and centers, I am committed, to paraphrase Segovia, to the postmodernist sense of diversity by which I mean that there is no truth outside a perspective and that one among many perspectives or lenses for truth is the

---

C H Interplay between context and hermeneutics for the author.

C Cultural concerns of the author.

C Social commitments.

C H Postmodernism and author's hermeneutic.

sociohistorical and sociocultural grounding of myself.[3] I thus foreground my lived reality across cultures as a valuable life-context for interpretation. Rather than as a sharply demarcated, self-contained, homogeneous, and integrated whole, culture in my postmodern experience is "a ground of contest in relations" and a historically evolving, fragmented, inconsistent, conflicted, constructed, ever-shifting, malleable and permeable social reality.[4]

C In this contest of relations the role of power in the shaping of cultural identity has importance. This role is mostly eclipsed in modern concepts of culture which tend to regard culture as a "given" to be discovered by the anthropologist or as an innocent set of conventions by which many diverse individual parts can function as an orderly whole. I tend to regard culture as a reality of *lucha* (struggle) in which the colonizers, the powerful, the wealthy, the well-fed, the victors, the dominant obliterate the beliefs and values of the colonized, the weak, the poor, the starving, the vanquished, the subjugated. The role of power is, as Foucault has argued, central in the formation of knowledge and hence identity.[5] In the formation of cultural identity the role of power is even more extensive, since culture is inscribed by groups of people with conflicting interests, and the winners dictate their cultural terms to the losers.

Postcolonialism

C H The issues of power and empire in the Americas leads me to claim postcolonialism as part of my life-context, the sense of postcolonialism, as defined by Said, seeking to raise awareness that the categories of knowledge and meaning through which colonizing Western nations seek to analyze and understand other cultures are primarily acts of Western imperial cultural construction in which acts of representation and the exercise of power are "inextricably conjoined."[6] Hence, it is impossible to divorce culture, a powerful source of identity, from the relations of intercultural domination in my context. My commitment as a reader of established Euro-centric interpretations of texts/cultures is not only to unmask their imperialism but also to draw out my voice among those who have been elided, silenced and marginalized in these interpretations.

To this postcolonial context I add the important nuance to "culture" articulated by Bhabha. For him, culture is not something pre-existent to be irenically transmitted, but a "third space" to be constructed amid the struggle for survival, between the self and other, beyond colonizer and

---

C Power in shaping cultural identity.

C H Postcolonialism and author's hermeneutic.

colonized. Bhabha locates such contrarian identities in the same individual or group: we are all colonizers and colonized insofar as we are both drawn to and repulsed by imperial promises. This "third space" is always fragmentary, conflictive and multiple. It is characterized by a "double vision" acquired by the marginalized and immigrants: an awareness of both the promises of the encounter between the imperial and the local cultures and their contradictions.[7]

Latina/o Religious Hybridity

C In keeping with my postmodern deconstruction of universal, neutral interpretations and reconstruction of truth as a function of particular interests, I present here a particular, socially interested religious experience as a reflection of another commitment I bear as a biblical interpreter in the church and in the academy: the commitment to nurture the growing religious hybridity among my community of Latinas/os. In my recent pastoral religious experience as Director of Hispanic Ministry for the Roman Catholic Archdiocese of Saint Louis, Missouri, I attended a number of midweek worship services organized by Spanish-speaking Latin American evangelical preachers in the inner-city of Saint Louis in order to nourish myself with preaching experiences inculturated to my everyday Latina/o reality in addition to the preachings in Catholic worship on Sundays. Most of the "regular" congregation, numbering around one hundred, were Latinas/os whom I saw on Sundays in Catholic churches for *misa* (Mass) in Spanish. I find tremendous resonance between this experience and one cited by Espinosa with reference to a Latino pastor plying his ministry at weekday services for Latinas/os:

> 'We preach the Truth' pastor Pedro Romo thundered to his emotionally spent audience one hot Friday night in southern California. 'We will take you to the Truth . . . because we have the Light!' Romo, like so many other Latin American evangelists, offers 'Truth' and 'Light' in what he believes is a hopelessly confusing and dark world. He sells *his church* as the one that offers the wayward traveler and desert immigrant hope in this life and in the life to come. Refusing to be bound by any creed other than his own, he held up his church as the Ark that contains the remnant of God's faithful. As he stated in his preachings, he was not Evangelical, Protestant, or Catholic; he was simply a 'Christian.' After attending his services I walked away with the

---

C Latina/o religious identity.

distinct impression that he did not want to be bound by any walls that might tarnish his image and standing in the Latino community. By eschewing traditional denominationalism and the confines of religious orthodoxy (he taught that God created the world on the third day) he could create his own distinctive yet inclusive message that would enable him to cast his evangelistic and marketing net much broader than many of his religious colleagues.[8]

C My experience echoed in Espinosa's experience with Romo is not unique. Romo's inroads into the Latino/a community in the United States represents a trend toward denominational pluralism that is challenging the Catholic Church's dominance of the Latina/o religious marketplace in the United States. I foreground two relevant findings from a demographic study published this year, *Hispanic Churches in American Public Life*, (hereafter "HCAPL") which ground that trend and which I claim as part of my social location for reading Romans: (1) the growth in the number of Roman Catholics in the United States from the increasing number of Latinas/os, and (2) the Pentecostalization of Latina/o Catholicism in the United States largely from the growth of the Latina/o Protestant and Catholic Charismatic movement in the United States.[9]

C The United States Census of 2000 reported that the Latina/o population increased by 58 percent between 1990 and 2000, reaching 35.3 million and on track to surpass the African-American community (36.4 million in 2000) as the largest minority group in the United States by 2005.[10] HCAPL finds that the number of Roman Catholic Latinas/os is increasing as the overall percentage of Latinas/os who identify as Roman Catholic has remained fairly constant at 70 percent over the past thirty years (almost 25 million in 2002).[11] The apparently stable proportion percentage-wise and growth number-wise, according to this study, is largely due to the significant influx of Catholics into the United States from Latin America and especially from Mexico, which has the highest rate of Catholics among all Latin American countries. The relatively high overall percentage of Catholics is also attributed to the creative work of a growing number of liberationist and activist Latino priests, Catholic youth programs, social programs geared toward the need of the poor and immigrants, increased lay participation, and the growth in the Pentecostal/Catholic Charismatic movement.

C Espinosa's experience.

C Latina/o population in the USA.

C The last point underscores the second finding to which I draw attention: the growth of the Latina/o Catholic Charismatic movement from, and its increasing re-association with, the growing Latina/o Pentecostal Charismatic movement in the United States. The Latina/o Protestant and Catholic Charismatic movement has grown from just a handful of Mexicans at the Pentecostal Azusa Street Revival in 1906 in Los Angeles to more than 150 million men, women and children throughout Latin America (141 million) and the United States (9.2 million) in 2002.[12] HCAPL found that of all U.S. Latinas/os 3.8 million identified as Pentecostal Charismatic and 5.4 million as Catholic Charismatic; that is a total of one in four Latinas/os identifying as Charismatic, and those numbers and percentages have been increasing over the last fourteen years.[13]

Although the Catholic Charismatic movement is an outgrowth of the Protestant Pentecostal movement, I am not concluding that it has simply brought Protestant Pentecostalism into Latina/o Charismatic Catholicism. Catholic Charismatic groups present their beliefs in light of traditional Catholic teachings.   But increasing Catholic hybridization with Pentecostal Charismatic movements is attested to in the literature and in my pastoral religious ministry experience in Saint Louis.[14] Moreover, the Catholic hierarchy has stressed that the Catholic Charismatic renewal must remain under clerical control because it has been too lay driven and interactive with Pentecostals. As Hallum writes,

> The Pope sought more control over the charismatic movement by moving the World Catholic Charismatic Headquarters from Belgium to the Vatican.   He also appointed "shepherd" coordinators for different countries to direct the local movement. The charismatic meetings and crusades especially among Latin American immigrants in the United States were instructed not to allow Protestant speakers and to demonstrate loyalty to Catholic doctrines by singing songs to Mary and the saints. Ironically the Vatican's response to the charismatic groups is similar to its response to Latin America's Christian base communities—initial support, developing ambivalence, and attempts to reassert control.[15]

C From those religious trends in my social location, I see two issues: the disestablishment of Roman Catholicism as the defining cultural ethos of Latinas/os and the re-Christianization of United States society with the

---

C Latina/o Catholic Charismatic movement.

C Cultural ethos.

increase in numbers and Charismatic movements across denominations.
C H The impact of such trends on my reading of the Bible follows: I
read for issues of hegemony, the dominance or disestablishment of one
religious movement over another in light of the religious pluralism or
hybridity in which I live. Furthermore, these issues are not merely of
concern for Latinas/os or for religious-minded groups. HCAPL surveyed
responses to questions of social and political debates in order to gauge
trends of social and political engagement in the "quiet revolution" of the
Latina/o demographic boom in the United States. The authors of the
survey note,

> Democrats and Republicans have good reason to court the Latino
> vote. We found that Latinos tend to be morally and ethically
> conservative but politically and economically liberal. Thus each
> party can make the claim that they represent the Latino
> community. With some notable exceptions, Latino Catholics and
> Protestants shared similar educational, moral and political
> opinions. For this reason Latino Catholics and Protestants may be
> able to join forces in American public life on key educational,
> moral and political issues, while at the same time respecting and
> not having to water down their own unique theological differences
> and traditions.[16]

My cultural-religious location is a harbinger of potentially significant
change in the formation of challenging and surprising new hybrid
political coalitions in my social landscape.

Assimilation by Latina/o Academic Elites

C I add another piece of cultural study which further locates the life-
context woven above through my academic and ecclesial experiences:
the threat of assimilation by Latina/o professional theologians. This
threat of assimilation is Bhabha's fragmented space between the
universal and the local. It comes from the uncertainty and violence
experienced by a United States-*dominicano* hybrid like myself located in
both United States and Latin American societies which reject any mixed
version of themselves with the pejorative labels "impure" or "half-
breed." This is the case, for example, when *dominicanas/os* and so-called
"Americans" dismiss United States-reared *dominicanos* like myself, the
former calling me "*gringo*" or "Dominican-York"[17] and the latter also
mistakenly labeling me as "Mexican." Moreover, I have found myself
minoritized in United States Latina/o communities whose majority is

---

C H Cultural factors influencing one's interpretation.

C Life context.

(culturally, idiomatically, religiously, geographically) *mexicana/o* and prefers monolingual communication in Spanish.

Within this life-context of multiple identifications and dismissals, there is a "politically/economically-correct" identity claimed increasingly by bilingual, United States-reared and college-educated persons like myself: Latina/o. However, as such an identity is born of rejection from "pure" spaces or categories, it serves as an adaptation to dominant spaces or categories by negating my cultural and historical particularities. When I use the "Latino" label for myself, I am aware that I thus suppress my *dominicano*-United States particularity in the name of methodological expediency and assimilation into a modern United States academic and social culture which creates the abstract individual citizen and negates the hermeneutical self-understanding of specific ethnic groups in the name of maintaining the rules of a universal, neutral scientific method. **C** Why do I suppress my own hybridity for the sake of the universal? Is such assimilation the inevitable thrust of my identity politics in my struggle for recognition, for a pass to the great game of "the pure"?

Especially now that Latinos/as are building a critical self-interested mass in academic and church leadership in the United States, arriving at boards organized with funds, networks and other expressions of power, I see clearly that my scholarly discourse here has a particular social investment and interest in the world of the Latina/o professional intellectual which I engage in my reading here. As I play a role in the construction of my analysis, I find myself once again with a hybrid identity full of promise and contradiction. On the one hand, as intellectuals Latinas/os are situated in a dominant position among a dominated people; but, on the other hand, as Latinas/os we are situated in a marginalized position in an academic world dominated demographically and intellectually by the Euro-centric claims of empires of old and present.

H Not surprisingly then, I see myself as an elite susceptible to assimilation via an academic career. Specifically and materially as a Latino theologian, I relate to the real, living suffering of Latinas/os. From such suffering I withdraw, among other things, a currency of abstraction with which I enrich myself in as much as the academy and church recognize my ability as a biblical interpreter to engage in abstract discourses based on real, material suffering. Moreover, I agree with Althaus-Reid's assessment of the price of such abstraction:

C Critical reflection of one's context.

H Latina/o theologian.

The [theological discourse] process gives value to human suffering as merchandise, objectified as an abstract commodity and sold for a price: the continuation of oppressive political systems in alliance with ecclesiastical ones. Meanwhile, suffering becomes ontologically and theologically devalued. The richer the theologian grows as a person by the world's recognition of her ability, the poorer become those whose experience of suffering is the subject of reflection.[18]

With the professional development of my abstraction power comes promotion and gain. My gain is access to a members-only glut of resources off-limits to the overwhelming majority of Latinas/os and other peoples of the world in the *lucha* for subsistence.[19]

C Given the Latin American and now Latina/o experience of centuries-long colonial exploitation by Euro-centric powers in the past and presently under the economic, political, military, and cultural domination of the United States as the only surviving superpower, I realize as an elite I am in cahoots with hegemonic powers and so have much to lose from being "liberated" from dominant intellectual and material systems. I see the temptation to eclipse the question of power even though such would distance my theologizing from the everyday struggles of my economically, culturally, and politically dominated United States Latina/o reality. In fact, more than a temptation, it is a reality already. The majority of Latinos/as are much poorer and less educationally certified than myself.[20] Leaving my home country, family, church and neighborhood—bracketing them and laying such aside—allowed me to successfully navigate post-secondary educational "Ivy" institutions, the bedrock of my intellectual and economic credentials. Thus, my assimilationist tendency is contradictory and self-negating: I make the move to blend in because of an awareness of interest and power and their relation to my particularity, and yet in doing so I also collude in silencing my and others' questions of interests and power and particularity.

Having detailed my postmodern, postcolonial, religiously hybrid and academically assimilating social commitments which impact my biblical moorings, questions and quests, I now turn to reading Romans and other readers of Romans in order to construct my own interpretation in dialogue with the world in which I live as a flesh-and-blood reader. For the following section I opt to engage a socially located interpretive lens regarding traditional readings of Romans, a lens which resonates with my own critical interest in provoking a dialogue between established

---

C Latin American culture and colonial culture.

interpretations and those historically at the margins of academic and ecclesial institutions.

Different Viable Choices for Romans 9-11

C A H Marking further my interpretation as particular and hybrid one, I choose to engage the description of three interpretive "families" in the history of interpretations on Romans as presented by Patte in his commentary on Romans in the *Global Bible Commentary.* Patte presents the history of interpretations in terms of hermeneutical, analytical and contextual choices of scriptural criticism made within each interpretive "family":

> Forensic interpretations (often supported by "Lutheran" scholars) use philological historical-critical approaches to elucidate the theological argument of the letter—an argument that provides "forensic" evidence for the justification of the guilty (sinners) before God, the righteous judge, and through faith in Christ.
>
> New Covenant interpretations—also know as those of the "New Perspective" developed after World War II, depart from the preceding by using a combination of rhetorical and socio-historical analyses to read the letter as a discourse through which Paul seeks to convince his readers to change behavior, especially in Jewish-gentile relationships. Through Christ's faithfulness, the Gentiles are now in a covenantal relationship with God similar to that of the Jews.
>
> Apocalyptic Gospel interpretations start with a more pessi-mistic post-Word War II outlook, use methods of history of religions and structural studies to clarify the religious experience and symbolic world presupposed by the letter and characterized by convictions about the Gospel as the power of God for salvation from apocalyptic powers. In Christ and Christ-like people (from Abraham to "the body of Christ"), through resurrection-like interventions God defeats the powers of sin, death, and other evil.[21]

Patte further relates these three interpretive perspectives to "ways the text affects its readers/hearers" in terms of what such readers lack and

---

C A H Global biblical interpretation that makes use of the three frames.

listen for in Paul's communication: respectively, knowledge, will, power. As Patte comments succinctly,

> [Forensic] Paul conveyed to the Romans certain kinds of information—a theological knowledge—about the gospel he proclaimed;
> [New Perspective] he attempted to convince them—tried to establish their will—to do certain things, including to change their behavior toward each other in their community and to support his mission to Spain;
> and [Apocalyptic] he empowered his readers by sharing with them his deepest convictions concerning God's power manifested in Christ, in the gospel, and in the believers' lives.[22]

C H Among such distinctive interpretive perspectives and communication foci with Romans, I seek my own response to how I as a hybrid Latino academic theologian best repudiate assimilation. I choose to situate myself among those perspectives conscious and wary of the Euro-centric basis for this schematic analysis. Patte takes responsibility for his structuring interpretive practices in terms of hermeneutical, analytical, and contextual choices as he explicitly situates this structure in the particular social location from which he writes his commentary on Romans: a post-World War II, French Huguenot theologian coming to terms with how Christians in the name of their religious beliefs and biblical interpretations were complicit in the horrific rise of the Holocaust. He aims his commentary toward making the case that religion could instead serve to resist such legitimation of the Holocaust by means of a distinctly ethical interpretation of Romans. I engage Patte's schema with ambivalence. I proceed conscious of the Euro-centric elite academic context within which I do my present study and wary of the long history of totalizing, colonizing projects full of missionary urges rising out of that context.

    A H I focus the conversation on repudiating assimilation within Romans 9-11 because between my reading and those of others, I find two points of common ground on which to compare and contrast our readings: (1) Those chapters form a distinct section in Romans directly addressing tensions between two culturally and religiously distinct (albeit related) groups, namely, Israelites and Gentiles, within the context of Roman imperial rule, and (2) The tensions bespeak of one group over another in terms of arrogance, dominance, and treatment by God (9:4-6;

C H Latino interpretation and cultural context.

A H Interpretation of assimilation within Romans 9-11.

11:18, 25). Such a text, then, appears to be fertile ground for a critique of the logic of hegemony I hope to elicit as a hybrid Latino academic theologian. I now proceed to elucidate, within the frame of the three interpretive perspectives, the different hermeneutical (theological), analytical (textual) and contextual choices grounded in Romans 9-11 in response to my concern for repudiating assimilation in a hybrid cultural life-context.

"Forensic" Choices

I In this section I explore the perspective that assimilation is due to a lack of knowledge in terms of theological themes, textual choices and the presupposed particular context in which this text meets the particular needs of particular believers. I draw on Stuhlmacher's commentary on Romans to ground this perspective in the letter's chapters 9-11. In keeping with the historical-critical hermeneutical basis for this perspective, Stuhlmacher frames the meaning of Romans 9-11 in terms of the historical context behind Paul's letter to the Romans: a Pauline-Petrine dichotomy regarding "works of the Law," observance of practices prescribed for Jews by the Torah, which created among other things a crisis of authority and identity in the early church movement.[23]

C Stuhlmacher surmises that the author of the letter to the Romans is the elder Paul now victorious yet apologetic toward those conversant if not also practicing in the rituals of Judaism. Significantly, Stuhlmacher includes in that Jewish context of his historical reconstruction Rome's Jewish Christians, whom he argues were likely and largely from the devout group of "God-fearers" on the edges of Rome's synagogues. As a result, according to Stuhlmacher, Paul has to contend with his reputation for being an apostate Jew bearing a false teaching in front of a Roman Gentile Christian audience hybridized with Jewish sensibilities.[24]

With this apologetics frame in mind, Stuhlmacher entitles his comments on Romans 9-11, "The Righteousness of God for Israel," and develops his analysis between two counterbalanced theological themes: (1) The gracious acts of God—God's free election (9:6-13), God's free mercy (9:14-29), God in Christ (9:30-10:21), God's mystery of salvation for all (11:25-32)—and (2) Israel's rebellion against such acts (for now)—lament for Israel (9:1-5), Israel's taking offense (9:30-33), Israel's failure to recognize the righteousness of God (10:1-13), Israel's disobedience to the Gospel (10:14-21), and Israel's temporal hardening against God (11:11-24).[25]

I Three frames used.

C Stuhlmacher's interpretation.

The two explicitly positive remarks about Israel having "the chosen remnant" (11:1-10) and being assured of "the salvation of all Israel" (11:25-32) come at the end of the section and are hedged with mystery: Who exactly are the remnant and how is that plan of salvation to be realized exactly? No details are forthcoming other than that it is a mystery assured of success by God's free mercy (11:25). This serves to highlight the climax of Romans 9-11 according to Stuhlmacher's analysis expressing the basis for Paul's claim that his teaching is true: a hymn of praise for the mysterious way of God (11:33-36) whose very mystery relieves the cognitive tension about Paul's relationship to the Jewish matrix of early Christianity.

C The thrust of the apologetic according to Stuhlmacher is aimed at imparting theological knowledge to a Gentile-Jewish hybrid community, knowledge about (1) why large parts of Judaism found suspicious and ultimately rejected Paul's doctrine of justification based on grace rather than on the basis of works (11:6) and (2) why God's free mercy and election will bear fruit for Israel nevertheless.[26] Paul wants to assure that "his" gospel teaching does not result in the damnation but rather in the salvation of Israel. Paul thus seeks to buttress belief in God's faithfulness in light of the promise which God gave to Israel, "an issue of far more fundamental concern than the matter of the accompanying salvation and deliverance of the Gentiles."[27]

C A Nuancing the importance of this apologetic tone and its relation to the identity and authority of Paul, the style in 9:1-3, 10:1, and 11:1 is uncharacteristically and consistently personal compared to other sections of the letter. As Paul laments "for the sake of my own people" (9:3), he claims that what happened was a problem of knowing: Israel misunderstood that God's mercy and election were given freely; but by God's design Israel's deficient knowledge of such a gift highlights that it is a gift (11:11-13), and such cognitive deficiency will be overcome through hearing the word of Christ (11:17). Thus, God is not revoking God's word of promise; Paul's mission work as the apostle to the Gentiles can be seen as "for the sake of Israel" with Paul's teaching on God's ways with Israel.[28]

C The contextual implications for this forensic perspective on Romans 9-11 are apropos for the question of how a hybrid Latina/o academic theologian may resist assimilation. The hybridity is broken down into a starkly contrasting "us vs. them" (Gentile vs. Israel) with a common frame (God's plan) presumed present yet still unknown if not

---

C Stuhlmacher's apologetic thrust.

C A Identity and authority of Paul in Stuhlmacher's interpretation.

C Contextual implications for Latina/o theologian.

misunderstood. I read that the basic need projected here for the believer is relief from cognitive dissonance. The conjoining of two very different worlds raises the questions, "Who am I in such a confusing and conflicted hybrid world?" and "What do I need to know to answer that question?" The teaching of Romans 9-11 in this perspective can plausibly be that **H** there is an unknown, mysterious metanarrative and higher canon of a common God-graced/given identity only glimpsed at dimly in our historical roots and modeled by Paul's teaching of what is true: Rest secure in that God has a plan to resolve the seeming contradictory worlds in my hybrid location.

H How do I read resistance to assimilation in this perspective? By turning to a selfless sense of self with a renewed quest for a universal, neutral re-mapping of the contemporary intellectual and socio-historical contentions about truth and authority, a re-mapping seeking to order what at present seems to be a jumble/jungle of antinomies. This quest becomes a matter of attaining an enlightenment (10:2) which orders the common zeal to choose sides in the politics of identity, even the side of not choosing. The quest is no longer about my personal, mutable experience of self: in God's plan there is a principled way out of the chameleon-scorpion dichotomy. "Let us study that plan in order to realize such principles which are neither Jewish nor Greek but timeless and universal (10:12)." Hence, the question—"What do I need to know?"—subsumes the other—"Who am I?"—with confidence that the tools found in a response to the former will provide firm ground for my ever evolving and ever hybrid labels of self which frustrate a definitive answer to the latter. **I** My reading of Stuhlmacher's historical reconstruction is that the Christian community in Rome was assisted by Paul with "their" idea of God as consistent and true (with Judaism as necessary backdrop, not foreground to justification by faith not works) rather than with "their" choice of one identity over the other as demarcated sharply in the Pauline-Petrine politics of Antioch and Jerusalem. The example of God's righteousness is the focus across changing identities of time, geography, nation and apostle. Knowing God, as distinct from Israel, is the aim of this *apologia*.

C H A Following a reconstruction of Paul's historical life-context wherein he had practical need for support and thus showed his

---

H Mysterious metanarrative.

H Resistance to assimilation for the author.

I Interplay between author's interpretation and Stuhlmacher's interpretation.

C H A Concern for Paul's historical life-context and author's context in one's interpretation.

authoritative connection with tradition through the re-appropriation of Jewish election, salvation and deliverance by God, I, as a hybrid Latino academic theologian, may quickly attend to the issue of assimilation as an important one if I am to be taken seriously and supported in the academy and church as an impartial, universal authority on the biblical canon as a lamp to the feet of the academy and the church. If I as a Latino follow the forensic reframing of the assimilation struggle as a surmountable deficiency in knowledge, I may contribute the following to the ongoing search for metanarratives: the concept of hybridity as a universalizing gift of God for a growing humanity. I suspect from my experience there are academic theological work-settings seeking such a colleague in the pursuit of an abiding "true" teaching in an increasingly relativist and secular social United States setting.

"New Perspective" Choices

H In this section I explore the perspective that assimilation is due to a lack of will in terms of theological themes, textual choices and the presupposed particular context in which this text meets the particular needs of believers. I draw particularly on the respective works of Stendahl and Gager to ground this perspective in the letter's chapters 9-11. In keeping with the literary-critical hermeneutical basis for this perspective, Stendahl and Gager frame the meaning of Romans 9-11 in terms of rhetorical strategy in Paul's letter to the Romans: an ethical concern for the relations between Gentiles and Jews.

There is historical context supposed in this perspective related to the forensic theological focus on justification by faith. However, such a focus is narrowed in "the New Perspective's" historical reconstruction. Consider Stendahl's contention, "Justification by faith was hammered out by Paul for the very specific and limited purpose of defending the rights of Gentile converts to be full and genuine heirs to the promises of God to Israel."[29] As a result, the presumed immediate historical context for the letter to the Romans is important for the development of a different choice in theological themes, textual analyses and contextual resonance with particular believers today. In the "New Perspective" of Stendahl, the immediate historical context is a well-developed Gentile Christian community distinct yet in social relationship with the Jewish community at the epicenter of Roman imperial stratification of one social group over another. Thus, the question is the relation between the two communities and "not the attitudes of the gospel versus the attitudes of the law."[30] Regarding Romans 9-11, the concern is about a sense of superiority in the Gentile community toward the Jewish community.

H Literary-critical hermeneutics.

With this backdrop in mind, Stendahl succinctly states a theologico-rhetorical theme of Romans 9-11: "Paul's reference to God's mysterious plan is an affirmation of a God-willed coexistence between Judaism and Christianity in which the missionary urge to convert Israel is held in check."[31] His analysis proceeds to highlight a more positive view (almost defense) of Israel on its own terms in order to check Gentile arrogance (11:18):

> It should be noted that Paul does not say that when the time of God's kingdom, the consummation, comes Israel will accept Jesus as the Messiah. He says only that the time will come when "all Israel will be saved" (11:26). It is stunning to note that Paul writes this whole section of Romans (10:18-11:36) without using the name of Jesus Christ. This includes the final doxology (11:33-36), the only such doxology in his writings without any christological element.[32]

Rather than the forensic focus on God's righteousness in contrast to Israel's "No", the focus here is on warning Gentile Christians against conceit. Rather than the "timeless answer [of justification by faith] to the plight and pain of the introspective conscience of the West," the human predicament specific to the hybridization of Christian communities over and against Jewish communities receives an interpretive response.[33] This "New Perspective" is not directed to a Jewish-Christian but rather to a Gentile-Christian who feels so "other" to the former in a superior way. As the most direct critique of such conceit, Stendahl and Gager consider Romans 9-11 to be the rhetorical climax of the letter in terms of Paul's knowing contribution to a community he has yet to visit.

C Gager contributes in particular a detailed analysis of how Paul follows socio-rhetorical conventions of raising reader expectations only to end with a stunning reversal of the expected argument—the most stunning of which is that whereas Gentiles depended on Jews in God's plan to bring salvation to all, now Jews depend on Gentiles to be included in that promise (11:1-33). His assessment is that forensic perspectives dismiss the seeming "contradictions and inconsistencies" of Romans 9-11 in light of Romans 1-8 (read as a denunciation of Jewish law and works) because Romans 9-11 presents Paul's most positive affirmations about the law and Israel's salvation (9:4-5, 11:1) on top of his most personal and emotional identification as a Jew (9:5). As he notes pointedly, "To conceive of Paul's representation as a Jew is

---

C Gager's interpretation.

essential for it reveals that the letter does not contrast Jews and Gentiles but Jews who represent opposing solutions to the Gentile problem."[34]

Gager deconstructs that false dichotomy—of Gentiles over and against Jews—with his analysis that 9:6-10:21 sets up the Gentile reader's expectation for an etiology of why Jews are confused regarding God's plan of salvation through Christ (9:30-33: Gentiles have attained righteousness while Israel did not fulfill "even" the law of righteousness). As he argues, the very confused reversals associated with God's ways with Jews are essentially rhetorical traps for the Gentile reader about to have the reversal of expectations in 10:21-11:36. For example, the reference to the Zion-stone placed in Israel's way (11:9) is usually read as a reference to Christ and not Torah. But in conjunction with Stendahl's analysis of reading the multiple citations of the Hebrew Testament (e.g., 9:13-17, 9:25-29, 9:33) as references to God and Israel and not Christology, Gager finds it a stunning reversal rhetorically for Gentile readers to encounter the subsequent claim in 11:11 that Israel has not fallen. The stumble over the Zion-stone only served as part of God's plan to relate Israel to the Gentile mission. Even Gager's word analysis of Christ as the *telos* (10:4) of the law in terms of goal and not termination nor cancellation adds to his interpretive pursuit of a Pauline critique of a Gentile superiority-complex that eclipses the "still very much valid and living reality" of the Jewish communities' dignity and on-going significance for God's plan for all nations.[35]

ǀ The contextual implications of this perspective are also apropos to the life-context of a hybrid Latino academic theologian looking to resist assimilation. In contrast to the introspective turn of the West regarding the heuristic basis for knowing, the "New Perspective" turn to the "other presumed to be inferior" projects a basic need for desire or will to include "the other." As a result, the questions in the face of assimilation are, "With whom do I belong? Who wants to be with me? Whom do I want to be with?" In short, in contrast to the forensic, "What do I know?" it is now "Who do I know? Who is my ally?"

I perceive these questions of a will-to-belong address the experience of status inconsistency in my life-context as a hybrid Latino academic theologian—a hybrid of membership among the dominant and the dominated, across nations (superpowers and colonies), across global and local cultures, across communities of religious belief and practice. What option is there to the chameleon-scorpion dichotomy in such seeming confusion and contradiction? There is the option of willing—acting—to build community across such divisions. It means using my privilege of having professional relationships across borders to gather a group of people of disparate ideologies and asymmetrical power to sit as "equals"

ǀ How scholars' interpretations influence a Latino interpretation.

around a common project. The resistance to assimilation herein lies in joining together what social status keeps apart.

The "New Perspective" reading of Romans 9-11 rhetorically makes present in a way unexpected to Gentile readers the contemporary reality of God's ways with Israel as still essential for the universal plan of salvation. By turning to a sense of self-stitched-with-the-other, the quest becomes one of decentering my old sense of self as essentially having to choose between being a member of one group or the other and constructing a new sense of self from a calling to respect by re-specting, seeing in a new perspective, the other. Practically for myself as a hybrid Latino academic theologian in the church and the academy, the willful response to this calling may be raising consciousness among colleagues about the need to establish multicultural ground rules for encouraging active group participation in ministry, preaching, and institutional policy-making deliberations in light of differences—e.g., cultural assumptions about communications, distance-to-power, mutual-invitation discussion models.

This ground-rules initiative assumes optimistically that everyone can partake equally in a common professional process of participation and that then they will participate. Another assumption here is an optimistic assessment of that hybrid Latino's abilities as a leader to facilitate such engagement across disparately-identified groups. Yet another assumption is that belonging to a multicultural community takes work especially on processes. The idea stirs in me that if we work hard at coming together, we will find a common ground for reconciliation across our differences. My thinking in this context could be, "It takes work to hold in myself disparate memberships; thus, I want to belong to a multicultural community that synergizes with my efforts to make it happen with others." Contextually, this hybrid Latino academic theologian may appeal to Scripture as a family album animating our embattled spirits to see connections where we thought there was none. I suspect such "animating" work entails many committee meetings in an institutional setting that values community-building activities as essential seed for the harvest of a settled, cohesive identity.

"Apocalyptic" Choices

H In this section I explore the perspective that assimilation is due to a lack of *poder* (power/ability) in terms of theological themes, textual choices and the presupposed particular context in which this text meets the particular needs of believers. I draw on my ideological reading of

---

H Revelatory hermeneutics.

Romans 9-11 and the work of others with Romans in order to present this interpretive perspective. In keeping with the revelatory hermeneutical value given to ideologies in front of the text within this perspective, I frame the meaning of Romans 9-11 in terms of an ideological reading of Paul's letter to the Romans: exposing and subverting the Roman Empire's brutal political, economic and social hegemony as cause of almost unspeakable suffering for millions. **A** In other words, Paul opposes Caesar and his Roman imperial order with the Messiah of Israel and the subversive fulfillment of God's promised deliverance to Israel by drawing all nations into that deliverance. **H** Hermeneutically I read such a critique through the lens of my currently partaking in community organizing work by Latinas/os striving to build an alternative social order to expose and subvert the hegemony of a brutal United States Empire. Whereas hermeneutically religion and geopolitics have been separated (albeit with an a posteriori relationship in a few scholarly views) in Forensic and New Perspective approaches, in the Apocalyptic approach I see them as essentially related and underlying Paul's own conflicted, hybrid relationship as a Roman citizen and a Jew within Roman imperial order.

H I organize my own apocalyptic reading around two theological themes in Romans 9-11: (1) a justice from God and (2) a politicized solidarity with the oppressed, both in the context of an unjust and alienating Roman imperial order. I glean such themes from my reading of Romans as a three-step rhetorical move: presentation of the problem—the hegemony of an inherently unjust social order (1:1-8:39), climactic response—the just response of God's universal and nationalistic solidarity with the oppressed nation of Israel (9:1-11:36), and instructions for practical, strategic witness to such dangerous yet hopeful solidarity in an unjust social order (12:1-16:15). I owe this rhetorical structuring of the text to my reading of Tamez's reframing the traditional Euro-centric justification-by-faith debates on Romans as ones fixed to a common textual analysis of 1-8 as the center (climax at chapter 8) with the rest of the letter as excursus. I find her critique convincing that such a common structuring of the textual analysis results from an *a priori* thematic choice about what justification means ever since Luther's theologizing on his sense of salvation and not what it means ever since the *Pax Romana*'s brutal infliction of so-called justice, deadly for the oppressed majority masses.[36] Hence, I structure my textual analysis with Romans 9-11 as Paul's climactic response to the brutality and conceited

---

A Paul and Caesar.

H Author's interpretation.

H Author's apocalyptic reading.

deceit of the Roman imperial order, which is expounded by contrast to God's justice in Romans 1-8 and further characterized in terms of strategic response by the Christian community in Romans 12-16. Hermeneutically, my experience with biblical criticism has often left me with a fragmented, isolating sense of text—abstracting a particular from the whole without reference back to the whole. It is engaging for me here to break out of that solipsistic experience of dealing with a particular part of the text as if it were the whole. The rest of the whole is not mere excursus to Romans 9-11.

Within Romans 9-11, I read the articulation of Paul's climactic case as follows: God made an abiding promise of justice to suffering Israel (9:1-29), justice as the breaking of injustice's death grip (in the death and resurrection of the Messiah) is the *telos* (10:4, goal rather than cessation) of God's promised order for Israel (9:30-10:21), and all nations will be saved for the sake of God's promised justice to Israel (11:1-36). In this structured analysis I see three particular textual considerations which draw my reading Romans 9-11 as a warning against Gentile anti-Semitism as a form of reinscribing imperial injustice: (1) Two points of translation: *telos* as noted above, and *dikaiosynê* as socially responsive justice rather than an introspective, self-justifying righteousness and rather than a vocational call to facilitate peaceful communal relations (e.g., 9:30; 10:3, 5-6); (2) The shift from Paul's reference to Judaism from "the Jews" (e.g., 1:16) predominant in 1-8 to the chosen-nation ideology in his reference to "Israel" laden with personal pathos (9:1-4) and predominant throughout Romans 9-11; and (3) The strengthening, not abrogation, of God's promise of justice to Israel from the metaphor of athletic racing using "stumbling block" imagery (11:7-12) to urge Israel on in the contest of relations with Gentiles. The thrust of these textual considerations adds force to my reading that Romans 9-11 is explicitly addressed to Gentiles: God's ways with Israel are not Gentiles' denigrating ways with Israel, the subjected elect people of God, whose promise of deliverance is still theirs.

However, I do not reduce Paul's reframing Gentile-Israel relations for Gentile readers as merely, "Be nice. Play with one another." I do not see Paul addressing a generic individual Gentile of faith. I see his addressing a particular political social (dis)order. **C** In my reading of Paul's socio-economic political context, he speaks knowingly of this disorder, to use Tamez's terms, as "a plural subject"—a diaspora Jew, privileged intellectual, artisan with acute economic needs, highly mobile traveler with contact experience in the teeming ghettoized urban *barrios* of beggars, slaves, manual laborers, sailors and other "dregs of society" on

---

C Paul's context.

top of the scorn and stigma of being imprisoned multiple times under Roman justice.[37]

Thus, beyond seeing Paul admonish anti-Semitism, I see his relating a rather nationalistic promise in Israel to a hope for a mass of suffering humanity across the Roman Empire. Despite the structured, systematized brutality of the imperial order, Israel still bears the election, mercy and justice of God. God's promise to them still stands; God has not "rejected" (11:1) the oppressed. All Israel will be saved (11:29) as "the gifts and the call of God are irrevocable" (11:29).

But why would this matter to a Gentile hearer? The warning of Paul against Gentile conceit takes on apocalyptic political tones against Gentiles who would reap insult on top of Israel's suffering. Gentiles face the same prospect of stumbling like Israel for not perceiving what mystery (11:25) reveals: **A** God is still in charge and has caused only temporarily the "hardening" of Israel to bring all nations under God's sovereign plan. The border is drawn to cross through the shame associated with siding with Israel: "For I am not ashamed of the gospel; it is the power of God for deliverance to everyone who has trust, to the Jew first and also to the Greek. For in it the justice of God is revealed" (1:16-17).

H A In framing the Gentile-Israel contest in terms of aiming to side with the power of God versus the power of imperial social disorder, I read the choice as both political and atypical in the Roman imperial order whereby one group is either dominant over or dominated by another. As Elliott states succinctly, "Paul has not dissolved Israel's covenant in a sea of theological universalism."[38] The political-economic context of competing nationalisms is evoked against Roman hegemony with reference to Israel's contradictory sufferings and promise as a nation chosen by God. In Romans 9:30-10:4, Israel's "fall" is not about works-righteousness but about Israel's exclusivist sense as a nation that the promise is theirs alone. The issue with nationalism is then an ethnocentric exclusion which is contrary to and does not "submit to the justice of God" (10:4). Counter to the divide-and-conquer hegemonic logic of imperialism (taken here by me as the domination of the one remaining superpower nation over all other nations), Paul integrates a universalism (God will save all) and nationalism (for Israel) with a tension. It is a tension between contradicting the nativist-assimilationist dichotomized system of imperial global/local governments and promising the fragmentary, conflictive event of God's justice against any social organization of terror by which such governments exact the

---

A God's sovereign plan.

H A Gentile-Israel issue in one's interpretation.

suffering of millions. At last, as Tamez notes, there is good news for the oppressed majority that is bad news for the oppressor minority who would rather hear a seemingly "depoliticized reading of good news" in Paul which leaves unquestioned the structural sin of social domination.[39]

H Thus I read Paul's message in Romans 9-11 revealing for a Gentile social movement the role of solidarity with the oppressed as essential to God's ways of deliverance with Israel. I agree with Horsley that the decolonizing apocalyptic rhetoric of "restoring the imprisoned nation to itself" repoliticizes Paul for social action in seemingly depoliticized Western Pauline theologies fixated with "the paradigmatic hero of faith, *homo religiosus*, who obsessed with his own striving for perfection, finally surrendered his will in faith in Christ yielding a personal release and the freedom of the soon-to-be-sovereign individual person in the West."[40] Resisting assimilation into an unjust social order then is not just awaiting the end of Roman rule but also alternately conceiving such order as already decentered by God's solidarity with the oppressed. As Horsley notes, once Paul had become convinced that in Jesus God "had inaugurated the fulfillment of history that had been running through Israel all along, he understood his own role to be not simply the preaching of the 'good news' of that fulfillment, but also the organizing of communities of people in anticipation of the imminent advent of direct divine rule" contrary to all appearances under the Roman imperial order.[41] Building an alternative society entailed more than talking about it as Paul organized people and money ("to Jerusalem in a service to the saints," 15:25) alongside his letter-dictating activity.

I The contextual implications for this perspective are also apropos to the life-context of a hybrid Latina/o academic theologian looking to resist assimilation. The problem of knowing in the politics of identity is reframed in light of the lack of *poder* (power/ability) to step out of systemic internalized oppression with which I collude knowingly and unknowingly. Rather than "What do I know?" or "Who do I know?", there is an existential shaking of my own optimism that the alternative I construct to the chameleon-scorpion dichotomy will lead the way out of suffering and causing the suffering of others. The question now becomes, "Can I know or believe such that it would make any real difference?" I bear this question with a suspicion that the mere abstract form of the question may suspend action toward transgressing unjust policies, practices and procedures. Not to know the way out can lead to a damning "paralysis of analysis" in a world where who lives and who dies is a matter of, among other things, concrete praxis.

H Hermeneutical implication of solidarity with the oppressed.

I Interplay between text, context, and interpreter.

The politicized apocalyptic perspective I render to Romans 9-11 locates my self-identity in social movements that address oppression as a function of systemic power asymmetries between constantly-negotiating interests. As such, the teaching of this reading for my life-context is to place on negotiating tables (Eucharist, classroom, kitchen, assembly, boardroom) my self-interests (e.g., nationalism as dual citizen of the United States and the Dominican Republic) with an ethnorelativist sense of self-interest as "self-inter-est," i.e., being myself among or in relationship with others.[42] This "Apocalyptic" self-inter-est stands in contrast to the "Forensic" selflessness or the "New Perspective" self aiming for full, essentialist settlement or integration in community. Practically one "Apocalyptic" implication for my life-context is to organize people and money around issues of (in)equity as part of the flesh-and-blood, life-and-death struggle for power. **H** Resistance to assimilation in the chameleon-scorpion hegemonic dichotomy may take the shape of scholarly and ministry action to destabilize dominant biblical interpretations and construct interpretations of a new sort—responsibly "self-inter-est-ed"—from the perspective of an interminable struggle against hegemony in my reality as a Latino. The theological, interpretive work then is not mere scholars' play detached from the world of hard, exploited labor underlying contemporary social structures of hegemonic control and collusion. Scripture here serves as empowering word but not in the way I am used to seeing power as a zero-sum "given" to be held onto at all cost in fear of another's power against my own. The sense of power I construct in Romans 9-11 is not to be wielded from a fortress to silence disruption or dissension. The power I construct is the power to reveal and conceal the system of competing social interests within my hybrid space. Inasmuch as that system goes without critique, injustice is deemed the inevitable lot of humanity.

Best Interpretation for Chosen Life-Context

H C At this point in my argument I hold as both dear and suspect the expectation that if the chosen life-context is my life-context, then my "Apocalyptic" interpretation above should "naturally" be the best interpretation. However, taking hybridity seriously, I do not claim such hegemony. Indeed to claim such is a trapdoor back to the chameleon-scorpion "choice." I do see the "Forensic" and "New Perspective" readings above as viable choices relevant to and interrelated on issues of knowledge, desire and power identified by me as significant aspects of my struggle with assimilation. Then, what is the basis of my choosing

---

H Power and resistance in biblical interpretation.

H C Contextual frame and hermeneutical frame in biblical interpretation.

one over another? First, I have a choice: my own reading is a hybrid choice knowingly cross-fertilized with diverse "texts" from my social location, Romans, scriptural criticism, and various readers of Romans. Second, there is a project which I attend to now with a sense of urgency, importance, and need, but furthermore with a sense that I have a chance for success in making a decolonizing difference in society: the work of faith-based community organizing among Latinas/os in grassroots inner-city settings in keeping with the "Apocalyptic" choices I reconstruct above within cultural studies.

H I choose my "Apocalyptic" reading as the best in offering socio-political strategies against the essentialist challenges of power I currently face in the politics of identity in my location within the academy and the church. How do I repudiate assimilation? (1) I guard against essentializing my social location as the definitive site of construction for who/what/where Latinas/os are. (2) I draw public attention to human and ecological dimensions of my academic wealth: in particular, the politico-economic-religious interrelationship of oppressions across multiple identities (e.g., gender, color, sexuality, religion, class) and the hierarchy of such oppressions ("I am more oppressed than you so be quiet") which masks and so perpetuates an underlying hegemonic organizing principle in my reality. For example, how easy it is to elide the work and voices of Latinas distinct from my own under my reference to "Latina/o reality," eclipsing the subjugation of women and girls in the subjugation of the poor, of people of color, and of *la tierra* (the land). (3) I make ongoing analysis and praxis within the social settings of Latinas/os a constitutive element of my professional work as a biblical interpreter and pastoral agent. I join professional associations with companion voyagers who brave ecumenical and interdisciplinary contentions about our declared and unspoken commitments to the societies from which we abstract our theologies. (4) I join my own theologizing work to the work of faith-based community organizing initiatives with an aim to build material possibilities for the recruitment and sustenance of more activist Latina/o academic theologians, especially among young adults.

C Aware of multiple identities and power asymmetries across those identities, I do not join the "Forensic" readings' strategic search for metanarratives. Such a search aims to fix my sense of self in a universal, neutral and informed identity. The adoption of scientific methods comes from a suspicion and recognition of the refractive power of location on all perspectives and interpretations. However, such an adoption remains quite naïve and dangerous as it disguises its own socio-historical

---

H Apocalyptic reading.

C Acknowledging multiple identities.

conditioning in the claim to transcend all such conditioning. To join that unreflective claim is to further the dehumanization project of colonization parceling out land and peoples according to "Manifest Destiny" master plans.

The "New Perspective" reading above, on the other hand, does offer a strategy to ground and stabilize my sense of self in terms of claiming membership in a self-consciously multicultural community. But my own sensibilities at present are steeped in reading my past and living my present in terms of the material matrix of Latin American colonial history laden with broken promises and the self-serving claims of *patrones* (patrons) that peace will come through bloodshed. Such a reading and living of history leaves me with constant unease and flickering moments of outright cynicism about how the value of stability or social cohesion in community is co-opted and plays into the hands of imperial control of intellectual contradiction and social conflict, both of which are germane to my critical struggle against assimilation now. What the "New Perspective" reading promotes is not an "alter-native" reality to stand between Jews and Gentiles but the elimination of all "other", of all ethnic, religious identities for all people and all time.

H The "New Perspective" multiculturalism's avowed ethno-relativism appears to make space for difference. However, ethnocentrism is part and parcel of the nativist-assimilationist dichotomy which appears in my intellectual life-context in the claim that all cultures are equally valid and thus above critique from any other culture. This claim is itself a homogenizing rhetoric which deals with difference either by isolating it as an insular, separate existence or reduces solidarity to a self-aggrandizing and destructive essentialism. Agreeing to disagree seems to me like talk of reform without structural change, like essentialism in the guise of universalism. I know well the diplomacy of elites at tables with multicultural agendas (e.g., a bilingual Catholic Mass to feign inculturation) which score victories for the status quo and pacify my own angst about being included. Yet, I wish to engage my own contradictions and ambivalence at those norm-setting tables for I speak, to use Bhabha's expression, with a tongue though "forked, not false."[43]

Then, what does norm-setting look like in my life-context when I no longer claim the politics of the melting pot? I do not pretend to have any *a priori* universal, in-the-know surety with my "Apocalyptic" reading. My cross-fertilized "Apocalyptic" reading relies on the walls of a scriptural criticism schema which initially struck me as alien and occidentalist in its construction. I read such schema, as another familiar Western land claim to make space for Euro-centric interpretive traditions within contemporary cultural torrents of interpretive pluralism,

---

H Multiculturalism in "New Perspective" reading.

isolationism and cacophony across academies and churches. As such, this schema appears more imperial omniscience than colonial contingency; more finished product than ideologically-conditioned process; more oriented toward synthesis than contention; more consensus-driven than site of struggle; more universal, logocentric, introspective principle of order than lived, contradictory experience of subaltern, emancipating social human agency; more Columbian Discovery than Cuban Revolution.

C Yet, I engage such a schema because I claim as a norm the impossibility of essentialism in my experience and understanding of hybridity. By my critique of essentialism in such schema I do not claim to stand outside my interest and location in order to feign objective distance and surety. My choice to cross-fertilize my reading with such an alien construct serves to provoke socially-committed reflection and action on an issue in my hybrid space: assimilation. It took an alien construct; yet, one evocative of metaphors so familiar and rarely named in my flesh-and-blood, Western and non-Western reality: chameleons and scorpions. It is evocative, but not the last word.

Conclusion

H Not said-and-done, my theologizing as a biblical interpreter is an ephemeral one ineluctably situated in a relentlessly particular material struggle for the well-being of Latinas/os. Politically, economically, and religiously, immigrant though I am, I belong to a super-buying/firepower exercising oppressive control over the world even to the point of outright military occupation. The task of socio-political and economic critiques of imperial hegemony is a constitutive element of my hybrid theological location, identity, discourse and action. Such a task is timely for Latinas/os growing in number and in religious impact on the United States social landscape. I theologize and interpret as a chameleon, as a scorpion, and also as a Latino, by which I mean the identity I construct *a posteriori* from a struggle with assimilation as an activist theologian engaged in both collusion and resistance. Locating my Latino identity with an "Apocalyptic" reading of Romans 9-11 gives me a chance to succeed in being publicly critical about and responsible for academic and ecclesial socialization processes which suppress hybrid peoples and our

---

C Essentialism.

H Author's biblical interpretation.

interminable, conflictive ways of knowing and constructing the world in which we live.

Notes

1. I refer to the method of Scriptural Criticism presented by Cristina Grenholm and Daniel Patte, "Overture: Receptions, Critical Interpretations, and Scriptural Criticism," in C. Grenholm and D. Patte ed., *Reading Israel in Romans: Legitimacy and Plausibility of Divergent Interpretations* (Vol. 1 of Romans Through History and Culture Series; Harrisburg: Trinity Press International, 2000), 1-54.

2. Grounded in the overt gender inflections of Spanish and in my more covert construct of masculinity, I use "Latina/o" to refer more inclusively to Latinas and Latinos, by which I mean, respectively, those girls and boys, women and men of Latin American heritage who reside in the United States as immigrants, transient migrants, resident aliens, and naturalized or native-born citizens.

3. Fernando F. Segovia, "Theological Education and Scholarship as Struggle: The Life of Racial/Ethnic Minorities in the Profession," *Journal of Hispanic/Latino Theology* 2 (1994): 6.

4. Robert J. Schreiter, *The New Catholicity: Theology Between the Global and the Local* (Maryknoll, New York: Orbis Books, 1997), 54. See also analysis of postmodern theories of culture by Peter C. Phan, "U.S. Latino/a Theology and Asian Theology: Partners in the Postmodern Age?," *Journal of Hispanic/Latino Theology* 10 (2002): 8-11.

5. Michel Foucault, *Politics, Philosophy, Culture: Interviews and Other Writings*, ed. L. Kritzman, trans. A. Sheridan (New York: Routledge, 1988), 12-37.

6. Edward Said, *Culture and Imperialism* (London: Chatto and Windus, 1993), 21.

7. Homi K. Bhabha, *The Location of Culture* (London: Routledge, 1994), 53-78.

8. Gastón Espinosa, "The Impact of Pluralism on Trends in Latin American and U.S. Latino Religions and Society," *Perspectivas* 7 (Fall 2003), 9-10. Used by permission of the Hispanic Theological Initiative.

9. Gastón Espinosa, Virgilio Elizondo, and Jesse Miranda, *Hispanic Churches in American Public Life: Summary of Findings* (Notre Dame, Indiana: Institute for Latino Studies at the University of Notre Dame, 2003). Hereafter *HCAPL*.

10. Espinosa *et al.*, *HCAPL*, 11.

11. *Ibid.*, 14.

12. *Ibid.*, 15.

13. *Ibid.*, 16.

14. Brian H. Smith, *Religious Politics in Latin America: Pentecostal vs. Catholic* (Notre Dame, Indiana: University of Notre Dame Press, 1998), 2-3, 64, 74-75; Espinosa *et al., HCAPL*, 16.

15. Anne M. Hallum, *Beyond Missionaries: Toward an Understanding of the Protestant Movement in Central America* (New York: Rowan & Littlefield, 1996), 89-90.

16. Espinosa *et al., HCAPL*, 12.

17. This relates to the *dominicana/o* synecdoche *"Nueba Yor"* designating New York City for the whole of the United States. Hence, any Dominican strongly associated with the U.S. is hyphenated as a "Dominican-York" or "Dominican-*Yor*."

18. Marcella Althaus-Reid, *Indecent Theology: Theological Perversions in Sex, Gender and Politics* (London: Routledge, 2000), 27-8. For a similar critique of scholarship as social practice see also Manuel J. Mejido, "Propaedeutic to the Critique of the Study of U.S. Hispanic Religion: A Polemic against Intellectual Assimilation," *Journal of Hispanic/Latino Theology* 10 (2002): 58-61.

19. For case studies indicating that 75 percent of the world's population living in the "Two-Thirds" World are losing their access to safe water as this life-sustaining common good is converted into a profitable commodity for the 25 percent of the population in the "One-Third" World see Diane Raines Ward, *Water Wars: Drought, Flood, Folly, and the Politics of Thirst* (New York: Riverhead Books, 2002).

20. See the dismal 2003 statistics gathered by Richard Fry, *Hispanic Youth Dropping Out of U.S. Schools: Measuring the Challenge* (Washington, D.C.: Pew Hispanic Center, 2003), ii-iv: 16 percent of U.S. born Latina/o 16- to 19-year olds drop out before completing high school, double the rate of "white" teenagers and second only to the 30 percent rate for immigrant Latina/o teenagers (40 percent for Mexican immigrants); of the 529,000 Latina/o teenagers who have dropped out, 175,000 (a third) are immigrants; and the average "dropout" earns per year US$7,300 (whites), US$6,500 (U.S. born Latinas/os), and US$10,000 (immigrant Latinas/os).

21. Daniel Patte, "Paul's Letter to the Romans," in D. Patte ed., *The Global Bible Commentary* (Nashville: Abingdon Press, 2004). Used by permission. The book will be available from Cokesbury.com in October 2004. See a related, earlier developmental stage of this tri-partite schema by John K. Riches, *A Century of New Testament Study* (Valley Forge, Pennsylvania: Trinity Press International, 1993), 125-149.

22. Patte, "Romans" (2004). Used by permission.

23. Peter Stuhlmacher, *Paul's Letter to the Romans: A Commentary* (trans. S. J. Hafemann; Louisville, Kentucky: Westminster/John Knox, 1994), 142.

24. *Ibid.*, 144.

25. *Ibid.*, 142-74.

26. *Ibid.*, 142.

27. *Ibid.*, 144.

28. *Ibid.*, 147.

29. Krister Stendahl, *Paul Among Jews and Gentiles: And Other Essays* (Philadelphia: Fortress, 1976), 2.

30. *Ibid.*, 4.

31. *Ibid.*, 4.

32. *Ibid.*, 4.

33. *Ibid.*, 4.

34. John G. Gager, *Reinventing Paul* (New York: Oxford University Press), 130.

35. *Ibid.*, 134.

36. Elsa Tamez, *The Amnesty of Grace: Justification by Faith from a Latin American Perspective* (trans. S. Ringe; Eugene, Oregon: Wipf and Stock, 1991), 19-21.

37. *Ibid.*, 48-58.

38. Neil Elliott, *Liberating Paul: The Justice of God and the Politics of the Apostle* (Maryknoll, New York: Orbis Books, 1994), 176.

39. Tamez, *The Amnesty of Grace*, 165.

40. Richard A. Horsley, "Submerged Biblical Histories and Imperial Biblical Studies," in R. S. Sugirtharajah ed., *The Postcolonial Bible* (Sheffield, England: Sheffield Academic Press, 1998), 163.

41. *Ibid.*, 165.

42. I draw this "self-inter-est" nuance from community organizing training I received from the Gamaliel Foundation (www.gamaliel.org).

43. Bhabha, *The Location of Culture*, 85.

Works Cited

Althaus-Reid, Marcella. *Indecent Theology: Theological Perversions in Sex, Gender and Politics.* London: Routledge, 2000.

Bhabha, Homi K. *The Location of Culture.* London: Routledge, 1994.

Elliott, Neil. *Liberating Paul: The Justice of God and the Politics of the Apostle.* Maryknoll: Orbis Books, 1994.

Espinosa, Gastón. "The Impact of Pluralism on Trends in Latin American and U.S. Latino Religions and Society." *Perspectivas* 7 (2003): 9-55.

_____, Virgilio Elizondo, and Jesse Miranda. *Hispanic Churches in American Public Life: Summary of Findings.* Notre Dame: Institute for Latino Studies at the University of Notre Dame, 2003.

Fry, Richard. *Hispanic Youth Dropping Out of U.S. Schools: Measuring the Challenge.* Washington, D.C.: Pew Hispanic Center, 2003.

Gager, John G. *Reinventing Paul.* New York: Oxford University, 2000.

Grenholm, Cristina, and Daniel Patte. "Overture: Receptions, Critical Interpretations, and Scriptural Criticism." Pages 1-54 in *Reading Israel in Romans: Legitimacy and Plausibility of Divergent Interpretations.* Edited by C. Grenholm and D. Patte. Harrisburg: Trinity Press International, 2000.

Horsley, Richard A. "Submerged Biblical Histories and Imperial Biblical Studies." Pages 152-172 in *The Postcolonial Bible.* Edited by R. S. Sugirtharajah. Sheffield: Sheffield Academic Press, 1998.

Hallum, Anne M. *Beyond Missionaries: Toward an Understanding of the Protestant Movement in Central America.* New York: Rowan & Littlefield, 1996.

Mejido, Manuel J. "Propaedeutic to the Critique of the Study of U.S. Hispanic Religion: A Polemic against Intellectual Assimilation." *Journal of Hispanic/Latino Theology* 10, no. 2 (2002): 31-63.

Patte, Daniel. "Paul's Letter to the Romans." In *The Global Bible Commentary.* Ed. D. Patte. Nashville: Abingdon Press, 2004.

Phan, Peter C. "U.S. Latino/a Theology and Asian Theology: Partners in the Postmodern Age?" *Journal of Hispanic/Latino Theology* 10, no. 2 (2002): 5-30.

Riches, John K. *A Century of New Testament Study.* Valley Forge: Trinity Press International, 1993.

Said, Edward W. *Culture and Imperialism.* London: Chatto, 1993.

Schreiter, Robert J. *The New Catholicity: Theology Between the Global and the Local.* Maryknoll, New York: Orbis Books, 1997.

Segovia, Fernando F. "Theological Education and Scholarship as Struggle: The Life of Racial/Ethnic Minorities in the Profession." *Journal of Hispanic/Latino Theology* 2, no. 2 (1994): 5-25.

Smith, Brian H. *Religious Politics in Latin America: Pentecostal vs. Catholic.* Notre Dame: University of Notre Dame Press, 1998.

Stendahl, Krister. *Paul Among Jews and Gentiles: And Other Essays.* Philadelphia: Fortress, 1976.

Stuhlmacher, Peter. *Paul's Letter to the Romans: A Commentary.* Transl. S. J. Hafemann. Louisville: Westminster/John Knox, 1994.

Tamez, Elsa. *The Amnesty of Grace: Justification by Faith from a Latin American Perspective.* Translated by S. Ringe. Eugene: Wipf and Stock, 1991.

Our Struggle as *Mestizos*

A Response to Escarfuller, "Repudiating Assimilation in Reading Romans 9-11"

Elsa Tamez

———— ◆ ————

Reading Juan Escarfuller's article, "Repudiating Assimilation in Reading Romans 9-11," has shaken me (has made an impact on me). From my social and cultural location as a *mestiza* (mixed) in Latin America, I observe the rereading of Romans 9-11 done by a person who, from the beginning to the end of his investigation, offers an internal, almost existential, struggle for establishing the dignity of the perspective of hybridity in the scientific analysis of a biblical text. Escarfuller places all of his cards on the table (chameleon-scorpion), he submits himself to the rules of the game established by the circle of biblical scholars (Forensic, New Perspective, and Apocalyptic Interpretations), utilizes the Western *logos,* imposed in the academic world, and with this he plays a clever card: he discovers what Romans 9-11 could say to his Latino world in the United States. From Latin America I join him in preferring the apocalyptic interpretation.

His investigation reminds me of our discussions about Latin American thought, especially our struggle as *mestizos* to go to our indigenous roots, to our cultural heritage, in search for another *logos,* our own, with the intention of avoiding the obligation of saying what we want with borrowed tools. We have not achieved it, and perhaps we will never achieve it due to our divided identity: white-indigenous, full of nostalgia for the past and of fascination—some times hidden—for the western academia. In the world of philosophy, Leopoldo Zea, a Mexican philosopher, already resolved this "justification of humanity," or, as he puts it, this "bargaining of humanity," by saying: "Let's do philosophy without excuses." To me this means that when practicing biblical rereading we have to recognize and accept who we are and where we are, as Escarfuller does so well, and from there establish our own rules, borrowing—without shame—only those rules which will illuminate the ones we invent for ourselves. I believe that in this way the dignity of hybridism is established and we lose the fear to assimilate. This is so because, I think, one stops being "on guard" all the time under the scrutiny of the "dominant other." I know that from my Latin American context this is easy for me to say but I imagine that it is very difficult to apply it in the context of Latinos and Latinas who live in the academic circles of the first world, a world that demands, as the price for entering it, the mastery of its own rules. Conscientious Latinos/as see constantly the need to establish the dignity of their hybridity/hybridism and of not "lowering their guard" in front of assimilation.

From Latin and Caribbean America, a place where the poor and the excluded ones abound more and more due to the neo-liberal economic politics, I would like to share some of my rereading of Romans 9-11, which takes another route. I take again the classic theme of election and I reread it in light of the excluded ones, by what I mean the poor, Indians, blacks, women, homosexuals, lesbians and others. The chosen ones of the market are not the same as the chosen ones of God. God chooses the excluded ones so there might be no more exclusion.[1]

God's election is by grace. Merits or any privileged status do not count for being chosen. That is why Paul writes: "So it depends not on human will or exertion, but on God who shows mercy" (Rom 9:16). When merits or privileges come to play, competition arises, the "exertion" among human beings, which creates simultaneously exclusion. For that reason grace has priority over merit.

God rejects exclusion and chooses by mercy precisely because God chooses the excluded, the powerless, the discriminated, the ignorant, in order to avoid all exclusion. If God chose Israel as God's people, it was because Israel was small and oppressed by other empires. God chooses in order to include and liberate. Deuteronomy 7:7,8 expresses this clearly.

In Rom 9:13 Paul repeats the tradition: "The elder shall serve the younger." It refers to God's gratuitous preference for Isaac and Jacob. They both were the younger brothers and only because of that fact God has a preference for them, not because they had done good or bad (Rom 9:11). With this attitude God is not excluding or rejecting the elder (when in 9:13 it says "I have hated Esau" that simply means, in Hebrew thought, that God preferred the other one). What we reread is that God enters in solidarity with the younger, the downtrodden and the discriminated. That is God's free way of acting in history. Of course, when the younger becomes arrogant and starts excluding others, he ceases to be God's preferred one. Israel went through this experience many times and Christians even more and are always subject to this temptation (Rom 11:20).

We could even ask ourselves, why does God have to choose? Wouldn't it be better to treat everyone equally without having to prefer some? The answer is to affirm that in a divided society in order for God's merciful purpose to be fully accomplished (that is, that no one stays out of God's liberating will), God has to prefer those whom society excludes. They are the ones who need more of God's solidarity. They, by being chosen by God in a preferential manner, witness the love of God, which does not discriminate people. The excluded and discriminated ones will always be God's chosen ones. This is the guarantee that God's mercy may reach all, peoples and persons, and God's liberating will may be fulfilled.

In the Hebrew Bible, God chooses personages or people in order to testify to God's mercy and make God's power known in the face of all injustice. In this sense, election is visibly manifested in the conduct of the chosen ones and this privilege is maintained as long as the chosen people remain faithful to God's merciful testimony. When they do not do so, when they do not follow God's ways of justice, election is suspended until the people return to God's ways and make visible God's mercy. Paul mentions the cycle exclusion-inclusion in the parable of the olive trees (Rom 11:18-22).

To be chosen, as an act of God's solidarity, makes the excluded one to feel dignified and included in God's liberating will. The awareness of being elected, chosen by God recreates the strength to face the hostilities one is subject to, the hope in view of an uncertain future and a praxis of liberation. In addition, God's merciful election of the excluded ones moves others also to act in accordance with this mercy. This rereading de-authorizes those readings that manipulate the concept of election with the purpose of dominating other peoples, communities or persons.

Note

1. Here I include some paragraphs from my article: "Eleccion, exclusion y misericordia de Dios," *Revista de Interpretacion Biblica Latinoamericana* (RIBLA, n. 12, 1992).

* The volume editor wishes to extend appreciation to Osvaldo Vena for providing an English translation of the original Spanish response of Elsa Tamez.

– F I V E –

Subjection, Reflection, Resistance

An African American Reading of the Three-Dimensional Process of Empowerment in Romans 13 and the Free-Market Economy

Monya A. Stubbs

I had reasoned it out in my mind, there was one or two things I had a right to—freedom or death. If I could not have the one, I would have the other, but no man would take me alive. I would fight for my freedom as long as my breath lasted, and when the time come for me to go, the Lord would let them take me (quote by Harriet Tubman).[1]

C Life is replete with revelatory moments. We experience events, meet people, or encounter ideas that transform or clarify our purpose in the world. Lerone Bennett's discussion on Harriet Tubman's life (1820-1913) gave me such an occasion. When asked why she returned to the South some nineteen times, helping more than 300 slaves escape to freedom, Tubman responded with the above quotation. Her words have long intrigued me. She reveals through her statement three important aspects of her character that now serve as a paradigm, framing how I comprehend and engage the world. Tubman understood herself and those she rescued as subject to a "governing authority," namely, the institution of slavery. To "fight" for freedom, first she had to recognize that she was subject. Second, Tubman valued the process of careful examination that leads to a conviction. She "reasoned it out in her mind" that the institution of slavery denied her the dignity warranted by her humanness. After carefully reflecting on the condition she shared with her enslaved cohorts, Tubman became convinced that slavery stood outside the will of God. Third, and finally, as a response to her recognizing her subjection and reflecting upon it, Tubman resisted the subjection. She seized her own freedom by escaping from the slave South and then returned

---

C Contextual frame influenced by Tubman.

repeatedly, leading other slaves to the metaphoric "promised land." Tubman's statement therefore reflects a three-dimensional process of empowerment that I define as Subjection-Reflection-Resistance. Although the institution of chattel slavery did not end by Tubman's resistance alone, her subjection-reflection-resistance did prove that slavery was not absolute for either the slaves or slave owners. Ultimately, through this process, Tubman envisioned and created a faith reality beyond her slave experience.

The Paul in Tubman

C A H I experienced this Tubman revelatory moment during my junior year of college. Now, years later, I sit staring at Romans 13:1-7, trying to make sense of Paul's supposed call for Christian "subjection" to civil and state authorities. This is no simple task. As learned from the preceding years of the Romans Consultation through critical studies as biblical scholars, we must assume responsibility for our interpretations by explicitly identifying the frames and categories we employ to make sense of the text. Interpreters should make clear not only the analytical frame[2] used to ground a particular reading in textual evidence, but should also identify two other frames that critical interpretations often fail to explain: the hermeneutical frame(s), used to circumscribe the dialogue with the text, as done in theological commentaries; and the contextual frame(s), used to relate life and text—the frame commonly emphasized in believers' interpretations and sermons. Considering these issues, this paper revisits Romans 13:1-7, and presents the view that if this passage is read in light of its surrounding verses (12:1-13:14), it reads less like a prescriptive demand and more like a call for Roman Christians to acknowledge their social reality in relation to the Roman state which is part of the existence of life in the Christian community. This broader text shifts the emphasis from subjection as a single hermeneutical frame and expands the frame to include subjection-reflection-resistance as a three-dimensional process that Paul espouses for empowering those who may feel powerless in their relationship with governing authorities.

C H The paper is divided into two major sections: the contextual frame and the hermeneutical frame. The paper's first section, the contextual frame, outlines the author's perspective of the free market economy and its present role as the "governing authority" today. Economics or the way in which money influences the human condition concerned both Paul and the Christian community at Rome. For instance,

---

C A H Interplay of three frames in biblical interpretation.
C H Using two frames to read Romans.

Romans 12:13 reminds the community to support the needs of each other. Romans 13:6 speaks of the Christians' duty to pay taxes. Romans 13:7 refers to the responsibility of Christians to discharge all dues, including taxes and other types of revenue owed to the state or to an individual. Therefore, considering the importance of economics (finances) to the first century world of the text, it is reasonable to employ the free market economy as a contextual frame that helps me to recognize as particularly significant the way in which the text integrates economic, political, and social power structures and their implications for human relationships.

H The hermeneutical frame is subdivided into three parts. Part A discusses *subjection*, the first step in the three-dimensional process of empowerment. First, it offers a brief analysis of Paul's usage of "subjection" throughout Romans, noting the ambiguity in Paul's usage of the term, vacillating between voluntarily offering self in subjection to an authority and offering self to an authority because of coercion. Second, the paper examines "subjection" in Romans 13:1, where one faces the challenge of deciding if Paul wants *pasa psychê exousiais hyperechousais hypotassesthô* understood as an imperative middle (let every soul subject her or himself to governing authorities) or as an imperative passive (let every soul be subjected by governing authorities). Ultimately, I argue that although the Christians at Rome act as agents in their subjection, they do so because of the ideological influence the governing authority holds over their lives. Finally, I briefly consider the implications for modern readers whom the free market economy subjects.

Section B on *reflection* discusses Paul's call for the Christians at Rome to reflect upon the perceived conception of their relationship with the "governing authority." It further argues that Paul challenges them to a careful reflection that leads to the conviction that God dwells both in and beyond their subjection. The analysis pulls important textual support from Romans 12:2 and Romans 1:1-23, showing these texts' significance to Romans 13:1-7 as an empowering passage for those in a subjected relationship to governing authorities. Section B ends with a model for discerning resistance language and/or actions within Paul's seemingly pro-empire comments.

Finally, section C argues that Paul offers in Romans 12 and Romans 13:8-14 resistance language that denies the absolute authority of the Roman system of authority and (re)defines love as "debt of love" or the voluntary commitment one makes to addressing the physical and spiritual needs of both self and others. In closing, section C analyzes the

---

H Hermeneutical interest on freedom.

free market economy in light of Paul's call to resist governing authorities as absolute. The discussion characterizes the free market doctrine as an absolute, highlights features of the free market ideology, points out its contradictions, and finally offers Paul's "love of neighbor" (13:9) for envisioning and creating a reality beyond our subjection by and to the free market economy and its culture.

The Contextual Frame: — C
The Ethos of the Free Market Economy

C The free-market economy functions as the ethos of our social and economic context, whether actively or passively, voluntarily or involuntarily, we are "subject" to its rules and demands. Since 1989, and the fall of USSR (communism), the free-market economy reigns as what appears to be the absolute system of maintenance in which the world functions. The United States, however, since its inception, has promoted a free-market economy. It is the transcendent economic order of history and it represents a development through which human beings have sought to meet their economic needs (food, clothing, shelter). At the same time, the free-market economy has served as a historical development through which individuals, or groups, or classes, or races have sought to gain a privileged position at the expense of others. This economic order will therefore present anytime in history a development in which there is much that is good and much that is evil.

The free market economy, however, is not driven merely by the dynamics of market production nor does the term economy refer solely to the economic power in capital itself. The free-market economy relies on a specific type of culture to support it. "Thoroughly privatized, the American economy only moves in response to personal initiatives to invest in productive enterprises, to mobilize resources for work, and to save or spend according to individual dictates."[3] Appleby, Hunt and Jacob argue that the American economy is sustained by cultural models such as "individual fortitude, prosperity, agricultural abundance, open opportunity, hard work, free choice, inventive genius and productive know-how."[4] These models, according to Appleby, Hunt and Jacob, permeate the historical consciousness of America. The people of America have come to understand or accept these "coerced" values as natural:

> History texts have provided American children with exemplary
> models of trailblazing initiatives, disciplined efforts, and

---

C On free market economy.

individual sacrifices for progress. Beginning with the accounts of nation-building in the revolutionary era, national history has imparted the kinds of moral lessons that have enabled capitalism to flourish, but like the roots of a plant, this vital cultural sustenance is hard to see.[5]

The force of the free-market economy lies in its ability to appear fundamental to the human condition or as essential to the human exchange of services and goods. The deception, masked in the ideal of "freedom" and fueled by the presumed naturalness of self-interest, creates an environment where the very act of "commercial transactions appear voluntary and its participants feel as if they are free to choose." Appleby, Jacob and Hunt provide a simple yet profound example:

> The fact that people must earn before they can eat is a commonly recognized connection between need and work, but it presents itself as a natural link embedded in the necessity of eating rather than as arising from a particular arrangement for distributing food through market exchanges. Despite the fact that men and women must buy and sell in order to live, the optional aspects of the market remain most salient.[6]

It is the specific individual or the specific group who decides to take certain actions and suffers the misfortune or enjoys the benefits. Nevertheless, as Appleby, Hunt and Jacob remind us, because we have become so accustomed to natural and personal (freedom/voluntary) presentations of how people provide for the necessities of life, the "social and compulsory" aspects of capitalism elude us. The situation is comparable to recent discussions in biblical scholarship regarding proper modes of interpretation. For centuries the historical-critical method served as the normative model for biblical hermeneutics (the subjection). One was "free" to analyze any passage within the Bible; however that freedom was qualified by the underlining notion that biblical interpretation is that type of analysis that looks "behind" the text, seeking to uncover the meaning intended by the authors themselves. Although biblical scholars had conclusions about what a given text "meant," the methodology used for arriving at their conclusions and its "universal" intent were never questioned. Like the veiled significance of the free-market in the lives of Americans, the historical-critical method, until some thirty years ago was "the" way of being a biblical scholar, it was the governing system in which we lived and scholars were only "free" to follow the rules which governed historical-criticism.

Like the historical-critical method functioned as the governing authority for over a century in the world of biblical scholarship, the free-market economy and its culture functions as the "governing authority" in our current social structure. The marketplace-demand influences, even guides, our decision making process. It decides who will die of disease and who will receive adequate health care. It decides who will receive a viable education and become equipped with the appropriate information required for rational thought, judgment, and planning, and who will fall prey to the vultures of ignorance. The marketplace-demand decides who will be demonized as an enemy and who will be extolled as a friend. The free-market economy is the transcendent structure in which we live. We are "subject" to it and subjected by it. So, as we explore Paul's three-dimensional process for the relationship of Christians to the state or "governing authorities." Paul's opening statement, "Let every soul be subjected by/to authorities" sets the interpretive tone for the remainder of the chapter in that it introduces the first step (subjection) in our hermeneutical frame.

The Hermeneutical Frame — H

Subjection in Romans: The Imperative Middle or the Imperative Passive?

A Paul uses *hypotassesthô* in four different contexts within his letter to the Romans: 8:7; 8:20; 10:3; and 13:1. Romans 8:7 reads: "For the mind belonging to flesh is enmity against God: for it is not subject to the law of God, indeed it lacks the power." The flesh-oriented[7] concern of humanity is death, which directly opposes the "life" offered by God through the law of the Spirit in Christ Jesus (see 8:1). Therefore, those with a mind of the flesh resists what God desires. Building on 7:15-25, Paul asserts that the refusal by those whose minds are set on "this world" to "subject" to the will of God moves beyond the matter of one's personal *will*. Paul raises the question of *ability*. Flesh-oriented humanity, dominated by sin, lacks the power to free itself when confronted by the law of God.[8]

H Romans 8:20 offers a more concise example of subjection as a consequence of coercion: "For the creation was subjected to futility not of its own will, but by the will of the one who subjected it." The creation is subject to purposelessness through no fault of its own. Rather, it lacks the *ability* to free itself from the bondage of decay (v. 21). From this perspective, a pattern arises in Paul's employment of "subjection" which

---

A Historical-critical understanding of Paul's text.

H Subjection as consequence of coercion.

emphasizes his recognition that subjection can result both from acting as an agent by will, as well as from being acted upon because of a lack of power.[9]

Romans 10:3 also addresses "subjection" in relation to human ability or the lack thereof. In 8:7, Paul describes humanity as being dominated by sin. In 10:3 the consequence and manifestation of being dominated by sin is ignorance of God's righteousness. Paul writes: "For, being ignorant of the righteousness that comes from God, and seeking to establish their own, they have not submitted to God's righteousness." Here, Paul suggests that humanity wills not to subject themselves to God's righteousness. However, because humanity is subjected/dominated by sin, they lack the ability to know/recognize the righteousness of God. As in 8:20 we also find here Paul understanding "subjection" in a sense where subjection can be both an act of volition and imposition.

H The issue of subjection as both an act of volition and imposition is also central in Romans 13:1 where, in my analysis, a significant question one might ask of the text is: Why do people tolerate subjection?[10] Paul suggests that people *willingly* tolerate and perpetuate their subjection because they lack the ability to recognize or resist the influence of power. *Pasa psychê hypotassesthô* can be translated either as an imperative middle or an imperative passive. At first glance, the distinction between the translations may seem irrelevant. But, a closer examination uncovers, in my estimation, a central point of Paul's argument in Romans 13:1 and its co-text. If translated as a middle imperative, the phrase reads "every person subject herself or himself" to governing authorities.[11] On the other hand, if translated as a passive imperative,[12] taking into account the dative of means (*exousiais hyperechousais*), the phrase reads "be every person subjected" by governing authorities. The first reading suggests that Christians possesses the power to socially situate themselves within the order of their environment. "Subjection" then, is a matter of *will,* only. The second translation, on the other hand, suggests that the "governing authority" is a structure in which the Christian is placed or already exists and it acts upon the Christian existence. The Christian cannot but live within a preexisting social system that limits how one can best express one's Christian faith within the parameters of the "governing" structure. The power of Paul's logic does not, however, rest in the either/or of these two translations but in the both/and. Taking seriously the ambiguity embedded within the imperative mood as both middle and passive reveals a provocative alternative meaning: Christians act as agents,

---

H Subjection as act of volition.

tolerating and perpetuating their subjection to the "governing authority," because of its power upon them. Essentially, Christians subject themselves *to* the governing authority (middle imperative) because they are subjected *by* the governing authority (passive imperative). Paul's exhortation, in my hermeneutical analysis, is not a prescriptive demand for some sort of subjective action or an admonition to prevent subversive action against the state or civil authorities. Instead, Paul's comment calls the Roman Christians to acknowledge the social reality of their relation to the Roman state.

H Jan Botha's observations on the rhetorical effect of Romans 13:1-7 is helpful at this juncture. Not allowing Paul's comments to remain within the realm of narrative, Botha's conclusions forces the reader to look at the passage's ideological dimension. Botha argues that Romans 13:1-7 reflects the "existing and well-known values of Paul's Jewish audience." Values, he adds, which were "held more or less as self-evident truths in the wider context of the Hellenistic world."[13] Botha substantiates his claim by referring to Strobel and Van Unnik's works which demonstrate that the vocabulary used is that of the Hellenistic administration and that the Greek ideals of the just and honorable man are evidenced in Romans 13:1-7.[14] Furthermore, the ideals expressed in Romans 13:1-7 reveal certain universal values attributed to God and ascribed to authorities: everyone should submit to God; God punishes those who resist God's ordinations; God always does what is good; everything belongs to God. Thus, everyone should submit to governing authorities. God punishes through the governing authorities those who resist the governing authorities; the governing authorities always do what is good; everything belongs to God, therefore that which one gives to governing authorities, one gives to God. The power of the rhetorical analysis then, according to Botha, is that it brings to the "fore the implicit and unspoken/unwritten values which underpin the argumentation."[15] The rhetorical analysis illuminates the ideological underpinnings of Paul's statement. Reading Romans 13:1 as both an imperative passive (every soul be subjected by governing authorities) and an imperative middle (every soul subject him or herself to governing authorities) shifts Paul's statement from a prescriptive charge, advising on what people should and should not do, to a religious perception of the relations between God and humanity via worldly "governing authorities." In this light, the value system functioning in Romans 13:1-7 reflects an ideology in Louis Althusser's understanding of the term, according to which people are "always already subject" to the normative ideas or values which lay at the roots of particular societies.

H Botha's ideological dimension of Paul's text.

H Althusser maintains that ideology is a "representation of the imaginary relationship of individuals to their real conditions of existence."[16] In other words, ideology is that which is self-evident. Yet, that which is self-evident is a construct, is created through the imagination. The relevant question is what exactly is this ideological construct? It is a construct of a relationship to one's condition of existence. Using Romans 13:1 as an example, the construct, according to Althusser, is not the fact that governing authorities exist nor that they have power. The construct is the way in which human beings conceive of their relationship with the governing structure and to other individuals. The construct is the illusion of subjection. At the same time, however, illusion becomes reality as human beings accept the ideology as a natural ordering of human relations: the illusion equals the obvious. So, while Romans 13:1 describes the unspoken/unwritten values that underpin Roman social life, Althusser makes clear that this perceived relationship is an ideological construction of the community's perception of their relationship to the governing authority. This phrase read as both an imperative middle and passive recognizes that Christians are agents of their subjection (they subject themselves *to* the governing authority), because they are subjected *by* the governing authority. The combined reading takes seriously the enormity of the social and religious ideological weight placed on the lives of individuals within given communities.

A Romans 1:18-25 supports reading Paul's opening statement as both an imperative middle and an imperative passive. Humanity's wickedness, according to Paul, rests in its conspiracy to suppress the truth that we are indeed subjected by a governing authority: God the Creator. Paul argues that humanity has taken God's partial manifestation in nature as an absolute manifestation. Consequently, we suppress the truth about God in our glorification and worship of the creature rather than God, thus making it an absolute. The result is exploitive and destructive human relationships. Romans 1:21-24 describes these "false" governing authorities as *asynetos* minds,[17] proven "worthless and base in not recognizing God" for what God is (1:28). In the end, we subject ourselves to (imperative middle) the governing authorities, because we failed to acknowledge that we are subjected by (imperative passive) the governing authorities. In Romans 12:2 Paul calls for a "renewal of the mind" as a way of redeeming and resisting the evil indicative of humanity's current mind-set (this analysis continues in the reflection section).

H Althusser's understanding of ideology in reading Paul's text.
A Historical-critical understanding of Paul's text.

In our contemporary context, we too have created an absolute reality out of our constructed relationship with the free market economy (see section on contextual frame). Therefore, Paul's comments in Romans 13:1-2 fit well as consequences for one's cooperation with or negligence of the free market ideology. After Paul's opening charge, he moves into a more detailed discussion regarding the necessity and consequences of the community's voluntary, yet imposed subjection. "Every soul be subjected by and to governing authorities for there is no authority if not by God and the existing ones have been appointed by God. So that the ones to resist the authority resists what God has ordained, and those who resist shall themselves receive judgment" (vv. 1-2). Paul has presented a reality made possible by the social acceptance of the people's perceived relation to governing authority. To resist subjection to the authority of the free-market economy, to resist understanding and participation in the free-enterprise economic system (failure to gain prosperity is interpreted as a form of resistance) results in a person or a community receiving the wrath of God. In a free-market economy one is subject, therefore, free to pursue the aim of economic advancement: he or she is free to respond to the marketplace demand with the hope that one's response (creating a supply to meet the demand) will afford one (as an individual or a specific group) the opportunity to enjoy fortune and dispose of it as one chooses; without regard for other human beings and independently of society.

Moreover, according to Romans 13:2, systems of power are ordained by God. To resist the system is to resist God and live in a state of alienation from God. Alienation from God is manifested in misfortunes within the system of authority: "for if you do what is wrong or what is evil, fear, for the authority does not bear the sword in vain" (verse 4).[18]

C H In a free-market economy such alienation or misfortune, or the wrath of God often manifests itself in the forms of poverty and social, political and cultural disenfranchisement. Such an understanding of God's wrath within the free-market economy promotes the theory that poverty is caused by individual defects and is not the result of a mismanaged economic system. People are poor or experience the wrath of God because of their inability to succeed within the economic system. Their poverty is the result of their sin.

By drawing such conclusions, I am forced to ask: Is salvation characterized by economic advancement? Have we transformed an ideology into a reality by accepting as absolute the "illusion" that we are in a righteous or unrighteous relationship with God based solely on our economic prosperity? Has the free-market economy become a subjection that blinds us to a faith reality of a higher order of humanity and human

---

C H A move to cultural and hermeneutical frames.

relationships that brings us into a more perfect relationship with God and each other?

Discerning Awareness: Reflections on the Subjection

Subjection alone is an oppressive posture and mere submission forces one to remain in a powerless state. Therefore, acknowledging one's subjection by the governing authority represents the first step in Paul's three dimensional-process of empowerment, but, Paul moves a step further. He challenges the Christians at Rome to *reflect* upon the situation in which they live; he challenges them to engage in the process of careful examination that leads to the conviction that God dwells both in and *beyond* their "subjection by governing authorities." Paul makes clear the empowering quality of reflection within the lives of the Christian community at Rome in his comments in 12:2:

> and do not be conformed to the example of this world/age, but let yourselves be transformed by the renewing of your mind so that you may *discern (dokimazein)*[19] what is the will of God – the good and acceptable and complete (will of God) (12:2).[20]

H In light of the discussion on subjection, our first hermeneutical category, we see that Paul has already advised the Christian community against accepting as absolute the *apparent* order of "this world." Argentinean theologian Enrique Dussel's observations on morality are relevant here. According to Dussel, the term "this world" functions in the bible both as a reality and a category. He writes:

> *This* world, is a 'practical' totality (a totality constituted and characterized by relationships of praxis), a system or structure of prevailing, dominant *social* actions and relationships, under the hegemony of evil.[21]

"This world" for instance, referred to Egypt, not simply as a nation, but as a "system of practices" confronting or engaging Moses. "This world," Dussel notes, is self-totalizing, it lifts itself as an absolute system of authority which is opposed to the will of God. This world is under the domination of sin. Paul too, I suggest, employs "this world" as a means of referring to a system of social actions and relationships opposed to the will of God.

H Interpreting "this word" hermeneutically.

‖ Hence, Christians are not to be conformed to/by "this world/age." They are to recognize the prevailing norms of the society in which they live but not fashion their personal or communal behavior by it. Dunn notes that the significance of Paul's warning lies in its recognition of a "power or force which molds character and conduct. Paul in effect recognizes the power of social groups, cultural norms, institutions, and traditions to mold patterns of individual behavior."[22] At the same time, however, Paul recognizes that the mind is the seat of conformity. Therefore, he argues that Christians must have a renewal of mind, a change in their attitude, in their way of thinking. The renewing of the mind is evidenced by one's rational discrimination; therefore, Paul argues that one is able to discern the will of God, because one's thinking and attitude are renewed and no longer fashioned by the norms of "this world."

Finally, reflection is a process of discernment. Walter Wink's comments on discernment are worth noting here. Wink writes, "discernment does not entail esoteric knowledge, but rather the gift of seeing reality as it really is. Nothing is more rare, or more truly revolutionary, than an accurate description of reality."[23] Reflection, the renewal of the mind, empowers those oppressed by what I describe as an "illusionary relationship of subjection to the "governing authorities" or what Wink calls the "delusional power of the System of Domination" with the ability to discern that subjection to "worldly" authority is not absolute. Instead, the standard for Christian conduct is measured by a "knowledge" of what God desires. One does not "know" what is "right" or "wrong" through the normative values of "this age/world" whether it be Roman values or Jewish law. Instead, Paul suggests that it is in fact the renewal of Christians' mind(s) from these prescribed norms which allow them to "know" God's will. The significance of reflection, however, is not to end the subjection. Instead reflection prevents the Christians at Rome from making absolute the Roman political authority, thus worshiping it instead of God (worshiping the creature rather than the Creator, Rom 1:19-23). Or as Wink states, "the seer's gift is not to be immune to invasion by the empire's spirituality, but to be able to discern the internalized spirituality, name it, and externalize it."[24] The subjection remains, but not as an absolute reality within the life of the "seer." Consequently, humanity in a state of reflection stands in direct opposition to the state of humanity described in Romans 1:21: "for though they knew God, they did not honor him as God or give thanks to him, but they became futile in their thinking, and their senseless minds were darkened" (recall discussion in previous section). Reflective humanity, on the other hand, possesses the capacity to see anew, to

---

‖ Interplay between hermeneutical and analytical frames.

envision and understand realities of the power and presence of God beyond their immediate subjection.

H Comparing God with the artistic concept of negative space offers a powerful example of Paul's call for Christians to *reflect* upon their subjection in order to reach the conviction that God dwells both in and *beyond* the structure or the ordering of relationships that we deem absolute. Artists refer to the hollow, empty area surrounding the edges and contours of an object as "negative space." For instance, draw a circle on a sheet of blank paper and fill the circle with a solid color; the outer white space defines the edge of that circle. The white area is negative space because it is not recognizable. It is nothingness. Without this negative space, however, the viewer would not be able to identify a solid blue circle. The blue circle represents "positive" space, because it occupies an area of the negative space and is defined by that negative space.

At the same time, "positive" objects possess the capacity to *partially* frame negative space. Although positive space partially frames negative space, negative space cannot be transformed into positive space. A brief interactive exercise will help further clarify this point. Take your hands and bring them together into a praying posture. Slowly release your hands, allowing only your finger tips to touch, including your thumbs. Adjust your hands so that you create an upside down heart. Your eyes tell you that you see a heart. If you now completely pull your hands apart, however, do you see a heart? No. Your eyes really saw your two hands coming together to create a heart shape. Negative space always define your hands, regardless of the shape they take.

In the same way artists discuss negative and positive space, I argue that Paul speaks of God and human relationship. Like negative space, God is infinite and indefinable. Similar to the way negative space circumscribes the reality of the solid circle and the hands, God circumscribes and defines finite humanity. God reminds us that we are creatures within the boundaries of our finite existence precisely because we are able to construct more than a "heart," or a "circle,"—negative space reveals many revelations of itself through positive space. Likewise, God engages our humanness and offers other possible revelations of itself *beyond* what we presently see. According to Paul, reflection represents freedom. We argued in the previous section that "freedom" rests in one's participation within the governing structure as absolute. On the contrary, freedom as reflection involves participation in the governing structure with the *discerning awareness* that it represents *one* but not the *absolute* way of being in the world.

H Critical and theological reflections of Christians today.

Discerning the Resistance: A Foundation for Analysis

H Using James C. Scott's recent study *Domination and the Arts of Resistance: Hidden Transcripts* as a interpretive frame, the remainder of the paper explores how Paul's call to reflection leads to his ultimate call for the Christian community to respond to, in words and/or gestures, the empowering awareness that its subjection to the governing authority is but an illusion, an ideology. Scott suggests that in any given political situation where an elite class dominates segments of the population, there exists a public transcript of events managed by the ruling elites and hidden transcripts of the same events produced secretly by the oppressed. Scott defines "public transcript" as "a shorthand way of describing the open interaction between subordinates and those who dominate."[25] Hidden transcript, on the other hand, characterizes "discourse that takes place 'offstage,' beyond direct observation by powerholders."[26] Produced by the dominant class, public transcript presents "the self-portrait of the elite as they would have themselves seen."[27] Although each group has both a public and hidden transcript, the public transcript produced by the elites serves as the social/cultural ideological *subjection* which conforms to the "flattering self-image of the elite."[28] The oppressed group's survival usually depends on their seeming compliance and obedience to the "onstage" script and political play of the elite, hoping to find recourse for their interest within the "prevailing ideology without appearing in the least seditious."[29] Of course, the hidden transcript of the oppressed offers another form of political discourse, but it is relegated to the "offstage," beyond the purview of the powerholders. Therefore, the oppressed actions "onstage" seems consistently to affirm the *subjection,* limiting the hidden transcript of the oppressed to little more than a private venting mechanism. The power of the hidden transcript of the oppressed group, however, is that it is not limited to the "offstage." Rather, the oppressed hidden transcript functions as a "politics of disguise and anonymity that takes place in public view but is designed to have a double meaning or to shield the identity of the actors."[30] For instance, during the period of chattel slavery in America, spirituals functioned as hidden transcripts or resistance songs. Although these songs were sung in the public arena and employed the language of Christian piety, they were coded messages signaling revolt, rebellion, or simple disgust with the institution of slavery and the slave masters. For example, whenever Harriet Tubman planned an escape, the enslaved men and women often sang in the fields throughout the day, "swing low, sweet chariot coming for to carry me home" or "steal away, steal away to

---

H Critical analysis on resistance and power.

Jesus! Steal away, steal away home, I ain't got long to stay here" as an indicator of their impending flight to freedom. In essence, "Spirituals were the indispensable device that slaves used to transmit a worldview fundamentally different from and opposed to that of slaveholders."[31]

Resistance: How Much Do I Owe You?

H Whereas *reflection* makes obvious the *subjection*, and allows one to envision other possibilities of God's reality beyond subjection, *resistance* represents the state of transformation: It represents those acts that a person or a community makes, based on reflection, which places both their minds and bodies beyond the given subjection. Resistance is about acting and speaking in such a way that reflects commitment against conformity both to and by this world. Paul speaks of this metaphorically in 12:1 where he urges the Christians at Rome:

> I encourage you therefore brothers and sisters by the mercies of God and because of the mercies of God, to offer your bodies as a living sacrifice, holy and acceptable to God, which is your reasonable worship. (author's translation)

Worshiping God requires the giving of one's life and body.[32] In essence, Paul suggests that "worship" of God only happens as a consequence of resisting conformity to "this world." Because one has engaged the process of *reflection*, she is now able to offer her body as a living sacrifice—able to engage in speech and action which moves beyond the boundaries established by societal norms. Let us now, in light of Scott's concept of "hidden transcripts," examine more closely Paul's call to *resistance*. Reading Romans in light of its resistance features is not a common mode of interpretation. But, neither is it a novel one. William R. Herzog argues that Paul's exhortation in 13:1-7 to the Christian community at Rome represents "dissembling" speech. Paul's comments "feign obedience and loyalty to the colonial overlords while pursuing its own hidden agenda."[33] Herzog's study suggests that Romans 13:1-7 alone, functions as *resistance* text. Herzog builds his thesis around Paul's usage of *diakonos* (13:4) and *leitourgoi* (13:6), arguing that rulers, as "servants" stood diametrically opposed in the Roman world. Therefore, Paul's description of the rulers as servants is a "hidden transcript."[34] Paul specifies that the military, as servants of God, be used solely to suppress anarchy and wrong behavior. In reality however, the military and its sword functioned more as a "means of

---

H Critical analysis on resistance and worship.

intimidation and brutality that ensured that subjected populations would quietly endure the so-called Pax Romana."[35] Thus, by using this coded term, Paul suggests loyalty to a non-existent empire while actually critiquing it for not following the will of God.

Similarly, Paul characterizes the authorities as *leitourgoi,* a variant on *diakonoi.* These figures carried out the public and bureaucratic functions of the state. Thus, "just as the military devotes itself to physical control, the financial bureaucrats devote themselves to economic control."[36] So, Paul writes: "Pay to all what is due them, taxes to whom taxes are due, revenue to whom revenue is due, respect to whom respect is due, honor to whom honor is due" (v. 7). Financially, this implies resistance to conceding to the finance ministers, who were obsessive about extracting from the population everything but the barest necessities, more than is their due.[37] Likewise, Christians are to offer respect (*phobon*) and honor (*timên*), not as enthusiastic support of the empire. Instead, "Paul most likely means that Christians should always display the public deference that the oppressed show their masters."[38] Paul offers allegiance to empire that does not exist while using the "weapons of the weak to reinforce the survival skills of the fledgling community."[39]

I This paper broadens the textual range for examining the interaction between public transcripts and hidden transcripts, or between *subjection* and *resistance.* I propose that Romans 13:1-7 functions as the public transcript or the subjection and Paul's mentioning it reminds the Christians at Rome to acknowledge it as the ideological system in which they live because by not recognizing the system, they are not only subjected by it, but they also subject themselves to it. The hidden transcript surfaces not so much in 13:1-7 (although Herzog has proven this to be a legitimate claim), but in verses 8-10. In his summary statement on the Roman Christian community's relationship to governing authorities, Paul writes: "owe no one anything, except to love one another, for the one who loves another has fulfilled the law" (verse 8). Paul has just described in verse 7 that according to the public transcript of the Roman empire, giving all (military and financial bureaucrats) their expected dues is a service to both humanity and God. But in verse 8 Paul encourages his readers to discharge all debts except the debt of love. Herein lies Paul's resistance language, where the hidden transcript imposes itself upon the public transcript. Before offering an analysis of verse 8, let us explore Paul's utilization of *opheil-* in Romans.

A *Opheil-* (debt or obligation) or one of its derivatives appears seven times in Romans: 1:14, 4:4, 8:12; 13:7, 13:8, 15:1, 15:27. Paul uses the

---

I Interplay between analytical and hermeneutical frames, between resistance and subjection, between public transcripts and hidden transcripts.

A Historical-critical understanding of Paul's text.

term in varying contexts which affords the reader several interpretive options. For instance, Romans 4:4 describes one incurring a monetary debt to the one who performs a service for hire. The employer "owes" the employee for the work he has performed on behalf of the employer. Romans 15:27 describes a debt incurred out of an obligation to repay one group for what they have done for another. Gentiles are indebted to share their material resources with the saints at Jerusalem since the Jerusalem saints shared their "spiritual blessings" with the Gentiles. New Testament scholar Revelation Velunta clarifies Paul's usage of *opheil-*. Explaining the notion of debt from a Filipino perspective, Velunta notes that debts can be voluntarily incurred or imposed.

A debt incurred voluntarily arises either from the asking of a loan or favor. If the loan or favor is paid back in equivalent terms or with the margin agreed on, both parties can consider themselves discharged. Involuntary debts would occur when a loan or favor is offered or done without having been preceded by a formal request. Even here both loan or favor could be repaid in equivalent or with profit in order to be absolved of the debt.[40]

The subjection listed in Romans 13:7 concerning the payment of dues represents a type of imposed debt. Velunta rightly argues that involuntary debts, like taxes and tribute are exactly what Paul wants everyone to cancel. The problem for Paul is that one's continued indebtedness to the structures described in verse 7 forces one to remain a "debtor to the flesh," therefore living "according to the flesh" (Romans 8:12). Yet, Paul maintains that those empowered by the Spirit of God are no longer *opheiletai tê sarki* (indebted to the flesh). More importantly, Paul associates indebtedness with subjection. He suggests that if one is indebted to the "flesh" then the "flesh" possesses the authority to create the ideological presuppositions under which one must live. Paul is concerned here with right actions (including gestures and speech)—the world created by the flesh forces one to engage nature and other human beings in a manner that results in death (see 8:13). But, those no longer indebted to the flesh, no longer *kata sarka zên* (live according to the flesh) (8:12). In light of 8:12, one sees clearly how Paul's usage of debt (Greek *opheil-*) speaks to his call to *resistance;* he employs the language most indicative of Roman social, political, and economic structure[41] to describe how Christians ought not engage in relationship with each other.

Surprisingly, Paul returns to *ophei-* as a means of discussing human love for other human beings. Velunta suggests that there is yet another way of understanding *ophei-* which he calls *utang na loob. Utang na loob* refers to a debt of volition which is irresolvable.

C H *Utang na loob* is a unique kind of debt: however it may have been incurred, no matter how insignificant the debt, there is no way by which one is absolved of the debt except perhaps by having the "lender" him/herself incur a similar *utang na loob*. The debt goes beyond the legal-juridical framework; it creates an extra-legal but even more binding debt because it involves a personal debt, *one that can only be paid back not only in person but with one's person . . .* one is bound no longer by a single compensating act but binds him/herself voluntarily to be committed beyond repayment.[42]

Debt as a voluntary commitment sheds new light on Paul's use of what Fitzmyer calls oxymoronic language: "Paul states it strangely, speaking of love as something owed like a debt. Love does not constitute one being under an obligation to pay or repay another for something received."[43] Yet, debt is an appropriate representation of humanity's responsibility to one another. Paul moves beyond the traditional ideas of indebtedness and challenges the community to understand their debt to humanity as the logical consequence of love. The two terms, *opheil* and *agape*, actually redefines the other. Paul equates debt with love and love with debt as the voluntary commitment to love. The Roman state often characterized human relationships asymmetrically, associating "debt" with parties of an unequal status (= debtor to the flesh) (feeding off the classic patron-client dynamics).[44] Paul, on the other hand, offers a more horizontal model of human relationships in 13:9 where he summarizes proper human relationships as "love your neighbor." The aim now focuses on wholesome relationships amongst people with a commitment to use their talents and skills to effect qualitative good in the community rather than on relationships guided by selfish motivations for social status (12:3-21).

Ultimately, debt as a voluntary commitment to love functions as *resistance* ideology in the midst of Paul's seemingly pro-empire language. Paul's hidden transcript offers a supreme critique of "secular authority," suggesting that true servants or ministers of God occupy themselves with addressing the physical and spiritual needs of the citizens, not in exacting burdensome taxes and forced military might to maintain control of the masses of people for the benefit of the governing elite. Thus, Paul's juxtaposition of *opheil-* (debt/owe) and *agape* (love) challenges the Roman social structure as an absolute authority and offers "debt of love" as an alternative system of authority, as a measuring stick which gauges the actions and intentions of both individuals and governing institutions.

C H Between *utang na loob* and debt.

A Chapter 13 reaches its climax in 11b; subjection-reflection-resistance is made purposeful as Paul exclaims: "for now is nearer our salvation than when we (first) believed." The community of believers having acknowledged its subjection by the governing authorities, reflected upon the subjection and now are convinced that God exists both within and beyond their subjection, and finally, resisted their subjection by allowing "love of neighbor" to have dominion over their lives, the community has stepped into the process of salvation—it has come near (Paul does not say this is full revelation—love of neighbor—it just brings it closer to realization). Paul's understanding of salvation is best summarized in Romans 6 where he explains that on the one hand, salvation was made possible (in the past) through the death and resurrection of Jesus the Christ. However, salvation continues (the fruits of salvation) in the lives of those dedicated to the worship of God through their voluntary commitment to seek and serve the good of others (in the present and future). Paul begins his explanation of salvation in chapter 6, describing it as "walking in the newness of life" (6:4). We are unable to grasp the fullness of his soteriological argument until chapters 12 and 13 (particularly 13:9—love of neighbor as fulfillment of law). But, his argument against idolizing the law reflects his expectation that the Christian community, in their process of salvation, would change (through the grace and power offer by God through the Holy Spirit) both their habit of thinking and their habit of living. He explains:

> We know that Christ, being raised from the dead, will never die again; death no longer has dominion over him. The death he died, he died to sin, once for all; but the life he lives, he lives to God. So you also must consider yourselves dead to sin and alive to God in Christ Jesus. Therefore, do not let sin [function as the governing authority in your mortal bodies], to make you obey its passions. No longer present your members as instruments of wickedness, but present yourselves to God as those who have been brought from death to life, and present your members to God as instruments of righteousness (6:9-13, NRSV; see also 8:10-11).

The language and the implications of this passage are reminiscent of what we have already discussed regarding the community of Christians at Rome being "transformed-nonconformist."[45] But, what is central here is that like in 12:1 or 8:12 or 13:9, Paul is concerned with *resistance*. He wants the community of believers to act in a manner that gives priority to personhood in God, not to the judicial or legalistic prescriptions of the

---

A Historical-critical understanding of Paul's text.

law or the hierarchal and exploitive social relations of the Roman state.
Being raised from the dead, raised from a death-sleep—a state where
love of neighbor is not a vigorous, operative power—speaks to the
essence of Paul's soteriological stance in that it reemphasizes the
connection he establishes between humanity's relationship with God and
their relationship with one another.[46] Ultimately, "salvation comes near"
in the process of subjection-reflection-resistance, empowering the
Christians at Rome to break through the idolatries of "worldly"
structures and build a community and an ideological stance grounded in
offering their minds and bodies to the worship of God through the
(voluntary indebtedness) "love of neighbor."

Resistance and the Free-Market Economy

H C In light of "love of neighbor" as a model of resistance, let us
revisit my earlier argument which suggests that as world citizens at the
end of the 20th century, the power(s) which govern our lives is the free-
market economy and its culture. Full participation within the "aim of
economic advancement" is imperative for the salvation of an individual
or a community. The economic structure itself, however, is not God.
Therefore if one seeks full participation in it without at some point and in
some way resisting the structure, the free-market economy is forever
perpetuated and affirmed, therefore deemed absolute. In our modern
context, to be subject by/to the aim of economic advancement and to
fully participate, without resisting is idolatrous. This paper argues,
however, that although the historical circumstances which surround our
20th century situation within the *subjection* by/to the free-market
economy differs from those about which Paul was writing, the command
to love remains the same. Let us now explore a few examples as to why
"love of neighbor" is needed as a model of resistance in order to counter
the free-market economy as absolute—as a "demonic spiritual force."[47]

Six basic arguments contribute to the authoritative dominance of the
free-market economy in contemporary society: (1) The freedom to
consume; (2) The freedom of the seller; (3) The freedom of the producer;
(4) Freedom from government interference; (5) Lower costs; (6)
Promotion of democracy. John McMurtry explores each of these
arguments noting the incoherency in the market's doctrine because it
fails to consider the power of "external influence in the production and
exchange of goods between buyers and sellers who agree to the
transaction."[48] As explained in the section on *subjection,* this essential
"freedom" to buy and sell applies to every aspect of our lives, therefore it
is critical that we examine, and as McMurtry advises, *reflect* on how the

---

H C Hermeneutical interest of free-market economy.

"veiled" inconsistencies of the doctrine contribute to the betterment or detriment of human lives and relationships and at those points where we find detriment make the necessary steps towards resistance.

It is beyond the scope of this paper to present McMurtry's analysis of each of the arguments. However, let us briefly consider two of the arguments along with McMurtry's counter-arguments. First, the free market doctrine maintains that individuals are "free" to consume. But, freedom to consume presupposes one has the money to buy those things she needs or desires. "Under the rules of the free market, need without effective demand (i.e. the purchasing power of money) is not recognized. It counts for nothing. Need with no money to back it has no reality or value for the market . . . . The 'freedom of the consumer' in the free market, is really only the freedom of those who have enough money to demand what they need or want."[49] And so it seems that under the rules of the free market those without the money to purchase the things they need do not have the right to live.

Second, the free-market argues that it reduces the costs of production and distribution. In a free market, producers and sellers must compete to produce and sell their goods at the lowest price, thereby ensuring lower costs for consumers. The problem with this argument is that "it looks only to lower costs for the consumers, not to the way these lower costs are achieved."[50] For instance, private businesses can lower their costs by avoiding or eliminating pollution control, minimum wages, workers' benefits, health and safety standards, etc. McMurtry points to the highly controversial NAFTA as an example of how businesses promote lower costs at the expense of the environment and human integrity. New trade laws established by NAFTA have encouraged the recent trend of major companies relocating to areas where they are not required to pay the costs of protecting human life and the environment. For instance, many private corporations move to the Maquiladora Zone "where wages are a small fraction of what they are in Canada or the United States, effective pollution controls are non-existent and taxes for public health and education have been reduced or abolished."[51] Moreover, under the rules of the international free market, the obvious consequence of companies relocating is that unemployment increases in the home country and lowers the price of labor. Ultimately, lower costs to private businesses results in lower wages paid to employees.

A further way of reducing costs in the free market is by "economies of scale."[52] The danger here is that small producers or businesses, without "economies of scale" are unable to compete in the price of their goods. Consequently, these smaller, "home town" businesses are forced to close. These negative aspects of the free market are referred to as "externalities" which means they are not recognized as business costs.

Ultimately, consumer goods for sale in the market may carry a lower price for those who can afford to purchase them, but all suffer the social costs produced by these non-factored "externalities:"

> While consumer goods may become less expensive, though this is by no means assured by the current oligopoly conditions of competition, the shared goods of life such as our air and water, social conditions, mutual security and cultural diversity deteriorate, with no limit in free market doctrine to their decline.[53]

In the end, McMurtry likens the current free market doctrine to an "absolutist religion." The inevitable hand of free trade governs human events "with an omniscient logic 'which cannot be interfered with'." Those loyal to this true faith will be rewarded with prosperity, perhaps immediately, or in some indeterminate time in the future. On the other hand, those who resist its strict necessity suffer the "wrath of God." The responsibility of failure rests on the shoulders of those under the doctrine's rule and "no amount of human suffering or natural destruction exacted by the doctrine's implementation can alter its prescriptions or prove it false because its truths are eternal and not subject to falsifying evidence."[54] Salvation, then, can only be won by *successful* participation in the free market system. And those who participate in that system, life to them grows more desperate (the majority of those under its rule). They are characterized as *sinners,* undeserving or unworthy of the blessings offered by the free-market economy and its culture.

A As in the time of Paul, "love of neighbor" serves as a resistance ideology against an absolutist structure which rules out any social alternative. It functions as a hidden transcript because it challenges us to make decisions and take actions based not on the minimization of costs and the maximization of profits, but on how we can best maximize our service in helping to feed the hungry, clothe the naked, heal the sick, educate the illiterate. **A H** Love of neighbor as resistance ideology disrupts policies and ideologies that promote the (inalienable) "freedom to consume," yet denies this freedom to those unable to afford it. It critiques the logic of profit for private investors as the ruling absolute of global life:

> the free market in fact flourishes by the dynamic new outlets for investment which social crisis provide: producing and selling arms to the combatants; selling ever more narcotic stimulants; producing and selling costly new pharmaceuticals to the

---

A Historical-critical understanding of Paul's text.
A H Paul's text and the modern world.

environmentally diseased who can afford them . . . generally making the rich richer, the poor poorer and the environment more uniform and more degraded.[55]

I Unchallenged, the free market increasingly becomes an unethical structure or in Paul's words, a system of sin. Ultimately, love of neighbor calls us to "internalize the externalities." That is, social responsibility must accompany "the aim of economic advancement." Social responsibility resists the free market economy as a transcendent power upon individuals through the recognition of our "debt" of love as the love of neighbor evidenced in our voluntary commitment to the service of humanity. Yet, "debt of love" cannot be manifested in a simple appendixed welfare system. Instead, it must be incorporated into the fabric of our society, allowing, inviting even, love of neighbor to dominate our hearts and minds. We must subject ourselves to love, so that we are subjected by love. In this way, humanity pays homage to God. In this way, we experience the nearness of salvation.

C A H Reading Romans 13:1-7 in light of subjection-reflection-resistance is my way of entering into the dialogue that deals with the challenges of the world economic order. Creating a language and a focus to address the economic displacement and dysfunction of the dominant economic system is vital. We have become immune to the old language (socialism, marxism, communism have become demonized). Entering the 21st century Christian believers face the wondrous challenge of identifying, acknowledging and resisting our subjection to the notion that salvation is reflected in economic prosperity. The means of resistance are not yet clear, and will only become clear as we prioritize "love of neighbor" *in light of* our subjection.

Notes

1. Lerone Bennett, Jr., *They Came Before the Mayflower* (New York: Penguin Books, 1984), 166. Bennett quotes Harriet Tubman.
2. Discussion of the analytical frame will come mostly in footnotes and references to other texts.
3. Joyce Appleby, Lynn Hunt, and Margaret Jacob, *Telling the Truth About History* (New York: W. W. Norton & Company, 1994), 120.
4. *Ibid.*, 119.

I Interplay between Paul's text and our modern world.
C A H A holistic reading of Romans.

5. *Ibid.*, 120. For a more theological analysis of this concept read Walter Wink, *Engaging the Powers: Discernment and Resistance in a World of Domination* (Minneapolis: Fortress Press, 1992), particularly chapter 5.

6. *Ibid.*, 120-121.

7. I borrow this term from Joseph Fitzmyer, *The Anchor Bible. Romans* (New York: Doubleday, 1993), 489.

8. I do not read humanity's lack of power as either a result of an inherent sinful nature (see Fitzmyer, *Romans*, 489; Peter Stuhlmacher, *Paul's Letter to the Romans: A Commentary* [Louisville: Westminster/John Knox Press, 1994], 121) or only as a result of an egocentric preoccupation with its own satisfaction and desires (C. E. B. Cranfield, *On Romans* [Edinburgh: T&T Clark, 1998], 34-35). Humanity's lack of power springs from a refusal to acknowledge its creatureliness which ultimately produces dominating attitudes and actions that can "lock so tightly into a mind-set that it takes a disruptive revelation to shatter the imprisoning mold in which those attitudes have become set" (J. D. G. Dunn, *World Biblical Commentary. Romans.* Vols. 38a and 38b [Dallas: Word Books, 1988], 427).

9. I am not concerned here with the source of or reason for creation's subjection but only with Paul's understanding that subjection can be an act of volition or imposition.

10. Wink, *Engaging the Powers*, 87-104.

11. Fitzmyer translates the term as an imperative middle: "Paul recommends submission in earthly matters" . . . (*Romans*, 665). Cranfield also reads this phrase as an imperative middle: "The term implies more than simple obedience but it also carries the sense of recognizing that one is placed below the authority of God" (71). Both Fitzmyer and Cranfield's readings suggest that subjection is primarily a matter of *will*.

12. Dunn leans more toward reading the text as an imperative passive. He writes, "Such counsel to disciplined acceptance of the realities of social status and of what that entailed for the social inferior was a regular part of early Christian paraenesis, . . . it may well be the case that such submission is an inevitable or inescapable outworking of the Christian grace of humility (*Romans*, 761). Jan Botha's definition of the phrase further emphasizes an imperative passive understanding of the term. Romans 13 means, "to submit to the orders or directives of someone. . . It does not have specifically the semantic feature of a voluntary action . . . It is not a means of conforming to rules and regulations (Jan Botha, *Subject to Whose Authority?* [Atlanta: Scholars Press, 1994], 46).

13. Botha, *Subject to Whose Authority?*, 185.

14. *Ibid.*

15. *Ibid.*, 187.

16. Louis Althusser, *Essays on Ideology* (London: Verso, 1984), 36.

17. The term is actually "senseless hearts" but functions like the term "mind." See Fitzmyer, *Romans*, 127-128 for detailed discussion.

18. See section on resistance for more discussion on verse 4.

19. Other possible translations are "test," "prove" or "examine." Dunn suggests that "discern" refers to the "capacity of forming the correct Christian ethical judgment at each given moment." The point is, however, that it is not simply forming a correct judgment but also acting in a responsible manner (*Romans*, 714). Fitzmyer, on the other hand, limits his definition to "knowledge" of what God desires (*Romans*, 641). My argument stands closer to Fitzmyer's position in that I read discernment as a process of examination which leads to "awareness."

20. Length constraints on the paper do not allow me to develop the possible connection Paul makes between *dokimazein* in 12.2 as "discerning awareness" and *syneidêsis* in 13.5 as "discerning awareness." I hope to develop this perspective in a follow-up project.

21. Enrique Dussel, *Ethics and Community* (Maryknoll: Orbis Books, 1988), 29.

22. Dunn, *Romans*, 712.

23. Wink, *Engaging the Powers*, 89. Although I agree with Wink's position on the importance of discernment as an accurate description of "reality," I add that every description of reality is clouded by an ideological presupposition which must be made explicit. People's descriptions of reality are largely based on their relationship to their conditions of existence.

24. *Ibid.*, 89.

25. *Ibid.*, 2.

26. *Ibid.*, 4.

27. *Ibid.*, 18.

28. *Ibid.*

29. *Ibid.*

30. *Ibid.*, 18-19.

31. Katie Geneva Canon, "Surviving the Blight," in Gloria Wade-Gayles ed., *My Soul is a Witness* (Boston: Beacon Press, 1995), 23.

32. I realize the underlining danger in such a statement for those "accustomed to patterns of submission to the desires of others and of denying their own worth" (Beverly Gaventa, in Carol H. Newsome and Sharon H. Ringe ed., *Women's Bible Commentary* [Louisville: Westminster/John Knox Press, 1992], 319). However, Paul's call for the community to present their whole selves as a "living sacrifice" challenges those limited by societal norms to seek the liberative power and presence of God *beyond* the confines of their present relationship to their conditions of existence.

33. William R. Herzog, "Dissembling, A Weapon of the Weak: The Case of Christ and Caesar in Mark 12:13-17 and Romans 13:1-7," *Perspectives in Religious Studies* 21 (Winter, 1994): 341.

34. *Ibid.*, 356.

35. *Ibid.*

36. *Ibid.*, 358.

37. *Ibid.*

38. *Ibid.*, 359.

39. *Ibid.*, 360.

40. Revelation E. Velunta, "Ek Pisteos Eis Pistin and the Filipinos' Sense of Indebtedness," *Seminar Papers of Society of Biblical Literature* (Atlanta: Scholars Press, 1998), 46.

41. See Richard A. Horsley ed., *Paul and Empire: Religion and Power in Roman Imperial Society* (Harrisburg: Trinity Press International, 1997), 96-97.

42. Velunta, "Ek Pisteos Eis Pistin and the Filipinos' Sense of Indebtedness." 47.

43. Fitzmyer, *Romans*, 677.

44. See Horsley, *Paul and Empire*, chapter 5.

45. Martin Luther King, Jr. *Strength to Love* (Philadelphia: Fortress Press, 1981), 2.

46. Length constraints on the paper prevented me from doing an analysis of 13:11a. Paul's call for the community to arise from its "sleep" points back to the discerning awareness called for in 12:2 and 13:5.

47. Old Testament scholar Walter Brueggemann argues in his article "The Liturgy of Abundance, the Myth of Scarcity" that consumerism is more than a marketing strategy, it has become a "demonic spiritual force" and he asks does the gospel have the "power to help us withstand it." ("The Liturgy of Abundance, the Myth of Scarcity" in *Christian Century* (March 24-31, 1999): 342-347.

48. John McMurtry, "The Contradictions of the Free Market Doctrine: Is There a Solution?" *Journal of Business Ethics* 16 (1997): 645.

49. *Ibid.*, 646.

50. *Ibid.*, 658.

51. *Ibid.*

52. A situation where the greater the investment and purchasing powers, the capital infrastructure of labor-saving machinery, the division of labor and specialization, the volume of goods produced, and the international linkages of production and distribution, the cheaper the per-unit costs of the commodities produced and sold (Ibid.,, 649).

53. McMurtry, "The Contradictions of the Free Market Doctrine," 649.

54. *Ibid.*, 657.

55. *Ibid.*, 652.

Works Cited

Althusser, Louis. *Essays on Ideology*. London: Verso, 1984.
Appleby, Joyce, and Hunt, Lynn, and Jacob, Margaret. *Telling the Truth About History*. New York: W. W. Norton & Company. 1994.
Bennett, Lerone Jr. *They Came Before the Mayflower*. New York: Penguin Books, 1984.
Botha, Jan. *Subject to Whose Authority?* Atlanta: Scholars Press, 1994.
Cranfield, C. E. B. *A Commentary on Romans 12-13*. Edinburgh: Oliver and Boyd, 1965.
_____. *On Romans*. Edinburgh: T&T Clark, 1998.
Dunn, J. D. G. *World Biblical Commentary. Romans*. Vols. 38a and 38b. Dallas: Word Books, 1988.
Dussel, Enrique. *Ethics and Community*. Maryknoll: Orbis Books, 1988.
Herzog, William R. "Dissembling, A Weapon of the Weak: The Case of Christ and Caesar in Mark 12:13-17 and Romans 13:1-7." *Perspectives in Religious Studies* 21 (Winter, 1994): 339-360.
Horsley, Richard A, ed. *Paul and Empire: Religion and Power in Roman Imperial Society*. Harrisburg: Trinity Press International, 1997.
Fitzmyer, Joseph. *The Anchor Bible. Romans*. New York: Doubleday, 1993.
King, Martin Luther, Jr. *Strength to Love*. Philadelphia: Fortress Press, 1981.
McMurtry, John. "The Contradictions of the Free Market Doctrine: Is There a Solution?" *Journal of Business Ethics* 16 (1997): 645-662.
Scott, James C. *Domination and the Arts of Resistance: Hidden Transcripts*. New Haven and London: Yale University Press, 1990.
Stuhlmacher, Peter. *Paul's Letter to the Romans: A Commentary*. Louisville: Westminster/John Knox Press, 1994.
Velunta, Revelation E. *"Ek Pisteôs Eis Pistin* and the Filipinos' Sense of Indebtedness." Pages 33-54 in *Seminar Papers of Society of Biblical Literature*. Scholars Press: Atlanta, 1998. [Revised as Chapter Seven in this volume.]
Wink, Walter. *Engaging the Powers: Discernment and Resistance in a World of Domination*. Minneapolis: Fortress Press, 1992.

A Subversive Reading of Paul

A Response to Stubbs,
"Subjection, Reflection, Resistance"

Kathy Ehrensperger

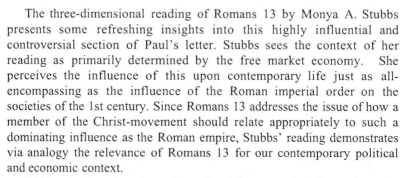

The three-dimensional reading of Romans 13 by Monya A. Stubbs presents some refreshing insights into this highly influential and controversial section of Paul's letter. Stubbs sees the context of her reading as primarily determined by the free market economy. She perceives the influence of this upon contemporary life just as all-encompassing as the influence of the Roman imperial order on the societies of the 1st century. Since Romans 13 addresses the issue of how a member of the Christ-movement should relate appropriately to such a dominating influence as the Roman empire, Stubbs' reading demonstrates via analogy the relevance of Romans 13 for our contemporary political and economic context.

Stubbs develops her three-dimensional hermeneutical frame from the different context of 19th century slavery in the South of the United States, a context which nevertheless is structurally similar enough that it can legitimately be applied to the situation of first century Christ-believing groups. In applying this three-dimensional hermeneutical framework of subjection-reflection-resistance Stubbs thus avoids a one-dimensional reading of the passage which focuses almost entirely on the subjection aspect and thus contributes to an image of Paul as someone who unconditionally supported the established authority irrespective of its character.

Stubbs does not deal with the most controversial part of this passage (Rom 13:1-7) in isolation but analyses it in relation to its immediate textual context (12:1-13:18). She thereby sets her face against a reading of this text as a general statement of Paul about the Christian's appropriate relation to state or governing authorities which is universally applicable. Paul is not seen as arriving at his statements in a social vacuum but in the wider context of the concrete implications of a life in Christ which Paul offers to the Christ-believers in Rome. According to Stubbs' reading, Rom 12:1-2 is perceived as setting the pattern and is seen as the presupposition of the following section, whereas 13:8-18 functions as the summary of an "alternative system of authority" over against the Roman imperial system. Stubbs demonstrates that thereby 12:1-2 relativizes and at the same time contextualizes the statements of 13:1-7: Christ-believers are reminded that their primary commitment is not to any other authority than God. Stubbs demonstrates convincingly that this is a call to reflection which distances Christ-believers from any straightforward identification with the Roman imperial system. Thus the subjection section 13:1-7 is seen as being relativized in that it is a descriptive statement about the social reality of the Roman Christ-believers under the imperial authorities rather than constituting a prescriptive demand. The *opheilô* terminology of 13:7-18 accentuates the distancing aspect in relation to the Roman state. When it acknowledges the debt owed to Rome, it at the same time sets an alternative emphasis by making it clear that the greatest debt that Christ believers owe is not that owed to the state but the debt of mutual support in love. As distinct from the traditional reading, Stubbs views the debt language as the language of a "Hidden Transcript" of resistance which does not only mention different kinds of debt owed in different situations, but sets the different discourses in mutual relation whereby *the latter inherently relativizes the former*. It thus emerges as a hidden discourse of resistance against the imperial state "in the midst of Paul's pro-empire language."

Stubbs' approach provides us with an alternative, even subversive reading of Paul's statements concerning the authority of the state. I find her argumentation particularly convincing in that she does not negate the subjection aspect in Rom 13:1-7 in order to come to her alternative reading. She perceives Paul as not denying the necessity to accept the social reality of the Roman imperial order but makes it very clear—with the help of the three-dimensional hermeneutical framework and the theory of "Hidden Transcripts of Power" by James C. Scott,[1] that this must not be equated with a positive acceptance or support of this dominating power. On the contrary, this acceptance must be seen as the realistic starting point of reflection, distancing and resistance in a situation where there is little option for changing the social reality as a whole. Nevertheless the strategy Stubbs discovers in Romans 13 is far from mere subordination and servile acceptance of the situation. She rather finds that Paul provides the Roman Christ-believers with means and ways to maintain their own dignity, and ability to live and act according to Christ under adverse circumstances, resisting the imperial order without encouraging a suicidal uprising.

Being in basic agreement with Stubbs' reading, I would nevertheless indicate some aspects which could have been developed further and some which could highlight and provide additional support for her particular approach. Stubbs develops her analysis of the contemporary economic situation quite extensively but fails to do so for the first century context. Since economic factors are perceived as a central aspect of the twenty-first century context it should prove fruitful to consider these very same aspects also with regard to the early period, especially since Paul himself addresses the economic impact of a life in Christ most prominently in his collection project (Rom 15).[2] Taking the economic aspect into account, the admonition to "love of the neighbor" has then not a mere interpersonal individualistic connotation but encompasses an economic-political and, moreover, corporate dimension as well. Love, then, includes the economic support of those in need. Perceived in this light, the hidden transcript of resisting power gains a much stronger dimension since the dominant Roman imperial order constituted not only political but strong economic pressure as well.

More attention could have been paid to the actual context of the Christ-believers in Rome as living at the centre of imperial power.[3] Paul's admonitions in 13:7 read in this light oscillate at the margin between subjection and resistance. To "render to all their due . . ." is not only an admonition to give to the authorities what they require but also an inherent hint not to give anything more than that. It is moreover implied here by Paul that the authority granted to those in power is not their own, nor is it established by their own will but only by the will of God. This is a clear *limitation* and thus *relativising* of any absolute power claims. The situation of the divergent groups of Christ-believers in Rome and their interaction might be an important contextual aspect to be taken into account as well.[4]

One aspect I consider specifically significant is the apocalyptic dimension of Paul's theologizing. Rather than referring only to general Hellenistic patterns of relating to the governing authorities, the Jewish apocalyptic background is also an important aspect of Paul's arguing when we recognize that he interpreted the Christ-event from within an apocalyptic framework. The perception that governing authorities were given power for a limited time until God himself would intervene at the turn of the ages would support Stubbs' argument that Paul argued for a relative acceptance of the dominating authority of the Roman emperor within the specific limits of time. I further see here a closer relation of Paul to his own Jewish context—rather than to general Hellenistic values "which were held more or less as self-evident truths in the wider context of the Hellenistic world." Stubbs, in her reading here, seems to be struggling to differentiate her stance from a traditional promotion of straightforward subjection to the authorities. I cannot see all that much difference between a "prescriptive charge advising on what people should and should not do" and "a religious perception of the relations between God and humanity via worldly governing authorities." Even as an ideological construct of the community (which is by no means self-evident), it is a call to subjection, not merely a statement about the actual reality of power under which the community lives. If we take the apocalyptic context of these statements into account, that involves a perception of "this world" as passing away and awaiting the "coming triumph of God."[5] The power and authority of "the rulers of this age" is thus extremely limited and will actually come to an end in the near future. We are not then faced with evidence of the Greek ideals of the just and honorable man but with an apocalyptic relativisation of the power of the "rulers of this world." This concurs with the alternative ethics Paul tries to establish as normative among the Christ-believing groups. It is an ethics that is thoroughly Torah oriented, as the will of God as transmitted via Christ to the believers in Rome and elsewhere.[6]

Despite these few critical remarks, I find Monya A. Stubbs' study a very important contribution to the debate about this highly influential Pauline text. She demonstrates that a traditional reading of Romans 13 which emphasizes subjection to the authorities is still relying on the hermeneutical presuppositions of the dominating discourse. She convincingly argues that there is sound historical reason for a reading from different hermeneutical presuppositions which are derived from the margins. The implications of her reading contribute to an ethics of critical distancing from any dominating powers.

Notes

1. Cf. his *Domination and the Arts of Resistance: Hidden Transcripts* (New Haven; London: Yale University Press 1990).

2. On this see, for example, my "The Language of Grace in Paul's Letters—a Call for Subordination? A Feminist Approach" paper given at the Contemporary Approaches to the Bible conference at the University of Wales, Lampeter, April 2004.

3. See William S. Campbell, "Zwischen Synagoge und Staat: Identitaet und Konflikt in den paulinischen Gemeinden," in Gabriella Gelardini, Peter Schmid ed., *Theoriebildung im christlich-juedischen Dialog. Kulturwissenschaftliche Reflexionen zur Deutung, Verhaeltnisbestimmung und Diskursfähigkeit von Religionen* (Stuttgart: Kohlhammer Verlag 2004), 151-170.

4. See William S. Campbell, "Divergent Images of Paul and His Mission," in Cristina Grenholm and Daniel Patte ed., *Reading Israel in Romans* (Harrisburg: Trinity Press International 1999), 187-211. Also Philip Esler, *Identity and Conflict in Romans* (Minneapolis: Fortress

Press, 2003) and my *That We May Be Mutually Encouraged: Feminism and the New Perspective on Paul* (Harrisburg: T&T Clark International 2004).

5. This is J. Christiaan Beker's strong emphasis, cf. *Paul, the Apostle: The Triumph of God in Life and Thought* (Edinburgh: T&T Clark, 1980), 351-367.

6. I cannot find any reference of an argument "against idolizing the law" in Romans, or against "legalistic prescriptions of the law"—these views seem to have slipped into Stubbs' argument presupposing a specific reading of Paul which is not discussed in this otherwise fine article.

PART 3

ASIA

– S I X –

Reading Romans in Southeast Asia

Righteousness and Its Implications for the Christian Community and Other Faith Communities

Daniel C. Arichea, Jr.

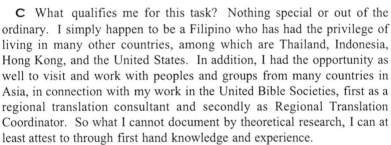

C What qualifies me for this task? Nothing special or out of the ordinary. I simply happen to be a Filipino who has had the privilege of living in many other countries, among which are Thailand, Indonesia, Hong Kong, and the United States. In addition, I had the opportunity as well to visit and work with peoples and groups from many countries in Asia, in connection with my work in the United Bible Societies, first as a regional translation consultant and secondly as Regional Translation Coordinator. So what I cannot document by theoretical research, I can at least attest to through first hand knowledge and experience.

A Nevertheless, I have to express apprehension in dealing with the letter to the Romans. This letter is not one of the favorite biblical books in Southeast Asia. For one thing, it is one of the most difficult books in the whole New Testament. Having worked with the United Bible Societies for twenty-six years, I know that translators don't want to touch Romans until and unless they have to, and often that means never! The Gospels are much easier to translate than the letters anyway, and Romans is much more complicated than the other letters, perhaps with the exception of 1 Peter.

H It is not that Romans is not used. In fact, it has been used as a tool for evangelism, with concentration on specific verses that are combined with other verses in the New Testament to come up with neat formulas for salvation. Thus, the more well known verses from Romans are 3:23,

---

C Contextual frame of a Filipino.

A The text of Romans.

H Hermeneutical interest of evangelism.

6:23, and 10:9. Combine these three verses with Acts 2:38, Acts 16:30, and conclude with John 3:16, and one has the formula of salvation in a nutshell!

Righteousness in Romans

A The concept of righteousness is one of the most important aspects of the letter, and consequently, it has been the focus of attention for the understanding and interpretation of the letter. Many commentaries are organized according to this concept. Here are two examples:

Thomas R. Schreiner, *Romans* (Grand Rapids, Baker Books, 1998)
I.   The Gospel as the Revelation of God's Righteousness (1:1-17)
II.   God's Righteousness in His Wrath against Sinners (1:18-3:20)
III.   The Saving Righteousness of God (3:21-4:25)
IV.   Hope as a Result of Righteousness by Faith (5:1-8:39)
V.   God's Righteousness to Israel and the Gentiles (9:1-11:36)
VI.   God's Righteousness in Everyday Life (12:1-15:13)
VII.   The Extension of God's Righteousness through the Pauline Mission (15:14-16:23)
VIII.   Final Summary of the Gospel of God's Righteousness (16:25-27)

Peter Stuhlmacher, *Paul's Letter to the Romans: A Commentary* (Louisville: Westminster, 1994)
The Introduction to the Epistle (1:1-17)
Part One: The Righteousness of God for Jews and Gentiles (1:18-8:39)
Part Two: The Righteousness of God for Israel (9:1-11:36)
Part Three: The Testimony of the Righteousness of God in the Life of the Community (12:1-15:13)
Conclusion (15:14-16:27)

It is not the aim of this paper to present a thorough discussion of the concept of righteousness in Paul or in his letter to the Romans. I agree with Douglas Campbell when he notes that the debate about the Pauline concept of *dikaiosynê* and its cognates "is so widespread and complex it defies any exhaustive analysis."[1]

One important element in this discussion is the necessity of recognizing the multiplicity of meanings that are included in the term

---

A Concept of "righteousness" in Romans.

dikaiosynê together with the verb form *dikaioô*, as well as the adjectival form *dikaios*.

James Dunn gives us a table of the occurrences of these terms:[2]

	Paul	Romans	NT as a whole
Dikaiosynê	57	44	91
Dikaioô	27	15	39
Dikaiôma	5	5	10
Dikaiôsis	2	2	2
Dikaiokrisia	1	1	1

A H The first usage that needs to be taken into account is when *dikaiosynê* is directly related to God. The obvious example is *dikaiosynê tou theou*, which is used by Paul in Romans 1:17, 3:21, and 3:22. But also included are expressions like "God's righteousness," which appears in Romans 3:25 and 10:13.

Secondly, there is the verb form *dikaioô*, with God as the actor or subject. In many cases, the verb is in the passive voice, but it is clear enough that the implicit subject is God.[3]

Thirdly, there are instances in which *dikaiosynê* is used of people; in some cases, this describes the relationship of people to God; in other cases, it refers to a person's character.

Fourthly, there is the adjective *dikaios*, sometimes qualifying God, and at other times qualifying people. It is used in the former sense only once in Romans (3:26), and six times in the latter sense. The adjective is used once to describe the law (7:22), and once to describe God's judgment (2:5)

The debate on righteousness has been primarily on the first and second category, namely, the term "*dikaiosynê theou*" and the verb "*dikaioô*" specifically when God is the subject either explicitly or implicitly. While these terms are different on the formal level, on the semantic level, they have practically the same meaning. Let me explain.

In Romans 1:17, Paul asserts that the righteousness of God has been revealed in the gospel. This could be read in such a way that righteousness is a description of God's character, in which case God has the attribute of righteousness. On the other hand, if *dikaiosynê* in this context can be read not as an attribute of God, but primarily as an activity of God, then the primary meaning is not that God is righteous, or that God is just, but that God does what is right, or God rights something that is not right. Barclay Newman states it thus:

A H Summarizing concept of "righteousness" in Romans.

> In this context . . . 'the righteousness of God' does not refer to God's own righteous character, but to his saving activity whereby he puts men in the right (as a judge declares a man innocent), or whereby he puts men in a right relationship to himself. . . . Traditionally, this reference to "the righteousness of God" has been explained as "forensic righteousness," that is to say, "God declaring men right." . . . However, the theological focus at this point seems not to be so much on God's declaration of man's imputed innocence as on the fact that he puts men in a new relationship to himself. It is man's confidence in God which puts men in a new relationship to himself. It is man's confidence in God which puts him in a new covenant relationship with God and thus establishes his 'righteousness.'[4]

The term *dikaioô*, on the other hand, is also used by Paul to refer to God's activity of making things right. Again, to quote Newman:

> So far the verb has appeared three times in this letter (2:13; 3:4, 20), while its related noun form has appeared four times (1:17; 3:5, 21, 22). The verb itself is a causative stem, and means something like "to make right." The analogy that Paul has in mind is that of a law court. This then is not an ethical term, as though God's pronouncement made men morally upright or virtuous; rather it is used to indicate that God pronounces men acquitted or not guilty in his sight. In other words this is merely another term used to describe the way in which God forgives. The simplest way to express this idea in today's English is to say that God puts man into a right relationship with himself.[5]

When taken this way, the distinction between *dikaiosynê theou* and *dikaioô* as an act of God disappears, for both refer to the same act of God in making something right. Some translations of the Bible reflect this understanding, as for instance,

1:17
NEB: "God's way of right and wrong," 3:24
Goodspeed: "God's way of uprightness"
TEV: "how God put people right with himself"
CEV: "God accepts everyone."
Jerusalem Bible (JB): "the justice of God," but with a footnote: "the saving justice (cf. Isaiah 56:1) of God, 3:26, who fulfills his promise to save by giving salvation as a free gift."
Dikaioô, 3:24
CEV: God freely accepts us.

TEV: God puts right everyone.

As already noted, there is one occasion where the adjective *dikaios* is used as a qualifier for God. In this case, the term could refer to the character of God as just, or more probably to the character of God as one who puts things right. If this is the case, the term would be grouped semantically with *dikaiosynê tou theou* and *dikaioô* as primarily referring to God's activity of putting things right.

Finally, another thing to consider is when *dikaios* is used as a qualifier of people. When people are described as *dikaios*, what does that mean? In some cases, *dikaios* is primarily a relationship term, referring to people who are "put right" by God, or in other words, who are accepted by God as being in a right relationship with God. In some other cases, the term is used in an ethical way, describing the proper lifestyle of people who have been "justified" by God. This latter meaning is of prime significance, as we shall see later in this paper.

With all these nuances of meaning, it is not difficult for us to see the richness of the concept of righteousness in Paul and the difficulty of communicating such richness to people who are primarily dependent on translations for their understanding.[6] The impression seems to be given at times that *dikaiosynê* and its cognates are monolithic terms, or in other words, that every time the terms are used by Paul, they mean the same thing. This is reinforced by translations of the Bible known as form-correspondent translations. Let me explain further.

Bible Translations on Righteousness in Romans

C A Most, if not all, translations of the Bible in Asia before 1970 follow the principle of one-to-one correspondence, which means that a term in the source language (in this case, Greek or Hebrew) is translated consistently by one corresponding term in the receptor language. To give a concrete example, in the Indonesian Bible of 1972, *dikaiosynê* is almost always rendered as *kebenaran*, and *dikaios* as *benar*, *dikaioô* as *membenarkan* or *dibenarkan*. It is very easy for a person using this translation to assume that *dikaiosynê* has only one meaning in Paul's letters, and in fact, in the whole New Testament, since *dikaiosynê* in Matthew 6:33 and Romans 1:17 are translated in exactly the same way. Furthermore, the word *kebenaran* does not include the component of "justice," which in Bahasa Indonesia is an entirely different word, namely, "*keadilan*." The situation gets more complicated when another

---

C A Translations that pay attention to contextual and analytical frames.

factor is considered, and that is, that *kebenaran* itself is ambiguous in Bahasa Indonesia, for it is the same word that translates *alêtheia* (truth). In such a translation, one would not know whether in Matthew 1:19 Joseph is a righteous man or a true man! And what did Jesus say in John 14:6? Did he say, "I am the way, the truth, and the life," or "I am the way, the righteousness and the life"?

It is imperative then to help Asians to better understand the Pauline concept of *dikaiosynê* not only in using secondary sources, but also in directly going to Paul's letters. However, it is not enough for them to use what we have already referred to as formal correspondent translations. Fortunately, through the efforts of the National Bible Societies, and with the help of the United Bible Societies,[7] new kinds of translations are now available. **C A** These are referred to as dynamic (or functional) equivalent translations, and bear one or more of the following characteristics:

1. They are interconfessional translations, involving many churches, including the Roman Catholic Church.
2. They are common language translations, which means they are easier to understand than formal equivalent translations.
3. They are meaning-oriented translations, which means that they are more interested in making clear the meaning of the biblical text rather than retaining its form.

It is in these translations that technical biblical terms are translated according to their meaning in specific contexts. For the purposes of this paper, let us look at a few examples of how the concept of *dikaiosynê* is treated in two Indonesian translations, namely the formal correspondence translation that was printed in 1972, known as the Terjemahan Baru (TB, or New Translation), and the dynamic equivalent translation that was published in 1978, known as the Bahasa Indonesia Sehari-hari (Everyday Indonesian) or BIS.

Romans 1:17 *dikaiosynê theou*
TB: kebenaran Allah (righteousness of God)
BIS: Allah menunjukkan bagaimana hubungan manusia dengan Allah menjadi baik kembali (God shows how the relationship of people with God can be put right).

3:5 *dikaisynê theou*
TB: kebenaran Allan (righteousness of God)

C A Dynamic equivalent translations that are faithful to contextual and analytical frames.

BIS: keadilan Allah (the justice of God)

3:21 *dikaisynê theou*
TB: kebenaran Allah
BIS: Allah sudah menunjukkan bagaimana manusia berbaik dengan Dia (God has already shown how people can be righted with him).

4:3 *eis dikaisynên*
TB: kebenaran
BIS: orang yang menyenangkan hati Allah (people who make glad the heart of God)

6:19 *doula te dikaisynê*
TB: hamba kebenaran (slaves of righteousness)
BIS: hamba bagi kehendak Allah (slaves for the will of God).

Implications for Southeast Asian Communities

C H It remains for us now to single out specific aspects of the concept of righteousness and apply them to the situation in Southeast Asia.

1. One thing that is quite helpful and readily applicable to the Southeast Asian situation is the observation that Paul's concept of *dikaiosynê* is related to the Old Testament concept of *tsedhaqah*.[8] This concept focuses on the relationship between God and God's covenant people, and defines God's faithfulness to the covenant as well as to the covenant community. So Dunn writes,

> The righteousness of God . . . denotes God's fulfillment of the obligations he took upon himself in creating humankind and particularly in the calling of Abraham and the choosing of Israel to be his people . . . God's righteousness could be understood as God's faithfulness to his people. For his righteousness was simply the fulfillment of his covenant obligation as Israel's God in delivering, saving, and vindicating Israel.[9]

This has tremendous implications for Southeast Asia, and for that matter, all of Asia. Christianity came to Asia by way of the West, primarily through Western missionaries. This statement is true both of

---

C H Meaning of "righteousness" to cultural contexts of Southeast Asia.

Roman Catholics and Protestants. However, I will limit my discussion to the Protestant side. In general, Protestant missionary activity has focused on the individual rather than the group. There are, of course, reasons for this. For one thing, this focus on the individual seems to be supported by the New Testament itself, especially the letters of Paul. For another thing, Western culture tends to give greater attention and importance to the individual. This is one of the bases for the emphasis on individual human rights. As a result of all this, the message proclaimed by Protestant missionaries was aimed at the individual rather than the group, so much so that individual response to the gospel was sought, and this often created tension and conflict in the group.

C Asian culture, on the other hand, tends to focus on the group rather than on the individual. Since the group is of prime importance, the individual can be sacrificed for the sake of the group. The basic social group is the family, and beyond that is the extended family, then a group of families, and so on.

There is, therefore, a tension between the individualistic message of the Christian faith and the Asian focus on community. Thus many Asians have become "schizophrenic" when it comes to their faith. As individuals they are believers, but their faith is limited to themselves and their relationship to God; it has nothing to do with their relationship to the society in which they live. There is a sharp distinction between church and world, between soul and body, between heaven and earth, with faith being relevant only on one side of the equation. The holistic view of the world, which continues to be present in Asian society, is somehow undermined by the Gospel with its primary message to the individual.

H We can see then how important it is to recapture this relationship component that is contained in Paul's concept of righteousness. This would mean that the gospel could once again speak not only to the individual, but also to society in general. Furthermore, this would mean taking the gospel message seriously not only in "spiritual" or "religious" areas, but also in secular concerns, such as politics, government, economics, the environment, and other concerns related to the whole created universe.

It is here where we see the importance of some theological developments in Asia, where Asian values are taken seriously and where the Gospel is interpreted through Asian eyes and Asian hearts. While there is a great deal of diversity in Asia, there is at least one element that seems to be in common in all the attempts of doing theology in Asia,

---

C Asian culture.

H Biblical text speaking to cultural contexts.

namely, the emphasis on the importance of people in community.[10] **H**
Two examples of these theological developments are the Min-Jung
theology in Korea, and Dalit theology in India, where clearly the focus is
not the individual but the mass. It is also here where we see the
importance of focusing on the life of Jesus in the Gospels rather than on
the letters of Paul. The Gospels present a Jesus who was with the *ochloi*,
the crowds, and who interacted with all kinds of people in society,
including those who were despised by society, such as tax collectors,
prostitutes and people afflicted with leprosy. **I** Jesus thus becomes the
model for Christian life, and his teachings become the new law of the
new community. It is this aspect of Christology that many Asian
theologians are rediscovering.[11]

2. Secondly, **A** a recovery of the real intent of *dikaiosynê theou* and
dikaioô in Romans has tremendous implications for Christians in
Southeast Asia as they relate to people of other faith communities. Let
me elaborate.

A The concept of *dikaiosynê* in Paul is sometimes (even often)
understood as a judgment on those who are not in a faith-relationship
with Jesus Christ or with the Christian God. For example, Romans 1:17
is interpreted as an invitation for everyone to put their faith in Christ, and
those who reject the invitation will suffer the judgment of God. While
this can be deduced as part of the meaning of the text, yet this is not its
primary intention. Here Krister Stendahl is very helpful in his assertion
that the main focus of Paul's concept of justification, especially as found
in the letter to the Romans, is to give a rationale for the Gentile mission,
that is, for the acceptance of Gentiles as part of God's people.[12] If
Stendahl is correct, and I think he is, then to use Romans 1:17 as a way
of excluding non-Christians from the orbit of God's grace is to
misunderstand, misinterpret and misuse Romans 1:17. Instead of being a
text of exclusion, Romans 1:17 is in fact a text of inclusion, opening up
the possibility of non-Jews to be counted among God's people without
going through the process of first becoming Jews through the "works of
the law." "Law" in this expression refers to the Jewish Law, the Torah,
in which case "the works of the law" do not refer to any human effort,
but actions that result from following the Jewish Law. Does this mean
then that following the Jewish law is wrong, and that it is a way of

---

H *Min-Jung* theology and *Dalit* theology.

I Interplay between biblical text and cultural context.

A Real intent of biblical texts.

A Paul's understanding of "righteousness."

seeking salvation by one's own efforts? This indeed is the popular understanding, in which case, following the law is lumped together with any human effort in order to obtain the blessings of God.

A There is however another way of interpreting this expression and its meaning, and that is, that the Law itself is a product of God's grace, and therefore, doing the "works of the law" is a legitimate response to God's initiative of calling Jews to become God's people. Here E. P. Sanders is very helpful. In his book *Paul and Palestinian Judaism,*[13] he proves very convincingly that Judaism is indeed a religion of grace rather than of works. It was God who chose the Jews to be God's people, and therefore following the law was not a way of becoming God's people but rather a way of staying within the covenant community. Sanders terms this "covenantal nomism," and defines it as "the view that one's place in God's plan is established on the basis of the covenant and that the covenant requires as the proper response of man his obedience to its commandments, while providing means of atonement for transgression."[14] He further writes, "Election and ultimately salvation are considered by God's mercy rather than human achievement."[15]

But if the Jews were not mistaken in doing the works of the law as a response to God's grace, then why would Paul cast aside following the law as the way of experiencing God's grace and being included among God's people? Paul gives an answer. God is one, and therefore God is the God not only of Jews but also of Gentiles. Now, if the way to be put right with God is only through the works of the law, then God would only be the God of the Jews, and Gentiles would be excluded, unless of course they first become Jews, and then they would be justified by their obedience to the law.[16]

A But again, if the Jews did what was right in pursuing righteousness through the works of the law, then why all this negative attitude towards them as God's people? Again, James Dunn offers help: Doing the "works of the law" "came to re-enforce the sense of Israel's privilege, the law as marking out this people in its self-apartness to God."[17] This statement is supported by the text. Paul rebukes the Jews because of their arrogant attitude as a result of their relationship with God. He notes that the Jews "boast" of their "relationship to God" (2:17b). Instead of understanding their being chosen to be God's people as something undeserved and as a call to responsible service to the world, they have used it instead as an occasion for pride and even arrogance. Instead of understanding their being chosen as God's people as a call to be a blessing to all nations, they have instead used it as a reason to be

---

A Paul and Palestinian Judaism—covenantal nomism.
A Righteousness through works of the law.

separated from other nations. **A** It is to check this kind of attitude that a new way of righteousness has been revealed. So 3:21-31:

> [21] But now, apart from law, the righteousness of God has been disclosed, and is attested by the law and the prophets,[22] the righteousness of God through faith in Jesus Christ for all who believe. For there is no distinction, [23] since all have sinned and fall short of the glory of God; [24] they are now justified by his grace as a gift, through the redemption that is in Christ Jesus, [25] whom God put forward as a sacrifice of atonement by his blood, effective through faith. He did this to show his righteousness, because in his divine forbearance he had passed over the sins previously committed; [26] it was to prove at the present time that he himself is righteous and that he justifies the one who has faith in Jesus.
> [27] Then what becomes of boasting? It is excluded. By what law? By that of works? No, but by the law of faith. [28] For we hold that a person is justified by faith apart from works prescribed by the law. [29] Or is God the God of Jews only? Is he not the God of Gentiles also? Yes, of Gentiles also, [30] since God is one; and he will justify the circumcised on the ground of faith and the uncircumcised through that same faith. [31] Do we then overthrow the law by this faith? By no means! On the contrary, we uphold the law. (New Revised Standard Version)

C Isn't it interesting, that when we examine the situation in Southeast Asia, the attitude of the Jews as portrayed above is often seen and acted out by Christians. **H** It is Christians, and not Jews who are legalistic, who demand from people a special response in order for them to be part of God's people. It is Christians and not Jews who condemn anyone who dares to disagree with the "Christian" position.

Of course these are generalizations, and generalizations are usually dangerous. But the attitude does exist, and is fueled by no less than the doctrine of justification by faith.

That is why it is so important to recover for Southeast Asian Christians and the Christian community as a whole, the real meaning and intent of Paul's concept of the righteousness of God. Such a recovery will contribute tremendously to a better attitude of the Christian community to those who belong to other faiths. The assertion that the

---

A New way of righteousness.

C Southeast Asia context.

H A Christian response.

righteousness of God was not meant to exclude but rather to include will mean that the Christian community will have to struggle with the challenge of making the gospel of faith much more inclusive than it is now. If the righteousness of God made it possible for Gentiles to become part of God's people, and this possibility was primarily an expression of God's grace, apart from any human quality or merit, then that would lead the members of the Christian community into an attitude of humility and prevent them from assuming an attitude of pride or arrogance. And finally, **A H** if the righteousness of God has the intention of asserting that God is indeed One, and that God is the God of all peoples, then that would lead the Christian community to explore its relationship with other faith communities, engaging in dialogue and discovering areas of cooperative endeavors, while at the same time, continuing to play its role as a community that is touched and transformed by the gospel of Christ.

C Already this is happening. Let me just give one example. The Philippines is in the news these days primarily because of the turbulence in the South, particularly in the island of Mindanao, which is home to some five million Muslims.   The conflicts there are much more complicated than they are depicted in the media, which usually concentrate on the spectacular, and which often give the impression that the turbulence in the South is more widespread and covers more territory than it really does. But while the news is full of accounts of violence, murder, kidnappings, and displacement of vast communities, there is no mention of peace efforts that are promoted by no less than religious leaders in Mindanao. In addition to many dialogues among Christians and Muslims, Catholic, Protestant and Muslim leaders have come together to form the Bishops-Ulama Forum in 1996, which has held quarterly dialogues since then. In addition, there are marches for peace where Muslims and Christians walk hand in hand, and there are various interfaith social and economic programs going on in many parts of Mindanao.[18] I am sure that similar activities are happening in Indonesia and other parts of Southeast Asia.

3. A third (and final) element that we want to focus on is when *dikaios* refers to the actual quality of the lives of people who have been affected in a positive way by the righteousness of God. **A** It is here where Ernst Käsemann offers some very helpful insight. In his famous essay "The Righteousness of God in Paul,"[19] he resolves the tension in

---

A H Righteousness of God in Romans.

C Mindanao situation in the Philippines.

A Analytical frame of Käsemann.

the relationship of "declare righteous" and "make righteous" by describing the righteousness of God as both gift and power. So he writes:

> The gift itself has thus the character of power ... Paul knows no gift of God that does not convey both the obligation and the capacity to serve. A gift which is not authenticated in practice and passed on to others loses it specific content.[20]

A H What all this means is that there is an ethical dimension in the concept of righteousness, and therefore to say that a Christian is righteous means that the Christian is expected to live in such a way as to reflect God's righteousness. In other words, Christians are to reflect certain attitudes and virtues that define them as righteous, that is, as people who are reconciled to God and who now exemplify in their lives a certain lifestyle that defines them as God's people.

In the letter to the Romans, examples of such a lifestyle are found in the paranetic part of the letter, chapters 12 through 15. This paper will concentrate on chapter 12.

Chapter 12 is very interesting. It is definitely addressed to the Christian community as the people of God. A few observations will suffice. The tension of being in the world but not of the world (or more properly stated, being a part of the world but qualitatively different from the rest of the world) is stated in the first two verses. The chapter contains many negative admonitions: don't do this, don't be that. Two of these remind us of Paul's admonition to the Jews not to boast of their status as the chosen people of God. "I say to everyone among you not to think of yourself more highly than you ought to think." (v. 3) "Do not be haughty, but associate with the lowly; do not claim to be wiser than you are." (v. 16) Is it possible that even during Paul's time, Christians were beginning to boast about their special relationship with God?

A H But the main theme of the chapter is knowing the will of God as a result of God's transforming activity. Verse 2 says: "Do not be conformed to this world, but be transformed (by God of course!) by the renewing of your minds, so that you may discern what is the will of God—what is good and acceptable and perfect."

But what is the will of God? It has relevance for the individual, for the community of faith, and for those who are outside the faith community. The personal aspect is primary in verse 3, which is a plea for humility. The community aspect is emphasized in verses 4-6, with the focus on unity in the midst of diversity (many members and many gifts

---

A H Ethical dimension in "righteousness."

A H The "will of God" in Romans.

in the one body). Furthermore, the members of the community are exhorted to show genuine love and affection, to be zealous in serving the Lord, to persevere in their sufferings, to share their material resources with needy fellow Christians, and to extend hospitality to Christian travelers.

A But chapter 12 goes beyond the Christian community, and deals with the relationship of Christians to those outside the church. We see allusions here to the Sermon on the Mount in the Gospel of Matthew. Does this mean that Paul himself was aware of some of the teachings of Jesus? If it does, it would also mean that there is an aspect of the concept of righteousness in Paul that is parallel to the concept of righteousness in Matthew. In Matthew, righteousness primarily refers to what God expects and demands of people in order for them to be pleasing to God. That Matthew's concept of righteousness does not focus on God's act of restoring people to a right relationship with God is most probably due to the fact that Jesus was not talking to people who needed to be reconciled to God, since they were already part of God's people. But here again, there is a parallel between Paul and Matthew: in Paul, the ethical aspect of righteousness comes after God's act of making people right with Himself. The beginning of Romans 12 is intentional: "I appeal to you, therefore, brothers and sisters, by the mercies of God."

A If this position is valid, then the twelfth chapter of Romans helps to define the ethical relationship of Christians to their neighbors who are members of other faith communities. **H** This then would have tremendous implications for the Christian communities in Southeast Asia. We must bear in mind that in continental Asia, Christianity is a very small segment of the total population. In Southeast Asia, the only country that can be described as "Christian" in terms of its population is the Philippines. In the rest of Southeast Asia, Christianity is small and insignificant. If we go beyond Southeast Asia to East and South Asia, the minority position of Christianity is even more marked.[21]

Conclusion

Now a few words to sum up all of these things. First, if the righteousness of God is defined in exclusive terms, namely that it is a way of limiting those who can be considered part of God's people, then we have consigned to hell and damnation two thirds of the world's

---

A Gospel of Matthew and Paul.

A Ethical responsibility of Christians to their neighbors in Romans 12.

H Hermeneutical implications.

population. How can such a position agree with our conception of a righteous God, that is, a God whose will is to restore all people to a right relation with God?

Secondly, if righteousness has an ethical dimension, then that should influence the relationship of Christians to the rest of the Asian population, particularly to those who publicly acknowledge their membership in and adherence to other faith communities, such as Islam, Buddhism, and Hinduism. And here, as we have already said, Romans 12 is very helpful: "Ask God to bless those who persecute you, ask God to bless, not to curse." "If someone does you wrong, don't repay him/her with a wrong." "Don't take revenge . . . , instead, let God's anger do it." "If your enemies are hungry, give them something to eat, if they are thirsty, give them something to drink." "Don't let evil defeat you; instead, overcome evil with good."

We have a long way to go in order to show that we believe in a righteous God and we are God's righteous people!

Notes

1. Douglas A. Campbell, *The Rhetoric of Righteousness in Romans 3:21-26* (Sheffield: Sheffield Academic Press, 1992), 138.

2. James D. G. Dunn, *The Theology of Paul the Apostle* (Grand Rapids: Eerdmans, 1998), 341.

3. This term appears 8 times in the letter to the Galatians, where the meaning is the same as in Romans.

4. Barclay M. Newman and Eugene Nida, *A Translator's Handbook on Paul's Letter to the Romans* (London: United Bible Societies, 1973).

5. *Ibid.*

6. Western scholarship is not easily accessible to many Asians, considering the fact that books from the West are very expensive. Also, in some Asian countries, theological education is carried on with the use of indigenous languages. Some of the countries in this category are Indonesia, Thailand, Korea, Japan, and China. The countries that were colonized by English speaking countries continue to use English extensively in theological education. Included in this category are India, Sri Lanka and the Philippines.

7. The United Bible Societies is the umbrella organization for national Bible Societies throughout the world.

8. See Dunn, *Theology of Paul*, 341-342. Campbell (*Rhetoric of Righteousness*, 147-155) includes in his discussion the Qumran scrolls and intertestamental literature. See also E.P. Sanders, *Paul and Palestinian Judaism* (Philadelphia: Fortress Press, 1973).

9. Dunn, *Theology of Paul*, 342.

10. There are many publications describing theological development in Asia. A few can be mentioned: Douglas J. Elwood ed., *Asian Christian Theology: Emerging Themes* (Philadelphia, Westminster Press, 1980); R. S. Sugirtharajah ed., *Frontiers in Asian Theology: Emerging Trends* (New York: Orbis Books, 1994); Yeow Choo Lak ed., *Doing Theology and People's Movements in Asia* (Singapore: Chopmen Publishers, 1987); T. Dayanandan Francis and F. J. Balassusndaram ed., *Asian Expressions of Christian Commitment* (Madras: Christian Literature Society, 1992).

11. An example of this is represented by Carlos Abesamis, *A Third Look at Jesus* (Quezon City: Claretian Press, 2000). He says that his emphasis is more on telling the story of Jesus rather than "drafting formulas about Jesus and his nature" (p. 3). See also R. S. Sugirtharajah ed., *Asian Faces of Jesus* (New York: Orbis Books, 2001).

12. Krister Stendahl, *Final Account: Paul's Letter to the Romans* (Minneapolis: Fortress Press, 1995). He writes: "Paul only mentioned justification by faith when he discussed the status of his Gentile converts. Speaking about justification by faith was . . . his way of defending the right of the Gentiles to be included in the consummation and redemption now underway—by faith." (p. 4).

13. Philadelphia: Fortress Press, 1977.

14. Sanders, *Paul and Palestinian Judaism,* 75.

15. *Ibid.,* 422.

16. So Romans 3:27-31.

17. Dunn, *Theology of Paul*, 358. Dunn also makes the same point in "The Justice of God," *Journal of Theological Studies* 43 (1992), 11, where he remarks that the boasting that is mentioned in Romans 2:17 and 23, is "not the boast of self-confidence, but of Jewish confidence, the boast of one conscious of his privilege as a member of the people of Israel."

18. For a fuller account, see Hilario M. Gomez, Jr., *The Moro Rebellion and the Search for Peace: A Study on Christian-Muslim Relations in the Philippines* (Zamboanga City, Philippines: Silsilah Publications, 2000), especially page 205 to the end of the book.

19. *In New Testament Questions for Today* (Philadelphia: Fortress Press, 1965), 168-182.

20. Käsemann, *In New Testament Questions for Today*, 170.

21. I have appended to this paper the religious composition many countries of Asia and the Pacific. The data is from the 2002 *Bulletin* of the United Bible Societies.

Works Cited

Campbell, Douglas A. *The Rhetoric of Righteousness in Romans 3:21-26.* Sheffield: Academic Press, 1992.

Dunn, James D. G. *The Theology of Paul the Apostle.* Grand Rapids: Eerdmans, 1998.

Käsemann, Ernst. *In New Testament Questions for Today.* Philadelphia: Fortress Press, 1965.

Newman, Barclay M., and Eugene Nida. *A Translator's Handbook on Paul's Letter to the Romans.* London: United Bible Societies, 1973.

Sanders, E. P. *Paul and Palestinian Judaism.* Philadelphia: Fortress Press, 1973.

Appendix
Religion in Asian Countries
(Source: United Bible Societies Bulletin, 2002)

Afghanistan
    Population 23.7 million
    Islam – 98%
    Christianity – undetermined

Bangladesh
    Population 129.2 million
    Islam 85.8%
    Hindu 12.4%
    Christian 0.7%
    Buddhist 0.6%

Brunei
    Population 322,000
    Islam 64.4%
    Buddhist 9.1%
    Christian 7.7%

Cambodia
    Population 11.4 million
    Buddhist 95%
    Islam 2.2%
    Christian 0.4%

China
    Population 1.2 billion
    Non-Religious 50.3%
    Traditional beliefs 32.6%
    Buddhist 8.4%
    Islam 1.5%
    Protestant 6.5%
    RC 0.6%

East Timor
    Population 885,000
    RC 89.9%
    Protestant 2.3%

Fiji
    Population 813,000
    Christian 56.8%
    Hindu 33.3%
    Islam 6.9%

Hong Kong
    Population 6.7 million
    Non-Religious 58.5 %
    Taoist 15.5%
    Buddhist 14.9%
    Protestant 5%
    RC 4%
    Islam 0.9%

India
    Population 1 billion
    Hindu 82.8%
    Islam 11.8%
    Christian 2.3%
    Sikh 2%
    Buddhist 0.8%

Indonesia
    Population 203.5 million
    Islam 82.2%
    Protestant 6%
    RC 3.6%
    Hindu 1.8%
    Buddhist 1%

Iran
    Population 66.1 million
    Islam 98.8%
    Christian 0.4%
    Bahai 0.5%
    Jewish 0.1%

Japan
    Population 126.7 million
    Shintoist 50.2%
    Buddhist 42%
    Protestant 0.8%
    RC 0.3%
    Islam 0.2%

North Korea
    Population 22.3 million
    Non-Religions 71.2%
    Confucian 12.9%
    Traditional 12.3%

Christian 2.1%
Buddhist 1.5%

South Korea
Population 47.7 million
Non-religious 40.3%
Buddhist 23.1%
Protestant 18.1%
RC 6.6%
Unification 1.1%

Laos
Population 5.6 million
Buddhist 48.8%
Traditional Beliefs 41.7%
Non-religious 5.4%
Christian 2.1%
Chinese Folk Religion 1.5%
Islam 0.4%

Macau
Population 437,000
Non-religious 60.9%
Buddhist 16.8%
Roman Catholic 6.7%
Protestant 1.7%
Mormon 0.1%
Bahai 0.1%

Malaysia
Population 22.2 million
Islam 47.7%
Chinese folk religion 24.1
Christian 8.3%
Hindu 7.3%
Buddhist 6.7%
Traditional Beliefs 3.4%

Maldives
Population 269,000
Islam 99.2%
Buddhist 0.6%
Christian 0.1%

Micronesia
Population 440,162
RC 84.2%
Protestant 26.6%
Buddhist 1.6%
Mormon 1.5%
Traditional Beliefs 2.1%

Mongolia
Population 2.4 million
Non-religious 39.7%
Traditional beliefs 31.7%
Buddhist 22.5%
Islam 4.8%
Christian 1.3%

Myanmar
Population 50 million
Buddhist 89.3
Christian 4.9
Islam 3.8
Hindu 0.5
Traditional beliefs 0.2

Nepal
Population 24.3 million
Hindu 76.7%
Buddhist 8.2%
Traditional Beliefs 6.9%
Islam 3.9%
Christian 2.4%

Pakistan
Population 130.5 million
Islam 96.1%
Christian 2.5%
Hindu 1.2%

Papua New Guinea
Population 4.9 million
Protestant 65.1%
Catholic 30.6%
Traditional beliefs 3.6%
Bahai 0.8%

Philippines
Population 76.5 million
RC 83%
Protestant 9%
Islam 5%

Samoa
Population 220,000
Protestant 65.2%
RC 21.9%
Mormon 9.1%
Bahai 2.3%

Singapore
	Population 4 million
	Chinese folk religion 42.7%
	Islam 18.4%
	Buddhist 14.5%
	Christian 12.2%
	Hindu 5.1%
	Non religious 4.7%

Sri Lanka
	Population 18.7 million
	Buddhist 68.4%
	Hindu 11.3%
	Christian 9.4%
	Islam 8%

Thailand
	Population 60.6 million
	Buddhist 93.3%
	Islam 4.8%
	Christian 1.7%

Taiwan
	Population 23.5 million
	Buddhist 82%
	Taoist 13%
	Protestant 3%

RC 1.5%

South Pacific
	Population 2.5 million
	Protestant 56.4%
	RC 21.2%
	Hindu 11.4%
	Mormon 2.9%
	Islam 2.6%
	Bahai 1.4%

Solomon Islands
	Population 455,000
	Protestant 77.5%
	RC 22.1%
	Bahai 0.4%

Vietnam
	Population 77.3 million
	Buddhist 49.5%
	Non-religious 20.5%
	Traditional Beliefs 9.5%
	Christian 8.3%
	Chinese Religions 5.3%
	Islam 0.7%

"Quasi-Lutheran" Considerations

A Response to Arichea,
"Reading Romans in Southeast Asia"

Douglas A. Campbell

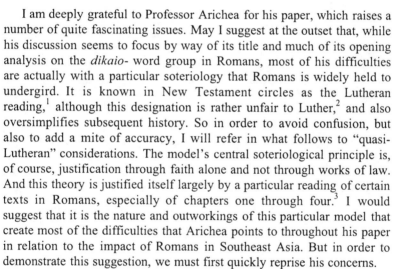

I am deeply grateful to Professor Arichea for his paper, which raises a number of quite fascinating issues. May I suggest at the outset that, while his discussion seems to focus by way of its title and much of its opening analysis on the *dikaio-* word group in Romans, most of his difficulties are actually with a particular soteriology that Romans is widely held to undergird. It is known in New Testament circles as the Lutheran reading,[1] although this designation is rather unfair to Luther,[2] and also oversimplifies subsequent history. So in order to avoid confusion, but also to add a mite of accuracy, I will refer in what follows to "quasi-Lutheran" considerations. The model's central soteriological principle is, of course, justification through faith alone and not through works of law. And this theory is justified itself largely by a particular reading of certain texts in Romans, especially of chapters one through four.[3] I would suggest that it is the nature and outworkings of this particular model that create most of the difficulties that Arichea points to throughout his paper in relation to the impact of Romans in Southeast Asia. But in order to demonstrate this suggestion, we must first quickly reprise his concerns.

Arichea details nine issues in his paper—and he is especially concerned with the last four:

(1) the use of Romans for evangelistic proof-texting (specifically 3:23, 6:23, 10:9);[4]

(2) its avoidance by translators;[5]

(3) the use of a *dikaio-* theme to structure the entire letter's argument;[6]

(4) the skewed New Testament distribution of *dikaio-* terminology, which is dominated by Paul and, within his corpus, by Romans;[7]

(5) the translation possibilities (the verb and noun phrase arguably overlap in terms of God "making something right");

(6) the standard translation conundrum between formal correspondent and dynamic or functional equivalents;

(7) the individualism of much of the Protestant missionary movement, which jars with Asian culture's strong emphasis on the group and especially on the family, and the consequences of this individualism, notably theological dualism, that mutes any constructive Christian impact on culture—this has also elicited various, partly reactionary, indigenous, or alternative theological, programmes by way of response;[8]

(8) the strong implication of judgment, and allied attitudes of condemnation, to outsiders that promote Christian arrogance and undermine inter-Faith co-operation;[9] and

(9) the complementary undermining of a humble and non-violent ethic towards outsiders.

It will be clearest to begin our more detailed demonstration with Arichea's final issues, i.e., seven through nine (and these comprise three of his four major concerns in any case).

The quasi-Lutheran model of salvation is inherently individualist. It focuses throughout on an essentially rational individual who deduces a number of very important points from the cosmos, concludes on the basis of these that she is in very deep trouble with God, and consequently makes the decision to appropriate the generous, and apparently quite manageable, Christian offer of salvation through faith alone. This journey, from dawning theological awareness, through the mounting awareness of sin, to the climactic point of decision and conversion, is necessarily individualist throughout. And it is the basis of all Christian existence. Hence this, I would suggest, namely, the central dynamic of quasi-Lutheran soteriology, is clearly one powerful source of the individualism that Arichea finds so problematic in the Southeast Asian context.

I also found his aside in this connection concerning dualism especially interesting. Arichea characterizes this as a response to the tensions created by reconciling an individualist model with an irreducibly social and familial context—and I am sure he is right to point to this. But dualism is also an inherent propensity within the quasi-Lutheran model. The individual who makes her reflective journey to salvation is also struggling throughout with the horrors of repeated transgression—it is this dark reality that drives much of the journey. Hence some form of dualism really must be introduced to safeguard the intellectual purity of this journey from the contamination of sin—if the individual's rational faculties are fundamentally distorted, she will be unable to undertake the appropriate rational steps, and the model will not work; the journey will not take place. In short, a quasi-Lutheran alliance between semi-Pelagian soteriology and Dualism is entirely predictable.[10]

We turn then to the second of Arichea's major difficulties, with a set of problematic attitudes in the Christian posture towards outsiders.

And here it needs to be recognized that the quasi-Lutheran model is also inherently judgmental, although the precise nature of this judgment must be noted carefully. As we have just seen, this model emphasizes the rational and moral journey of the individual to Christian salvation strongly, hence it can place quite considerable rhetorical pressures on the individual within the pre-Christian phase to convert—this is one of the model's apparent strengths. It is, quite simply, the correct rational and moral decision to choose salvation, because conversion will result in the forgiveness of sins and the avoidance of eternal punishment. However, it follows necessarily from this argument that those who resist this decision are immoral and irrational—that is, essentially, the recalcitrant are stupid and dissolute.

Now I do not want ultimately to deny that some sense of judgment vis-à-vis outsiders will arise from Paul's writings (although this needs to be carefully debated, and it must be still more carefully considered if he is being absolutely consistent in so arguing).[11] Nevertheless we ought to distinguish between the dynamic that arises from a strong judgment of culpability that derives from one's fundamental theological position, as in the quasi-Lutheran model, over against a mitigated judgment that is the reflex of a fundamentally non-judgmental position established by grace. If one's fundamental posture is conditioned by grace, then one's basic attitude towards outsiders is solidarity, not condemnation—in George Whitefield's famous phrase: "there but for the grace of God go I." Ongoing recalcitrance by some is then a tragedy more than anything else. However, the quasi-Lutheran model delivers a strongly condemning message towards outsiders; they are directly culpable for their failure to convert—"theirs is a mistake that we Christians have not made", it says.

So I would suggest that Arichea's various difficulties with the attitudes of Christians towards outsiders are also explicable in large measure in terms of the quasi-Lutheran model. Firstly, as we have just seen, it is inherent in this model to condemn outsiders in strong terms. Concomitantly, there are few resources present that generate solidarity with outsiders (as well as, arguably, any related sense of humility). Secondly, the model also offers few (or no!) checks on the endorsement of violence against outsiders. It suggests that the recalcitrant *deserve* punishment, and are also ultimately *destined* for punishment, so present violence against them, justly conceived, is not really offensive in theological terms.[12] And again, concomitantly, few if any resources are provided for the potentially highly costly endorsement of a non-violent and even actively loving response to outsiders. Indeed, the very connection within the model between conversion and a Christian ethic of self-sacrifice is notoriously difficult to establish or to discern. While, even granting its establishment, it does not in and of itself directly empower Christians to pursue it. This ethic requires the resources of the Spirit; something the quasi-Lutheran model initially necessarily excludes, and later includes only by way of an optional extra. So, once again, I would suggest that quasi-Lutheran soteriology lies in large part behind Arichea's difficulties.

If Arichea's main concerns, with individualism, dualism, judgmentalism, and arrogance over against benevolent ethical action, all turn out to be difficulties inherent within quasi-Lutheran soteriology, what of his more narrowly lexicographical questions?

Arichea argues, I think correctly, for a dynamic or functional approach to translation. However, this approach places a premium on context. Hence the construal of the surrounding argument will clearly now be even more important for the translation of the individual *dikaio*-terms that stud its progressions than it was previously within a formal correspondent approach. And indeed the influence of the quasi-Lutheran model on the dynamic Indonesian translations he lists is plainly apparent (and it is not absent from his list of formal translations either, but there it exerts its influence, rather typically, via the selection of stems). Similarly, the overlapping translations that he selects earlier on for *dikaiosynê theou* (usually translated "the righteousness of God") and *dikaioô* (usually translated "justify") also clearly reflect a quasi-Lutheran agenda.[13] And note that the very designation of these signifiers as strategic or critical is a consequence of quasi-Lutheran concerns! Once again, then, the influence of the model seems paramount.

This influence also clearly explains why certain key verses from Romans end up proof-texting evangelistic systems so frequently, as well as why certain commentators suggest that the theme of righteousness (or some closely related notion) can structure the argument of the letter as a whole—it is entirely predictable that advocates of quasi-Lutheran soteriology would attempt to extend the control of their model from its key texts over the arguments of the rest of the letter.[14]

Hence, as far as I can tell, only one of Arichea's nine concerns, the avoidance of Romans by translators—and even then only arguably[15]—remains unexplained by the influence of quasi-Lutheran soteriology.

I hope that it is also quite clear by now that I am wholly in agreement with Arichea's suggestions that quasi-Lutheran soteriology possesses a number of deeply problematic aspects.

But we need now to press our analysis in some further, rather intriguing, directions, again following Arichea's lead. In particular,

What roles do the cross-cultural perspective, and the cultural dimension, play here?

Arichea's paper highlights clearly that culture is a critical dimension within this whole, deeply problematic, dynamic. Six brief, related, points in my view flow from this basic observation.

(1) It needs to be admitted that the quasi-Lutheran model *is* characteristically western, and also distinctly modern, in that it came into being specifically in the early sixteenth century, shortly after the first stirrings of European modernity.[16] At its heart is a God of retributive justice who endorses a universe structured in terms of law; arguably a distinctively mediaeval Catholic conception of society. Salvation is an agreement—in effect, a contract—between God and humanity, although one that passes through two forms. The first is strict and difficult and leads inevitably to failure.[17] Fortunately, the second, rather easier, contract, offered by the church's preachers, is effective (and here the model tends to depart from its Catholic antecedents). It is, moreover, directed towards an individual who chooses to embrace it on the basis of their own deductions. This entire system is defended by its protagonists on the basis of their own investigations of the Scriptures in which they decide for themselves, if necessary against the church and its traditions, what those authoritative writings mean.

These emphases on the autonomy of the individual and their investigations suggest to me especially that this model is a post-Renaissance, European one (and one also deeply indebted to Humanism, although not identical with that movement). Hence the language of contract and consent—and even of rights—if not intrinsic to it, does carry its sense forward accurately.[18] And this distinctive marriage creates certain important dynamics for the model's later reception by Western scholars.

(2) Clearly a reciprocal endorsement between the model and certain aspects of Western culture can take place. We should note in particular the way the model reinforces the West's typical critique of monarchical tyranny, as overriding individual rights and consent. Indeed, a form of this critique is often deployed against those who propose an alternative to quasi-Lutheran soteriology, as if the only alternative to quasi-Lutheranism is divine despotism! (One suspects that there are other alternatives, in the case of God.)

Symmetrical to this potential cultural endorsement (which always has a vicious potential) is (3) the increased difficulty many western scholars have recognizing the problems within the model, because this is tantamount to recognizing problems within one's most cherished cultural commitments. It is at times to seem, for example, anti-American, or some such. Hence one might expect a degree of myopia in relation to the model's difficulties for interpreters located in the West. (We might say that a hermeneutic of generosity exists towards the model's validations, but a hermeneutic of suspicion concerning any putative difficulties or problems.)

Hence (4) I would suggest that one of the most significant contributions of a cross-cultural interrogation like Arichea's is to expose some of these difficulties by standing (partly) outside the main cultural equation (that is, insofar as this is really possible in an increasingly westernized world, and the latter especially where higher education is concerned). We see our own western difficulties more clearly when this process is aided by non-western eyes.

But (5) his paper also suggests that it would be a mistake to go on to assume that this model's particular difficulties, which are caused in part by its distinctively western commitments, are therefore culturally limited as well. Unfortunately, it would seem that this model causes damage wherever it goes, whether east or west. So, Christian condemnation of the unsaved as stupid and immoral tends to cause difficulties in some sense wherever it is suggested. Put bluntly, bad theology is destructive of humanity *per se*, although doubtless with cultural differences of emphasis, and this clearly irrespective of a model's exact cultural origins.

What then are we to do?

Finally, it is a further intriguing dimension of his paper that Arichea, in an act of supreme charity, appeals for help to several of the classic western critiques of quasi-Lutheranism, which propose different ways forward in relation to the key texts.[19] And indeed a long tradition of dissent against the quasi-Lutheran reading of Paul is discernible in the West. Hence I would suggest following Arichea's lead once again in considering first whether these alternative western resources can assist us with our difficulties. Unfortunately, time precludes any detailed interaction with these resources here, and much as I would like to pursue this. (This is a complex question in its own right).[20] But at least we sense from this appeal by him the perception within some in the East that the West might ultimately be able to contribute to the healing of the theological and social damage it has inflicted on the church, and on the world, through its quasi-Lutheran offspring, and so make a degree of reparation, however long overdue.

Notes

1. Terminology popularized especially by Krister Stendahl, "The Apostle Paul and the Introspective Conscience of the West," *Harvard Theological Review* 56 (1963): 199-215; *idem, Paul Among Jews and Gentiles, and Other Essays* (Philadelphia: Fortress, 1976).

2. Cp. C. E. Braaten and R. W. Jenson, ed., *Union with Christ. The New Finnish Interpretation of Luther* (Grand Rapids: Eerdmans, 1998).

3. Specifically 1:16-5:1; but we should note also esp. chap. 10, specifically 9:30-10:17.

4. He also observes that these are combined with Acts 2:38, 16:30 and John 3:16. See Daniel Arichea, "Reading Romans in Southeast Asia: Righteousness and its Implications for the Christian Community and Other Faith Communities," paper presented to the Romans Through History and Cultures Seminar, SBL/AAR General Meeting, Toronto, 2002 (18 pp.), 1.
See http://www.vanderbilt.edu/AnS/religious_studies/Romans.htm.

5. Along with 1 Peter (Arichea, "Reading Romans in Southeast Asia," 1).

6. Arichea ("Reading Romans in Southeast Asia," 2) specifically cites the commentaries of Peter Stuhlmacher Peter, *Der Brief an die Römer* (Göttingen & Zürich: Vandenhoeck & Ruprecht, 1989; ET 1994 S. Hafemann; Louisville: Westminster/John Knox) and Thomas A. Schreiner, *Romans* (Grand Rapids: Baker Books, 1998).

7. Citing evidence collated by James Dunn, *The Theology of Paul the Apostle* (Edinburgh: T&T Clark; Grand Rapids: Eerdmans, 1998), 341 (Arichea, "Reading Romans in Southeast Asia," 3).

8. Specifically, *Min-Jung* and *Dalit* theology, and an emphasis on the historical Jesus as a moral exemplar in the work of scholars like Abesamis and Sugirtharajah (Arichea, "Reading Romans in Southeast Asia," 7-9).

9. Concrete expressions of the latter in the Southeast Asian context are the peace efforts, and the inter-religious socio-economic programs and dialogues, currently taking place in Mindanao (the southern part of the Philippines) (Arichea, "Reading Romans in Southeast Asia," 12-13).

10. In the light of Dualism's notorious social ineffectiveness, it is also hardly surprising to encounter the further reactions that Arichea speaks of like *Min-Jung* and *Dalit* theology that have already been mentioned. But the argument of Romans, correctly construed, may ultimately not be especially sympathetic to any foundational reification of indigenous perspectives, eastern or western, although it should warmly endorse incarnational theological responses, and especially where these involve interrelational or interpersonal as against either individual or corporate

and collective visions. Similarly, any flight from Paul to the ethics of Jesus, as if these two perspectives are both fundamentally different and happily separable, is also ill-advised (Arichea, "Reading Romans in Southeast Asia," 9, esp. n. 11). Unfortunately now is not the time to address these particular questions in detail—for some further brief but apposite remarks, see A. J. Torrance, "Response to Jürgen Moltmann (at 'Christ and Context' [Knox Theological Hall, Dunedin, New Zealand, 1991])," in H. Regan and A. J. Torrance ed., *Christ and Context: The Confrontation Between Gospel and Culture* (Edinburgh: T&T Clark, 1993), 192-200; perhaps also Douglas A. Campbell, "Response to John de Gruchy (at "Christ and Context" [Knox Theological Hall, Dunedin, New Zealand, 1991])," in *Christ and Context: The Confrontation Between Gospel and Culture*, 159-76.

11. See esp. Martinus De Boer's insightful study ("Paul and Apocalyptic Eschatology," in J. J. Collins ed., *The Encyclopedia of Apocalypticism. Volume 1: The Origins of Apocalypticism in Judaism and Christianity* (New York: Continuum, 1999), 345-83, esp. 371-75.

12. Arguably the model contains other potentially violent components and endorsements as well, although it must be appreciated that I am not arguing that the model itself is *inherently* committed to violence; I am suggesting that it provides few or no safeguards against it.

13. Arichea, "Reading Romans in Southeast Asia," 4-7.

14. However, note also that while this is easy enough to claim in terms of some summary structure, it is a more difficult thing to demonstrate in relation to the actual texts at the crucial argumentative points of transition, notably into chapters five, nine, and twelve.

15. That is, Is it the deep unpalatability of some of the model's theological consequences that leads, at least in part, to this?; a phenomenon allied perhaps with the difficulty of grasping in detail how this model *does* shift into the arguments of chapters five, nine, and twelve following.

16. Stendahl, in my view, did not help us at this point, that is, the model's relationship with Augustine is not direct and possibly even antithetical.

17. However, no one, whether Christian or not, is released from the ethical demands of this contract and its consequences; hence, non-Christians are still bound by the rule of law, a useful point in relation to political society.

18. See here in particular two seminal essays by James B. Torrance ("Covenant and Contract, a Study of the Theological Background of Worship in Seventeenth-Century Scotland," *Scottish Journal of Theology* 23 (1970): 51-76; *idem*, "The Contribution of McLeod Campbell to Scottish Theology," *Scottish Journal of Theology* 26 (1973): 295-311, and usefully reprised also in his "Introduction," in J. McLeod Campbell,

The Nature of the Atonement (Edinburgh: Handsel [1856], 1996), 1-16. See also two fascinating analyses by J. Lockwood O'Donovan, "Historical Prolegomena to a Theological Review of 'Human Rights'," *Studies in Christian Ethics* 9.2 (1996): 52-65; *idem*, "The Poverty of Christ and Non-proprietary Community" (Paper presented to "Theology and Ethics," a conference held at King's College London, 28-30 April, 1997); cp. also C. B. MacPherson, *The Political Theory of Possessive Individualism. Hobbes to Locke* (Oxford: Clarendon, 1962).

19. Specifically he cites Krister Stendahl, "The Apostle Paul and the Introspective Conscience of the West"; *idem*, *Paul Among Jews and Gentiles, and Other Essays*; *idem*, *Final Account: Paul's Letter to the Romans* (Fortress: Minneapolis, 1995); E. P. Sanders, *Paul and Palestinian Judaism* (Philadelphia: Fortress, 1977); J. D. G. Dunn, "The Justice of God: A Renewed Perspective on Justification by Faith," *Journal of Theological Studies* 43 (1992): 1-22; *idem*, *The Theology of Paul the Apostle*, and E. Käsemann, *New Testament Questions of Today* (London: SCM, 1969): 168-82. Many more studies could be added here, perhaps most notably, Heikki Räisänen, *Paul and the Law* (Tübingen: J. C. B. Mohr [Paul Siebeck], 1983); Dunn, *Romans 1-8* (Dallas: Word, 1988) and *Romans 9-16* (Dallas: Word, 1988); Neil Elliott, *The Rhetoric of Romans: Argumentative Constraint and Strategy and Paul's Dialogue with Judaism* (Sheffield: JSOT, 1990); Bruce Longenecker, *Eschatology and the Covenant: A Comparison of 4 Ezra and Romans 1-11* (Sheffield: JSOT, 1991); Stanley K. Stowers, *A Rereading of Romans: Justice, Jews, and Gentiles* (London & New Haven: Yale University, 1994); John D. Moores, *Wrestling with Rationality in Paul: Romans 1-8 in a New Perspective* (Cambridge: University Press, 1995); Anthony J. Guerra, *Romans and the Apologetic Tradition* (Cambridge: University Press, 1995); Terrence L. Donaldson, *Paul and the Gentiles: Remapping the Apostle's Convictional World* (Minneapolis: Fortress, 1997); N. T. Wright, *The Climax of the Covenant: Christ and the Law in Pauline Theology* (Edinburgh: T&T Clark, 1991); *idem*, "Romans and the Theology of Paul," in D. M. Hay and E. E. Johnson ed., *Pauline Theology. Volume III: Romans* (Minneapolis: Fortress, 1995), 30-67; *idem*, "Romans," in ed. L. Keck *et al.*, *The New Interpreter's Bible* (Nashville: Abingdon, 2002), 10: 395-770, and Wendy Dabourne, *Purpose and Cause in Pauline Exegesis: Romans 1:16-4:25 and a New Approach to the Letter* (Cambridge: University Press, 1999) (although can one sense a tailing off of interest in these questions in recent years, Wright excepted?).

20. These and all the related issues that Arichea's paper, and my response, touch on, will be rehearsed in full in a forthcoming study.

SEVEN

"*Ek Pisteôs Eis Pistin*" and the Filipinos' Sense of Indebtedness (*Utang Na Loob*)

Revelation Enriquez Velunta

◆

In Memory of Her:
A Contextual Translation of Romans 1:16-17

> For I am not ashamed of the gospel;[1] it is the power of God to save[2] everyone believing,[3] to the Jew first and to the non-Jew.[4] For in it the solidarity[5] of God is revealed[6] from faith to faith;[7] as it is written, "the just by faith[8] will[9] live"[10] (modified NRSV).

C Romans 1:16-17 were my late Nanay's (mother's) favorite Bible verses. She grew up in a predominantly Roman Catholic community where protes[11] children were discriminated against and were not allowed to attend religion classes in public schools (of course, the reverse was equally true in predominantly Protestant communities). Lola (grandmother) was United Methodist. Lolo (grandfather) was a nominal Catholic.[12] Their children, Nanay being the eldest, chose to go where Lola went to church. This did not make Lolo very happy and he poured all his frustrations on the children, especially on Nanay.

C But Nanay stood her ground, not "ashamed" of the gospel that she lived by. She eventually won Lolo over, though not with words but with deeds. He became a Methodist. When Nanay decided, against Lolo's wishes, to go to seminary instead of finishing her business program, the verses from Romans, again, gave her support. Protestant pastors, then and now, have always lived near the poverty line. Nanay disappointed many people who had high hopes for her when she went to seminary. She disappointed even more when she married a classmate, another

---

C Family background influences author's understanding of the biblical text.

C Nanay lived out her understanding of the gospel.

future pastor. Their marriage literally "lived by faith" until her death at 49 in 1984.

C H It was Nanay who taught us, her three children, about *utang na loob*[13] as a legitimate translation of faith. She saw the Christian life as a life lived in a state of perpetual indebtedness, that is, also a state of perpetual gratitude.[14] To a lot of people, many of her life choices could have been interpreted as *walang utang na loob* (having no sense of indebtedness), *walang hiya* (shameless), or *makapal ang mukha* (thick-faced). She was the eldest in a brood of six.[15] **C** Philippine society expected her to help with the schooling of her younger siblings. Society expected her to help her parents in their old age. Society expected bright children to pursue medicine or business so that she might offer her family a taste of the good life, and more importantly, her future success would bring honor to the family name. Society expected her to obey her parents' wishes.[16] And society expected her to be ashamed of what she eventually did. But she was not. What she did instead was offer her life to her siblings, her own family, her parishioners, the people around her.[17] And, instead of being ashamed, she was really proud of what she did.

C H Her life was lived as an offering of thanksgiving to God because this was the only way she could ever "repay" God for everything she "owed" God, for everything God has done for her, for God's *kagandahang loob*.[18] Thus she lived not trying to cancel her debt to God, which, of course, she could never have done. What she did was try to "repay" God by "owing" people love (cf. Romans 13:8-9). Her sense of *utang na loob* was not reciprocal, in the strictest sense of the word but channeled or funneled. The only way she could ever repay her parents for what they did for her was to be a good parent herself. And she was. The only way I could ever repay her for everything she did for me is to be a good parent to my sons, Lukas and Ian. The only way Nanay could ever repay God for what God did for her was to take good care of God's children. And she did.

The relevant teaching of the text for me—as read through my mother's legacy—is that Paul's concept of faith can be translated in Filipino as *utang na loob* (as compared to the widely used *pananampalataya* which roughly means risk-taking or taking a gamble). **C A H** "Faith-ing" as a dynamic response of gratitude to God's *kagandahang-loob* (mercies, justice, grace) liberates humanity from the

---

C H Interplay between cultural context and one's biblical hermeneutic.

C Philippine society.

C H Interplay between cultural context and biblical interpretation.

C A H "Faith" understood in three frames.

clutches of sin and death. Also, God's *kagandahang loob* is revealed—the divine passive—by faith to faith, from *utang na loob* to *utang na loob*, by one indebted and thankful generation to the next. It is through people who live their lives as debts of gratitude that God's liberating acts are revealed. This is equally true of the counterpoint to God's justice; God's wrath is revealed by the lives of people who do not have any sense of gratitude or indebtedness (*walang utang na loob*), by one ungrateful generation to the next.

A Critical New Testament Study that Brings to Critical Understanding

A Pro Me *Interpretation*

C H Does this traditionally "unacademic" reading—Nanay's appropriation of a two-millenium-year-old text through the lens of a Filipino value system—qualify as a legitimate and valid interpretation? I have always considered her interpretation as a devotional reading—what others might call a *pro me* interpretation—which characterized the daily Bible-reading of many Filipino evangelicals—both lay and clergy. Believers come to the text (which many consider as a "direct line" from the Almighty) and try to discover for themselves God's challenge/message/teaching for them for this particular moment in their lives. The same is true about worship. People come to church expecting to receive God's distinct message for today either from the music, the reading, the sermon or the benediction. For many, the blessing at the end of the service is the most important part because it means being assured of God's protection for the coming work-week.

A H Having been trained in historical-critical discourse, like most graduates of Union Theological Seminary since its founding in 1907, I looked at these interpretations as interested and subjective readings into the text, pure *eisegesis*. I have always tried to discover what the text meant in the most neutral and objective way I could possible can. For a long time, I have engaged the text through foreign lenses, never even bothering to see if my own eyes could see without those foreign-made specs.[19]

A Traditional historical-critical work has been "from text to text," a process of objectively dissecting the text to arrive at a universal truth. This model is a Euro-American/Androcentric construct whose after

---

C H *Pro me* interpretation.

A H Tension between historical-critical discourse and *pro me* interpretation?

A Analytical frame of historical-critical work?

effects are still felt in most of the Two-Thirds World where Bible studies are still held in order to search for the one, more often than not, individualistic, status-quo-maintaining, true interpretation.[20] **A H** But interpretation, by definition, is always perspectival and particular. We know that there is no disinterested reading. Whether we admit it or not, any critical study starts and ends with interested interpretation.[21] Whether we admit it or not, any critical reading starts and ends with *pro me/pro nobis* interpretations. Thus by working with varied interpretations and the value judgments that go along with them, we do not end up with a reading that all of us need to live by. What we do end up with are alternative readings that inform[22] our particular situations (the term "particular" by definition can never mean "universal" thus debunking any reading's claim to privilege). And then we choose among these readings and respond to the question: "Why did we choose this over the rest?" Some have called this move as "taking a stand and being both responsible and accountable" for such a particular stand.

    C H A In order to demonstrate the legitimacy of my mother's interpretation, I will work with three different set of judgments: Is there textual evidence to support her reading? Does her reading make sense of the text? Is her reading relevant for me and my community at the present time? Patte has asked, "Does this reading amount to projecting upon the text something that is foreign to it? Is it plausible to interpret this text in terms of epistemological categories provided by the Filipino concept of *utang na loob*?"[23] Will *utang na loob* really work as a reading lens for this text? Will Romans work as a reading lens for *utang na loob*?

    C H I am prepared to argue that both will work because both already have. Nanay drew strength and inspiration from Paul's faith conviction. She lived by this passage. But bringing *utang na loob* into the interpretative process not only transformed her perception of faith, it also transformed mine. Not only that—and this is most important to many of my female colleagues in the Philippines who despise Paul—it transformed my attitude toward Paul.[24] But the opposite is equally transforming. Reading *utang na loob* from Romans helps conjure up images of the covenantal character of *utang na loob*—the human response to grace—which, unfortunately, have been relegated in the present Philippine society to the sidelines by a "degenerated idea of petty legalism and reciprocity."[25] Equally important, for me as a Filipino

---

A=H? Interpretations are perspectival; no disinterested reading.

C H A Using three frames to justify an interpretation.

C H Author's primary interests.

Christian, is that "reading" *utang na loob* from Romans reveals the One who is deserving of *utang na loob*, God.

Ek Pisteos Eis Pistin

A Faith or grace, depending on who is describing and defining it—like love, salvation, righteousness and similar words—can mean everything, anything and nothing. I agree with Kwok Pui-lan who argues that the way a people's language is structured influences their mode of thinking.[26] Her broad sketch of how the Asian psyche works applies to Filipinos. **C** Filipino logic is very different from Aristotlelian logic. The traditional type of subject-predicate is absent in Filipino logic. Plato's world of ideas that is eternal and unchanging—which thus provides an Archemedian point (focused on "being")—is totally opposite to the Filipino's world of perpetual flux and change (focused on "becoming"). **C** Dionisio Miranda, in *Buting Pinoy*, effectively argues that Filipino philosophy, instead of speculating about abstract propositional truth or constructing theories of metaphysics, focuses more on pragmatics—on the correct use of language to provide guidance for action (*gawa*), to shape social relations (*pakikipagkapwa*), and to transmit a moral vision of society (*magandang hinaharap/kinabukasan*). Miranda continues: In Filipino thought there is no separation of the transcendent and the immanent, the human and the natural, the historical and the cosmological. Filipinos understand the self as one among many centers or circles of relationships (a community of *loobs/pakikipag-kapwa*), not an isolated entity. Salvation (*kaligtasan*) involves the broadening of the self to embody (*bigyang katawan/katawanin*) an ever-expanding circle of relatedness. According to Ferdinand Anno: for the Igorots of the North which number about one million—land, life, *Kabunian* (the Great One), the spirits of their ancestors, and nature are communing essences (*loobs*) in their world in the Cordilleras.[27] This kind of orientation, which does not seek absolute truths but seeks wisdom for life in the "nitty-grittiness"[28] of the everyday, allows more room for dialogue, for difference, and for multiplicity.

C H It is with this Filipino concept of interlocking circles, of dynamic images that we come to understand Nanay's reading of Romans 1:16-17. Three images play important roles in her interpretation: grace (*kagandahang loob*), debt (*utang*), and faith (*utang na loob*), and all

---

A Polyvalence of "faith"? Language and thinking.
C Different cultural frames.
C Contextual frame of Filipino worldview.
C H "Earthy" interpretation of faith, debt, and grace.

three would help us understand and appreciate—what I call—her "earthy" interpretation of "from faith to faith."

Grace and Kagandahang Loob

C H *"Kagandahang loob* (in a first approximation, goodwill or beneficence) is the most important indigenous Filipino value."[29] According to Miranda, the mechanism most related to this concept is *utang na loob*. The latter is really not a value in itself; it is explainable and understood only in terms of *kagandahang loob*. *Utang na loob* is a response to *kagandahang loob*. One who is truly *magandang loob*[30] deserves *utang na loob*. *Utang na loob* is not the primary value; at best it is a secondary value, a response.

Miranda argues that *Kagandahang loob* is absolute unselfishness, or self-forgetfulness; it is acting purely for the sake of others. It never imposes, never forces, is completely free. *Kagandahang loob* is compassion. It is the natural sensitivity to the pain of a fellow human being, one's *kapwa*. *Kagandahang loob* is not exclusive but responds to all cries of pain. *Kagandahang loob* is pity. Pity is the instinctive response to another's pain. *Kagandahang loob* is most evident vis-à-vis the suffering. *Kagandahang loob* is mercy. It soothes the bitterness of humiliation. It cheers the sad, warms the heart, makes peace and understanding. *Kagandahang loob* is, in one word, grace.

Understandings of God's Grace Compatible with Kagandahang Loob

A H Most interpreters agree on what Romans 1:16-17 is all about: the most concise crystalization of Pauline conviction. They, on the whole, agree on what the text is saying: that salvation, for Paul, is about God's grace, God's agenda from start to finish, and that what is left for humanity is to respond in faith.

Beverly Gaventa's commentary on grace in Romans isolates its most important characteristic as God's impartiality and care for all people: If God is not partial to the rich over against the poor, to the child with a family over against the orphan, then it follows that God also is not partial to the Jew over against the Gentile.[31] She continues to say that, "When Paul refers to the righteousness of God, he refers to a characteristic of God (that is, God is righteous) and the implications of that characteristic for human beings (that is, God freely gives to human beings the gift of God's own righteousness)."[32] She calls it God's radical grace for all people. In dealing with this text that is widely accepted as the heart of

---

C H Grace and *Kagandahang Loob*.

A H What Paul meant in Romans 1:16-17.

Paul's theology, Gaventa highlights its theocentricity. Her concept of radical grace is encompassed by *kagandahang loob.*

Several other scholars propose related interpretations, which nevertheless, emphasize another aspect of God's righteousness. Ernst Käsemann writes about God's righteousness in terms of power, God's saving power in loyalty to God's covenant, overthrowing the forces of evil and vindicating God's people.[33] N. T. Wright's understanding is similar. For him, God's righteousness is "essentially the covenant faithfulness, the covenant justice of God who made promises to Abraham, promises of a worldwide family characterized by faith, in and through whom the evil of the world would be undone."[34]

These scholars emphasize other aspects of God's *kagandahang loob.* Yet like Gaventa, they consider righteousness as a fact about God and that this fact has a dynamic meaning. **A** Righteousness refers to the way God acts and relates to human history and thus to God's gracious activity, to God's *kagandahang loob.*

Problematic Hermeneutical Appropriations of God's Faithfulness as *Kagandahang Loob*

This apparent easy identification of God's righteousness with God's *kagandahang loob* breaks down when one considers more closely **H** the theological categories used to make sense of this concept, especially in hermeneutical appropriations of the Romans text. From his theological perspective, Karl Barth argues that the passage teaches us about God's omnipotent power; that this power is active "unto salvation to everyone who believes, to the Jew first and also to the Greek."[35] Barth comments that the phrase "from faith to faith" is simply about God's faith (God's faithfulness) to our faith.[36] God's grace always comes first, ours is never other than a response. He then continues to say that the content of this power is Jesus Christ. Jesus, his salvific act is, therefore, the background of the text. Without Jesus Christ the text has no meaning. Salvation is "by faith unto faith" and is really about God's faithfulness aimed at the trust, the faith of the Jewish and Greek people who hear it.[37] Over against *kagandahang loob*, Barth's reading—of God's faithfulness made possible in the redeeming work and the person of Jesus Christ—is not very helpful for me. Where is God's radical impartiality? **A H** Locating God's revelation only in Jesus Christ may be good news for the

---

A Righteousness and God's faithfulness.

H Theological category in hermeneutics.

A H Interplay between textual meaning and modern audience.

Christians that compose 3% of Asia's population, but bad news for the remaining 97%.[38]

Similarly, according to Charles Hodge, verse 16 teaches us that: "The salvation of men [i.e., humankind], including the pardon of their sins, and the moral renovation of their hearts, can be effected by the gospel alone. The wisdom of men during four thousand years previous to the advent of Christ, failed to discover any adequate means for the attainment of either of these objects; and those who, since the advent, have neglected the gospel, have been equally unsuccessful." With verse 17, he continues: "The power of the gospel lies not in its pure theism or perfect moral code, but in the cross, in the doctrine of justification by faith in a crucified Redeemer."[39] Hodge and Barth both agree that the true revelation of God's *kagandahang loob* is found in Jesus Christ and in him alone. But Hodge goes further when he explicitly denies any possibility of discovering God's activity, God's liberating acts, God's *kagandahang loob* in the midst of humanity's past, present and future struggles outside the Christian experience. Good news for dispensational premillenialists but bad news, I think, for the majority of Christians; horrifying news for all Jews, for Muslims, Buddhists, and peoples of other faiths.

John Stott also does a *kagandahang loob*-focused reading. He focuses on God's righteousness and thinks of it as a divine attribute (our God is a righteous God), an activity (God comes to our rescue), and an achievement (God bestows on us a righteous status). But he also offers something everyday Filipinos can identify with: *utang* or debt.

Debt and Utang

H Stott does a very good job of reading Romans 1:16-17, Paul's basic faith conviction, from the perspective of the other side, from the perspective of the recipients of God's grace, from the perspective of someone in debt, *may utang*. What he does is anchor his interpretation on verse 14: "I am a debtor both to Greeks and barbarians, both to the wise and to the foolish." (NRSV) It is about Paul being a debtor (as translated in the NRSV above and the AV) trying to cancel his debt. He notes that many translations follow the NIV's "I am bound" and the RSV's "I am under obligation" probably because people might have problems equating Paul's motivation for sharing the gospel with the concept of debt cancellation. He then proceeds to explain what kind of debt Paul was trying to repay.

H Stott's hermeneutic.

As Stott points out; there are two ways of getting into debt. The first is to borrow money from someone; the second is to be given money for someone by a third party. Using Stott's illustration, if I were to borrow $1,000 from you, I would be in your debt until I paid it back. Equally if a friend of yours were to hand me $1,000 to give to you, I would be in your debt until I handed it over. In the former case I would have got myself in debt by borrowing; in the latter it is your friend who has put me in your debt by entrusting me with $1,000 for you. For Stott, it is this second sense that Paul is in debt. He has not borrowed anything from the Romans which he must repay. But Jesus Christ has entrusted him with the gospel for them. It is Jesus Christ who has made Paul a debtor by committing the gospel to his trust. Similarly we are debtors to the world, even though we are not apostles. If the gospel has come to us, we have no liberty to keep it to ourselves. Nobody may claim a monopoly of the gospel. Good news is for sharing. We are under obligation to make it known to others. Such was Paul's first incentive. He was eager because he was in debt. It is universally regarded as a dishonorable thing to leave a debt unpaid. We should be as eager to discharge our debt as Paul was to discharge his.[40] Murray offers a similar interpretation. He argues that the terminology cannot be divorced from the idea of an obligation that must be met or discharged.[41]

   C One of the first things that struck me about America when I got here in 1996 was the culture of indebtedness. Almost everyone I knew had mortgages to pay, credit card bills to settle, and loans that needed refinancing. It is almost the complete opposite in the Philippines. In many of situations in the United States, a person's worth was based on his/her credit history. Stott's comment that it is universally regarded as a dishonorable thing to leave a debt unpaid might very well be true but his statement that we should be as eager as Paul to discharge our debt as Paul was to discharge his might not work very well in a society that thrives on credit. At any rate, eager or not as far as repayment is concerned, the debt eventually gets discharged.

   My problem with Stott's *utang* metaphor is that I do not believe the debt Paul is describing is one that can ever be discharged. Using Stott's own illustration of the thousand dollars, a loan creates a debt situation. A gift does not. A gift evokes a grateful response. What motivates Paul's classic faith confession in 1:16-17 is not *utang* in 1:14 but *utang na loob*. Frederic Godet echoed this notion of a debt of gratitude for a priceless gift when he said, "All those individuals, of whatever category, Paul regards as his creditors. He owes them his life, his person, in virtue of the grace bestowed on him and of the office which he has received."[42]

C Culture of indebtedness.

C H The possibility of a reading from the perspective of *utang na loob* can be developed from most of these scholars' definition of grace as a gift freely given. Therefore there is no *utang*; there is no debt that needs to be cancelled. But because the gift is unearned and unmerited then a different kind of debt is created, a debt of gratitude, *utang na loob.*

Miranda notes that *Utang na loob*, as a response to grace, has two strands: In the contractual sense there is a symmetry, a mutuality of duties and obligations or expectations. In brief, reciprocity of the same sort detected by Western and Western-educated Filipino social scientists. By contrast, in the covenantal sense, the reigning attitudes are complete trust and fiduciariness; the exchange is one of gift and gratuity.

Faith and Utang Na Loob

H Miranda argues that debts, *utang* can be incurred in a variety of ways: consciously or unconsciously, voluntarily or involuntarity.[43] A debt incurred voluntarily arises either from the asking of a loan or a favor. If the loan or the favor is paid back in equivalent terms or with the margin agreed on, both parties can consider themselves a *manos* or "quits" (discharged in Stott's terms). Involuntary debts, like taxes, would occur when a loan or favor is offered or done without having been preceded by a formal request. Even here both loan or favor could be repaid in equivalent or with profit in order to be absolved of the debt. **A H** This is the kind of *utang* or *opheilei* Paul wants everyone to be absolved of (he does not want anyone to be beholden to anyone or to any structure except to Christ). This is the kind of *utang* or *opheilei* that people can and must cancel (Rom 13:7).

Miranda continues: *Utang na loob*, on the other hand, is a unique kind of debt: however it may have been incurred, no matter how insignificant the debt, there is no way by which one is absolved of the debt except perhaps by having the "lender" him/herself incur a similar *utang na loob*. The debt goes beyond the legal-juridical framework; it creates an extra-legal but even more binding debt because it involves a personal debt, one that can only be paid back not only in person but with one's person. *Utang na loob* as a debt of gratitude is not absolved legally but through a personal involvement which acknowledges the unmerited and unsolicited graciousness.

C H Reading from the perspective of *utang na loob.*

H Modern understanding of debt.

A H *Opheilei* and *utang.*

C *Utang na loob* has also sometimes been translated, according to Miranda, as a debt of volition probably because one is bound no longer to a single compensating act but binds him/herself voluntarily to be committed beyond repayment. *Utang na loob* is not merely autonomous in the sense of independence, but also in the sense of self-binding. This kind of debt is not imposed per se; it binds only to the extent that one allows oneself to be thus bound (as Paul himself does in Rom 1:14). *Utang na loob* between familiar persons is usually not recognized as *utang na loob* precisely because it is so spontaneous. But *utang na loob* between strangers or non-intimates reveals another characteristic whereby it ceases to be a socially accepted value and turns into a burdensome social norm. Filipinos do not want to be considered, even unjustifiably, as *walang utang na loob* (having no sense of indebtedness). That would be equivalent to implying that a person has no sense of personal honor. This is probably one reason that Filipinos have culturally instituted the "repeated refusal" before one finally relents and allows the loan to be pressed on oneself or permits the favor to be imposed on oneself. Because the debt appears to have been accepted under duress, the person feels less obliged to consider it as *utang na loob*, and merely as *utang*; the moment the *utang* is repaid he can consider himself freed of *loob* obligations. But precisely because of its intensely binding character and disproportionate terms of repayment, there is the temptation, consciously or unconsciously, to make another enter into such an *utang na loob*. Instead of building up relationships based on human responses to grace, what is created is alienation fueled by legalism and forced reciprocity. To call it value in this form is to distort the meaning of words.

Faith, Miranda continues, also binds in a pattern similar to *utang na loob*. Without our having been asked, without our even wanting, despite our lack of merit, God, or *Bathala*, or *Kabunian* has given us life, sustains that life, and wishes us to enjoy the fullness of life. A Christ has redeemed us from all evil and sin; indeed even when we were yet sinners (Rom 5:8) Christ willingly gave his life for us. The Spirit allows us to call God "Abba" (Rom 8:15) and Christ "Lord," (I Cor 12:3) assuring us that God's offer of life for us renewed in the redemption by God's Son will not be frustrated. A greater debt than this no one can incur; greater gratitude no one can show that one lays down one's life for God. H This *utang na loob* incurred vis-à-vis God, precisely because it involves life and precisely because it is incurred vis-à-vis God, can never

---

C *Utang na loob.*

A Meaning of Paul in Romans.

H Reading of Romans from the perspective of *utang na loob*.

be absolved. One can only give tokens of the will to recognize this indebtedness by a life-long repayment, a repayment that can occur only in symbols because its real repayment is impossible (Paul echoes this symbolic repayment in Rom 12:1).

According to Miranda, this theonomous claim is at once value and norm. It is value because it is only in God that life ultimately has meaning, and therefore it is also reasonable that it be a norm, the better to guarantee its fulfillment. But God, by making it clear that all this is a gift (Rom 6:23), also returns our freedom to ourselves so that acceptance of the *utang na loob* is a conscious and voluntary binding, not a forced one. This binding of ourselves implies at least two things. First, we should not think that we can involve God in a similar *utang na loob*. Nothing we can do, no holiness that we can attain, no sacrifice that we can make, can ever bind God to us. God is not susceptible to *utang na loob* to humanity because God is *kagandahang loob*. Second, theonomou*s utang na loob* obliges us, negatively, not to behave in the same way as the unforgiving servant (Matt 18:23-35); positively, to imitate the mercy and graciousness of God (owe no one anything but love, Rom 13:8). Faith as *utang na loob* is an appropriate response to God's eminent *kagandahang loob*.

From Faith to Faith: *Utang Na Loob* to *Utang Na Loob*

A H This identification of faith with *utang na loob* challenges the theological categories traditionally used to make sense of "faith" in Romans. Martin Luther in commenting about the teaching of the phrase "from faith to faith" offers that "the righteousness of God is entirely from faith, yet growth does not make it more real but only gives it greater clarity." He continues: "And just so also, 'from faith to faith,' by always believing more and more strongly, so that he 'who is righteous' can be justified still . . . and so that no one should think that he has already apprehended and thus ceases to grow, i.e., begins to backslide."[44] Luther's reading does not directly address either *kagandahang loob* or *utang na loob*. What it does is focus on the individual's growth in faith, from one level of faith to another, like the United Methodist's doctrines of justification, sanctification, and glorification.[45]

A Frequently Paul is made to say that faith increases, that one activation of faith gives rise to another and that the latter, again, is faith

---

A H New interpretation in tension with traditional interpretation.

A Paul's meaning in Romans.

rather than seeing. Other interpretations distribute the occurrences of pistis to different believers: "Because of God's faithfulness in regard to the individual's faith, on account of the faith of Jesus in the faith of Christendom, from the faith of the teacher to the faith of the hearers."[46]

Stott, as an evangelical, offers the traditional four interpretations of the phrase "from faith to faith."

> The first relates to faith's origin, from the faith of God who makes the offer to the faith of the men who receive it. . . . Secondly, the spread of faith by evangelism . . . from one believer to another. Thirdly, . . . from one degree of faith to another. Fourthly, faith's primacy as an unfolding process, by faith from first to last or by faith through and through.[47]

However appealing and high-sounding most of these readings are, they are in a foreign language (an imposed language), using concepts (like faith, righteousness, etc.) that, as stated earlier, can mean everything, anything and nothing to the common *Tao* (human in Filipino).

C H In the Philippines, as Miranda point out, the criterion of ethical value is not to be found in isolation (like Luther's individual on a faith journey) but in interpersonal relationships and communal interaction. It is the other *tao* (human), the equal *tao, kapwa* (neighbor, fellow human), that is the primary objective and external reality that tests the humaneness of humanity. The ideal of *loob* is *kabuuan* (wholeness, integrity, harmony) or *kapwa/kapatiran* (the collective body of *loobs*).[48] In the New Testament, the church has often been described as the body of Christ. According to Melanio Aoanan, "body" takes on so many meanings when translated into the vernacular.[49] Leonardo Mercado points out that in Filipino thought, this body symbolism is most important because the body and body parts have always been used to symbolize the Filipino.[50] For example, the English "You worthless ingrate" is *Walang hiya* (shameless) or *Makapal ang mukha* (thick faced). Both translations are about "face." A man without honor is "*walang bayag*" (no balls) in Filipino.

C H According to Aoanan, the most important part of the Filipino human body is the *loob*. The center, the core of one's *loob*, is his/her *lamanloob* or *bituka* (the intestines—roughly the equivalent of the Greek *splagxnon* which literally means "guts" or "entrails"). The most concrete example of its use as a term for connectedness, for the community of *loobs* is the word *kapatid* (brother/sister/sibling). The word is a

---

C H Ethical value in Filipino interpretation.

C H Filipino interpretation.

contraction of the Tagalog *patid ng bituka* (cut off from one intestine). The word in Visayan is *igsoon* (*igsumpay sa tinai*) and *kabsat* (*kapugsat iti bagis*) in Ilocano. Therefore siblings come from one and the same intestine![51] To children who get bruised or who are bleeding from minor cuts, their elders say in a soothing tone: *Huwag kang mabahala, malayo sa bituka* (No need to worry, the wound is far from your intestine). But more than being body-related concepts, these terms do not just describe individual parts but communal body parts.[52] Thus a small wound is not just far from the center of one's *loob* but also peripheral and insignificant as far as the center of the community of *loobs* is concerned. Those soothing words from our elders simply mean: "Children, we (meaning the community and its collective experience) know about little cuts like these and we do not worry about them, so you do not have to worry about them too."

This is the reason why most Filipinos greet each other with "*Kumain ka na ba?*" (Have you eaten?)[53] instead of the Western form "How are you?" And this is not just a perfunctory greeting. Filipinos are renowned for their hospitality. Closely linked to this "relational" practice, according to Aoanan, is the *padigo* or *patikim* where neighbors share with neighbors what they have cooked.

C When my brother, sister and I were children, we could not understand why Nanay had to share food with our neighbors. We also had to leave some food on our plates for our pet dogs and cats. She used to tell us that food shared fills up more than one's stomach. When I was a teenager working with urban poor communities in the garbage dumps of Tondo, Manila, I met a girl, a young scavenger. She was probably around twelve. I offered her the remaining half of the Coke I had on that hot, humid morning. She drank a third of it. Realizing that she might not be accustomed to having a soft drink all to herself, I told her, "Drink all of it; that's all yours." She smiled back and asked (and I remember this scene as if it were yesterday), "Can I bring this home? I have two little brothers who would love to have a taste of Coca-Cola."

H According to Virgilio Enriquez, "Relationship or *pakikipagkapwa* is evidently the most important aspect of Filipino life. As codified in the language, eight levels of interaction have been identified: (a) *pakikitungo* (transaction/civility with); (b) *pakikisalamuha* (interaction with); (c) *pakikilahok* (joining/participating with); (d) *pakikibagay* (in-conformity with/in-accord with); (e) *pakikisama* (being along with); (f) *pakikipagpalagayan/pakikipagpalagayang-loob* (being in rapport with/understanding/acceptance with); (h) *pakikiisa* (being one with).

C Family situation.

H Filipino hermeneutics.

These levels of conceptual and behavioral differences are most concretely manifested in Filipino food-sharing, in the context of meals."[54]

It is in these relationships where *kagandahang loob* and *utang na loob* are most concretely encountered. What is most surprising is that all these acts of *pakikipagkapwa* are motivated by *utang na loob*. Each one does something for another because he or she responds in gratitude for something he or she has received. The initiators say that they do what they do because of *utang na loob*. But observers and the recipients of the gift describe these acts as *kagandahang loob*.

H   Daniel Patte comments: "Through faith believers discover manifestations of the righteousness of God, manifestations of God's power for the salvation of the believers (Rom 1:16). This revelation of God's righteousness is through faith (discovered and actualized through faith) and for faith (for those who have faith), as is expressed in 1:17a. This is the positive intervention of God in the believers' experience (involving other people) which is discovered and actualized in a life in the right relationship with God (1:17b)."[55]

For Patte, God is revealed primarily in the present experience of believers. Believers' faith is established through and because of God's interventions, God's breaking into their experience. He continues, "We need to remember that what we call the believer's experience is not limited to the private experience of an individual. It includes all that is related to this believer in daily life, and thus also other people who are parts of his or her life experience."[56]

What Patte does is locate God and God's activity within the locus of human experiences in the present. It is faith that allows people to "see" God's righteous interventions in their life, interventions via human agents. Along with Gaventa's God whose radical grace knows no bounds, Patte's interventionist God who reveals Godself in the midst of people's experiences present very appealing and affirming readings for peoples in the Philippines who, despite having to face the violence of poverty everyday, still manage to whistle happy tunes because they believe, no, they know that God is with them. They are not alone. They are never alone.

It is within the realm of people's acts of faith, of people's *utang na loob*, in the living out of what Paul calls his "debt" to peoples that God breaks in as *kagandahang loob*.

H   According to Miranda: God never, ever, comes face to face with humanity like everybody else or like anything else, yet humanity is to

---

H   Patte's interpretation.

H   Miranda's interpretation.

believe that God is revealed (the divine passive) as beyond reach (mysterious, transcendent) in every *pakikipagharap* (face to face encounters); yet that God is revealed as Immanuel (immanent) in every embrace of a person in care, responsibility, respect and knowledge. God cannot be embraced like anybody or like anything else, yet a person is to cling to God in the desire to be embraced, as God is already embraced in every experience of family, kinship, fraternity, justice, truth, peace, in every act of *utang na loob*. God, because God is absolute freedom (blowing wherever God wills), cannot be forced to respond, but because God is absolute love, God as *kagandahang loob* cannot be indifferent, so that people can seek to become worthy to be manifested to, spoken to, accepted and commended for every kindness and solidarity, for every sacrifice and generosity tendered to those whom God has called the least of God's children, our sisters and brothers.[57]

Notes

1. In traditional interpretations, the shame referred to is that which comes when one is disillusioned by something one has trusted in. Suggested positive renderings of the statement would be "I am proud of the gospel" (Moffat) or "I have complete confidence in the gospel" (see Barclay Newman and Eugene Nida, *United Bible Societies' Translator's Handbook on Romans* [Stuttgart: United Bible Societies, 1973], 19). I will challenge this understanding of shame.

2. Instead of the noun phrase "into salvation," thus focusing on God's saving activity. Can also be translated "the power of God saving all who are believing" so as to focus again on the acts, the dynamics of salvation and faith. Salvation in the Old Testament is often expressed as liberation from physical danger. In the New Testament salvation more often than not is equated with deliverance from the power or bondage of sin (Newman and Nida, *Translator's Handbook on Roman*, 19-20).

3. The NRSV, RSV and AV translate *panti tô pisteuonti* as "to everyone who has faith" which, for me, is a reading that equates faith to something one can possess; a thing, an object one has instead of an activity, an unfolding process. In Tagalog (a Filipino language used by about a third of the Philippine population), "faith" can be translated as *pananampalataya* (literally means habitual risk taking) which, in actual usage, is more of a verb than a noun. We don't say, "I have faith" but *Nananampalataya ako* (literally "believing or faithing I do" with emphasis on the act not on the possession of something). A study conducted by the SVD (Society of the Divine Word) seminary in Cavite, Philippines, on language shows that there are at least 300 prefixes and

suffixes one can add on a single verb stem. To illustrate this verb-focused language, let's take *ulan* (to rain) which can go *Umuulan* (is raining), *Uulan* (will rain), *Umulan* (it rained), *Uulanin* (will be rained out). All of these, by the way, are complete sentences.

4. Literally rendered "to the Jew first and to the Greek." This translation, though, would be problematic to most Filipinos who know who Jews are but who would identify Greeks as folks who live in Greece.

5. Traditionally *dikaiosynê* has been translated "righteousness" but even Paul uses the same verb to mean justification, see 3:24,26. In my particular context, the word justice (*katarungan*) conjures more concrete, earthy liberating images compared to righteousness (*katuwiran*) and its abstract, other-worldly connotations.

6. Paul, I think, puts emphasis on the connection between God's justice and God's wrath, vs.18, both of which is described as *apokalyptetai* (as being revealed) in human experience. Put another way, only in the realm of human affairs can one discover manifestations of God's justice and God's wrath.

7. The phrase can also be translated "starts from faith and ends in faith" (NEB) which is actually another rendering of "believing" as an ongoing process of trust in God, a more anthropocentric reading of the phrase. An alternative reading, which affirms God's power, is to focus on the fact that salvation is God's agenda; it is about God's faithfulness from "alpha to omega," a theocentric reading. This paper develops both.

8. An alternative would be "the just by believing will live" again to emphasize the action, the process of trusting completely.

9. I agree with Stendahl's choice to use "will" instead of "shall." He comments, "In the third person you express straight future by 'will,' and Paul reads this statement about the future. 'For that time will come—not as a principle, but as a statement—the time . . . when there will be this living faith'" (Krister Stendahl, *Final Account: Paul's Letter to the Romans* [Minneapolis: Fortress Press, 1995], 17).

10. The one whom God has put right with Godself because he or she trusts God, or because God is faithful, or both are faithful.

11. The Philippines was under Roman Catholic Spain for over three centuries; under Protestant America a century this year. Today, more than 80% of the population is Roman Catholic (from Michael Amaladoss, *Life in Freedom: Liberation Theologies from Asia* [New York: Orbis, 1997], 12). Protestant children were teased as being "*protês*" meaning "followers" of the protesting Luther. I had a taste of the discrimination in first grade. The religion teacher asked all the Protestants in class to raise their hands. I was the only one. I was asked to leave the room. I hated every moment of that daily routine. This Catholic-Protestant tension still exists to this day. As an illustration, the

evangelical PCEC (Philippine Council of Evangelical Churches) was established as a reaction against the NCCP (National Council of Churches in the Philippines) because the group was perceived as being Catholic-lovers. Evangelistic crusades are held to "convert" (proselyte is the better term) Catholics.

12. By nominal, I mean one who went to church about three times a year (Good Friday, Christmas and on one's birthday). When Lolo got "converted," however, he became one of the most active United Methodist Men in Santiago, Isabela.

13. *Utang na loob* can be translated "sense of indebtedness" or "sense of gratitude." The "sense" comes from the term *loob* which literally means "inside." *Utang* is debt. In Filipino, the inside or "essence" is what makes one human. But *loob* is more than one individual's essence but the community's, the "collective essence." For the most comprehensive work on the Filipino *loob* read Dionisio Miranda, *SVD's Buting Pinoy* (Manila: Divine Word Publications, n.d.).

14. Tomas Andres in his *Positive Filipino Values* (Quezon City: New Day Publishers, 1989) offers the same translation of *utang na loob*: sense of gratitude.

15. Actually there were ten Enriquez children. The eldest, Jesus, nicknamed Susing, was killed in a vehicular accident when he was 16. Three children died very young. Among the surviving siblings, Nanay was the eldest.

16. Daniel Patte in his article "Whither Critical New Testament Studies for a New Day? Some Reflections on Luke 17:11-19," in A. Brown, G. F. Snyder, and V. Wiles ed., *Putting Body and Soul Together: Essays in Honor of Robin Scroggs* (Valley Forge: Trinity Press International, 1977), 275-296, talks about his encounter with the more common, reciprocal expectations regarding *utang na loob*: we have *utang na loob* toward our parents, our neighbors in the village because they have done and are doing so many things for us, from the time of our childhood. This means that we have the duty to express our gratitude toward them, by respecting them, offering them gifts, doing things for them, and taking care of them in time of need (291-292).

17. During her wake, a woman we did not know came weeping over her casket. When we went over to talk with her, she told us that she knew Nanay from 20 years back. She was a fish vendor and Nanay was her favorite customer. She talked about Nanay's thoughtfulness. This, for me, was a sign of Nanay's "*pagtanawang utang na loob*." Having been blessed, she became a blessing to others, a blessing to the fish vendor.

18. Her interpretation fits nicely with the "life offering" of Romans 12:1-2, and the challenge of 1 John 4:11, 19-21. God's mercies is translated *kagandahang loob* in Filipino translations of the Bible.

Kagandahang loob is the quintessential Filipino value (Miranda, *Buting Pinoy*, 182).

19. It was Melanio Grace Aoanan, my spouse who as a fellow Filipino, who urged me to use my own "eyes" to engage the biblical text instead of other peoples' lenses. It was Daniel Patte who challenged me to focus on *utang na loob* as a legitimate lens to use in reading this particular pericope. These two persons helped me remember my mother's reading.

20. Union Theological Seminary in Dasmarinas, Cavite, Philippines is a case in point. Up until 1994, the standard hermeneutical model taught there was the historical-critical method. Anderson's Introduction to the Old Testament has been the standard text since the 1960's. The faculty is almost half Westerners. Ninety-five percent of the books in the library are authored by European-American males. And only two of the present Filipino faculty have had books published.

21. From Patte, "Whither?," 279.

22. The suggestion that proposes that "a text should inform, instead of define behavior" is from Elisabeth Schüssler-Fiorenza's "The Bible as prototype not archetype" paradigm which she proposed in a series of lectures delivered at Union Theological Seminary, Philippines (January 1996).

23. Patte, "Whither?," 292-293.

24. A book that also helped me appreciate Paul more is Robert Jewett's *Paul: Apostle to America* (Louisville, Kentucky: Westminster/John Knox Press, 1994).

25. I am borrowing E. P. Sander's terminology in his excellent *Paul and Palestinian Judaism* (London: SCM Press, 1977), 419-421 where he discusses covenant and law which echoes *utang na loob's* two strands, the covenantal and the reciprocal.

26. For this particular section on language, I have drawn from Kwok Pui-lan's essay "Toward a Dialogical Model of Interpretation," a chapter from her excellent book, *Discovering the Bible in the Non-Biblical World* (New York: Orbis, 1995).

27. Ferdinand Anno, "Toward a Liturgical Approach to Theological Reconstruction," *Explorations in Theology, Journal of Union Theological Seminary* (Cavite, Philippines: UTS, 1996), Vol 1, No. 1, 81.

28. The term nitty-gritty denotes raw, hard and concrete realities (from Anthony Pinn, *Why Lord? Suffering and Evil in Black Theology* [New York: Continuum, 1995], 116).

29. See Miranda, *Buting Pinoy*, 182-183.

30. One who actualizes *kagandahang loob* is described as *magandang loob* (roughly, one who is kind or gracious).

31. Beverly Gaventa, "Romans," in Carol H. Newsome and Sharon H. Ringe ed., *The Women's Bible Commentary* (Louisville: Westminster/ John Knox Press, 1992).

32. Gaventa, "Romans," 315.

33. Ernst Käsemann, *Commentary on Romans* (1973; ET, Grand Rapids: Eerdmans, 1980), 23.

34. N. T. Wright, *The Climax of the Covenant: Christ and the Law in Pauline Theology* (Edinburgh: T&T Clark, 1991) 234.

35. Karl Barth, *A Shorter Commentary on Romans* (Richmond: John Knox Press, 1959), 20.

36. Karl Barth, *The Epistle to the Romans* (Oxford: Oxford University Press, 1933, 6th edition), 41.

37. Barth, *Shorter Commentary on Romans*, 22.

38. Kwok, *Discovery*, 2.

39. Charles Hodge, *Commentary on the Epistle to the Romans* (Philadelphia: William and Martin, 1861), 29-40. For Nygren, (*Commentary on Romans* [Philadelphia: Muhlenberg Press, 1949], 96) the pericope presents the juxtaposition of God's righteousness and God's wrath. God's righteousness is set not in contrast with humanity's unrighteousness but God's wrath (against unrighteousness and against the unrighteousness of the law). Thus, the text is really a teaching about God's activity. Again, this is a reading from the divine perspective but I don't have enough to correlate his interpretation with *kagandahang loob*.

40. Based on Stott's excellent discussion of Romans 1:14-15 in his *Romans: God's Good News for the World* (Morton Grove: InterVarsity Press, 1994) 58.

41. John Murray, *The Epistle to the Romans. The New International Commentary on the New Testament* (Grand Rapids: Eerdmans, 1959), 24.

42. Godet quoted in Murray, *The Epistle to the Romans*, 12-24.

43. This section adopted from Dionisio Miranda's *Lakbay Diwa* (Tagaytay City, Philippines: Divine Word Publications, 1987), 36-38.

44. Martin Luther, *Luther: Lectures on Romans*, The Library of Christian Classics, Vol XV, trans. Wilhelm Pauck (Philadelphia: Westminster Press, 1961), 18.

45. I learned about this three levels of one's faith development from attending youth camps sponsored by the United Methodist Youth Fellowship in the Philippines. We were taught that one is justified when one accepts Jesus as personal Lord and Savior. One is sanctified as one lives up to the ideals of discipleship. One is glorified when one gets to heaven.

46. Adolf Schlatter, *Romans: The Righteousness of God*, trans. Siegried Schatzmann (Peabody: Hendrickson, 1995), 25.

47. Stott, *Romans*, 63.

48. Miranda, *Buting Pinoy*, 81-83.

49. This portion is based on Melanio Aoanan's "Teolohiya ng Bituka at Pagkain: Tungo sa Teolohiyang Pumipiglas" (Explorations in Theology), *Journal of Union Theological Seminary* 1(November 1996): 23-44.

50. Fr. Leonardo Mercado discusses this in his *Elements of Filipino Philosophy* (Tacloban: Divine Word Publications, 1974).

51. Aoanan, "Teolohiya ng Bituka," 35.

52. Daniel Patte in his *Discipleship According to the Sermon on the Mount* (Valley Forge: Trinity Press International, 1996), 386, comments: "While conversing with students and colleagues at Union Theological Seminary (Dasmarinas, Philippines), who cannot think of themselves apart from the community to which they belong, it became clear to me that I was looking in the wrong direction. The word of God is never 'for me' by myself; it is always 'for us.'"

53. In its most literal sense, the greeting means, "How are your intestines?", because it is a question prompted by a situation of *kumakalam ang bituka* (hunger pangs).

54. See Virgilio Enriquez, "Kapwa: A Core Concept in Filipino Social Psychology," *Sikolohiyang Pilipino, Aganon and Ma. Assumpta* (Manila: National Bookstore, 1985).

55. Daniel Patte, *Paul's Faith and the Power of the Gospel: A Structural Introduction to the Pauline Letters* (Philadelphia: Fortress Press, 1983), 257.

56. Patte, *Paul's Faith*, 232-233.

57. See Miranda, *Lakbay Diwa*, 80.

Works Cited

Andres, Tomas. *Positive Filipino Values.* Quezon City: New Day Publishers, 1989.

Anno, Ferdinand. "Toward a Liturgical Approach to Theological Reconstruction," *Explorations in Theology, Journal of Union Theological Seminary* (Cavite, Philippines: UTS, 1996), Vol 1, No. 1, November 1996, 81-91.

Aoanan, Melanio. "Teolohiya ng Bituka at Pagkain: Tungo sa Teolohiyang Pumipiglas," *Explorations in Theology, Journal of Union Theological Seminary* (Cavite, Philippines: UTS, 1996), Vol. 1 No. 1, November 1996, 23-44.

Barth, Karl. *A Shorter Commentary on Romans.* Richmond: John Knox Press, 1959.

_____. *The Epistle to the Romans*. Oxford: Oxford University Press, 1933.

Enriquez, Virgilio. "Kapwa: A Core Concept in Filipino Social Psychology, " *Sikolohiyang Pilipino, Aganon and Ma. Assumpta*. Manila: National Bookstore, 1985.

Gaventa, Beverly. "Romans." *The Women's Bible Commentary*. Ed. Carol H. Newsome and Sharon H. Ringe. Louisville: Westminster/John Knox Press, 1992.

Jewett, Robert. *Paul: Apostle to America*. Louisville: Westminster/John Knox Press, 1994.

Käsemann, Ernst. *Commentary on Romans*. Grand Rapids: Eerdmans, 1980.

Kwok Pui-lan. *Discovering the Bible in the Non-Biblical World*. New York: Orbis, 1995.

Luther, Martin. *Lectures on Romans, The Library of Christian Classics*, Vol XV. Trans. Wilhelm Pauck. Philadelphia: Westminster, 1961.

Mercado, Leonardo. *Elements of Filipino Philosophy*. Tacloban: Divine Word Publications, 1974.

Miranda, Dionisio. *Lakbay Diwa*. Tagaytay City, Philippines: Divine Word Publications, 1987.

_____. *Buting Pinoy*. Manila: Divine Word Publications [no date].

Murray, J. *The Epistle to the Romans*. Grand Rapids: Eerdmans, 1959.

Patte, Daniel. *Discipleship According to the Sermon on the Mount*. Valley Forge, Pennsylvania: Trinity Press International, 1996.

_____. "Whither Critical New Testament Studies for a New Day? Some Reflections on Luke 17:11-19," in *Putting Body and Soul Together: Essays in Honor of Robin Scroggs*. Edited by A. Brown, G. F. Snyder, and V. Wiles. Valley Forge: Trinity Press International, 1977, 275-296,

_____. *Paul's Faith and the Power of the Gospel: A Structural Introduction to the Pauline Letters*. Philadelphia: Fortress Press, 1983.

Pinn, Anthony. *Why Lord? Suffering and Evil in Black Theology*. New York: Continuum, 1995.

Sanders, E. P. *Paul and Palestinian Judaism*. London: SCM Press, 1977.

Schlatter, Adolf. *Romans: The Righteousness of God*. Trans. Siegried Schatzmann. Peabody: Hendrickson, 1995.

Stendahl, Krister. *Final Account: Paul's Letter to the Romans*. Minneapolis: Fortress Press, 1995.

Stott, John. *Romans: God's Good News for the World*. Morton Grove: InterVarsity Press, 1994.

Wright, N. T. *The Climax of the Covenant: Christ and the Law in Pauline Theology*. Edinburgh, Scotland: T&T Clark, 1991.

A Postmodern Critique

A Response to Velunta,
" '*Ek Pisteôs Eis Pistin*' and the Filipinos'
Sense of Indebtedness (*Utang Na Loob*)"

Troy W. Martin

◆

I am grateful to Revelation Enriquez Velunta for his cross-cultural reading of Romans from a Filipino perspective and for opening his private faith and religious traditions for public discussion. His reading offers an insightful opportunity to examine postmodernism as a context for cross-cultural readings of sacred texts. I offer my response in the spirit not of criticism but rather of consideration and conversation.

Adopting a postmodern critique of the historical-critical interpretive approach, Velunta seeks to legitimate and validate Nanay's reading of Paul's phrase *ek pisteôs eis pistin* (Rom 1:17) as *utang na loob*, rendered in English as sense of indebtedness or sense of gratitude. Velunta recognizes his mother's reading is a particular or *pro me* reading that differs from the usual Filipino translation of this phrase as *pananampalataya*, rendered in English as risk-taking or taking a gamble. However, he attempts to legitimate her reading by arguing that there is textual evidence to support her reading, that her reading makes sense of the text, and that her reading is relevant both for him and his community. He defends her reading as not projecting something foreign upon the text but as being a Filipino reading lens that works as a translation of *ek pisteôs eis pistin*. Each of these aspects of Velunta's cross-cultural reading of Romans from a postmodern critique merit response.

The concern for a legitimate reading reflects the postmodern critique that Velunta has adopted, for legitimacy is a major concern of postmodernism. This critique, however, complicates Velunta's goal of legitimating his mother's reading by discounting any authority beyond his mother that would be capable of legitimating or validating her reading. Velunta correctly articulates the postmodern critique when he describes his mother's reading as "perspectival and particular" and as one among several alternative readings that informed her particular situation. Lacking her particular life situation and perspective, others can understand and appreciate but not legitimate her reading.

The postmodern critique also complicates Velunta's goal, for it raises the question of whether legitimation, whatever it means and if it could be granted, is necessary or even possible. Velunta espouses the postmodern tenet that no reading can claim privilege over another. Since legitimate Filipino readings would have inherent privilege over illegitimate Filipino readings, seeking to distinguish Filipino readings by these categories is at least unnecessary and at most impossible according to a postmodern critique since all readings of this Pauline phrase by Filipinos would have equal claim as legitimate Filipino readings.

Velunta's adopting a postmodern critique particularizes the conception of the cross-cultural Filipino reading that he attempts to legitimate. He admits that Nanay's reading of *ek pisteôs eis pistin* as *utang na loob* (sense of interestedness or gratitude) is not the way other Filipinos read this phrase. Indeed, every reading according to postmodern critique is particular to the reader. What claim, therefore, does Nanay's reading of *ek pisteôs eis pistin* have of being a Filipino reading beyond her being Filipino? What even constitutes a Filipino reading? Is *utang na loob* essentially a Filipino reading of *ek pisteôs eis pistin* or is the sense of indebtedness conferred or at least conditioned by Spanish Roman Catholic influence? Reading this phrase as "sense of indebtedness" is certainly consonant with Roman Catholic piety. According to the postmodern critique, Nanay's reading should probably be specified as a colonial Filipino reading and further specified to indicate its particularity to her time and life situation. This critique raises the question of how such particular readings can claim to be representative of Filipino culture and a legitimate cross-cultural Filipino reading.

A postmodern critique hinders much of Velunta's argument for legitimation by removing the very text upon which he seeks legitimation. He argues that there is textual evidence to support Nanay's reading, that her reading makes sense of the text, and that her reading does not project something foreign upon the text. In a postmodern critique, there is no "the text," for readers never read the same text, but texts are always mediated by readers' agendas, interests, experiences, perceptions, and a host of other factors. So much is foreign to a reading of a text that distinguishing foreignness from innateness becomes extremely difficult for a postmodern critique. Of course, Velunta's arguments are perfectly valid if "the text" is Nanay's text. It follows logically that her reading has textual support from her text, makes sense of her text, and does not project anything foreign upon her text. Of course, Velunta argues much more than that Nanay's reading is a valid reading of her text, but a postmodern critique hinders such arguments.

Velunta's adoption of a postmodern critique of the historical-critical interpretive approach not only hinders his arguments for the legitimation of Nanay's reading but also challenges certain assumptions of her reading. Why did Nanay, a Filipino, privilege Paul's letter to the Romans over Filipino texts and oral traditions? By leaving her legacy of Paul's concept of faith to her children, Nanay assumed a Christian tradition that relies on a decisive revelation in history and passes this revelation to successive generations of Christians. Such a tradition necessitates an understanding of that revelatory moment and imbues that revelatory moment with an authority lacking in other historical events. The historical critical method developed in an attempt to "recover" that revelatory moment and to "discover" its inherent authority as a means of challenging the status quo. This method is certainly not perfect, and perhaps it has been co-opted by those interested in maintaining the status quo. Nevertheless, some means of recovering the past seems necessary for establishing legitimate readings, for otherwise the Christian tradition is severed from its past, and Nanay is separated from Paul and the Christ to whom she devoted her life. Thus, Velunta's adoption of a postmodern critique challenges the assumptions of Nanay's reading of *ek pisteôs eis pistin* in Rom 1:17.

As I stated in the beginning, I offer my response in the spirit of conversation, for I sympathize with Velunta and with all who attempt to legitimate specific readings of sacred texts in a postmodern world. A postmodern critique undermines not only the historical critical method, the traditional means of legitimating readings, but also faith communities' norms and controls, the traditional impetus for legitimating readings. Velunta rejects the historical critical method as being a foreign lens through which to view the text and as an Euro-American Androcentric construct used to interpret the text. Perhaps, his postmodern critique is just as Euro-American and as Androcentric as the historical critical method. Velunta's attempt to legitimate Nanay's reading of *ek pisteôs eis pistin* in Rom 1:17 as *utang na loob* certainly offers an insightful opportunity to examine postmodernism as a context for cross-cultural readings of sacred texts but leaves unresolved the question of whether a postmodern critique provides for genuine third-world readings of texts or is yet another imposition of a first-world structure of thought on third world thinkers.

– E I G H T –

Messianic Predestination in Romans 8 and Classical Confucianism

Yeo Khiok-khng (K.K.)

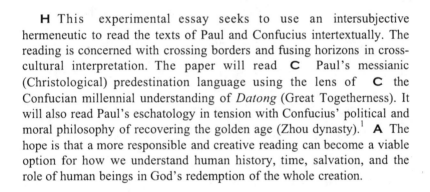

H This experimental essay seeks to use an intersubjective hermeneutic to read the texts of Paul and Confucius intertextually. The reading is concerned with crossing borders and fusing horizons in cross-cultural interpretation. The paper will read **C** Paul's messianic (Christological) predestination language using the lens of **C** the Confucian millennial understanding of *Datong* (Great Togetherness). It will also read Paul's eschatology in tension with Confucius' political and moral philosophy of recovering the golden age (Zhou dynasty).[1] **A** The hope is that a more responsible and creative reading can become a viable option for how we understand human history, time, salvation, and the role of human beings in God's redemption of the whole creation.

Intersubjectivity of Cross-cultural Interpretation[2]

H An intersubjective reading assumes a rhetorical-hermeneutical reading process that is interactive and persuasive in its communication. In *Rhetorical Interaction in 1 Corinthians 8 and 10* I allotted a considerable amount of space to spelling out the significance and process of an *interactive* model in biblical reading and cross-cultural hermeneutics based on rhetorical theories.[3] The rhetorical interaction

---

H Intersubjective hermeneutic.

C Paul's context.

C Confucius' context.

A Responsible and creative reading.

H Intersubjectivity of cross-cultural interpretation.

among text, writer, and reader is based on rhetorical and literary theories which are *less intentional and articulate in noting the significance of multitextual influence, the subjectivity of a text and its reader as well as laying out a two-way reading process.* In this paper, I wish to draw on the insights of intertextuality and intersubjectivity to supplement my rhetorical construct of a reading process to read Romans 8.

The term "intertextuality" was coined by Julia Kristeva to indicate that a text does not exist in a closed system of its own but in interrelation with other texts through quotations, references, allusions and influences of various kinds.[4] The intersubjective influence conveyed through the medium of a "text" is clearly seen in the "various cultural discourses"[5] because "the text is a tissue of quotations drawn from innumerable centers of culture."[6] The assumed locus of meaning-production in this inter-subjective process has shifted from the author to the reader. Both axis of intertextuality—via the writer (who is the first reader) and the readers (who are co-producers of textual meaning)—allow the "dialogism" or "heteroglossia" (exchange of language in M. Bakhtin's understanding) of texts to work in the genesis of meaning.[7]

The processes of reading- and meaning-production are always dialogues between the writers and the readers. The authority of interpretation does not reside in the frozen text or in the first writer, but is to be found in the interactive process of the text, involving both the writer and the reader, which I have previously termed "rhetorical interaction."[8] Gadamer writes of the intersubjective and inter-interpretive understanding process which is productive and reproductive:

> The actual meaning of a text, as it speaks to the interpreter, is not dependent on the occasion represented by the author and his original public. At least it is not exhausted by it; for the meaning is also determined by the historical situation of the interpreter, and thus by the whole of the objective course of history. . . . The meaning of a text goes beyond its author, not only occasionally but always. Understanding is therefore not merely reproductive, but also productive.[9]

This reproductive and productive process of reading allows and requires the text/writer and the reader/interpretation to be intersubjective. A text not only carries meaning but allows readers to create meanings. Similarly, readers not only interpret text, they are being read by texts, viz., their stories are made meaningful by the texts. Because understanding and reading processes are reproductive and productive, a writer cannot control the meaning of a text and limit it to *just* his own "original" intention.

The question then is: to what extent does this intersubjectivity between text and readers exist? On the extreme case, one may argue that any text can be "rewritten" by readers, as reader-response theories have shown.[10] For example, Roland Barthes would even argue for "the death of the author," thus putting the authority of interpretation only on the text and the readers.[11] Similarly, Culler writes, "There are no moments of authority and points of origin except those which are retrospectively designated as origins and which, therefore, can be shown to derive from the series for which they are constituted as origin."[12] This argument sounds shocking—the hope for significant, meaningful, substantive communication is entirely lost, but this proposal is understandable if seen in the reaction of reader-response theories to meaning in a determined text, the hegemonic control in ideological and authority structure, and the dualistic thinking of the interpreter Subject. At the least, the identification of an intertextual and intersubjective reading process is an act of interpretation that subjects to doubt the idea of a *determined* text, the ideology of authority, and the real and causative source of the text.

Confucian Messianic Expectation, *Datong*, and Recovery of the Golden Age

C H Both motifs of messianic consciousness and national salvation are present in biblical (Jewish and Christian) and Confucianist utopian history, but the dynastic change and hope of the return of the golden age is quite distinctive of Chinese history. Yet the Confucian political ethics and the biblical (especially Pauline) theology are intertextual lenses I often use to understand history. Jewish and Christian views look to a transcendental reign of God beyond national history. In those views, eschatological and millenarian hope is not only about national salvation, it is also about cosmic salvation (cf. Rom 1:20, 25; 8:20-22). In critiquing the domination of various empires, Jewish and Christian views portray the God of history whose intended will of salvation "invades" the world and becomes the *telos* (goal) of history. The question I often ask in reading Romans 8 is: Does Paul's argument regarding Christ as the *telos* (goal, purpose) of cosmic salvation provide a comprehensive narrative that excludes other narratives?

As we will see in this section, the majority of Confucianists, in contrast to the biblical view, see the Chinese Great Togetherness/ Harmony (*Datong*) as a realization of a past golden age. Is that Confucianist view too parochial?

C H Context of Confucius.

I We will take a look at both traditions rather independently before concluding with an intertextual reading of these two. My intention is *not* to make the claim that my reading of Romans 8 is the only valid, or even a better one, than those that have been offered by previous biblical scholars. My intention is to use my Confucianist lens to re-read Romans 8 and to argue that this is another plausible reading.[13] In the reading process, I also hope to use Romans 8 to offer helpful critiques to some of my Confucianist assumptions of history so that my Confucianist-Pauline hermeneutic will broaden my understanding of how God is at work in and beyond a particular cultural process and historical tradition.

H In contrast to the Pauline vision of Christ narrative of God's cosmic salvation, **H** the Confucian vision of national salvation posits a moral transformation of humanity in the hope of recovering the previous ideal dynasty. There are a few observations we can summarize regarding the Confucian view of salvation. These observations will serve as lenses for me to read Romans 8. I must admit that my selective understanding of Confucian political ethics is influenced by my interest in some of the themes in Romans 8 as well.

Recovery of the Golden Age *(Datong)*

First, the recovery of the golden age as the *Datong* in Confucian thought looks backward at history for the ideal goal within its social-political context. **H** This strikes me as a prominent spatial-temporal frame that Romans 8 also uses. Confucius (or known to the Chinese world as Kong Zi, 551-479 BCE) regarded the Western (Earlier or Former) Zhou (1050-770 BCE) as the "golden age," only 200 years or so earlier than "Spring and Autumn" (Chun Qiu 770-476 BCE) when he was born. Later Confucians were also fond of looking to antiquity as a prototype of an ideal age to which people in a disintegrating society should look. To them, antiquity was not a pre-civilization Garden of Eden but the golden age of Zhou as the era of highest human achievement.

Confucius' understanding of *Datong* is not nostalgia for the good old days. His messianic hope of recovering the golden age of the past served primarily as a backward stretching of the imagination of Chinese who were living in a state of cultural and moral deterioration. Confucius wanted the Chinese to contemplate the Great Harmony (i.e., *Datong* in

---

I   Interplay of two traditions.

H   Paul's meaning.

H   Confucius' understanding.

H   Use *Datong* to read Romans.

Chinese) in the perfect world. His *Datong* utopian hope was a critique of their chaotic and deteriorating society.

Continuing the tradition of Confucius, Mencius' social utopian understandings combine to form a government that is responsible to the people; Mencius also teaches that a royal government (*wangdao*) seeks to benefit all by distributing resources fairly according to the "well field system" (*jing*), and requires all to contribute according to their abilities.[14] It is a socialist system of government based on division of labors, consideration for others, and communal solidarity.[15]

Self-Perception as Heaven-Sent

H Second, the self-perception of Confucius as the "messiah" (heaven-sent and heaven-chosen) to bring about the ideal of the golden age is a distinctive ethos in Chinese philosophy. "Messianic" consciousness is not just a biblical or Pauline concept; it is evident in Confucianism as well. Bauer's research into this messianic concept in Chinese history shows Confucius as a self-conscious, "predestined messiah" of his own society:

> Confucius was firmly convinced of his world-shaking, 'heaven-sent' mission. He may already have known of a tradition whose existence during the century following his death is verifiable beyond a doubt and according to which the realm would be saved and restored every five hundred years by a truly spiritual ruler. Along with his . . . theories concerning the messianism of the oracle priests, Hu shih has [shown] . . . the existence of such a tradition for the period following Confucius. . . . Similar to the belief in a heavenly 'mandate' to rule the world being passed from one dynasty to the next, the conviction that a great restorer would appear every five hundred years thus more probably arose from the precedent created by Confucius's repeated emphasis on the close tie between himself and the duke of Zhou.[16]

Thus, Confucius identified himself with the duke of Zhou (Zhou Gong), the brother of the founder of the dynasty, Wuwang ("Warrior King"), who was regent for Chengwang, Wuwang's son and successor. *Lun Yu* (The Analects) often mentions the duke of Zhou, and some scholars have suspected that perhaps Confucius longed to be such a personality and restore the lost golden age.[17]

The self-perception of messianic consciousness seems to be the legacy of Confucianism, subsequently every Confucianist has the

---

H Self-perception of Confucius as sent by Heaven (*tian*).

conviction and aspiration to serve one's country after completing a moral education. That legacy also makes Confucian moral philosophy political in function. After all, the political semantic domain of the title, *Zi (tzu)*, being the title of Confucius (*Kong Zi [Kung-tzu]* is his name in Chinese), reflects an assumption of Chinese reality. The title *Zi* was first used to refer to royal princes and kinsmen, then to wise counselors of feudal lords, and finally to philosopher-teachers.

The significant point in Confucius' yearning for the restoration of peace and order in the world is his understanding of the heavenly mandate, i.e., the calling that is from the world beyond for him to fulfill, and the mission of saving the society in which he lives. Throughout Chinese history, few people had as clear a calling as Confucius. In *Shi Ji* (*Historical Records*), there is an account of Confucius as the ideal ruler:

> Three months after Confucius had assumed the government of the state [*Lu*], even cattle dealers no longer cheated others by demanding excessive prices; men and women walked along different sides of the road, and objects lost on the streets were no longer picked up. Strangers came from the four directions of heaven, but when they arrived in the towns, they never found it necessary to turn to the police, for they were treated as if they were in their own country (*Shi Ji* 47:667b)[18]

Confucius did have the ambition to be a political leader, but the hope was unfulfilled.[19] Confucius' despair is recorded in the Analects 9:9: "The phoenix does not come; the river gives forth no chart. It is all over with me!" The phoenix is a mythical creature belonging to the heavenly realm that sends forth messages concerning the arrival of sage-king Shun. The river chart is a gift given to Zhou king during his enthronement, the chart maps out his territory indicative of a peaceful reign.[20]

Political Morality in Confucian Datong

C Third, the intended purpose of heaven for Chinese society in Confucian thought focuses on political morality as a consummation of salvation of that society. Of course, the concern of salvation is the main theme of Paul's letter to the Romans; salvation, as related to the righteousness of God, is about creating the people of God who will live a life of holiness in Christ.

The assumption of this political morality is that the Confucian *Datong* vision as a trans-historical reality can be seen in Confucius'

C Political morality of Chinese society.

teaching of *Tian Dao* ("the Heavenly Principle" or "the Heavenly Way"). How did the uncrowned king reign and bring about *telos* in Chinese history? He reigns by being and teaching other to become *ren ren* (persons who love). Thus Confucianism emphasizes moral education rather than warrior nobility, political virtues rather than political prosperity, relational harmony rather than kingship kinship. Confucius believed that *Tian* not only gave birth to the people but continued to regenerate and sustain them. Thus, in terms of morality, Confucius regarded *ren* (love) as the fountainhead of all virtues. He exhorted all to actualize *Tian-ming* (mandate of Heaven) by committing themselves to *ren,* because *ren* is what makes human beings human. In terms of political morality, he emphasizes that the sage-rulers are to be virtuous, providing an example for others to follow, and thus bringing about the renewal of the society (*Great Learning* [*Da Xue*] 1:1). The *Doctrine of Mean* (*Zhong Yong*) likewise states that if a sage-ruler knows how to cultivate his own character, he will know how to govern other people (20:11).

As a result of his vision of political morality, Confucius did not popularize a patriarchal lineage of royal succession. Rather, he advocates virtues of *ren* and righteousness. He mentioned that Yao and Shun were regarded as virtuous rulers who left their thrones not to their sons but to the best qualified candidates. Analects 4:13 recounts, "If [a king] is able to govern his state with the disposition of modesty and propriety (*li-rang,* i.e., "yielding") [possibly including the idea of readiness to give it up], what trouble can he have? If he is unable to govern the state with modesty and propriety, what has he to do with the rites and propriety?"[21]

C In imagining the existence of goodness and beauty in a perfect society, Confucius' *Datong* vision emphasized music, propriety, character, and harmonious interpersonal relationships, because the Zhou dynasty is the prototype of *Datong*. The King of Zhou employed two principles as the common ground for unifying the people: *yue* (music as the harmony of emotion/feeling) and *li* (cultured behavior expressed artistically as propriety). Confucius believed that beauty and goodness were the foundations or the source of music and propriety, and that the potential for beauty and goodness resided in every person.

Mencius (372-289 BCE) is the first person who fully developed Confucius' ethical and social philosophy in the political realm. His sense of a vocation to save the world is also clear, even though the time cycle for him has not come. He explained his commitment based on two reasons: First, he believed in the goodness of human nature, that every human being should have a messianic consciousness. His

---

C Confucian context of Datong.

democratization of an inherently good human nature motivated the conscience of the people toward social responsibility. Second, he believed in the "quasi-mystical notion of a salubrious force pulsating through all beings"[22] (*hao-ran zhi qi*), i.e., because "heaven does not speak . . . people are the only court of appeal and decide whether or not a dynasty has the 'mandate.' A new ruler must be 'introduced' to both heaven and the people before he can be certain of his office. It is therefore a basic premise of every ideal government that the prince own everything in an 'equal manner' with the people."[23] His second point is also a democratic one, but of the mandate of heaven. Such a view suggests that the validity of heavenly mandate needs approval from the people.

Cyclical Movement of History

H Fourth, the Confucian democratization of messianic consciousness of all people for their society works and continues in the cyclical movement of history. The typical Chinese cyclical worldview works well with the periodization view of history. Since the view of historical time is cyclical, the periodization cannot be progress but instead a spiraling alternation between order and disorder. Long ago, Mencius said: "Since the appearance of the world of men, a long time has indeed elapsed, consisting of alternating order and disorder" (3B, 9). Not in keeping with that worldview, Mencius (2B, 13) delineates cycles of history in the following dispensations: (1) from the sage-kings Yao and Shun and Yu (24th-23rd centuries BCE) to the founder of Shang, (2) from the founder of Shang to the founders of Zhou (23rd-12th century BCE), and (3) from the founders of Zhou to Confucius (12th century to 551 BCE). The alternating sequence of old-new periods is attempted in the Qin dynasty, and the old-new-old pattern becomes evident in the earlier Han dynasty (206 BCE-6 CE).[24]

Given this Chinese cyclical/spiraling understanding of history, national salvation involves the rule of law and the propriety of virtuous rulers and democratized rule of virtue by all self-perceived educated Confucianists. As such, sage (philosopher) and ruler are inseparable, i.e., crowned kings have to be virtuous and virtuous persons (*ren ren*) can be uncrowned kings.

A popular Confucianist understanding of political messianism in China is that in a five-hundred-year cycle there would supposedly be a ruler vested with the heavenly mandate to reign over China. Bauer gives examples of messianic consciousness in Chinese history, and not all these figures are strictly political rulers. The first is the duke of Zhou

---

H Chinese understanding of time and national salvation.

(who died in 1105 BCE according to traditional chronology); next is Confucius (551-479 BCE); then the historian Sima Qian (Ssu-ma Ch'ien, ca. 145-90 BCE); the illegal emperor Wang Mang (45 BCE -23 CE); and the philosopher-emperor Yuandi (508-555) of the Liang dynasty.[25] Bauer notes,

> Curiously enough, men who did not live during these periods of renewal also believed that this messianic idea applied to them, particularly Mencius. He is the first to explicitly discuss this five-hundred-year rule (Mencius 2B, 13 and 7B, 38).[26]

This Confucian messianic mandate of saving the world lies in the consciousness of the political commitment of his moral philosophy. Confucian moral philosophy serves its political purpose of bringing about peace in the world through the process of self-cultivation, family harmony, and nation governing.

The Narrative of Christological Predestination for "Jews and Gentiles" in Romans 8

A Turning to Romans, we note the thesis of Romans 8:28-30 to be a discussion of the eschatological community of sonship created by the Spirit. Perhaps, **C** the Confucian emphasis on the mandate of heaven fulfilled in the ethical life of a community has guided the way I read Romans 8. **I** From my reading I understand that the ethical life force saves a community as it forms harmony in a world of suffering and moral deterioration.

C H Leaving aside the difference between *recovering* history (alternating cyclical view of history) and *looking forward* to the future (eschatological view of history), the Confucian vision of *Datong* is similar to the ideal presented in Romans 8:18-30, which spells out the salvific hope (Rom 8:20, 24-25) or future glory (Rom 8:17, 18, 21, 23, 30; cf. 1:23) of all God's people (Jews and Gentiles) together with creation in the context of present suffering (8:17, 18-23, 26). Paul encourages the audience to hope as the children of God (Rom 8:18-30).[27] Paul assures the community of faith that human weakness is overcome by the intercession of the Spirit and the loving purpose of God.

A Eschatological community of sonship created by the Spirit.

C Mandate of heaven in Confucian understanding.

I Interplay between Confucian ethic and Romans 8.

C H Between Confucian recovering history and Paul's eschatology.

A Focusing on Romans 8:28-30, we note a few key insights of Paul, which may be similar or different from the teachings of Confucius:

Sovereignty of God (Theos) and Transcendence of Heaven (Tian)

First, in the context of an imperfect world, **A H** the sovereignty of God (*Theos*) speaks of the *comprehensiveness* of God's purpose in creation; this is similar to the *macro* vision of Confucius' political ethics and its grounding of ethics in the transcendental *Tian* (heaven). The point of God's comprehensive purpose will extend Paul's understanding of predestination in a cosmic dimension later (vv. 29-30), and there, the language of predestination is set in the context of encouragement and not judgment. Here (v. 28), Paul argues that "all things work together for good for 'those who love God,'[28] who are called to his purpose" (8:28).[29] "All" (*panta*) includes suffering, sin, weaknesses, adversity, or bearing of the cross.[30] "Works together" (*sunergeō*) means assist or profit towards benefit.[31] Not all things serve the comfort of the people of God, but all things work together to their salvation. God does not cause everything but God uses every event, good or bad, towards an eventual greater good. *Eis agathon* is goodness realized eschatologically, goodness being understood as the *telos* of God's creation.[32] Nothing will be meaningless and stay outside God's purpose (eschatologically; cf. Rom 14:16). Cranfield summarizes the point well:

> We understand the first part of the verse, then, to mean that nothing can really harm—that is, harm in the deepest sense of the word—those who really love God, but that all things which may happen to them, including such grievous things as are mentioned in verse 35, must serve to help them on their way to salvation, confirming their faith and drawing them closer to their Master, Jesus Christ. But the reason why all things thus assist believers is, of course, that God is in control of all things.[33]

All things do not work together for good *on their own*, but God's sovereign act is the undergirding force behind God's absolute control and omniscient (all knowing) power over everything.[34] God is able to bring good out of all things, and that is the Christian hope.[35] Paul gives the faithful assurance that the future belongs to the children of God. This assurance strengthens the people of God as they struggle with sin and suffering. The future is secured because it is grounded in the eternity of

---

A Romans 8:28-30.

A H Sovereignty of God.

God. The eternal counsel/purpose of God in creation becomes the very purpose of humanity.

Eschatological Adam (Christ) and Ideal Community (Datong)

Second, for Paul cosmic salvation is inextricably connected with **A H** God's *primordial goal of transforming the fallen world* by means of the eschatological Adam. Analogously, the mandate of heaven (*tian-ming*) is to transform the morally corrupted world for Confucius. I understand the eschatological Adam as the realization of an ideal community (*Datong*) rather than a salvation by means of an individual. I also understand Romans 8 to mean that the power of God's gospel redeems the *whole* creation. The power also revealed the righteousness of God (Heaven). The ultimate purpose of God's righteousness is to restore all to wholeness and to bring the totality of creation back into loving relationship with God.

I Paul begins with God's love for believers through God's sovereign election and calling, and ends with God's divine purpose of our glorification through Jesus Christ (see the five aorist verbs in vv. 28-30). This is a narrative that speaks of the Oneness of God who is impartial and whose righteousness revealed in Jesus Christ is based on grace. Even though the first point (on the narrative of Christ for the cosmic salvation) may look hegemonic to (post)modern readers, the second point (on grace and faith) qualifies the first point by grounding the narrative within the socio-political context. I believe the Confucian moral critique of political ideology has given me a helpful lens to read Romans 8 with a political perspective also.

C Against the Roman ideology of violence because of polytheistic faith, Paul's narrative lifts up the Christ event as just/fair because it is based on a principle of "from faithfulness [of Christ] to faithfulness [of Christians]" (1:18). Romans 8:28-30 seem to underline the hope of cosmic salvation which "characterizes the life in the Spirit to be the life of those who are righteous by faith."[36] Against the competitiveness and boasting of house-churches in Rome (e.g., Jewish and Gentile Christians)—a manifestation of similar Roman ideology of boasting— Paul appeals to the narrative of Christ as the unifying force for them to welcome one another based on grace.

H But why isn't the narrative of Christ as articulated by Paul an imperialistic one? The narrative of Christ has its universal effect ("Jews

---

A H God's primordial goal of transforming the world.

I Between the contexts of Paul and Confucius.

C Roman ideology in the context of Paul.

H Is Christ's narrative imperialistic?

and Gentiles"), but it does not seek to "conquer," it seeks to include all by means of grace. Though it is *one* narrative for all, it does not have to be seen as imperialistic. Having *multiple* narratives cannot guarantee that they will not conquer each other; in fact, conflicts among these narratives will more likely result in violence if divine grace is not their driving force. The narrative of Christ is one championed by the grace of God. If there is one narrative of the eschatological Adam (ideal community, also Christ) sent by the Creator to be the way for co-existence of many, then that plan of salvation deserves consideration by all. The question is: who is that eschatological Adam? What is the plan of salvation?

"Pre-horizoning" of Christ and Predestination of Individuals

I Third, in light of the moral freedom I find in Confucian political ethics, I see the same moral freedom in the language of predestination in Romans 8. I know it is possible to see the predestination language as a doctrine that separates believers from unbelievers (sheep and goats), but I want to suggest another plausible reading. That is, the predestination language is a theological understanding of God's cosmic salvation through *pre-horizoning* of Christ as the ultimate purpose. This is a comprehensive narrative for humanity, including the vision of Confucius and others, while at the same time differentiating these narratives for the sake of enriching the whole.

H The problem is that, the language of "predestination" or "pre-horizoning" looks parochial to many. Grayston argues that, "The old word is 'predestined' (as in NRSV)—which means that the destination is chosen, but not the names or the number of those who will reach it. The Greek word might be Englished as 'pre-horizoned'—meaning that God has marked out the limits but not those who stray beyond them."[37] Predestination means to mark out a boundary or horizon beforehand to serve as a goal or purpose. The verbs *protithêmi* and *proorizô* and the noun *prothesis* refer to planning, purposing, or resolving to do something. All of these terms convey the idea of initiating an action.[38] The program of God's salvation for humanity is set in motion as God marks out the purpose, without predetermining every action in the process. In other words, it is plausible to read Romans 8 as describing the beginning in which God marks out a destiny for humanity—such as the Confucian understanding that to be human is to actualize virtue in a community. That *telos* (goal) or destiny, in this biblical text, is Christ who is God's paradigmatic Savior of the world (righteousness of God) through faith by grace. The paradigm is qualified by "through faith by

---

I Between ethics of Confucius and predestination language of Paul.

H The meaning of "predestination"—pre-horizoning.

grace." Therefore, what is predestined is primarily not believers or unbelievers but Christ, the purposeful creation of God by means of God's ideal community characterized by faith and grace.

"Firstborn" and Virtues of Faithfulness and Love

I Fourth, analogous to the ethical salvation of Confucian society via virtue and becoming *ren ren* (loving persons), Christ was portrayed in Romans 8 as the first born (*prototokôs*) and the defining horizon. Humanity will be formed (*proorizô*) and become sharers (*summorphous*; cf. Phil 3:21)[39] in the image (*eikôn*) of God's Son.[40]

H "Firstborn" speaks likewise of the resurrection life of the new age; Christ as the first born "implies his preeminence but also his sharing of sonship with numerous Christians."[41] The image of the "firstborn" as used in the Old Testament refers to one who receives the birthright, thus one who is the heir having a position of preeminence, prestige and power. The term is also used often in the Old Testament to refer to Israel as God's chosen, beloved one, instrumental in God's salvific plan.

"Firstborn" is also a messianic term, an epithet for the Davidic King (cf. LXX Psalm 88 [89 in English Bible]:28) who will restore Israel.[42] When this messianic term is used for Jesus, its nationalistic (David) and ethnic (Israel) connotations seem to be overturned into an *inclusive paradigm* of salvation for all who believe. Jesus trusted in God and was faithfully obedient in suffering and now is the pioneer of salvation for all who respond in love to God's call to believe and follow in Christ's footsteps.[43] The narrative of Christ is for the Jews and Gentiles, Greeks and barbarians, male and female, and all social classes. The Christological means of salvation has its goal that all will be made in the likeness of the Son, set right with God and glorified at the parousia.

Foreknowledge of God and His Purposeful Acts

I Fifth, *predestination* is often understood as predetermination of the individual decision process. It can also mean the sovereign purpose of God's salvation for creation—sovereign in final outcome and sovereign in full control of the process. After all, Heaven (*Tian*) is sovereign, transcendent and all knowing.

H Foreknowledge can mean to choose individuals beforehand for a special relationship, such as foreknowledge of the faithful response of

---

I Between virtue in Confucian thought and image of firstborn in Paul's theology.

H Meaning of "firstborn."

I Between purposeful act of salvation (Paul) and sovereign Heaven (Confucius).

H Meaning of "foreknowledge."

selected individuals.[44] But my reading understands foreknowledge to be foresight concerning the purposeful act of salvation in which believers will respond faithfully. Indeed, because of the sovereignty of God and eschatological view of history, foreknowledge can be understood as the Hebraic understanding of "knowing" with affection and predilection.[45]

God has foreknowledge, God knows all, all the time, in all time. God knows the sweep of history in a moment—"line" of history in a "dot." Yet when God creates, God is involved in history, God unfolds the moment into a spiral movement of history—recovering eschatological telos *and* re-imagining the golden age. What God knows and does in eternity appears to us as prior action. Throughout the unfolding of God's plan, "light falls from the divine past and the divine future."[46] In Romans 8:28-30, the Christian's hope rests in God who has been there for the people of God even before God's call was known.[47] Nothing is accidental in God's plan, nothing is sheer luck or chance, everything has a purpose in God's creation.

One ought to be careful not to read the language of predestination as a divine prediction and a closed system of static fate; otherwise, the narrative of Christ could be comprehensive and yet rigid, or could be specific and yet exclusive. This language of predestination and foreknowledge is a reassuring one for those in suffering, weakness, and in need of grace. And foreknowledge of God should be understood in the eschatological view of history, i.e., God intends *all* humanity to have an affectionate relationship with God as children of God.

The Love and the People of God in Christ

I Sixth, the Christian hope is knowing that, though God foreknew the costs of creating through the suffering and giving of his Son, yet because *God is love* and wills all humankind into loving relationship, God calls his Son(s) into obedience. So God creates. This is similar to the general Chinese understanding that Heaven has empathy and passion (*tian you qing*) for all.

More importantly, the Confucian messianic consciousness helps me to understand the divine mission of believers in-Christ. The "in-Christ" destiny is probably not an election to mere privilege but more a call to responsibility that gives birth to the mission of God's community. Election/calling means being called to a responsibility, assuming an office for duty.[48] Verses 29-30 phrase God's plan in four parallel clauses with the repeated key words "foreknew, predestined, justified," and the climax of God's salvific plan is the connecting verb "glorified."[49] Those who respond to God's call to be in loving relationship with God are

---

I   Between passionate *Tian* (Confucius) and the love of God (Paul).

justified by the gift of God's grace to be the bearers of God's purpose.[50]
The link of justification brings the reader back to the central theme of
stressing faithfulness/faith in Romans chapters 1-4.

H Paul's conviction of God's plan progressing towards its goal
makes him assert that the future glorification of humankind (Adam
theology again, cf. Ps 8:5; Heb 2:8-10) is a completed action (gloried in
the *aorist* tense) as far as God's sovereign plan of salvation is concerned.
In this way Paul seems to assure Christians of their hope in the proleptic
consummation of God's plan. This is the ultimate confidence Christians
can have while living in the present and neither fully glorified nor totally
released from the power of death, sin, and the law. Paul encourages
them that the Spirit is working at this eschatological age, and God's
intention is to bring to glory all who have been justified by faith in
Christ. As the redemptive process and unification of all creation of God's
plan continues, the readers are assured of being called as divine agents to
proclaim the gospel and to transform the world.

Intertextual Reading of Pauline and Confucian Horizoning of Human History

H The intertextual reading of the Pauline and the Confucian texts has
not been explicit. I want to show how intertextual reading helps us
differentiate each text from the other as well as cross borders for creative
interpretations.

Intertextual Reading Between Confucius and Paul

A There are several rationales for intertextual reading based on the
nature of textuality and the reading process of the text. First, the writers
are not absolute and autonomous egos who merely produce the text.
The writers, such as Paul, Confucius, and Mencius, are already readers of
many texts who bring with them other textual influences (e.g. tradition of
linguistic usage, worldview) and their social-historical backgrounds.
Second, the reading process, e.g., that of this paper, never involves only
a text and a reader (as if in abstraction), but includes also a cross-
fertilization of other texts from the authors and readers' backgrounds. In
other words, even though I present my reading of Romans and
Confucianism separately, I have in fact read these two texts side by side
in my understanding. Third, writers and readers are not transcendental

---

H Paul's understanding of God's plan.

H Hermeneutical interest of intertextual reading.

A Rationales for intertextual reading.

egos that only produce and search for meanings in texts; writers and readers are themselves the productions of texts already embedded in their historical contexts. For example, Paul, Confucius, and I are interpreters within our historical settings, and the texts of our interpretation are, together with us, the subjects that effect and produce one another. Fourth, readers re-write the texts as they bring their horizons and experiences into the language codes. In the same light, the text itself is "reading" the readers in a new context of the readers' life-world. Of course, the mutual reading process between text and reader works as far as the collective language allows; the collective language serves as both their contact point and their boundaries.

A I am aware of the huge differences between Paul and Confucius, Romans and the Analects, but I am challenged to try an intersubjective reading because that is an honest way I can read Romans 8 and Confucian classics as a Chinese-Christian. The intersubjective reading of Romans and Confucianism does not mean that the two cultures and theologies are all similar or the same. **H** Intersubjective reading only means that a Chinese-Christian reader allows his full subjectivity (thus his cultural repertoire) to come in full contact with the subjectivity of the text (thus textual context). It will be shown that the intersubjective reading has allowed the use of language not only to describe but also to recreate meaning of a particular text. For example, Paul's highly theological and Jewish understanding of human beings, sin, Torah, Christ, salvation, are not the same as the humanistic and moral connotation of Confucius' political philosophy. Yet they can be brought to dialogue, and as a result of this dialogue, Paul's christological lens is colored with the social and moral aspects of ethics and politics, and Confucius' humanistic lens is colored with the theological necessity. **I** Let me summarize my discoveries thus far.

In-Group and Communal Language

1. The intertexuality of the in-group language in Romans 8 and the communal understanding in Confucianism:

I Reflecting upon the process of struggle in my reading of Romans and Confucianism, it is fair to say that I take my reading clues from both texts in many respects. Two of the most influential aspects are the proleptic understanding of the in-group language of predestination in Romans 8 and the communal understanding of Confucianism.

A Assumption of differences between the two horizons.

H Intersubjective reading.

I   Interactions between Paul and Confucius.

I   Interactions between the use of group language.

Paul is talking about those in Christ already; therefore it is an "in-Christ" language necessitating us to be very cautious, if not prohibiting us, to speak of the final destiny or salvation status of "those who are not in Christ." How do we know they are not in Christ? To speak this message to non-Christians might cause misunderstanding or confusion. It is a language of *posteriori*, in the sense that only when one is in, and only from the perspective of the in-group, can one look forward to the assured state of glory. It is therefore not a language of prediction, as if history is a linear process.

Both Pauline theology and Confucianist ethics have their universal appeal. Unfortunately, the narrative of Christ in Pauline theology has been used in Christian missionary movements to prejudge or condemn the destiny of others and rigidly exclude other narratives that might correct or enhance the narrative of Christ. After all, the purpose of Paul's rhetoric in Romans 8 is to unite Jewish and Gentile Christians and proves the impartiality of God in the salvation of all humanity.

Similar concern of hegemonic violence could be raised regarding Confucianist ethics. Though limited in its cultural ethos, the Confucianist ethic has reigned in Chinese political history to the point where Chinese rulers abuse their power by barring any questions regarding their ethical behaviors, and some Confucianists use ethics to justify their political power to rule over their "inferior." These are distortion and abuses to both Paul's and Confucius' understanding.

The Pauline language of predestination is not an eternal comprehensive decree of God to discriminate between believers and unbelievers. It is, as I interpreted above, a communal understanding of the goal of conforming to the firstborn of creation. In other words, Jesus Christ does not simply represent himself, an individual identity. Rather, Christ, as the "pre-horizon" of God's boundary of salvation, represents the *corporate identity* in which humanity will be called to conform, be transformed, justified, and glorified the Great Harmony (*Datong*) of God's creation. The Son of God has the group identity of sons of God. Paul's theology emphasizes shared sonship. The designations of Jewish and Gentile believers—"those who love God," "saints," "called," "those God foreknew, predestined, justified, gloried"—have the identity of solidarity of *ren ren*.

I know Paul's understanding of theology, Christology, ecclesiology is communal. Yet I must confess that because of my formal training in biblical studies in the West and my enculturation into the assumptions of modernity, I am often tempted to read Paul with an individualistic perspective. Doing a comparative study between Paul and Confucius helps me to overcome my bias.[51] Confucius is helpful to my reading of Paul and vice versa. Confucius understands a human as a social being with personal selfhood. Confucius says, "Virtue does not exist in isolation; there must be neighbors" (Analects 4:25). "In order to establish oneself, one helps others to establish themselves" (Analects 6:28). Confucius' understanding of the socialization process is that one authenticates one's being, not by detaching from the world of human relations, but by making sincere attempts to harmonize one's relationship with others. Similar language is used by Paul to speak of Christians being "pre-horizoned and conformed to the likeness of God's Son" (8:29). The participation in the death and resurrection of Christ in Romans 5-6 speaks of a similar Christian socialization process whereby Christians authenticate their beings by imitating Christ.

Spiritual and Ethical Humanity

2. The intertextuality of the spiritual-ethical humanity in Pauline and and Confucian societies:

I The notion that Paul speaks only of theology and Confucius speaks only of humanism is simply not true. They both speak of theological ethics of a particular community, be that in Roman house churches or in ancient China. We have seen that the Confucian understanding of being human is to live out the mandate of heaven, to be *ren ren* ("loving persons"). To be *ren ren* is to be courteous, diligent, loyal, brave, broad-minded, kind (Analects 13:19, 14:5, 17:6)—virtues that are to be actualized in public. To be a *ren ren* is to express and to participate in the holy as a dimension of all truly human existence. Fingarette writes, "Human life in its entirety finally appears as one vast, spontaneous and Holy Rite: the community of man [humanity]."[52] The human is transformed by participation with others in communal ceremony. And that is the mandate of heaven, that all may live in righteousness and orderliness in relation to others as a society of sacredness. Many of these ethical teachings of Confucius are helpful lenses for me to understand the ethical dimension of a spiritual community in Romans.

Thus Paul advocates different factions of the Roman house-churches to "welcome one another in Christ" (15:7) and to "greet one another with a holy kiss" (16:16) despite their differences. People are called into the "fiduciary community" (Confucian language) of sharing intentions, values, and meanings. This fiduciary community of sharable values is the "beloved of God" (Rom 1:7, 9:25) community in Christ to whom the Jewish and Gentile Christians in Roman house-churches belong. The fiduciary community advocated in the Analects does not have the notion that all persons will always finally agree. On the contrary, it is natural that diverse personalities will have differing visions of the Way.[53] Similarly, the "strong" and the "weak" in Romans are not encouraged to

---

I   Spiritual-ethical humanity in Paul's and Confucius' contexts.

be other than themselves as they must hold true to their own "measuring rod of faith." The singularly crucial point for both groups is "the continuous process of symbolic exchange through the sharing of communally cherished values with other selves."[54]

This similar emphasis in Paul and Confucius is presupposed by their social/communal understanding of human nature. In the Analects, for example, the self is a center of relationships rather than the center of an isolatable individual. The self is a dynamic, open organism which actively seeks human community for wholeness of life and is transformed through the work of Christ. In Romans 8, those God foreknows are the Christians, called into conformity to the firstborn, also having a communal identity of God's new creation. The group is prior to individual; therefore Christ is prior to Christian.

Oneness of God and Violent Ideology

3. The intertextuality of Oneness of God (Heaven) in both Confucian and Pauline ideals in the context of violent ideology and polytheism:

H Confucius' preoccupation with political ethics has its "antireligious" tendency (Analects 5:13, 6:22, 7:21, 11:12) because of the violence and manipulation of "gods and ghosts." Confucius is living in an age when superstition dominates peoples' lives, thus his rationalistic tendency is to critique the archaic supernatural beliefs of the past. It is more accurate to describe Confucius as "unreligious rather than irreligious." His wisdom is to advise people to keep an appropriate distance from spirits and earnestly attend to ethical responsibility toward others (Analects 6:20). And Confucius has his own religious life of praying and offering sacrifice (Analects 2:5, 3:13, 17, 7:34). Confucian *Tian* is both the creator and the field of creatures. Confucius thinks *Tian* is awesome and respected by all sages (Analects 16:8), *Tian* has intentions (Analects 9:5, 3:24), and *Tian* possesses understanding (Analects 14:35, 9:12). And more importantly, for Confucius, *Tian* is the source of moral power (Analects 3:24, 7:23, 9:5, 8:19, 9:6,12, 11:9, 14:35). Confucius transfers the *tian-ming* ("Mandate of Heaven") from a highly political claim of the ruling family to a universally appropriated one for all. That is, Confucius seeks to popularize that elitist and political mandate of *tian* so that everyone can cultivate virtues and bring about universal peace and prosperity. As for the rulers, Confucius emphasizes that the sage-rulers are to be virtuous, providing an example for others to follow, and thus bringing about renewal of the society. Confucian ideals discussed here are good reminders to Christians that preoccupation with eschatological hope without attending to ethical

---

H "Theological" understandings in Confucian and Pauline ideals.

responsibility to our neighbors is a weak faith. And religiosity without ethic can bring about violence that is often sanctioned in the name of one's god(s).

For Confucius, the social understanding of being human speaks of the necessity of cultural pluralism but only within the boundary of cultured teaching (*wen, jiao*)—that of *li* (ritual propriety), *yue* (music), and *ren* (love) and other virtues. Confucianism will regard those who do not practice cultured teaching as immature persons (*xiao ren*, literally means "little persons") or barbarians (non-Chinese). Similarly, the Pauline theology of the Oneness of God seems to pose a comprehensive narrative that does not condone polytheism. This is a difficult issue regarding the boundary of cultural and religious pluralism, and I will offer my tentative reflections.

H C The Oneness of God and the impartiality of God go together, and theologically they serve to respond to an inherent ideology of violence of the dominant Roman Empire. The cultural problem of Romans 8 is the polytheistic ideologies of patriarchy (in familial and societal structures), hierarchy (in institutional power structures), imperialism (in Roman, Herodian and even priestly politics), oppression (between the ruling elite and marginalized peasants), and colonialism (in racial tension and immigration situations), which resulted in violence—socially, politically and religiously.

The Roman ideology of polytheism and conquest is displayed in the splintered nature of Roman house-churches, evident by the various boastings (Rom 4:2, 11:18) of Jews and Gentiles. Paul argues that the will of God for Jewish and Gentile Christians in Rome is the righteousness of God. How can the Jew and the Gentile and the many factions within the Roman house churches live in harmony? Based on the Oneness of God (Rom 3:30, 16:27, cf. 5:15-19) of both Jews and Gentiles, Paul's christology in Romans 8 emphasizes the sovereignty of God in creation; thus the narrative of Christ is evident in Paul's understanding of the salvation of Jews and Gentiles. The sovereign love of God creates by means of Christ's redemption, and the predestined Christ in loving obedience is *the* divine plan of God's creation and redemption of the world. Christ as the eschatological Adam (new humanity) has saved the first Adam (old humanity) from the bondages/slavery of sin, death, and cultural boastings.

Jews and Gentiles alike are addressed using the same terms (saints, those who love God, firstborn, called, predestined), so the promise, inheritance, and privilege of Israel are opened to all. The Adam christology (Christ as the image of God) is inclusive of all because all shared the sonship with Christ. The Pauline answer is the Oneness of

---

H C Paul's hermeneutic in response to his context.

God, the impartiality of God, the righteousness of God by means of grace.

This question of co-existence for humanity was also Confucius' concern in the splintered society of his days. Confucius answers the problem of ethnic conflict, cultural deterioration, and moral confusion: "The person of humanity is naturally at ease with humanity" (Analects 4:2). In a Chinese-Christian terminology, the answer is that God's Spirit (Rom 8:1) wills the faithful (all God's people) to become fully human in loving relationship with others (*ren ren*), and the firstborn (Christ) makes it clear and possible for humanity to co-exist based on the principle of grace and faith (trust) rather than on cultural boasting. The power of God's gospel is that it grants righteousness to all who place their faith (trust) in Heaven. That faith and grace is concretely expressed in our "faith" (trust) and "grace" towards one another. Leaney expresses it well:

> We are released from all ceremonial demands in the Law; our salvation does not lie in our conformity even to the laws of the universe but in God's conforming us not to his creation, not even to a restored and flawless creation, but to himself in his Son and those whom God foreknew he has already foreordained by baptism to share the image—not of the restored Israel with a perfect system of worship in a restored Temple, but of his son, so that he could be not the Messiah of their expectation, a new and final lawgiver, but the firstborn among many brothers, the beginning of a totally new order .... We do not wait for our Messiah. He has come and the new age has already begun.[55]

The conviction of Paul's christological predestination as the only plan of God's salvation could be exclusive and even hegemonic. **I** Yet we see that the subversion to and reversal of power overcomes the problem of exclusivism similar to the Confucian ethic of virtue (*de*) as the prerequisite for a person to become a ruler. If christological predestination explains God's interruption in human history (as seen in the death and resurrection of the Christ-event), then the Christ-event allows us to discern the meaning and intended goal of history. Thus **A** an *analogical or metaphorical understanding* of how God is at work in Christ becomes a key hermeneutical tool. For God's work is not limited by culture and language, but God's Spirit transcends culture and language while working in them. In other words, just as I see Confucian

---

I Christological predestination of Paul and ethical understanding of Confucius.

A Analogical or metaphorical understanding.

ethics being practiced in other societies, I also see how God-in-Christ is at work in other cultures and traditions.

God's involvement in history through his firstborn of creation is the narrative and *mythos* of deciphering meaning out of chaos, redemption out of violence in all societies. No matter how great the magnitude of violence and destruction is in the final conflict of human history, the *ren ren* (full humanity in loving others) and the Crucified God in his death as the firstborn do not accept the "will to power" of any ideology: not the violence of the Pax Romana, the murderous jealousy of Cain (Gen 4), or the Lion of Judah (Revelation). The *ren ren* will rule by means of virtue and not physical force. Confucius' political ethics of *de* (virtue) has the drawing force of virtuous rulers guiding the nation by means of his moral excellence, without exerting physical force. Analects 2:1 writes that "those who rule with *de* (moral force) are like the North Star that seated in its place yet surrounded by multitude of stars."

H The Crucified God incarnated as the Lamb of God does not accept tragedy, but establishes redemptive meaning. The resurrection confirms Abel's and Christ's innocence. The voice of Abel, the "son of Man" was raised up to heaven. Confucius may die without realizing his aspiration of finding a virtuous ruler, yet his political ethic reigns in China for two millennia. Confucian *de* (virtue) can be self-sacrificing, and the Cross is a "violent" event, but they do not condone violence. The end of the crucified Christ was the beginning of new life. "Christian eschatology follows this christological pattern in all its personal, historical and cosmic dimensions: *in the end is the beginning.*"[56] There is hope amid all historical ambiguities because God's future transcends history and God is the actor in history.

C Confucius' anthropological and moral ideals are grounded, and thus legitimized, in the partriarchal kinship and ancestral cult. Thus, we see on one hand, the moral vitality and cultural inclusiveness of Confucian vision of national salvation; on the other hand, we see the rigidity of propriety and the violence of predeterminism. It is not a surprise to see that Confucius' philosophy is a political and moral one, and that he is worshipped as an "uncrowned king" and the greatest teacher. The irony is that at times his moral philosophy seems unable to transform his assumptions regarding the political reality and rigidity of tradition; thus the result is that many are taught to observe their places and to maintain proprieties within the given culture.

The Confucian vision of national salvation for China is a noble one, and his vision of retrieving the golden age in the Shang and Zhou

---

H Hermeneutics that overcome violence.

C Context of Confucius.

dynasty can supplement Paul's eschatological emphasis. Unfortunately, Confucian retrieval of the golden age was often taken in a linear view of history. In the next point I will discuss the Confucian view of time and that of Paul.

Paul's and Confucius' Understanding of Times

4. The intertextuality between Paul's and Confucius' understandings of time:

I H Confucius' vision of the ideal regent is of an ethical but not a religious person, largely because of his preoccupation with the society, and because of the changes in worldview from the Shang to the Zhou: the new worldview emphasizes the here and now—a helpful critique of the preoccupation of the future in Paul's eschatological theology. The Chinese concept of time is cyclical, or rather, a spiral of two interlocking sets of "heavenly stems" and the "earthly branches."[57] Confucianists view history as moving in a spiral motion, unlike the linear view of Paul. Confucianists have a dynamic understanding of time, unlike the modern, scientific view that time is merely a linear progression of past, present, and future—the past is taken to mean the passing of the present, future is the prolongation of the present, and the present is the only possession one has. Chinese seldom talk about absolute time but time associated with events—dynamic time. Fang explains this view of time:

> The essence of time consists in change; the order of time proceeds with concatenation; the efficacy of time abides by durance. The rhythmic process of epochal change is wheeling round into infinitude and perpetually dovetailing the old and the new so as to issue into interpenetration which is continuant duration in creative advance. This is the way in which time generates itself by its systematic entry into a pervasive unity which constitutes the rational order of creative creativity. The dynamic sequence of time, ridding itself of the perished past and coming by the new into present existence, really gains something over a loss. So, the change in time is but a step to approaching eternity, which is perennial durance, whereby, before the bygone is needed, the forefront of the succeeding has come into presence. And, therefore there is here a linkage of being projecting itself into the prospect of eternity.[58]

In the Confucian process of production and reproduction, time never comes to an end or repeats itself.

I H   Interaction of different understandings of time.

A H The linear view of time is too static; the cyclical view is too closed a system. A synthesis of both views can be done if we understand the biblical understanding of past, present, and future as not tenses but modes of existence and aspects of action.[59] In other words, God's narrative in human historical time is what predestined christology is about. The present is our spontaneous and continuous experience of the Holy despite our current historical ambiguity and despair. The past refers to realized acts of God in history. The future is the coming (advent or parousia) of the radically new creation of God assured by the past and to be realized in the present. The manifest destiny of history through Christ is God's new creation towards wholeness. The dynamic understanding of God's working in history is not simply a linear or a cyclical but a spiral process. Redemptive event can happen at *kairotic* (opportune, meaningful time), thus repeating moments.

The traditional Confucian worldview believes in the constant flux of the universe following a "predictable pattern consisting either of eternal oscillation between two poles or of cyclical movement within a closed circuit. [So] . . . all movement serves in the end only to bring the process back to its starting point."[60] However, in Paul's view, historical events are dated backward to the beginning of Creation, and the end of history is defined by Christ. Dunn writes,

> Paul's view of history . . . is not cyclical, but more of a purpose, formed from the beginning, achieved *through* the process of history, moving toward an intended higher end, not simply returning to the beginning. As Paul has been at some pains to argue, God does not write of the intervening history as a total failure and useless; rather this purpose embraces it, works *through* it, through the travail of a creation subjected to futility, *through* the groaning of believers still beset by sin and under the sway of death, working to achieve not simply a return to pristine purity, but the fuller glory which Adam never attained, including life *from death*.[61]

C But in Chinese history events are dated cyclically every sixty years or from the rise of new emperors. And the dominant view in Chinese history is to look for a golden age in the past—in other words, the circle of degeneration characterizes Chinese history—and it is the circle of conscious cultivation of selves in harmony with society or cosmos that will bring back the golden age.

A H A new hermeneutic that synthesizes different understanding of time.

C Chinese history.

For 5000 years or so, Confucius has reigned without a crown, yet his moral philosophy is not subversive enough within the political culture to transform Chinese society seeking the recovery of the golden age. Looking backward without looking forward does not allow him to see the possibilities and hopes of the future. The conservatism of looking to the past will provide some guidance, but creativity in reappropriating the past could bring about freedom and hope as he would look to the future for openness and direction. Yao and Shun are exemplary rulers, but only within the historical contexts and problems. The notion of an uncrowned king may liberate the idea that kingship is not lineage and all can become kings, since education and wisdom are not limited to or by an elitist few. Yet, the question is whether the Confucian ideal of a philosopher-sage becoming a king is a philosophical legitimation of the old kingship, or a replacement of the old using a new paradigm of kingship.

Conclusion

I used to think Confucius and Paul were incommensurable (that probably is still true if an intertextual reading is not used), but a cross-cultural reading of the Pauline text and the Confucian texts has helped me understand that their differences can complement each other. Confucius' political context is a helpful lens for me to reread the political power of Paul's gospel mission—an ecclesial space that will transform and replace the larger political space. Confucius' ethical insights have led me to observe the communal problems faced in Romans with regards to group behavior and identity. Paul's theology of Christ clarifies the personal and political salvation of the Chinese. Paul's cross-cultural sensitivity with Jewish and Gentile Christians helps me overcome the possible ethnocentrism of working with monocultural texts such as that of the Analects, the Mencius, and Romans. Lastly, Paul's eschatological definition of the goal (the end) of history from the future supplements my Confucianist retrieval reading of history from the past golden age. The openness of the future will surpass the past, the New Jerusalem will transcend the Garden of Eden, but eschatology does not delete the golden age (e.g., *Datong*), just as future does not discount history. My Chinese-Christian worldview now has stretched to include past, present, and future in the full spectrum of dynamic time. Despite the recurring or spiral movement of dynamic time, it has a forward thrust towards the creation of God's people based on the incarnation of faith and grace. The virtue of Christ and Christians is faithfulness and love and hope for the salvation of humanity and the whole cosmos.

Notes

1. Unless otherwise noted, all translations of Confucian classics and Romans in this paper are the author's.

2. My intention in this paper is not to give a survey or theoretical understanding of biblical hermeneutics. It is not about a particular methodology called intersubjectivity. Rather, it is a discussion of the interpretation processes of biblical texts. On the survey of contemporary methods of biblical interpretation, see Carl R. Holladay, "Contemporary Methods of Reading the Bible," *The New Interpreter's Bible* (Nashville: Abingdon, 1994), 1: 125-149; on the theory of biblical hermeneutics, see Anthony Thiselton's magnum opus, *New Horizons in Hermeneutics: The Theory and Practice of Transforming Biblical Reading* (Grand Rapids: Zondervan, 1992). On the methodology of intersubjectivity, see Michael Morton and Judith Still ed., *Intertextuality: Theories and Practices* (Manchester and New York: Manchester University Press, 1991); George Aichele and Gary A. Phillips ed., *Intertextuality and the Bible, Semeia* 69/70 (1995).

3. Yeo Khiok-khng, *Rhetorical Interaction in 1 Corinthians 8 and 10: A Formal Analysis With Preliminary Suggestions for a Chinese, Cross-Cultural Hermeneutic* (Leiden: E. J. Brill, 1995), Chapter 3.

4. Julia Kristeva, "Word, Dialogue and Novel," in Toril Moi ed., *The Kristeva Reader* (New York: Columbia University Press, 1986); Kristeva, however, does not think that texts function for readers as an intersubjective network; they function only as intertextual networks.

5. Jonathan Culler, *On Deconstruction: Theory and Criticism after Structuralism* (Ithaca: Cornell University Press, 1982), 32.

6. Roland Barthes, *Image, Music, Text* (New York: Hill & Wang, 1977), 146.

7. "Dialogism" and "heteroglossia" are Bakhtin's terms in his work, Michael Holquist ed., Caryl Emerson and Michael Holquist trans., *The Dialogic Imagination* (Austin: University of Texas Press, 1981).

8. Yeo, *Rhetorical Interaction in 1 Corinthians 8 and 10*, as the title of the work indicates, see also pp. 15-49.

9. Hans-Georg Gadamer, *Truth and Method*, 2nd rev. ed. (New York: Crossroad, 1989), 261.

10. See the discussion in "Reader-Response Criticism," Elizabeth A. Castelli, Stephen D. Moore and Regina M. Schwartz ed., *The Postmodern Bible* (New Haven: Yale University Press, 1995), 20-69.

11. *Roland Barthes by Roland Barthes*, trans. Richard Howard (London and New York: Hill and Wang, 1977), 140.

12. Jonathan Culler, *The Pursuit of Signs: Semiotics, Literature, Deconstruction* (Ithaca: Cornell University Press, 1981), 117.

13. This paper does not deal with the question of "indeterminacy" and "completing plausible interpretations," which I dealt with in "Culture and Intersubjectivity as Criteria of Negotiating Meanings in Cross-cultural Interpretations," in Charles H. Cosgrove edited, *The Meanings We Choose* (Edinburgh: T&T Clark, 2004), 81-100. See also Charles H. Cosgrove, *Elusive Israel: The Puzzle of Election in Romans* (Louisville: Westminster/John Knox, 1997), 38-45 on "interpretive will and hermeneutical responsibility"; *idem, Appealing to Scripture in Moral Debate: Five Hermeneutical Rules* (Grand Rapids: Eerdmans, 2002), passim on rules of adjudication in moral debate of interpreting scripture. Cf. also, Daniel Patte, *Discipleship according to the Sermon on the Mount: Four Legitimate Readings, Four Plausible Views of Discipleship, and Their Relative Values* (Valley Forge: Trinity Press International, 1996).

14. Wolfgang Bauer, *China and the Search for Happiness. Recurring Themes in Four Thousand Years of Chinese Cultural History,* trans. by Michael Shaw (New York: Seabury Press, 1976), 24-25.

15. For example, Mencius (Meng Zi) taught King Xuan of Qi the reason of Wenwang of Zhou. He possessed a large piece of land and yet it was considered too small by his people. The reason was that Wenwang shared it with his people. Mencius 1B, 2. See James Legge, trans., *The Chinese Classics: With a Translation, Critical and Exegetical Notes, Prolegomena and Copious Indexes,* 5 vols. (Reprint; Hong Kong: Hong Kong University Press, 1960), 1:153-154.

16. Bauer, *China and the Search for Happiness,* 22-23.

17. Bauer, *China and the Search for Happiness,* 22.

18. Julia Ching, *Mysticism and Kingship in China. The Heart of Chinese Wisdom* (Cambridge: Cambridge University Press, 1997), 211-212.

19. This interpretation regarding Confucius is popular in the Tang (618-906) and Qing dynasties (1644-1912), see Ching, *Mysticism and Kingship in China,* 207, n. 7.

20. Ching, *Mysticism and Kingship in China,* 211. The Analects translation is that of Ching.

21. Ching, *Mysticism and Kingship in China,* 210.

22. Bauer, *China and the Search for Happiness,* 49.

23. Bauer, *China and the Search for Happiness,* 23. See Mencius 5A, 5. Legge, *The Chinese Classics,* 2:354-357. Translation of the Mencius is that of Bauer.

24. See Fung Yu-lan, *A History of Chinese Philosophy,* trans. Derk Bodde (Princeton: Princeton University Press, 1952), 160. Cf. *Shi Ji,* Chap 74.

25. Bauer, *China and the Search for Happiness,* 429-430, n. 44.

26. *Ibid.* See Legge, trans., *The Chinese Classics,* 2:232, 501-502.

27. Robert Jewett, *Basic Bible Commentary-Romans* (Nashville: Graded Press, 1984), 98.

28. "Those who love God" is the common designation in the OT of God's elect, the Jews (see Exo 20:6; Deut 5:10); this phrase is now used here to refer to Christians, Jewish or Gentile alike. See C. E. B. Cranfield, *A Critical and Exegetical Commentary on the Epistle to the Romans,* 6th ed. (Edinburgh: T&T Clark, 1975-1979), 1: 424 on "those who love God" as a designation of Jewish piety.

29. C. E. B. Cranfield, "Romans 8:28," *Scottish Journal of Theology* 19 (1966): 206.

30. On *"panta"* (not *Theos*) *as* subject, see discussion in J. D. G. Dunn, *Romans 1-8, Word Biblical Commentary* (Dallas: Word, 1988), 481; Joseph A. Fitzmyer, *Romans: A New Translation with Introduction and Commentary* (New York: Doubleday, 1993), 523; Brendan Byrne, *Romans* (Collegeville: Liturgical Press, 1996), 271-272.

31. Walter Bauer, William F. Arndt, F. Wilbur Gingrich and F. W. Danker, *A Greek-English Lexicon of the New Testament and other Early Christian Literature* [*BAGD*] (Chicago: University of Chicago Press, 1979), 795.

32. Or as Dunn puts it, "the temporal purpose . . . of moving history and through history to its intended end" (*Romans 1-8*, 482).

33. Cranfield, "Romans 8:28," 212.

34. Douglas J. Moo, *The Epistle to the Romans* (Grand Rapids: Eerdmans, 1996), 527-58.

35. John A. Zeisler, *Paul's Letter to the Romans* (London: SCM, 1989), 225.

36. Cranfield, "Romans 8:28," 204.

37. Kenneth Grayston, *The Epistle to the Romans* (Peterborough: Epworth Press, 1997), 75.

38. See Paul Jacobs and Hartmut Krienke, "Foreknowledge, Providence, Predestination," in Colin Brown ed., *New International Dictionary of New Testament Theology* [*NIDNTT*] (3 volumes; Grand Rapids: Eerdmans, 1975-1978), 1: 695-696. Also *BAGD*, 706, cf. Eph 1:11, 3:11, 2 Tim 1:9.

39. In Phil 3:21, the word is used to speak of the transforming body of lowliness to that of glory; thus, the resurrected humanity from the dead is emphasized.

40. *Eikôn* in Romans 8:11, 23 speaks of the resurrection body of God's Son despite death, i.e., the end (resurrection) determines the destiny (life) of humanity. Note the similar theology as expressed in Ephesians and Colossians: God seeks to transform the whole Cosmos through Christ as the "first born" of this new creation.

41. Fitzymer, *Romans*, 525.

42. See Byrne, *Romans*, 273. Cf. Heb 1:6; Rev 1:5.

43. Steve Mosher, *A Study in Romans* (Scottdale: Herald Press, 1996), 9.

44. *Proginoskô* signifies more than an advance knowledge or precognition, it suggests looking with favor, and is even used of sexual relations. See Francis Brown, S. R. Driver, and Charles Briggs, *A Hebrew and English Lexicon of the Old Testament* (Oxford: Clarendon Press, 1959), 394.

45. Dunn, *Romans 1-8*, 482; Fitzymer, *Romans*, 525. See Gen 18:19, Jer 1:5; Hos 13:5;Amos 3:2; Psalm 1:6, 1 Cor 8:3, 13:12; Gal 4:9, 2 Tim 2:19.

46. Ernst Käsemann, *Commentary on Romans* (Grand Rapids: Eerdmans, 1980), 244.

47. R. D. Kaylor, *Paul's Covenant Community* (Louisville: John Knox Press, 1988), 157.

48. See Brown, Driver, and Briggs, *A Hebrew and English Lexicon of the Old Testament*, 103-104; *NIDNTT*, 1:536-543.

49. Moo, *The Epistle to the Romans*, 530.

50. John A. Zeisler, *Paul's Letter to the Roman's* (London: SCM Press, 1989), 227.

51. See Yeo Khiok-khng, "Li and Jen (Torah and Spirit) in Romans," *What Has Jerusalem to Do with Beijing? Biblical Interpretation from a Chinese Perspective* (Harrisburg: Trinity Press International, 1998), Chap. 6.

52. Herbert Fingarette, *Confucius: The Secular as Sacred* (New York: Harper and Row, 1972), 17. Cf. Analects 3:17, 4:5, 6, 8.

53. Cf. Tu Wei-ming, *Confucian Thought: Selfhood as Creative Transformation* (New York: State University Press, 1985), 83.

54. *Ibid.*

55. A. R. C. Leaney, "Conformed to the Image of His Son (Rom. VIII. 29)," *New Testament Studies* 10 (1964): 479.

56. Jürgen Moltmann, *The Way of Jesus Christ: Christology in Messianic Dimensions,* trans. M. Kohl (London: SCM Press, 1990), x.

57. Ching, *Mysticism and Kingship in China*, 210. The English translation of Mencius is Ching's.

58. Thomé H. Fang, "The World and the Individual in Chinese Metaphysics," in Charles A. Moore ed., *The Chinese Mind: Essentials of Chinese Philosophy and Culture* (Honolulu: University Press of Hawaii, 1967), 240.

59. On especially the differentiation of future and advent as well as *novum*, see Moltmann, *The Way of Jesus Christ*, 22-28.

60. Derk Bodde, *Essays on Chinese Civilization* (Princeton: Princeton University Press, 1981), 239. On the oscillation theory, see Lao Zi's *Dao De Jing*: "The movement of the Tao is that of reversal" (Chap 40); "Passing on means going far away, and going far away means reverting

again" (Chap 25); "If diminished, it will increase; if increased, it will diminish" (Chap 42). On cyclical return, see *Zhuang Zi*: "All things are species which, through variant forms, pass one into another. Their beginnings and endings are like those in a ring—incapable of being definitely located. This is called the Equilibrium of Heaven." (Chap 27)

    61. Dunn, *Romans 1-8*, 484.

Works Cited

Bakhtin, M. *The Dialogic Imagination.* Edited by Michael Holquist. Translated by Caryl Emerson and Michael Holquist. Austin: University of Texas Press, 1981.

Barthes, Roland. *Image, Music, Text.* New York: Hill & Wang, 1977.

Roland Barthes by Roland Barthes. Trans. Richard Howard. London and New York: Hill and Wang, 1977.

Bauer, Walter, William F. Arndt, F. Wilbur Gingrich and F. W. Danker. *A Greek-English Lexicon of the New Testament and other Early Christian Literature.* Chicago: University of Chicago Press, 1979.

Bauer, Wolfgang. *China and the Search for Happiness. Recurring Themes in Four Thousand Years of Chinese Cultural History.* Trans. Michael Shaw. New York: Seabury Press, 1976.

Bodde, Derk. *Essays on Chinese Civilization.* Princeton: Princeton University Press, 1981.

Byrne, Brendan. *Romans.* Collegeville: Liturgical Press, 1996.

Ching, Julia. *Mysticism and Kingship in China. The Heart of Chinese Wisdom.* Cambridge: Cambridge University Press, 1997.

Cranfield, C. E. B. *A Critical and Exegetical Commentary on the Epistle to the Romans,* 6th ed. Edinburgh: T&T Clark, 1975-1979.

Culler, Jonathan. *The Pursuit of Signs: Semiotics, Literature, Deconstruction.* Ithaca: Cornell University Press, 1981.

_____. *On Deconstruction: Theory and Criticism after Structuralism.* Ithaca: Cornell University Press, 1982.

Dunn, J. D. G. *Romans 1-8, Word Biblical Commentary.* Dallas: Word, 1988.

Fang, Thomé H. "The World and the Individual in Chinese Metaphysics." Pages 238-263 in Charles A. Moore ed., *The Chinese Mind: Essentials of Chinese Philosophy and Culture.* Honolulu: University Press of Hawaii, 1967.

Fingarette, Herbert. *Confucius: The Secular as Sacred.* New York: Harper and Row, 1972.

Fitzmyer, Joseph A. *Romans: A New Translation with Introduction and Commentary.* New York: Doubleday, 1993.

Fung Yu-lan. *A History of Chinese Philosophy.* Trans. Derk Bodde. Princeton: Princeton University Press, 1952.

Gadamer, Hans-Georg. *Truth and Method.* 2nd rev. ed. New York: Crossroad, 1989.

Grayston, Kenneth. *The Epistle to the Romans.* Peterborough: Epworth Press, 1997.

Jacobs, Paul, and Hartmut Krienke, "Foreknowledge, Providence, Predestination." In Colin Brown, ed., *New International Dictionary of New Testament Theology.* 3 volumes. Grand Rapids: Eerdmans, 1975-1978. 1: 695-696.

Jewett, Robert. *Basic Bible Commentary-Romans.* Nashville: Graded Press, 1984.

Käsemann, Ernst. *Commentary on Romans.* Grand Rapids: Eerdmans, 1980.

Kaylor, R. D. *Paul's Covenant Community.* Louisville: John Knox Press, 1988.

Kristeva, Julia. "Word, Dialogue and Novel." Pages 34-61 in *The Kristeva Reader.* Edited by Toril Moi. New York: Columbia University Press, 1986.

Legge, James trans. *The Chinese Classics: With a Translation, Critical and Exegetical Notes, Prolegomena and Copious Indexes*, 5 vols. Reprint; Hong Kong: Hong Kong University Press, 1960.

Moltmann, Jürgen. *The Way of Jesus Christ: Christology in Messianic Dimensions.* Trans. M. Kohl. London: SCM Press, 1990.

Moo, Douglas J. *The Epistle to the Romans.* Grand Rapids: Eerdmans, 1996.

Mosher, Steve. *A Study in Romans.* Scottdale: Herald Press, 1996.

Thiselton, Anthony. *New Horizons in Hermeneutics: The Theory and Practice of Transforming Biblical Reading.* Grand Rapids: Zondervan, 1992.

Tu Wei-ming, *Confucian Thought: Selfhood as Creative Transformation* New York: State University Press, 1985.

Yeo Khiok-khng. "*Li* and *Jen* (Torah and Spirit) in Romans." In Yeo, *What Has Jerusalem to Do with Beijing? Biblical Interpretation from a Chinese Perspective*, Chap. 6 (pp. 129-161). Harrisburg: Trinity Press International, 1998.

_____. *Rhetorical Interaction in 1 Corinthians 8 and 10: A Formal Analysis with Preliminary Suggestions for a Chinese, Cross-Cultural Hermeneutic.* Leiden: E. J. Brill, 1995.

Zeisler, John A. *Paul's Letter to the Romans.* London: SCM Press, 1989.

Cultural Studies and Intersubjective Work

A Response to Yeo,
"Messianic Predestination in
Romans 8 and Classical Confucianism"

Brian K. Blount

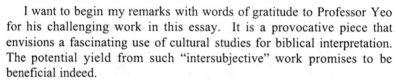

I want to begin my remarks with words of gratitude to Professor Yeo for his challenging work in this essay. It is a provocative piece that envisions a fascinating use of cultural studies for biblical interpretation. The potential yield from such "intersubjective" work promises to be beneficial indeed.

Yeo operates in three main stages. First, he defines the work of an intersubjective reading. By its very nature an *inter*subjective reading is a cross-cultural enterprise; it anticipates that the cultural space and perspective of the reader is as important a variable in the interpretative process as the grammatical and ideational markers in the text itself. Second, he applies this methodological understanding to his reading of Paul's narrative of Christological predestination in Romans 8. Third, he positions the Confucian Messianic expectation for the recovery of a national golden age as an interpretative, cultural lens for reading Paul's words across the chasms of time and place. Fourth, he contrasts Pauline and Confucian readings in an attempt to shed new light on the understanding of both.

There is much here to appreciate and relish. Yeo's approach is not a singular one; it operates on several methodological levels simultaneously. In making such a move he demonstrates that researchers need not be wed to a single approach in their interpretative endeavors, but can obtain rich produce by encouraging an investigative cross-fertilization in their work. Yeo's own efforts draw from the insights of intertextuality, intersubjectivity, and rhetoric.

The intertextual interest opens his discussion. Appealing to Kristeva, he notes that texts exist and develop meaning out of interaction with other texts. That interaction can take place through quotations, references, allusions and other means. When one looks at the discussion of predestination in Romans 8, then, one cannot assume that the hunt for meaning is limited within those textual borders; meaning also arises as ideas and themes inside the text intersect with ideas and themes from other texts. If Paul needs those *other* texts to produce meaning, careful readers must also appeal to those texts as they attempt to produce meaning in their own situations and circumstances.

That final point is a key one. Readers do not unearth meaning, as if Paul dug a literary hole and deposited a bone of thought inside that could be unearthed and retrieved intact in just the manner he'd left it. Yeo points us rightly towards the interaction that always takes place between readers and the text words they encounter. There is always what he calls "rhetorical interaction" between reader and text. A text does not have a single meaning; it has a range of meaning potential that can be accessed by a reader. As different readers approach this meaning potential from different contextual places with different situational identities and concerns, it is more than likely that they will be drawn to different aspects of that potential. They will refer to those different and perhaps competing aspects of the text as its "meaning." Meaning, then, is contextual. It is *produced* in the interaction of a text's grammatical and ideational markers and the reader's contextual emphases. This is why what is meaningful in and about a text for those in one community might be radically different from the meaning assessment produced by members of a community in a different cultural context.

This is the stuff of intersubjectivity. Not even the writer him or herself, Yeo warns, can control the meaning of a text so that it is limited to his or her original intention. Even if it is the case, as he points out, that the writer of a letter like Paul might *intend* that his words be understood in only one way, once he sets those words free in different contexts he must be prepared for the possibility, as Paul found in Corinth, that his words may produce meanings that he never intended or even anticipated. The apostle appears shocked that his Corinthian compatriots took his discussion about freedom in Christ Jesus to mean that all things were now lawful. Certainly, he must explain, that was not his original intent. But those were *his* words that had opened up the possibility of such an interpretation. He was the one who suggested that we are *free* in Christ. That language of freedom is a language filled will all kinds of uncontrollable meaning potential. Given the interaction of a Corinthian context of past pagan traditions and apparent *laisse-faire* moral attitudes with a new Christian perspective of being set free as a new creation, it seems from hindsight less than surprising that the Corinthians could have come up with such a "meaningful" interpretation of the apostle's teaching. This is because the text markers in his letters and speeches came alive contextually. Meaning is not discovered; it is produced, in the first century and in the twenty-first.

Of course, many have charged that such a realization puts us on that slippery slope of interpretative relativism that honors no shared meaning across cultural borders. The intersubjective approach subjects to doubt, as Yeo puts it, that there is a determined text whose meaning as produced by one particular culture can obtain hegemonic authority over all other culturally influenced readings. No one interpretation, then, can claim ultimate authority. Every interpretation must acknowledge that its own understanding has been produced through the lens of its contexts and interests. Every interpretation is forced, therefore, into conversation with other contextual productions in order to seek a fuller access to a text's meaning potential. And that is precisely why Yeo envisions a paper that has Confucian contextual interests looking alongside the methodology of the academic guild into the meaning potential of the predestination language of Romans 8. His paper wants to model the very cultural dialogue and exchange that it methodologically prescribes.

It is at this point that Yeo begins to demonstrate how a Romans 8 reading through the cultural lens of Classical Confucianism would look. His reading offers a fascinating view into the rich meaning potential in Paul's language of predestination. For example, on the predestination topic that I found particularly intriguing, he argues that we can read Paul in such a way that the object of his predestination language is not the believers in Christ but Christ himself. I, however, was not convinced that someone operating from a standard exegetical approach of unearthing Paul's original intent would ever agree to the conclusion that the text language is not talking about the predestination of believers. Obviously, as Yeo acknowledges, the idea of some being predestined to salvation and others not, can be most problematic and frightening. But even operating through the Pauline narrative of suffering with creation, I was not sure how one could override the language of the text which seems to have a specific people, not a single Christ figure, as the object of predestination language.

It is at just this point, though, that Yeo prepares us to read Paul's language through the Confucian lens. He makes his key interpretive move by appealing to the metaphor of the "firstborn." It is as the firstborn that Christ's individuality simultaneously, and paradoxically, operates collectively. As firstborn, Christ shares his sonship with the universal spectrum of Christians. From this Pauline perspective, even if predestination is oriented toward the people, because the people and the Messiah are metaphorically bound together, the potential for meaning is enlarged. Since, in the Confucian perspective, the people play the messianic role as a people, even though the leader generates the messianic process, the appearance of the Golden Age hinges on the role played by the people as messianic figure, or, perhaps, one might say, the messianic figure, who as firstborn, represents the people. When reading

Paul's language through such a lens, it would therefore not seem unreasonable to suggest that (as the grammar seems to suggest) the apostle has in mind the messianic predestination of a messianic *people* and not a single Christ figure alone. In this way, the Confucian corporate expectation could also allow one to believe that the predestination language could apply equally well to Christ as messianic agent and believers as a collective messianic agent. Predestination of believers, while still problematic, has in this case an intriguing explanation or *produced* christological meaning.

It is at just this point, though, that I would like to push Yeo as he pushes the boundaries of our interpretative process. As risky as his reading is, I would like to see him engage its principles more often and with more vigor. He does not, for example, show us enough detail from Paul's text to make the reading of Paul through the Confucian lens work as convincingly as it should. For example, he talks about the thesis of Romans 8:28-30 being the eschatological community of sonship created by the Spirit. Here would be a wonderful opportunity to speak directly to sonship as the process of democratization he had championed in his Confucian discussion. Instead of a provocative, close interpretive reading, however, he moves quickly to a more general discussion about the mandate of heaven. I am not arguing that this discussion isn't necessary. I am only suggesting that it would have had increased significance if it had followed upon a closer "Confucian reading" of the biblical text.

There are other places where I would have relished an opportunity to linger more with Professor Yeo over the biblical text as seen through the Confucian lens. He notes, for example, that the eschatological Adam is the realization of an ideal community rather than a salvation by means of an individual, but doesn't follow through by showing exactly how his reading reaches this conclusion. He tells the consequence of this reading ("the power of God's gospel redeems the *whole* creation") but doesn't help us see *how* the reading is reached. It is because of this lack of connecting the conclusions reached to the reading he is doing that it is difficult to agree when he makes a claim such as, "my reading understands foreknowledge to be foresight concerning the purposeful act of salvation in which believers will respond faithfully."

I believe the difficulty occurs because Yeo wants to make sure his readers can see the results of his work and realize its considerable impact. He remarks that "though I present my reading of Romans and Confucianism separately, I have in fact read these two texts side by side in my understanding." It is the mechanics and rhetorical strategy of that side by side reading that the reader misses seeing. For it is only in seeing how he reaches his conclusion that a reader can be convinced about the acceptability of that conclusion.

Finally, there seems to be one powerful example of these two strategies reading against rather than with each other that Yeo doesn't engage. (Note that Yeo does deal very helpfully with the different historical perspectives of the two strategies: the alternative cyclical view of Confucianism and the eschatological one of Paul.) The opposition is significant. If one were to dwell on these two opposing principles, one might be wary of thinking that one could or should even try to read one text's "theology" through the lens of the other. Yeo argues that the Confucian vision of *Datong* is similar to the ideal presented in Romans 8, which spells out salvific hope for all God's people even in the context of present suffering. There is indeed parallelism in the ends, but not the means. In the Confucian understanding as Yeo presents it, humans very much create the hoped for order by their acts of political morality. As Yeo presents Paul, God creates the hoped for goal through the power of grace. Humans may, and indeed ought to respond to what God has done, but they do not initiate the reality themselves. It would help, I believe, if Yeo could help readers see how this fundamental strategic difference could exist and nonetheless not prohibit reading of one strategy through the lens of the other, as he did with regard to the Pauline and Confucian views of history.

Despite these concerns, I am fascinated by Yeo's work. When one reads Paul's Christ narrative about God's cosmic salvation through the Confucian lens of a moral transformation of humanity in the hope of recovering an ideal dynasty, and vice versa, rich new possibilities for comprehending each "salvific" strategy emerge. Given my own confessional and professional drive to understand Paul more fully, I found Yeo's study on the recovery of the Golden Age as the contemplated *Datong* or Great Harmony to be fascinating. Its emphasis on a moral transformation that would begin with exemplary leaders and encourage the same kind of moral uprightness in the general populace creates a kind of democratization of messianism that I find very exciting. His reading is the old call for "power to the people" re-crafted in a christologically provocative way. And, in the process, it demonstrates the rich potential of cross-cultural reading.

– C O N C L U S I O N –

Charting the Course and Steering the Ship

Charles H. Cosgrove

◆

It is encouraging to see an increasing number of efforts to engage the Bible from multiple cultural perspectives in collaborative projects like this one, which brings together first-world and two-thirds world participants. The contributors who have navigated Romans through different cultural seas have steered their ships under a common charter from their patrons, who ask them to pay attention to four things: (a) the reasons for their own interest in a certain dimension of the text (the analytic frame); (b) the relation between the text (as they have focused it analytically) and a particular life context; (c) the religious tradition that guides their reading (the hermeneutical frame); and (d) a fundamental question about the possibilities for interpretations that arise from these multiple frames: "Why did I/we choose this interpretation rather than another one?"

As I understand the basic assumption here is that biblical texts can be fairly interpreted and appropriated in more than one way because, from our side, it is possible (and natural) to ask different questions of a text and to use different critical methods to answer our questions. Moreover, the biblical texts themselves are susceptible to multiple complementary and competing interpretations even for those operating with the same analytic frame, in the same context, and working out of the same religious tradition. K.K. Yeo talks about this semantic openness of the text in terms of "intersubjectivity;" Mark Baker and Ross Wagner appeal to Brian Blount's model for conceiving the semantic richness of the text, which can accommodate different readings in different socio-cultural settings. Revelation Enriquez Velunta stresses that all interpretation is interested and perspectival. Florin Cimpean celebrates the Spirit in Romans 8 as a sign of the semantic openness of Paul's theological categories, so that "[d]ifferent meanings are not condemned, but encouraged." None of these interpreters mean to suggest that any and all interpretations are justified. If I may use my own terminology, given a particular question and agreed-upon method, biblical texts typically yield a range of reasonable interpretations.

In view of this, it is also ethically important that we take responsibility for our interpretations. This requires acknowledging that the interpretation of a particular biblical text can go in a different, even an opposing direction, than where we have taken it, without being exegetically wrong. It also calls on us to give our reasons for choosing the interpretation we defend. It should be clear that those reasons are a complex of considerations from the various frames: our interest in a certain dimension of the text, our life context, and the religious tradition or perceptions that guide us.

The contributors to the present volume operate with varying orientations to the programme set out for them by the series editors, Cristina Grenholm and Daniel Patte. At least one (Velunta) works self-consciously within the method of "scripture criticism" that Grenholm and Patte have defined in various of their writings; others use the three frames in their own distinctive ways (see the markings of **C A H** and **I** on each essay). This variety is not surprising and fits the spirit of the editors, who have proposed some navigational charts for the voyage but have also encouraged the captains of these ships to follow their own lights.

The Cultural Seas in Which We Sail

We all know that Paul's letter to the Romans was shaped by his own cultural context, but a special virtue of the present volume is that it inquires into the ways Romans is or can be shaped by the present-day cultural contexts of interpreters. I say "is" or "can be" so shaped, because we face a navigational problem in charting the course of the interpretation of Romans through present-day cultures. This problem is the legacy of Western missionary interpretation in the non-Western cultural settings out of which Romans has been interpreted for this volume. The contributors are very much aware of this and attend to it. The legacy of Western missionary interpretation has clearly been an influential force in the African setting of Bishop Colenso's commentary on Romans (see the essay by Jonathan Draper), in Honduras (see the essay by Baker and Wagner), in Southeast Asia (see the essays by Daniel Arichea and Velunta), and in China (see the essay by Yeo). The essay by Cimpean looks at Romans in a Romanian context, using both a Romanian Pentecostal perspective, which I assume has some Western roots, and a Romanian Orthodox perspective (which is not a tradition founded by or influenced by Western missions).

In settings where the Western missionary legacy continues to operate very powerfully, an indigenous cultural reading is sometimes more a possibility than a reality. Baker and Wagner present what they see as a movement among a group of Honduran Christians away from the missionary theology in which they were raised toward a more indigenous reading of Romans. In some settings the missionary legacy has led to disinterest in Romans. Cimpean reports that Romanian Pentecostals have little interest in Romans and rarely preach from it. According to Arichea, Romans is not one of the favorite biblical books in Southeast Asian churches, although a certain Western evangelical way of interpreting Romans has shaped the way those churches understand salvation and carry out evangelism, namely, the use of Romans 3:23, 6:23, and 10:9, in combination with Acts 2:38, Acts 16:30, and John 3:16 to set forth "salvation in a nutshell." Some readers will recognize that the aforementioned passages from Romans belong to the so-called "Romans Road" of Protestant evangelicalism.

The Western missionary tradition has not only shaped but also been resisted and transformed in autochthonous readings of scripture. Velunta argues that devotional readings of Romans typical of Filipino evangelicals are not simply repetitions of missionary teaching but have become culturally indigenous. He seeks to both vindicate and deepen such readings through a method of interpretation that is closely attuned to Filipino culture but also draws on Western biblical scholarship. Velunta grounds his hermeneutical approach in the Lutheran formulas "*pro me*" and "*pro nobis*." He takes them to mean not only that God is "for me/us" (as revealed in the gospel) but also that scripture is "for me/us" in the sense that it is meant to be contextualized. Thus, there is an interesting blend of the Western tradition and the indigenous cultural interpretation in which Velunta proposes *utang na loob* (which involves "gratitude" as its core meaning) as a way of defining "faith" and *kagandahang loob* (absolute selflessness and self-forgetfulness) as a way of speaking about God's "grace."

Draper points out that colonial churches typically engage the Western missionary tradition in creative ways that are sometimes resistant or subversive. Indigenous Christian traditions are formed, often to the chagrin of the colonizers or missionaries. And sometimes a Western missionary becomes an agent of this kind of indigenous interpretation, as in the case of Bishop Colenso and his commentary on Romans for the Zulu people. K.K. Yeo compares Paul and Confucius in an effort to construct common ground and commensurability between the two. The resultant interpretation of Romans is a kind of Confucian take on the Paul of a Western scholarship, that is, an interpretation of Romans that uses the tradition of Western scholarship on Paul to work out a more indigenously Chinese (and more Confucian) Paul than one otherwise encounters in Chinese churches.

The example of Yeo's approach shows that the Western missionary legacy operates on multiple levels, which may compete with each other. In cultural identity, Yeo is a Malaysian Chinese but in terms of graduate education, he is a Western-trained Paul scholar. Yeo uses Western scholarship, along with his study of his own Chinese culture, to work out a Chinese Paul that in some ways is at odds with the traditional Paul of Chinese churches, shaped in varying degrees by the legacy of Western missions. Moreover, Yeo uses Western hermeneutical theory in a very sophisticated way to carry out his culturally-attuned "intersubjective" reading of Romans. A similar mixing of Western and non-Western background and training applies to some of the other contributors. In varying degrees and diverse ways, Arichea, Cimpean, and Velunta bring Western Pauline scholarship and Western hermeneutical theory to bear on Romans, redirecting and transforming elements of the Western scholarly tradition to serve non-Western churches and produce indigenous cultural readings. In some cases, but not all, Western biblical scholarship also serves as a lever against a legacy of Western missionary theology in non-Western settings.

Ideological Shoals

According to some contributors, the Western heritage of interpretation presents what might be called ideological reefs on which our Good Ship Romans is liable to founder and has often been wrecked. Draper describes colonial hegemony and ideology in African Christian settings. Cimpean refers to the conception of Romans on which he was brought up as a "false consciousness." In what follows I use the terms "ideology" in its traditional sense to mean a society's ruling value system, which people take for granted and that serves the interests of the more powerful at the expense of the less powerful. This differs from the usage of the term by some of the contributors, for whom an ideology appears to be simply another name for an organizing value system whether or not it serves the interests of the ruling class.

Ideological criticism is central to Monya Stubbs' essay. She advances a finely-honed interpretation of Romans 13 that criticizes capitalist (free-market) economies. Since Paul's letters (including Romans 13) have not usually been interpreted as a challenge to capitalism and in some circles have been seen as part of the intellectual foundations of the West that give rise to capitalism, Stubbs anti-capitalist reading of Romans 13 seems to imply that most Romans interpretation in the West has been more or less captive to capitalist ideology. If I understand her correctly, she believes that the free-market economy, as a kind of "governing authority" that determines social and political decisions in the West and provides "the transcendent structure in which we live," has also governed the interpretation of Romans 13. Romans 13 has served as a basis for obedience to the modern state (notoriously in institutional German church responses to the Nazi regime but certainly not only in this instance). Although Stubbs does not mention this history of interpretation, it is hard to imagine that she is not aware of it and did not choose Romans 13 as her focal text precisely in order to defeat the idea of submitting to the capitalist status quo at one of the very points where Paul's letters seem to support that kind of submission.

There are ironies and paradoxes in carrying out an ideological critique based on the assumption that texts are inherently open to multiple interpretations, including competing ones. Affirmations that all interpretation is perspectival, that the text harbors a surplus of meaning, that socio-cultural context inevitably and appropriately shapes interpretation, and that multiple different and sometimes competing interpretations are (or can be) equally valid—these all work against the assumptions and goals of certain kinds of ideological critique. If a "melanchthonian" conception of Romans is a false consciousness for Pentecostal Filipinos (see Cimpean), is it a false consciousness also for German Lutherans? Or does a postmodern approach to ideology relativize the concept of ideology so that what is ideological in one setting is not ideological in another setting? If Bishop Colenso managed to oppose hegemonic, colonial interpretations in an African context by giving Romans an indigenous nationalist reading, would that nationalist reading be an ideology if power relations at the times had been reversed? Or would his reading be non-ideological and therefore humane under any political arrangement among the Zulus? And if so, by what or whose standards of humane? When Stubbs interprets Romans 13 as a rhetorical strategy designed to encourage resistance to the state and to foster a new ethic of mutual obligations founded on a social vision very different from Caesar's, she refers to this alternative vision as "an ideological stance," which suggests that we have to do with two ideologies in Romans 13: that of the state and that of Paul. This is an example of using the term "ideology" in a non-traditional way (see above) and perhaps it reflects the relativizing influence on the concept exerted by postmodern perspectivalism. I hasten to add that I do not mean to suggest that Stubbs is a relativist when it comes to the weighty ethical matters she engages. Au contraire!

An explicit word against what I have been calling a relativist conception of ideology is found in Douglas Campbell's response to Arichea's essay. Speaking of Arichea's criticism of the "quasi-Lutheran model" for reading Romans as a Western imposition on Filipino Christians, Campbell comments that this model is not just bad for Filipinos but "causes damage wherever it goes." The problem is not just a failure of cultural contextualization but is rather more universal: "Bad theology is destructive of humanity per se, although doubtless with cultural differences of emphasis." Campbell holds that the quasi-Lutheran reading would be ideological (in the traditional bad sense) if it dominated in any cultural context, that it has been bad for humanity in the West, too. He therefore applauds the fact that the quasi-Lutheran view has recently come under severe attack in Western Pauline scholarship.

Charting a Course, Steering the Ship

Most of our contributors offer some preliminary hermeneutical comments which, for lack of a better word, I will characterize as "postmodern" in tendency (see Martin's response essay). Most (but not all) reject the modernist, historical-critical paradigm as inadequate by itself and, in certain ways in which it has been used, as distorting of the hermeneutical process. Hence, most also embrace some version of a postmodern hermeneutic that affirms the idea of the semantic openness of the text, embraces interpretive perspectivalism, and, therefore, assumes the constructive role of the interpreter (or community of interpreters) in making meaning out of the text in a particular socio-cultural context.

If what I have just described is a loose, common consensus about how to chart a hermeneutical course in diverse cultural waters, it is not always clear that our captains are following their own charts when it comes to steering their ships. Some of the contributors who seem to disavow the traditional historical-critical quest for the "one correct meaning" or "authorial intent" seem at times to argue as if they were after that meaning or had found it. That is, their mode of arguing sometimes seems very traditional and inconsistent with their hermeneutical convictions. Moreover, arguments cast in the rhetorical forms belonging to the traditional historical-critical quest for the "most probable" meaning also seem inconsistent with the basic hermeneutical assumptions on which the seminar and the series are said to proceed. What to make of this? In some cases we probably have to do with approaches that are in fact more or less traditional in looking for the historical Paul's intent (and arguing that this or that interpretation is most probable as a representation of that intent). In other cases, however, we either meet actual inconsistencies between hermeneutic theory and hermeneutic practice or, as I rather think, we see a manifestation of the difficulty of presenting an interpretation (with arguments and evidence) in ways that are rhetorically consistent with postmodern assumptions about interpretation. While we can talk in postmodern terms about the nature of interpretation, it's hard to do the rhetoric of interpretation in ways that reflect postmodern assumptions. Traditional habits of speech die hard, especially when it can be cumbersome to keep qualifying one's assertions and arguments in ways that make clear that one is not making claims about the historical Paul's intent or purporting to give an interpretation that is exegetically superior to all competitors and so forth. I know this from experience. Hence, I have great sympathy for those who take up the challenge of carrying out ethically responsible and rigorous interpretation on postmodern assumptions about locus of textual meaning. I am also grateful for the fine efforts of this volume by contributors who do seem to be wrestling responsibly with this challenge, even if they might frame the hermeneutical issues a bit differently than I have.

Contributors

◆

Daniel C. Arichea is bishop-in-residence both at Duke Divinity School (North Carolina) and Union Theological Seminary (UTS) Philippines. He worked for the United Bible Societies (1969-1994) first as translation consultant for the Philippines, Vietnam, Thailand, Malaysia and Indonesia, and then as regional translation coordinator for the Asia Pacific Region. In 1994 he was elected (in absentia) a bishop of the United Methodist Church in the Philippines. His wife is Ruth Mandac Arichea, who teaches music and worship at UTS.

Mark D. Baker is Assistant Professor of Mission and Theology at Mennonite Brethren Biblical Seminary, Fresno California. He was a missionary in Honduras for ten years, and is the author of three books, and co-author of *Recovering the Scandal of the Cross: Atonement in New Testament and Contemporary Contexts* (2000).

Brian K. Blount is Professor of New Testament at Princeton Theological Seminary. His publications include *Preaching Mark in Two Voices* (2002); *Then The Whisper Put On Flesh: New Testament Ethics in An African American Context* (2001); *Go Preach! Mark's Kingdom Message and the Black Church Today* (1998); *Cultural Interpretation: Reorienting New Testament Criticism* (1995); *Can I Get A Witness? Reading Revelation Through African American Culture* (forthcoming). He is an editor for the *Journal of Biblical Literature*, chairperson of the Program Committee and a member of Council for the Society of Biblical Literature.

Douglas A. Campbell is currently Assistant Professor of New Testament at The Divinity School, Duke University (2003). He has taught previously in the Department of Religious Studies at the University of Otago (New Zealand: 1989-96) and in the Department of Theology and Religious Studies at King's College London (United Kingdom: 1996-2003). His doctoral work on Romans was undertaken at the University of Toronto (1987-89). The thesis was published as *The Rhetoric of Righteousness in Romans 3:21-26* (1992).

FLORIN T. CIMPEAN, currently serves as Senior Pastor of Philadelphia Romanian Church of God in Chicago and Presiding Bishop of The Pentecostal Romanian Convention of USA and Canada. He is also a visiting professor at Institul Teologic Penticostal, Bucharest, Romania and founder and Academic Coordinator for Ekklesia Bible College in Chicago.

CHARLES H. COSGROVE is Professor of New Testament Studies and Christian Ethics at Northern Baptist Theological Seminary in Lombard, Illinois. He is the author of *Appealing to Scripture in Moral Debate: Five Hermeneutical Rules (*2002); *Elusive Israel: The Puzzle of Election in Romans* (1997); *The Cross and the Spirit:* A Study in the Argument and Theology of Galatians (1988); co-author with Herold Weiss and K.K. Yeo of the forthcoming *Cross-Cultural Paul* (forthcoming); editor of *The Meanings We Choose: Hermeneutical Ethics, Indeterminacy, and the Conflict of Interpretations* (2004), and co-editor with John T. Carroll and E. Elizabeth Johnson of *Faith and History: Essays in Honor of Paul W. Meyer* (1990).

JONATHAN A. DRAPER is a South African and Professor of New Testament at the School of Theology and Religion at the University of KwaZulu-Natal, Pietermaritzburg Campus, where he has taught for eighteen years. He holds his PhD from Cambridge University. He is editor of *Women Hold up Half the Sky: Women in the Church in Southern Africa* (1991); *The Didache in Modern Research* (1996), and co-author with R. A. Horsley of *Whoever Hears You Hears Me: Prophets, Performance and Tradition in Q* (1999). He has also edited Bishop J. W. Colenso's *Commentary on Romans* (2003), and *The Eye of the Storm: Bishop John William Colenso and the Crisis of Biblical Inspiration* (2003) and *Orality, Literacy and Colonialism in Southern Africa* (2003).

JAMES D. G. DUNN is currently Emeritus Lightfoot Professor of Divinity, University of Durham. He is a distinguished and prolific New Testament, particularly Pauline scholar, holding key leadership positions in biblical guilds and lecturing worldwide. Among his many contributions in monographs, journals, Festschriften, symposia and dictionaries are *Word Biblical Commentary, Romans* (2 vols., 1988); *The Theology of Paul the Apostle* (1998), and *Christianity in the Making. Vol. 1: Jesus Remembered* (2003).

KATHY EHRENSPERGER teaches New Testament at the University of Wales, Lampeter, United Kingdom. She was a pastor and religious educator of the Swiss Reformed Church for sixteen years. She is the author of *That We May Be Mutually Encouraged: Feminism and the New Perspective in Pauline Studies* (2004) and articles and essays including "Let Everyone Be Convinced in His/Her Own Mind: Derrida and the Deconstruction of Paulinism" (*SBL Seminar Papers,* 2002), and "Be Imitators of Me as I am of Christ: A Hidden Discourse of Power and Domination in Paul?" (*Lexington Theological Quarterly,* 2004).

JUAN ESCARFULLER is a doctoral student in New Testament at Vanderbilt University. He has taught courses in social analysis, homiletic enculturation, and multicultural ministry at Aquinas Institute of Theology. He also has directed the Office of Hispanic Ministry for the Catholic Archdiocese in Saint Louis, Missouri, with a focus on developing Latina and Latino leaders. His research and teaching interests include biblical hermeneutics, cultural studies, and community organizing.

TROY W. MARTIN is Professor of Biblical Studies at Saint Xavier University in Chicago. His works include *Metaphor and Composition in 1 Peter* (1992); *By Philosophy and Empty Deceit: Colossians as Response to a Cynic Critique* (1996); two recent articles in the *Journal of Biblical Literature*: "Paul's Argument from Nature for the Veil in 1 Corinthians 11:13-15: A Testicle instead of a Head-Covering" (2004) and "Covenant of Circumcision (Gen 17:9-14) and the Situational Antitheses in Gal 3:28" (2003). He has served as an officer in the Chicago Society of Biblical Research and as Regional Coordinator of the Midwest Society of Biblical Literature.

MONYA A. STUBBS is an ordained elder in the African Methodist Episcopal Church, is Assistant Professor of New Testament at Austin Presbyterian Theological Seminary. Her publications include articles on Mark and Matthew. She is one of four coauthors of Abingdon's *The Gospel of Matthew: A Contextual Introduction for Group Study* (2003).

ELSA TAMEZ is a Mexican living in Costa Rica. She is Professor of Biblical Studies in the Latin American Biblical University. Among her books translated in English: *Bible of the Oppressed* (1982); *The Scandalous Message of James* (1989); *Amnesty of Grace* (1993); *When the Horizons Close; Rereading Ecclesiastes* (2000).

REVELATION ENRIQUEZ VELUNTA, a Tagalog-speaking Filipino, is Professor of New Testament Studies at Union Theological Seminary (Philippines). He has taught at Southern Christian College, Philippine Christian University, and Vanderbilt University. He is one of four co-authors of Abingdon's *The Gospel of Matthew: A Contextual Introduction for Group Study* (2003).

J. ROSS WAGNER is Assistant Professor of New Testament at Princeton Theological Seminary. The author of *Heralds of the Good News: Isaiah and Paul 'In Concert' in the Letter to the Romans* (2002), his research focuses on the role of scriptural interpretation in the formation of early Jewish and Christian communities.

HEROLD WEISS is a native of Montevideo educated in Argentina and in the United States. He is professor emeritus of religious studies at Saint Mary's College in Notre Dame, Indiana, and an affiliate professor of New Testament at Northern Baptist Theological Seminary in Lombard, Illinois. Weiss is the author of *Paul of Tarsus: His Gospel and Life* and *A Day of Gladness: The Sabbath Among Jews and Christians in Antiquity.* He lives in Berrien Springs, Michigan.

GERALD O. WEST teaches Old Testament and African Biblical Hermeneutics in the School of Theology and Religion, University of KwaZulu-Natal. He is Director of the Institute for the Study of the Bible and Worker Ministry Project. His recent publications are *The Academy of the Poor: Towards a Dialogical Reading of the Bible* (1999; reprinted 2003) and co-edited with Musa Dube, *The Bible in Africa: Transactions, Trajectories and Trends* (2000).

YEO KHIOK-KHNG (K.K.), a Malaysian Chinese, is Harry R. Kendall Associate Professor of New Testament at Garrett-Evangelical Theological Seminary and Graduate Faculty advisory member at Northwestern University, Evanston. He is a visiting professor at major universities in China and has published in both English and Chinese on cross-cultural biblical interpretation—*Rhetorical Interaction in 1 Corinthians 8 and 10* (1995); *What Has Jerusalem to Do with Beijing? Biblical Interpretation from a Chinese Perspective* (1998), and *Chairman Paul Meets the Apostle Paul: Christianity, Communism, and the Hope of China* (2002).

Index of Scriptural References

◆

Genesis
18:19   *287*

Exodus
7-10   *136*

Deuteronomy
7:7-8   *169*

Number
25:6-13   *10*

Psalms
1:6   *287*
88:28   *271*
98:1-3   *107*
143:1-2   *106, 116*
145:7-9   *106, 116*

Isaiah
40:9-11   *107*
45:20-25   *107*
51:4-8   *107*
52:5   *13*
56:1   *208*

Jeremiah
1:5   *287*

Hosea
13:5   *287*

Amos
3:2   *287*
4:1-13   *136*

Matthew
1:19   *210*
18:23-25   *245*

Luke
12   *567*

John
3:16   *297*
7:53-8:11   *119*
14:6   *210*

Acts
2:38   *297*
5:34   *9*
7   *10*
7:58   *8*
8   *10*
8:1,3   *8*
9:1,4,11,17,30   *8*
9:4   *10*
11:25   *8*
16:30   *297*
18:3   *9*
21:1-16   *12*
21:39-40   *8*
22:2-3,7   *8*
22:3   *9*
22:7   *10*
23:6   *9*
26:5   *9*
26:14   *8, 10*

Colossians
1:1-4:18   *286*

2 Timothy
2:19   *287*

Hebrews
1:6   *286*

Revelation
1:5   *286*

Index of Names

◆

Index of Subjects

—— ◆ ——

322

Index of Subjects

Love, 11, 15, 17, 22, 36, 56, 67,
71-74, 99, 103, 109f, 114,
120, 170-74, 186-93, 199f,
218, 235, 238, 245, 247, 249,
265, 268-86

Mandate of Heaven, 263-93

Mencius, 263-87

Messiah. See also Christ, 10-12,
22, 68f, 153, 156f, 263, 279,
292

Messianic:
idea in Chinese culture, 263-
67, 290, 292
consciousness, 261, 265f
predestination, 259-93

Metanarrative, 151f, 162

Min-Jung theology, 213, 231

Minister, 46f, 57, 69, 135, 186,
188

Mission of Paul, of the Gospel,
3, 8-13, 283

Missionary, 8, 11, 13, 18, 58-
64, 68, 72, 74, 78-86, 90, 148,
153, 212, 226, 275, 296-98

Modernization, 6

Monotheism, 68

Moral, morality, 3, 5, 17, 22,
34, 41, 43-69, 99, 107, 134,
144, 175, 181, 208, 227-41,
259-62, 264-83, 294

Mystery, 24, 79, 82, 149f, 158

Narrative, 38, 63, 178, 261f,
267-94

Oneness of God, 269, 277-81

Opheilei. See also Debt, 186-
88, 199, 243

Origen, 17

Pastor, pastoral reading, 3, 13,
16, 27, 99f, 105, 128, 141,
143, 161, 234f

Patron, 162, 188, 195

Pentateuch, 58f, 62, 76, 80

People of God, 9-13, 70, 109,
117, 128, 135, 157, 217, 264,
268, 272f

Pharisees, Pharisaic, 9-14, 22

"Philistinism", 6

Philology, philological, 41, 147

Philosophy, 5, 17-28, 57, 164,
168, 238, 259, 263-89

Pistis. See also Faith, 74, 196f,
234-58

Pneuma. See Spirit

Politics, political, 3, 8, 18-22,
32, 40, 60f, 81f, 86, 123, 134,
138f, 144-46, 151, 156-67,
173, 180-87, 198-200, 212,
232, 259-83, 294, 298f

Postcolonial, 60, 84-92, 139-41,
159-61, 166f

Postmodern, 139-40, 256-58,
299-301

Power, 65-67, 75, 129-31, 136,
138-40, 148, 154f, 158-201,
217, 234, 240, 248, 250, 254f,
268f, 271, 273, 275, 277-80,
283, 293f, 299

Preacher, 104, 141, 229

Predestination, 259, 270f
Christological P., 267f

Pre-horizoning, 270-73

Pro me/nobis, 2, 31-54, 236f,
256, 297

Progress, 6, 24, 28, 67, 100,
175, 266, 273, 281

Psychology, 19, 254f

Solidarity, 13, 18, 39, 71f, 156,
159, 162, 169f, 227, 234, 249,
263, 275

Sonship. See also Adoption, 15,
18, 267, 271, 275, 278, 292f

Spirit, Holy Spirit, God's Spirit,
176, 187, 189, 228, 244, 256,
258, 267, 269, 273, 279, 287,
289, 295f, 304

Subjection, 2, 113, 171-201

Suffering, 35, 39, 49, 69, 98,
105, 111, 134, 145f, 156-59,
192, 218, 239, 252, 255, 267f,
271f, 292, 294

Telos (goal, purpose), 15, 154,
157, 261, 265, 268, 270, 272

Theology, theological, *passim.*

Tian Dao. See Heavenly Way

Tian-ming. See Mandate of
Heaven

Time and history, 281-83
Cyclical movement of
history, 266f, 282, 288,
294
Linear view of history, 275,
281f

Torah, Law. See Jewish
Tradition

Translation, 2, 7, 22-27, 48-50,
60-74, 89, 123-26, 157, 177,
195, 205, 208-10, 225, 228,
234f, 241, 246, 250f, 256,
284f, 286-89, 303
Versions of translation:
AV (Authorized Version),
241, 249
BIS (Bahasa Indonesia
Sehari-hari; Everyday
Indonesian), 210f

CEV (Contemporary English
Version), 208
JB (Jerusalem Bible), 208,
250
NEB (New English Bible),
250
NRSV (New Revised
Standard Version), 189,
234, 241, 249, 270
RSV (Revised Standard
Version), 9, 50, 249
TEV (Today English
Version), 208f
TB (Terjemahan Baru; New
Translation), 210f

Tsedhaqah. See Righteousness

"Two-thirds" world, 16, 165,
237, 295

Utang. See Debt, *Utang na loob*

Utang na loob, See also "Faith
to faith", 187f, 234-58, 297

uThixo, uYehova, uDio (God),
65f

uNkulunkulu (Great-Great-
One), 66

Uncircumcised, uncircumcision,
4, 12, 23, 27, 215

Violence, violent, 10f, 144, 216,
226f, 232, 248, 269f, 275,
277-83

Virtues, 4f, 115, 217, 242, 265f,
270f, 275-96

"Weak" and "strong", 12, 14-
16, 276

West, Western world, 2, 32, 36,
40f, 46, 49, 55, 59, 61, 63, 68,
70, 83-86, 88, 92, 140, 153f,
159, 162f, 168, 211f, 219,